Migration and Social Security Handbook

2nd edition

**Simon Cox, Duran Seddon, Helen Mountfield
and Simon Roberts with Elspeth Guild**

Child Poverty Action Group

First edition 1993 (*Ethnic Minorities' Benefits Handbook*) by Paul Morris,
Inderpal Rahal and Hugo Storey, edited by Janet Gurney

Published by CPAG Ltd
1-5 Bath Street, London EC1V 9PY

© CPAG Ltd 1997

A CIP record for this book is available from the British Library

ISBN 0 946744 87 4

Cover and design by Devious Designs, 0114 275 5634
Typeset by Boldface, 0171 253 2014
Printed by Progressive Printing UK Ltd 01702 520050

The authors

Simon Cox is a barrister with a London chambers. He practices in public law, specialising in immigration, social security and child support law. He was previously employed as the Free Representation Unit's social security and immigration caseworker, and is co-author of CPAG's *Child Support Handbook*.

Duran Seddon is a barrister with a London chambers and specialises in immigration and social security law.

Helen Mountfield is a barrister in a London chambers and specialises in public law, European law, and employment and social security law. She has worked extensively with CPAG in taking test cases to the European Court and has worked with other groups such as the Public Law Project.

Simon Roberts is a writer specialising in Europe and social security issues. He is a research fellow at the Centre for the Evaluation of Public Policy and Practice and a part-time lecturer in the Department of Government at Brunel University.

Elspeth Guild is a solicitor specialising in immigration and European law.

Acknowledgements

Grateful thanks to our editor Frances Ellery and to Beth Lakhani of the Citizens' Rights Office. They shouldered the burden of co-ordinating and combining the work of the authors and their ideas and comments were invaluable. Without their persistence and discipline this edition might never have appeared.

Many thanks also to Janet Gurney and Sue Shutter for reading and commenting on so much of the text. Thanks also to Katie Ghose, Laurie Fransman and Eileen Bye for their contributions.

Many people have contributed at different stages during the production of this book. Particular thanks are due to Richard Kennedy, who shaped and edited most of the text, and to Julia Lewis who edited Part 4. Thanks to Boldface for their typesetting, to Mary Shirley for checking footnotes, to Lynn Webster for compiling some of the appendices, to Kay Hart for the index, to Nadya Kassam for acting as locum marketing and production co-ordinator, and to our proofreader Paula McDiarmid.

We are grateful to the many colleagues in the fields of immigration and welfare rights for sharing their ideas, experiences and arguments and, in so doing, shaping ours. Thanks also to staff of the DSS and Home Office for answering queries and discussing both law and practice.

We are indebted to Paul Morris, Inderpal Rahal and Hugo Storey for the ideas and material we have drawn from the previous edition of this book, the *Ethnic Minorities' Benefits Handbook*.

This edition is dedicated to Inderpal Rahal who died earlier this year.

Contents

Glossary of terms used

Appellate authority The courts, tribunals, adjudicators that make decisions in appeals.

Applicable amount A figure representing your weekly needs for the purpose of calculating your benefit. For income support (IS) your applicable amount is the amount you are expected to live on each week. For housing benefit (HB) and council tax benefit (CTB) it is the amount used to see how much help you need with your rent or council tax. For family credit (FC) and disability working allowance (DWA) it is a fixed amount. For full details, see CPAG's *National Welfare Benefits Handbook*.

Association agreement A treaty signed between the European Community and another country which gives nationals of the other country (mainly business and self-employed people) preferential access to the countries of the EU.

Asylum A place of refuge; allowing a person to stay in one country because of the danger s/he would face if returned to the country from which s/he has fled.

Common travel area (CTA) The UK, Republic of Ireland, Isle of Man and the Channel Islands, between which there are no immigration controls.

Commonwealth countries Antigua and Barbuda, Australia, Bahamas, Bangladesh, Barbados, Belize, Botswana, Cameroon, Canada, Cyprus, Dominica, Gambia, Ghana, Grenada, Guyana, India, Jamaica, Kenya, Kiribati, Lesotho, Malawi, Malaysia, Malta, Mauritius, Mozambique, Namibia, Nauru, Nevis, New Zealand, Nigeria, Pakistan, Papua New Guinea, St Kitts, St Lucia, St Vincent and the Grenadines, Seychelles, Sierra Leone, Singapore, Solomon Islands, South Africa, Sri Lanka, Swaziland, Tanzania, Tonga, Trinidad and Tobago, Tuvalu, Uganda, Vanuatu, Western Samoa, Zambia, Zimbabwe.

Deportation (order) Sending a person out of the UK under an order signed by the Home Secretary after the person has remained in the UK without permission or broken another condition of stay, or has been convicted of a serious criminal offence, or because the Home Secretary has decided on public policy or national security grounds that the person's presence is 'not conducive to the public good'. The person cannot return unless the order has been revoked.

European Community (EC) In this book we refer to the legislation of the European Union (previously known as the European Community and before that the European Economic Communities) as EC law. For details see Chapter 22.

European Economic Area (EEA) covers European Union (EU) countries plus Iceland, Liechtenstein and Norway. EEA nationals have free movement within these and all EU member states (see below).

European Union (EU) member states are Austria, Belgium, Denmark, Finland, France, Germany, Greece, Ireland, Italy, Luxembourg, the Netherlands, Portugal, Spain, Sweden and the UK (the UK includes Gibralter for this purpose).

EU/EEA national In this book we use this term to describe citizens of EU member states and EEA countries (see above).

Family For benefit purposes, under British law who counts as your family are yourself, your partner (see below) and any dependent children who are members of your household. (For definition of household, see CPAG's *National Welfare Benefits Handbook*.) Under EC law, family members include a wider range of relatives, see p291.

GB Great Britain comprises Wales, Scotland, England and adjacent islands (but not the Isle of Man or Channel Islands).

Habeus corpus A legal remedy to protect personal liberty by requiring that a person who is being held in custody is brought before the court/judge giving the grounds for the detention. The court/judge can then test the legality of the detention and if appropriate direct that the person be released.

Habitual residence This is a condition of entitlement to certain social security benefits. It has acquired different meanings under domestic and EC law. *Under domestic law*, to be entitled to income support, income-based JSA, housing benefit and council tax benefit a claimant, but not her/his partner or child dependants, must be habitually resident in the common travel area (see above). To be habitually resident a person must have established an 'appreciable period of residence', which varies according to circumstances. For a fuller explanation, see p104. *Under EC law*, the term residence means habitual residence. Five main criteria are used to establish residence: the person's centre of interest; their employment record; their length and continuity of residence in another country; the reason for coming to the country where they are making a claim for benefit; their future intentions. These criteria have been established in case law concerning the entitlement to unemployment benefits for migrant workers within the EU/EEA. Details are set out in appendices to R(U) 8/88.

Partner A wife, husband or cohabitee (of the opposite sex) who is or is treated as a member of the same household as the claimant for benefit purposes.

Removal The procedure for sending a person refused entry or who is being treated as an illegal entrant away from the UK, against which there is no appeal.

Visa nationals People who always need to get entry clearance in advance of travelling to the UK, for whatever purpose, unless they are *returning* residents or are returning within a period of earlier leave granted for more than six months. For a list of countries covered, see JCWI *Immigration, Nationality and Refugee Law Handbook.* (Since publication of that book, Colombia has been added to the list.)

UK The United Kingdon comprises England, Wales, Scotland and Northern Ireland.

Abbreviations used in the text

AA	Attendance allowance
AO	Adjudication officer
AP	Additional pension
BDTC	British dependent territories citizen
BOC	British overseas citizen
BPP	British protected person
BS	British subject
CB	Child benefit
CTA	Common travel area
CTB	Council tax benefit
CUKC	Citizen of the UK and colonies
DLA	Disability living allowance
DSS	Department of Social Security
DWA	Disability working allowance
EC	European Community
ECJ	European Court of Justice
ECO	Entry clearance officer
EEA	European Economic Area
EEC	European Economic Communities
ELE	Exceptional leave to enter
ELR	Exceptional leave to remain
EU	European Union
FC	Family credit
GB	Great Britain
HB	Housing benefit
ICA	Invalid care allowance
ICB	Incapacity benefit
ILE	Indefinite leave to enter
ILR	Indefinite leave to remain
IS	Income support
JSA	Jobseeker's allowance
MA	Maternity allowance
NCIP	Non-contributory invalidity pension
NI	National insurance
SAL	Standard acknowledgement letter
SDA	Severe disablement allowance
SMP	Statutory maternity pay
SSP	Statutory sick pay
VOLO	Variation of leave order

About this handbook

This handbook is intended to bridge the gap between guides on welfare rights and those on immigration. It is designed to be used by migrants and their advisers wanting advice on benefit entitlement. By 'migrants' we mean people who have come or returned to Great Britain from abroad and people who have left Great Britain to live abroad, or are temporarily abroad.

The handbook covers the benefit rules which are most likely to affect migrant claimants and their families, and the practical problems they are likely to face. It is not a complete guide to the benefit rules and should be used together with general guides such as CPAG's *National Welfare Benefits Handbook*, *Rights Guide to Non-Means-Tested Benefits* and *Jobseeker's Allowance Handbook*.

How to use this book

Your benefit rights may depend upon your immigration status. In Part 1 we outline the immigration system and explain the terms used in immigration law which appear in the rest of the book. Part I aims to provide welfare rights advisers with a framework of immigration law (see Appendix 2 for comprehensive immigration law books). In some cases Part I may contain enough information for you to use the rest of the handbook to work out your benefit entitlement. However, if you are unclear about your immigration status or the effects of claiming benefit, you should if possible ask a specialist immigration adviser for immigration advice.

If your immigration status is clear, you should use Part 2 to work out your benefit entitlement. Use the chapter relevant to your immigration status.

If you are abroad, use Part 3. If you are planning to go abroad, use Parts 2 and 3.

Part 4 deals with EC rules as they affect benefits here and in Europe. Part 5 deals with reciprocal agreements with certain other countries which can be used by their nationals and residents.

The law covered was correct at 12 May 1997 and includes regulations up to that date. Where possible we have included changes to legislation and case law up to the beginning of August. For further updates, see CPAG's *Welfare Rights Bulletin*.

PART ONE

Immigration Law

CHAPTER ONE

Immigration control

This chapter covers:

1. WHAT IS IMMIGRATION CONTROL?

The term 'immigration control' refers to the system by which the ability of individuals to enter, stay and live in the UK for different purposes is restricted and regulated by the government. Control takes place by means of examination at ports of entry into the UK, but may, in certain circumstances, begin overseas at designated posts – eg, British Embassies and High Commissions. It may also continue to operate after a person has been admitted to the UK.

The stamps in your passport are evidence of immigration control. When a person is admitted to the UK, s/he acquires a particular immigration status. This may be changed at a later date. Rights – including access to employment and social security benefits – can depend on immigration status. Some people are not affected by immigration control and may freely come and go to and from the UK. This group is likely to qualify more easily for social security benefits.

Normally 'nationality' determines whether a person may freely come and go into a particular country. However, there are different classes of British national, and some British nationals are subject to immigration control (see Chapter 2). Certain groups of people are not subject to control or are subject to a partial form of immigration control or enjoy certain immigration advantages. This may be as a result of the particular nature of their employment or their nationality of certain other countries (see pp7 and 14).

Who immigration control affects

Everyone must undergo some form of examination by the immigration authorities, but the *extent* of immigration control varies greatly between different groups. There are two main groups:

- those who are 'subject to control' and who require specific permission or 'leave' to enter into or remain in the UK; *and*
- those who are not subject to control who do not require that permission.

The immigration authorities can also impose certain conditions and limitations (eg, access to work and time-limits) on people entering or staying in the UK who are subject to control and can, ultimately, force them to leave the UK. This is not the case with those not subject to control.

Movement within the 'common travel area'

The common travel area (CTA) is the UK, the 'Islands' (Channel Islands and the Isle of Man) and the Republic of Ireland.[1] Journeys within the CTA are not subject to control and, as a result, leave is not required. There are exceptions to this general rule of freedom of travel within the CTA. For example, people who simply pass through the Republic of Ireland on the way to the UK still need leave to enter the UK.[2]

The existence of the CTA means that citizens of the Irish Republic may travel to the UK without requiring leave to enter. However, they are still subject to immigration control and may, therefore, be deported and removed from the UK (see Chapter 6).

2. HOW IMMIGRATION CONTROL OPERATES

This section is relevant to people who require leave (permission) to enter/remain in the UK (for who requires leave, see pp6-7). In this section we summarise the basic mechanics of immigration control, the decision-making process and the personnel involved at different stages of the immigration process. Further detailed examination of relevant immigration controls in practice are given in Chapter 3.

Types of 'leave'

There are two kinds of leave:[3]

- **limited** leave to enter or to remain;
- **indefinite** leave to enter or to remain.

Depending on your circumstances, it is probable that certain conditions will be attached to your limited leave to enter or remain. No conditions may be attached to indefinite leave.[4] The conditions may relate to:

- your employment or occupation;
- maintaining yourself in the UK 'without recourse to public funds' (see p59);
- the requirement that you register with the police or report to a medical officer.

Personnel

In general, responsibility for the administration of both immigration and nationality laws lies with the Immigration and Nationality Directorate of the Home Office whose personnel are ultimately responsible to the Home Secretary (who may be referred to as the 'Secretary of State'). The main office is at Lunar House in Croydon (see Appendix 2).[5]

The most important personnel in immigration control are:

- **entry clearance officers**, stationed in overseas posts with responsibility for control prior to entry;
- **immigration officers**, including chief immigration officers and immigration inspectors, who are responsible for 'on entry' immigration control.[6] They also have the power to detain people on arrival for further questioning and to detain those refused leave to enter and illegal entrants.[7] They may also make initial decisions to deport people[8] (this is not the same as making a deportation order);
- the **Home Secretary** is responsible for 'after entry' immigration control (see p26)[9] and for making the immigration rules.[10]

Other personnel who play a significant part in immigration procedures are:

- the **Secretary of State for Education and Employment** – responsible for issuing work permits;
- the **Lord Chancellor** – responsible for the appointment of appellate personnel[11] and for making rules of procedure for immigration appeals;[12]
- **adjudicators, special adjudicators** and members of the **Immigration Appeal Tribunal** – all responsible for hearing and making determinations on appeals from decisions of entry clearance officers, immigration officers and the Secretary of State;
- **Home Office Presenting Officers** (HOPOs) – appointed by the Secretary of State and responsible for presenting the Home Office case at appeals;
- **police** – responsible for the registration of aliens,[13] the arrest of people

suspected of having committed criminal offences under the Immigration Act[14] and the arrest of people who may be detained under immigration law.[15]

Decisions about immigration and the 'immigration rules'

Decisions under the immigration rules

Decisions as to whether or not a person who is subject to immigration control:

- should be granted leave to enter or remain in the UK;
- upon what terms; *and*
- whether they should be required to leave the UK;

are generally made according to the immigration rules in conjunction with the Immigration Act 1971. (The Asylum and Immigration Appeals Act 1993, the Asylum and Immigration Act 1996 and other legislation passed since 1971 has modified the Immigration Act 1971 which is the foundation of current immigration law.) The immigration rules are not 'legislation' but rules of practice. The rules themselves are made by the Secretary of State and put before Parliament for approval.[16] The Secretary of State frequently issues statements of amendment to the rules and sometimes re-issues the whole of the rules in a different form. The last complete statement of the immigration rules was laid before Parliament on 23 May 1994 and is referred to as HC395. They came into effect on 1 October 1994, although there are certain transitional provisions.[17] Unlike social security regulations, the immigration rules are drafted in an informal style and the words used must be given their most natural and ordinary meaning.[18]

The rules set out:

- a series of 'requirements' which a person needs to satisfy in order to be granted leave in any particular capacity – eg, as a student, visitor or as a refugee;
- the length of time for which a person may expect to be admitted in any capacity and the 'conditions' which a person is likely to have attached to their leave;
- the process of deportation of persons who have had leave to enter or remain in the UK and who decline to leave when they are not permitted any further leave;
- which persons can generally claim social security benefits without affecting their right to stay. Most people who are here for a limited period are adversely affected by these rules (see pp21, 58 and 72).

Immigration decisions outside the rules

Certain people are admitted or allowed entry outside the rules. The rules represent the *minimum* standard of treatment that a person may expect and must be applied by entry clearance officers/immigration officers.[19] However, the Home Secretary has the discretion to waive certain requirements of the rules (and to authorise her/his officers to do likewise), and to treat some people more favourably than the strict letter of the immigration rules requires. A person given leave in this way has 'exceptional leave' (see Chapter 4). Exceptional leave may be given to asylum-seekers who are not granted refugee status and to a whole range of other people in different circumstances who cannot fit the normal requirements of the rules.

3. THE EXTENT OF IMMIGRATION CONTROL

People not subject to control

Persons who have the 'right of abode' (see glossary) in the UK are not subject to immigration control.[20] They are:[21]

- British citizens;
- certain citizens of Commonwealth countries (see glossary for list of Commonwealth countries).

Commonwealth citizens who have the right of abode are those who, prior to 1 January 1983, were:

- *either* Commonwealth citizens with a parent born in the UK;
- *or* women who had become patrial (see p13) through marriage.

For more information about nationality rules and the right of abode, see Chapter 2.

If you fall into one of these two groups you do not require leave to enter or remain in the UK. However, you may be obliged to undergo examination and provide evidence to establish that you have the identity and status claimed. The passports of people not subject to control are routinely checked by immigration officers on entry to the UK.[22] You may be able to prove that you have the right of abode with:[23]

- *either* a UK passport describing you as a British citizen or as a citizen of the UK and Colonies having the right of abode in the UK;
- *or* a certificate of entitlement issued by the UK government certifying that you have the right of abode.

People subject to immigration control

If you are not in one of the above groups (ie, with the right of abode), you are subject to immigration control. This means that to enter or remain in the UK you must satisfy the requirements of the immigration rules.

Special groups

In addition to the main division between those subject to control and those not subject, certain groups of people are treated differently under immigration law:

- nationals of states which are members of the European Union (EU) or a party to the European Economic Area (EEA) (see glossary);
- family members of EU/EEA nationals who would normally be subject to immigration control (see pp290-92);
- non-British citizen British nationals (see p14);
- non-visa nationals (see below);
- national of certain countries (see below);
- non-British citizen children born in Britain on or after 1 January 1983 (see below);
- diplomats and other embassy staff etc (see below);
- armed forces personnel (see below);
- ship and air crews.

The immigration rules distinguish between 'visa nationals' who require prior 'entry clearance', obtained overseas and 'non-visa nationals' who normally do not require prior entry clearance, unless specifically required by the immigration rules (see glossary and *JCWI Handbook*).

Nationals of other countries

Requirements for admission can vary according to nationality, depending on the purpose of your entry. For admission in *certain* capacities specified in the immigration rules, there are particular requirements relating to different nationalities. Thus, in certain circumstances, a national of one country may be in a better position than a national of another country. These circumstances are very much the exception rather than the rule. They are as follows:

- admission for an *au pair* placement can only be granted under the rules to citizens of Andorra, Bosnia-Herzegovina, Croatia, Cyprus, Czech Republic, The Faeroes, Greenland, Hungary, Macedonia, Malta, Monaco, San Marino, Slovak Republic, Slovenia, Switzerland, Turkey;[24]

- admission in the capacity of working holidaymaker is only open to Commonwealth citizens;[25]
- if Commonwealth citizens wish to seek employment they may be admitted on the basis of a grandparent born in the UK[26] thus avoiding the far more restrictive rules relating to work permits for other people subject to immigration control;
- nationals of Hungary, Poland, Bulgaria, Czech Republic, Romania and Slovakia may seek admission under the rules relating to people seeking to establish themselves in business under the provisions of an EC Association Agreement.[27] For citizens of Turkey, see Part 4.

Non-British citizen children born in Britain on or after 1 January 1983

Since the British Nationality Act 1981 came into force on 1 January 1983, certain children (see p17) born in the UK are not automatically born British citizens. Technically, they are subject to immigration control but this would only affect them if they left the UK. They would be subject to the ordinary provisions of the immigration rules if they wished to return. They do not require leave in order to remain in the UK. Because they have never actually been granted leave to remain they cannot be:

- deported from the UK as 'overstayers'; or as in breach of their conditions of leave;[28] *or*
- otherwise removed from the UK.[29]

In addition, these people can be forced to leave the UK if they are:

- deported as the part of the family to which they belong (eg, the parents are deported as overstayers) or, in rare cases, where it is 'conducive to the public good that the family be deported;[30] *or*
- first granted a period of limited leave and thus come within the normal immigration rules in which case they may, in due course, become liable for deportation.

For more details about enforcement of immigration controls and deportation, see Chapter 6.

Diplomats and staff of embassies, high commissions and certain international agencies

Diplomats and certain staff of embassies, high commissions and certain international agencies and their families are 'exempt' from immigration controls.[31] If you are employed by a high commission or embassy but pay local taxes (ie, UK taxes), then you are probably not within the category of staff who are exempt.[32] If you are privately employed by a member of the mission (rather than by the mission itself), the law is not clear as to whether you are exempt from control.[33]

For this category of people, there are no clear guidelines as to who is a member of the 'family' or who can be said to form part of the household. A judgement must be made on the facts of each case.[34]

There are further exemptions and partial exemptions from immigration control for:[35]

- consular officers or employees in the service of a foreign government;
- members of foreign governments or their representatives in the UK on official business;
- officials of international organisations such as the International Monetary Fund (IMF);
- people attending certain international conferences in the UK and certain Commonwealth officials.

In practical terms, if you fall into any of the above categories you are entitled to benefit from your exemption as soon as you arrive in the UK. However, the exemption only applies for as long as you retain the status for which it was granted.[36] So if, for any reason, you leave your post, you are no longer exempt from control. If you had some form of leave before being exempt, then that will continue to apply,[37] or else the Secretary of State may decide to grant you a period of limited leave so as to bring you back into the ordinary immigration system and you will have to satisfy the full provisions of the immigration rules from that point onwards.

Armed forces

If you fall into any of the following categories you are exempt from all immigration controls except deportation:[38]

- a member of UK armed forces;
- a member of a Commonwealth or similar force undergoing training in the UK with the UK armed forces;
- a member of a visiting force coming to the UK at the invitation of the government.

Ship and aircrews

If you arrive in the UK as the member of the crew of a ship or aircraft, hired or under orders to depart as part of that ship's crew or to depart on the same or another aircraft within seven days of arrival, then you may enter the UK without leave.[39] You may also remain in the UK without leave until the ship or aircraft is ready to leave. In order to be a 'crew member' you must be employed to carry out functions necessary to the running of the ship or aircraft.[40]

You will not benefit from this exemption if:[41]

- there is a deportation order against you; *or*
- you have at any time been refused leave to enter the UK and have not since been given leave to enter or remain in the UK; *or*
- an immigration officer requires you to submit to examination.

Nationality

This chapter covers:

I. DIFFERENT TYPES OF BRITISH NATIONALITY[1]

There are now six types of British national:

- British citizens
- British dependent territories citizens (BDTC)
- British subjects (BS)
- British protected persons (BPP)
- British nationals (overseas) (BNO)
- British overseas citizens (BOC)

The following is an outline of how these categories evolved.

Before 1948

People were divided into three groups:

- **British subjects** (BS) – born in a territory belonging to the Crown including the UK. Until 1962, these people had the right of abode in the UK and could freely come and go from the UK;
- **aliens** – non-British subjects;
- **British** protected persons – aliens under the protection of the Crown.

Then, as now, the last two groups had no right of abode.

British Nationality Act 1948

With the implementation of this Act, people were divided into five groups:

- **citizens of the UK and colonies (CUKC)** – this covered people born in or connected with the UK or a Crown colony;[2]
- **Commonwealth citizens** – this covered people born in or connected with a Commonwealth country that became independent and who became citizens of that country. CUKC status would normally be lost when the colony became independent. Some of these citizens were allowed to register as CUKCs on a discretionary basis;
- **British subjects without citizenship** – these people did not become citizens of the Commonwealth country in which they lived;
- **British protected persons** (BPP);
- **aliens.**

Until the 1960s, CUKCs, Commonwealth citizens and British subjects without citizenship could freely enter the UK. Note that you can no longer become a British subject or a BPP.

1960s: Commonwealth Immigrants Acts

The Commonwealth Immigrants Acts 1962 and 1968 affected the immigration position of CUKCs and Commonwealth citizens:

- **The 1962 Act** – this gave greater rights to people who had passports issued in the UK or on behalf of the UK government abroad, but denied Commonwealth citizens free entry to the UK.
- **The 1968 Act** – CUKCs who did not have parents or grandparents born in the UK lost the right of entry to this country; in particular, the effect was to deny entry to large numbers of East African Asians with CUKC status.[3]

Immigration Act 1971

This Act introduced the concept of people with 'patrial' status. Patrials had the right of abode in the UK, were not subject to immigration control and could therefore come and go freely. Most of the people who obtained patrial status were CUKCs, although some Commonwealth citizens also qualified.[4] Ancestry, status of husband, nature and duration of residence in the UK and how you acquired CUKC status dictated whether you were patrial. The 1971 Act separated 'nationality' from the most important immigration consideration – the right of abode and, with it, the right to enter the UK freely.

British Nationality Act 1981

The British Nationality Act (BNA) 1981 came into force on 1 January 1983 and created three new types of national (all were derived from patrial and non-patrial CUKCs):[5]

- **British citizens** – ie, patrial CUKCs;
- **British dependent territories citizens** (BDTC) – ie, non-patrial CUKCs who had a connection with a place which continued to be a colony or 'dependent territory';
- **British overseas citizens** (BOC) – ie, non-patrial CUKCs whose connection was with a place which had ceased to be a British dependent territory by 1983.

British citizens have the right of abode.[6] Until 1 January 1983, some non-patrial CUKCs (eg, East African Asians) were entitled to patrial status and therefore had right of abode after five years' ordinary residence in the UK.[7]

Non-British citizen British nationals – eg, some CUKCs, BPPs, British subjects without citizenship resident in the UK for five years have the right to register as British citizens if they satisfy certain conditions (see p18).[8]

Commonwealth citizens who were patrial on 1 January 1983:

- *either* by virtue of their having a parent born in the UK;
- *or* were women married to a patrial;

were classed simply as Commonwealth citizens with the right of abode in the UK.[9] Anyone born abroad after 1 January 1983 who would have qualified for the right of abode as a result of their parentage, now became British citizens 'by descent'.[10] Commonwealth women marrying British citizens before 1 January 1983 acquired the right of abode and were not subject to immigration control. After 1 January 1983, a Commonwealth woman marrying a British citizen did not have the right of abode.

Developments since 1981

Since the 1981 Act, there have been two important developments in British nationality law relating to the Falkland Islands and Hong Kong:

- **Falkland Islands** – Following the war in the Falklands, legislation converted most people born in the Falklands from British dependent territories citizens to British citizens by birth.[11]
- **Hong Kong** – Before Hong Kong was returned to the People's Republic of China in 1997, Hong Kong's British dependent territories citizens had the chance to register as a new type of national – British national (overseas).[12] In 1997, status as a British dependent territories citizen ended for those living in Hong Kong, but British nationals (overseas) will be able to continue to use British travel documents and will be able to register as British citizens following five years' residence in the UK having achieved settled status here.[13] The Secretary of State also registered as British citizens 50,000 residents of Hong Kong who

are 'heads of households'.[14] Selection was carried out by the Governor of Hong Kong under the provisions of a much publicised selection scheme.[15] In February 1997, the government accepted that British nationals who had no other nationality (ie, are not Chinese) may register to become British citizens after 1 July 1997.

Dual nationality

A 'dual national' is a person who is simultaneously a national of two countries. Some countries do not allow dual nationality so some people may be forced to choose between being a national of one country or a national of another. UK nationality law does not prevent a person from being both a British national and a national of another country.

Loss of citizenship

You can lose British citizenship in the following ways:

- If you obtained it by registration or naturalisation (see pp18-19). The government can make an order depriving you of British citizenship. This can only be done if you:[16]
  - obtained citizenship by deception;
  - have been sentenced to prison for 12 months or longer;
  - have acted treasonably.
- You renounce your citizenship where you are either a dual national or wish to obtain another nationality. The Secretary of State must be satisfied that you will obtain the nationality of the other country.[17]

In certain circumstances, the Home Office may also declare that a person has never been a British citizen. This may happen where citizenship was acquired on an incorrect basis or the authorities made a mistake.

2. BRITISH NATIONALS AND IMMIGRATION LAW

British citizens have the right of abode in the UK and are therefore not subject to immigration control (see Chapter 1). All the other types of British national (see p11) are subject to immigration control and in order to enter or remain in the UK must satisfy the various provisions of the immigration rules. However, some non-British citizen British nationals enjoy certain immigration advantages. These are set out below.

Right of re-admission

British overseas citizens granted indefinite leave to enter or remain in the UK by the immigration authorities any time after 1 March 1968 can leave the UK and qualify for indefinite leave to enter on their return. They do not have to satisfy the normal returning residents rules.[18] These rules apply to other people subject to immigration control. To satisfy the returning resident rules the person must:[19]

- have had indefinite leave to enter or remain when s/he last left the UK;
- not have been away from the UK for more than two years;
- not have received assistance from public funds towards the cost of leaving the UK;
- seek admission for the purpose of 'settlement' when s/he returns to the UK.

Special voucher scheme

This scheme applies to British overseas citizens. You can be admitted to the UK on an indefinite basis if you have:[20]

- *either* a 'special voucher';
- *or* an entry clearance valid for settlement.

Both these documents must have been issued on behalf of the UK government. Your spouse and children will be allowed to join you if you can maintain and accommodate them without recourse to public funds (see p59).[21] You can apply for a voucher at a British High Commission or a British Embassy.

The special vouchers were introduced at the same time as the Commonwealth Immigrants Act 1968. There is an annual quota which, in the past, has caused long waiting lists. There are no formal rules stating who will qualify for a voucher. In practice, the applicant must:

- have no other nationality available to them;
- be under pressure to leave the country in which they are resident. (This has mainly applied to people living in East and Central Africa and people who left those countries to go to India);
- be the head of a household (married women are excluded).

Admission of other passport holders

Any national of the five non-British citizen types (see p12) is entitled to be freely admitted to the UK on production of a UK passport issued prior to 1 January 1973 in the UK, Channel Islands or the Isle of Man or Republic of Ireland. The only exceptions are those people whose passports are endorsed to show that they were subject to immigration control.[22]

Obtaining citizenship

Non-British citizen British nationals have certain advantages in acquiring British citizenship and with it the right of abode, freedom from immigration control and thus greater access to social security benefits. For more details, see p18 on registration.

3. DIFFERENT WAYS OF ACQUIRING BRITISH CITIZENSHIP

British citizenship and birth

There are two main factors determining British citizenship:

- whether you were born before or after 1 January 1983 – the date when the British Nationality Act 1981 came into force;
- whether you were born inside or outside the UK.

The *method* by which nationality is obtained is also important:

- if you were born abroad and acquired British citizenship by virtue of the nationality of your parents (British citizens by descent), you cannot automatically pass your citizenship to your own children if they are born abroad;
- if you obtain your citizenship by birth, registration, naturalisation (British citizens otherwise than by descent), you can pass on your citizenship to your children even if they are born abroad. (Special provisions are made for children born to those living abroad who are working for the government);[23]
- BOCs, BSs and BPPs (see above) cannot generally pass on their citizenship, although BDTCs can pass on their citizenship in much the same way as British citizens (see below).

Born before 1 January 1983

Born in the UK

Children born before 1 January 1983 in the UK are British citizens as are those who were adopted here by a British parent. Only children born to diplomats and enemy aliens at times of war have not become British citizens.[24]

Born outside the UK

Children born:

- overseas to British fathers became British citizens if, at the time of the birth, the father was a CUKC other than by descent and the parents

were married. The father must have registered or naturalised;
- in non-Commonwealth countries whose father was a CUKC by descent are British, provided their birth was registered at a British High Commission or Embassy within a year of the birth. They are only British citizens if a grandparent was born in the UK;
- overseas to a British mother and non-British father would not become a British citizen, but the government has allowed such mothers to register their children as British citizens provided they do this before the child is 18.

Born on or after 1 January 1983

Born in the UK

- Children born in the UK after 1 January 1983 are only British citizens if, at the time of their birth, one parent is either a British citizen or is 'settled' (ie, ordinarily resident (see p99) with no restriction on their stay[25]) in the UK.[26]
- Children adopted under an adoption order made in the UK also become British citizens if either of the adoptive parents is a British citizen.[27]
- A child will be a British citizen even if the parent, upon whose citizenship the child relies, dies prior to the child's birth.[28]
- Children born in the UK who are not British citizens can apply to 'register' (see p18) as British citizens after they have been in the UK for 10 years or after either of their parents obtains 'settled' status.
- Children who do not have the nationality of any other country and are not born British, are 'stateless'. For the immigration position of children born in the UK, who are not British, see p8.

'Parent' for these purposes always includes the mother but excludes the father if he is not married to the mother at the time the child is born.[29]

Born outside the UK

- Children born outside the UK on or after 1 January 1983 are British citizens by descent if *either* their father or their mother:
  - is a British citizen by birth, registration or naturalisation (ie, otherwise than by descent);[30] *or*
  - gained the right of abode by living in the UK for five years or more and being settled in the UK before 1 January 1983.
- Children born abroad to parents who are British citizens by descent[31] do not generally become British citizens. These children have certain rights, but the law is complex. You should seek expert advice.

Applying for citizenship

You may be able to acquire British citizen status either by 'naturalisation' or by 'registration'. If you register and satisfy certain conditions for registration, the Home Office must give you British citizenship. If you apply to naturalise, the decision whether or not to grant citizenship is discretionary. The registration fee is £120. The naturalisation fee is either £120 or £150.

Registration

The following people can register:

- **non-British citizen British nationals** who have had settled status (see p33) for a year or more in the UK have a right to register as British citizens if they have lived lawfully in the UK for five years.[32] During that time, they must not have been out of the UK for longer than 450 days in total nor for longer than 90 days in the last year;
- **non-British citizen children** born in the UK have a right to register as British citizens if, while they are still minors, one of their parents becomes settled;[33]
- a child born in the UK, who is stateless, can be registered if s/he remains in the UK for 10 years;[34]
- people born overseas to British citizens who are British by descent can register in one of two ways. You should seek specialist advice if you are in this position.[35]

The Home Office retains a discretion to register all other children. It has been Home Office policy to register those born abroad before 1 January 1983 to British-born mothers provided the application is made while the child is still a minor.

Naturalisation

You can apply to the Home Office to be 'naturalised' as a British citizen if you fulfil all of the following criteria:[36]

- **Settlement** – You must have been settled in the UK – ie, with no restrictions on the length of your stay in the UK ('indefinite leave' to enter or remain – see p32) – for at least a year prior to your application.
- **Residence** – You must have lived lawfully in the UK for five continuous years without absences of more than 450 days (if you are married to a British citizen, three years without absences of more than 270 days) and, in all cases, not more than 90 days of absences in the last year.
- **Language** – If you are not married to a British citizen you must be able to show sufficient ability in either English, Welsh or Scottish Gaelic.
- **Intention to reside in the UK** – If you are not married to a British

citizen, you have to show that you intend to have your main home in the UK.

- **Good character** – You must be of 'good character'. Amongst other matters, criminal convictions may be taken into account.

4. WHAT YOUR PASSPORT SAYS

Passports give evidence of national status at the time they were issued. They are not necessarily conclusive evidence of your *current* status and they cannot account for any change of circumstance or status.

British citizens

If you have a passport issued before 1 January 1983, it should describe you as a CUKC (on page one) with the 'right of abode' (on page five). If you have a passport issued after 1 January 1983, it should simply describe you as a 'British citizen'. Although you have the right of abode, a statement to that effect is not endorsed on the passport.

Other British nationals

If your passport was issued:

- *before* 1 January 1983 and you are a BDTC or a BOC (see p13), it should describe you as a CUKC (on page one) but the statement of right of abode (on page five) will be crossed out or there may be no such statement;
- *after* 1 January 1983, it should describe you as a BDTC, BOC etc.

British subject/Commonwealth citizen with right of abode

If you are a British subject your passport will state this. If you are a Commonwealth citizen with the right of abode in the UK, any passport issued should have a stamp of 'certificate of patriality' (on page five) on passports issued before 1 January 1983. Passports issued after this date should be endorsed with a 'certificate of entitlement'.

Citizenship by registration/naturalisation

If you have been granted citizenship after having applied to register or naturalise, the Home Office will issue a certificate of naturalisation or registration as evidence of citizenship. You can apply to the Passport Agency for a British passport (which is now in the form of the common EU passport).

CHAPTER THREE

The process of controls and determining immigration status

This chapter covers:

This chapter describes the mechanisms for controlling immigration before entry to the UK, on entry and after entry. It also explains the different categories in which people may be admitted and allowed to remain in the UK and who may be able to obtain 'settlement' – ie, the right to reside permanently. In certain circumstances, it is possible to 'switch' categories while in the UK and these situations are detailed. This chapter also deals with the conditions that are attached to any leave, including 'public funds' conditions.

Finally, the chapter explains how to identify a person's immigration status. *This is for guidance only and it is important that advisers without immigration law expertise should refer clients to immigration specialists if there is any doubt about their position or they are seeking to change their status.*

Towards the end of the chapter (pp39-43) and in Appendix 5, the categories of leave and the corresponding conditions that can be attached are set out in tables for ease of reference.

I. HOW BENEFIT ENTITLEMENT IS AFFECTED BY CONTROLS

The following are a number of general points relating to benefit entitlement. See Part 2 for details.

After arrival at immigration control

A number of factors will influence benefit entitlement. After arrival you may be a person:

- who is not entitled to any benefits at all;
- entitled to a limited number of benefits including reduced rate income support (IS)/ jobseeker's allowance (JSA);
- entitled to all benefits provided you satisfy the residence, contribution and means tests.

Depending on your status on arrival and/or the purpose of your stay you may:

- be able to change your status after one year, after four years or at some stage during your stay;
- be able to acquire British citizenship (see p18);
- marry a person who is British, an EU/EEA national or a person with indefinite leave to remain.

If you change your status or you do any of the above, your benefit entitlement may change – for details, see Parts 2 and 4. You can lose the status of indefinite leave to remain (see pp32 and 71). If you are determined to have entered the country clandestinely, unlawfully or illegally this will affect your rights. If you seek to regularise your stay (ie, get permission to stay in a particular capacity) you may be entitled to benefit once leave is granted. This will depend on the nature of the leave you obtain. You may also have limited rights to benefit before you sort out your position but should not claim without getting advice.

In certain circumstances you may be deported. Before this happens there must be a decision in principle to issue a deportation order. You are unlikely to have a right to claim any benefits while you appeal against a decision to make a deportation order.

2. IMMIGRATION CONTROL BEFORE ARRIVAL

Entry clearance

If you are subject to immigration control you *may* need to obtain 'entry clearance' (permission to come to the UK) before arriving in the UK. Entry clearance consists of a number of alternative documents – a visa, an entry certificate or another document which is accepted as evidence of your eligibility to enter the UK.

- If you are a **visa national** (see glossary) entry clearance is in the form of a visa. (Visa nationals include stateless people and those without national documentation.)

- If you are a **non-visa national** your entry clearance is in the form of an entry certificate (or similar document).[1]

Visa and entry certificates are shown as endorsements on your passport[2] (see p46) and are valid for a certain length of time (often six months) from the date of issue. This means that you must arrive in the UK and present the entry clearance within the period specified. However, your period of leave to *enter* will run from the date the immigration officer stamps your passport after your arrival. An entry clearance, unless it is marked for multiple entry, may only be used once.

People who must get entry clearance

Whether or not you need an entry clearance depends on your national status and your reasons for coming to the UK. The general rules are:[3]

- **visa nationals** require entry clearance *whatever* their purpose for coming to the UK;
- **non-visa nationals** require entry clearance (or alternatively some other documentation fulfilling a similar function – eg, a valid Department for Education and Employment work permit) *for entry only for non-temporary purposes* – ie, categories which may lead to settlement (indefinite leave to remain).

If you are returning to the UK, within the time of a previous grant of leave, then you do not need an entry clearance as long as you are seeking entry for the same purpose as you were previously in the UK.[4]

There are important exceptions to these general rules in the case of refugees. For further information about how to obtain entry clearance see JCWI *Handbook*.

When entry clearance is optional

Although you may not *need* an entry clearance in order to obtain admission under the rules, you can choose to get entry clearance before travelling to be more sure of your eligibility for admission to the UK.[5] For example, the rules positively recommend that prospective au pairs obtain entry clearance prior to travelling.[6] In deciding whether to apply for entry clearance where this is not strictly required, you need to weigh up the additional cost and delay of getting an entry clearance against the risk of being refused on arrival in the UK when you arrive without it. You should also be aware that even if you have an entry clearance, admission to the UK on arrival is not guaranteed – see p26.

Obtaining entry clearance

You must be outside the UK when you make your application for entry clearance. Applications are usually made to a British Embassy, High Commission or Consulate[7] in the country in which you are living unless:

- there is no such post in that country; *or*
- you are applying to come to the UK as a visitor;

in which case you may apply to a post which accepts applications in that capacity.[8] You will not be considered to have made the application until you have paid the appropriate fee.[9]

To apply for entry clearance, you need to complete the relevant forms which may be obtained either from the British Embassy/High Commission or the Migration and Visa Department of the Foreign and Commonwealth Office in the UK. A sponsor or relative in the UK may fill in the forms but they must be signed and presented to one of the designated posts by the applicant. Often the entry clearance officer will interview the applicant and may conduct further investigations such as making enquiries at other agencies or even visiting relatives or neighbours.[10]

If the application is successful, the entry clearance is endorsed on the passport. If not, the notice of the refusal and the brief reasons for it should be given to you.[11]

Rules applied in entry clearance decisions

When deciding whether to grant entry clearance to a person in a particular category, the entry clearance officer (ECO) takes account of exactly the same requirements as govern leave to enter in that category[12] (see p24). The requirements in the rules are applied to the circumstances that exist at the date of the *decision* on the entry clearance application. The only exception relates to a child applying to join parents for settlement in the UK. In this instance, the child's age is taken to be the age at the date of application rather than the date of the decision.[13] These considerations are important as there is often a long delay between making an entry clearance application and the decision on that application. The fact that there may be long delays could have benefit implications. For example, the definition of 'family' for income support (IS) and jobseeker's allowance (JSA) purposes is affected by the period a couple are living apart (see p106).

The immigration rules always emphasise that leave *may* be granted if the particular requirements of the rules relating to the category in question are satisfied. In other words, even if you satisfy the requirements of the rules for the category in which you seek entry, you may still be refused an entry clearance under the 'general grounds' for which leave may be refused. These rules are similar for applications for entry clearance, leave to enter and leave to remain – see p45.

Revocation of entry clearance

Entry clearances may also be revoked if the ECO is satisfied that it was obtained by false representations, or a failure to disclose material facts, or that there has been a change of circumstances since it was issued, or if the person's exclusion is conducive to public good.[14]

Certificates of entitlement

If you are a British citizen or other person with the right of abode in the UK, you can obtain your certificate of entitlement from the entry clearance officer at a British post overseas.

3. IMMIGRATION CONTROL ON ARRIVAL

Examination on arrival

Immigration officers carry out examinations of people on their arrival at a port of entry to the UK in order to determine whether the person:[15]

- is a British citizen; *or*
- may otherwise enter the UK without leave; *or*
- if subject to control, should be granted leave to enter the UK and, if so, for what period and upon which conditions.

Note that if the person is in one of the first two categories s/he should generally be entitled to claim all social security benefits although s/he may have to satisfy a residence test. Whether a person in the third category qualifies will depend on the conditions attached to their stay. For full details, see Part 2.

Immigration officers may detain people required to submit to examination pending that examination, if it is not carried out immediately, and pending a decision to give or refuse them leave to enter.[16]

Sometimes a person applying for leave to enter is granted 'temporary admission'. Temporary admission is not leave to enter or remain in the UK; it is a restricted licence to be at large in the UK. A person with temporary admission may be treated differently for benefit purposes than a person with limited leave, especially for HB/CTB (see Chapters 15 and 16).

If you have been examined by an immigration officer, and no decision to give or refuse leave is made within 24 hours, you will be 'deemed' to have been granted leave to enter for six months with a condition prohibiting your employment.[17] However, the examination will not necessarily be concluded after a single interview. The process may continue for some time until immigration officers have carried out further investigations into your circumstances. For example, there is no prospect of an immediate decision for those who apply for asylum on entry. In order to decide whether or not such people may be granted leave to enter as refugees, the immigration officer has to refer the application to the Secretary of State for a decision.[18] As a result, asylum-seekers are invariably either given temporary admission or detained. If a person applies for asylum on arrival, s/he will qualify for means-tested benefits (IS, income-based JSA, HB, CTB); if s/he applies *after* entry s/he may not (see Chapter 17).

Evidence of leave to enter

Where leave to enter is granted, the immigration officer will place a rectangular date stamp in your passport together with a statement of the length of the leave (if there is any limitation) and any conditions attached to the leave. You may stay in the UK for the length of time indicated by the stamp. The leave period begins from the date of the stamp itself.

Indefinite leave to enter is usually signified by a rectangular date stamp with the words 'given leave to enter for an indefinite period'. Depending on the facts of your case, a date stamp with no time limit may not be enough to amount to an indefinite leave if, for example, the immigration officer did not intend to give you indefinite leave.[19]

- If the stamp in your passport is either unclear or illegible, you will be deemed to have been granted leave to enter for *six months* with a condition prohibiting you from taking employment.[20]
- If you arrived in the UK before 10 July 1988 and were given an unclear or illegible stamp in your passport, you are deemed to have been given indefinite leave to enter the UK.[21]
- If you are a person who requires leave to enter the UK and *no stamp* is placed in your passport (because, for example, you were simply waved through by the immigration officer), through no fault of your own you may be considered an 'illegal entrant'[22] (see p73).

Refusal of leave to enter

If leave to enter is to be refused, the immigration officer must first obtain the authority of either a Chief Immigration Officer or an Immigration Inspector.[23] You must be given written notice of any such refusal which must also inform you of any appeal rights.[24] After you have been refused leave to enter the UK and have had the opportunity to exercise any in-country rights of appeal (see Chapter 6), the immigration officer also has the power to set directions for your removal from the UK.[25]

Entry clearance and obtaining leave to enter

Even if you have valid entry clearance when you arrive in the UK, you can still be refused leave to enter if:[26]

- false representations were made for the purpose of obtaining entry clearance;
- material facts were not disclosed for the purpose of obtaining entry clearance;
- there has been a change of circumstances since the entry clearance was issued which removes the grounds for granting admission.

Returning to the UK during leave period

If you leave the UK and then return within the period of an existing leave then, unless you apply to return in a different category, the leave that you obtain on your return will usually be limited to the same period as the previous grant of leave and may be subject to the same conditions.[27]

When you are admitted in this way, you should have a stamp in your passport endorsed 'section 3(3)(b)' (a reference to section 3(3)(b) of the Immigration Act 1971). A previously unexpired leave to enter or remain is not a visa and you may still, therefore, be refused leave without the right of appeal when you re-enter the UK if you have ceased to meet the requirements of the rules.[28]

4. IMMIGRATION CONTROL AFTER ARRIVAL

Responsibility for control after arrival

Once you have entered the UK lawfully or unlawfully,[29] responsibility for regulating your immigration position passes to the Secretary of State for the Home Department (the Home Secretary acting through the Home Office).[30] You have not 'entered' the UK while you are temporarily admitted or detained under the authority of an immigration officer. Once you have entered the UK, any application for permission to stay longer is an application for leave to *remain*.[31]

Applying for leave to remain

If you are subject to immigration control and are granted only a limited leave to enter (or remain) in the UK, you may decide you want to stay for a longer period. Under these circumstances, you must apply to the Home Office for an extension of your leave *prior to the expiry of your existing leave*.[32] In other cases, you should, subject to proper legal advice, make an application as soon as possible. The application should be made direct to the Department for Education and Employment Overseas Labour Service if it concerns:[33]

- employment for which a work permit or a permit for training or work experience is required; *or*
- the spouse or child of a person who is making such an application.

For details about extending leave, see below. The circumstances under which you may 'switch' from one category to another are set out below. You should also note that in certain categories there is a limitation on the total amount of time you may spend in the UK (see p31). In addition, the Home Office may add, vary or revoke conditions attached to your leave.[34] If you do not apply 'in time':

- your application for further leave may be refused under the immigration rules;[35]
- any right of appeal you have if your application is unsuccessful will be lost;[36]
- you become liable for deportation as an 'overstayer'[37] and may be liable to criminal prosecution;[38]
- you may lose the right to claim IS/income-based JSA/HB/CTB (see Chapter 15).

No conditions will be attached to your leave if you are granted indefinite leave to enter the UK.

How to apply

Prior to 27 November 1996, there were no special rules as to what counted as an application for an extension of leave. Any clear and unambiguous request to the Home Office either in person or by letter accompanied by your passport or travel document was acceptable.[39] Since 27 November 1996, all applications to the Home Office for leave to remain other than asylum applications, work permit applications and certain EEA applications must be made on the appropriate Home Office application form.[40] The form must be properly completed and sent to the Home Office along with all the documents requested on the form or an explanation why such documents have not been supplied and when they will be sent.

If these procedures are not followed, then your application will not be valid and you *may* therefore have failed to apply in time – for the consequences of failing to apply in time, see above. You can get the appropriate application form by telephoning the Application Forms Unit at the Home Office (see Appendix 2). If you are sending your application by post you should send it by recorded delivery.

If you request the return of your passport in order to travel outside the common travel area (see p3) your application is treated as withdrawn.[41]

When the Home Office varies your leave (ie, grants or refuses leave or alters the conditions or time for which you can stay), it must give you a written notice of the variation and any rights of appeal.[42] Where leave is varied, this will be shown on your passport or travel document.

Automatic extensions of leave

The Variation of Leave Order 1976 (known as 'VOLO') automatically extends leave that would otherwise run out before the Home Office makes a decision on your application for an extension. Before VOLO, applicants who had made applications in time but were still awaiting a decision when their leave ran out became overstayers with no right of appeal against the decision.[43]

You can appeal against a refusal to vary leave if you have limited leave at the time the notice of appeal against the decision is given.[44] The effect of VOLO is to extend a period of limited leave from the day you make your application (provided the application is made in time) until 28 days after the date of the decision on the application.[45] This enables you to submit your notice of appeal while you still have a period of limited leave and thus ensures that the appeal is valid. You must still send off your appeal to arrive within the time-limits allowed by the appeals procedure rules.[46]

There are certain circumstances in which VOLO does not operate.[47] The most important of these is where the application is made at a time when the applicant enjoys a limited leave *only* by virtue of VOLO. So, if you make a further application for an extension of leave when your previous leave would have expired but for an extension brought into operation by VOLO, then VOLO will not operate *again* to provide you a further automatic extension of leave. You may still have a right of appeal in respect of this second application but only if the Home Office makes a decision on the application before your first VOLO extension has expired. The Home Office can easily avoid this outcome by delaying the decision on the application.

Time waiting for an appeal

VOLO only operates to ensure an applicant does not lose the *right* to appeal. After notice of appeal has been given, and the VOLO leave expires, you no longer have lawful leave to remain in the UK. However, you cannot be *required to leave* the UK while you are waiting for your variation appeal to be heard[48] (but see further the section on appeals in

Chapter 6 below). If you are appealing against a variation made to your leave, then normally that variation will not take effect while the appeal is pending.[49]

Example

A Sierra Leonian woman subject to immigration control had limited leave to remain until 1 July 1996 as a working holidaymaker. In May 1996, she married a British citizen and on 28 June 1996 applied for leave to remain as the spouse of a British citizen. The couple were interviewed by the Home Office in November 1996 but a decision on the application was not made until 1997. On 1 January 1997, the Home Office posted a notice of refusal to the woman which she received the next day. However, she did not deliver her notice of appeal until 25 January 1997.

Although the woman remained in the UK, she did not become an overstayer and could not be deported or removed from the UK after 1 July 1996 because her leave was extended by VOLO until midnight on 29 January 1997.[50] Because she submitted her notice of appeal at a time when she still had limited leave, the appellate authorities still had jurisdiction to hear her appeal against the refusal. However, the procedure rules state that notice of appeal against a refusal to vary leave should be given not more than 14 days after the refusal to vary.[51] As a result, before the woman's appeal can proceed, the Secretary of State or the adjudicator must be satisfied that, by reason of 'special circumstances', it is 'just and right' to allow the appeal to proceed.[52] On 1 March 1997, the Secretary of State decided that there were no special circumstances and so the matter came before the adjudicator on 29 June 1997 (a year after the original application). The adjudicator decided that, because the woman did not read or write English and because she did not have any legal representatives at the time she was informed of her rights of appeal, she was unaware of the time limits stated on the notice of refusal and, therefore, the appeal should be allowed to proceed.

After 30 January 1997, the woman did not have any 'leave' to remain in the UK but no steps could be taken to *require* her to exit the UK because she had an appeal pending against a refusal to vary her leave to remain.

Curtailment of leave

In certain circumstances, the Home Office can 'curtail' limited leave to enter or remain – ie, bring your leave to an end before it is otherwise due to expire. When your leave is curtailed you become a person with no leave (an overstayer) and this may have benefit implications (see Chapter 16). Leave may be curtailed in the following circumstances:[53]

- false representations are made or there is a failure to disclose a material fact for the purpose of obtaining leave to enter or a previous variation of leave;
- you fail to comply with any conditions attached to the grant of leave to enter or to remain;
- you fail to maintain or accommodate yourself and any dependants without recourse to public funds;
- it is undesirable to allow you to remain in the UK in the light of your character, conduct, associations or the fact that you represent a threat to national security;
- you make a claim to asylum which is rejected by the Secretary of State or if you are the dependant of such a person.

An indefinite leave to enter or remain may not be curtailed.[54]

After entry enforcement of departure

There are two basic methods of enforcing the departure from the UK of those who are subject to the ordinary requirements of immigration control:

- removal (after arrival or as an illegal entrant); *and*
- deportation.

You may be *removed* by the immigration officer after having been refused leave to enter the UK. You may also be *removed* having entered the UK if you are found to have entered the UK illegally – ie, in breach of the immigration laws or while a deportation order was in force against you.[55] If you enter the UK lawfully but *subsequently*:

- breach your conditions of leave; *or*
- stay beyond the time limited by your leave; *or*
- obtain leave by deception;

you may be *deported*.[56] It is also possible to be deported from the UK if:[57]

- your presence is not conducive to the public good (as being contrary to the interests of national security or otherwise);
- another person to whose 'family' (see p72) you belong is being deported;
- being 17 years old or over your deportation is recommended by a criminal court after you have committed an offence punishable with imprisonment.

Confusingly, the last stage of the deportation process is also removal. The main differences between the procedures relate to the rights of appeal and the fact that those who leave under a deportation order usually cannot return for at least three years (see Chapter 6 for details).

Police registration

As part of control after entry to the UK you may have to register with the police if:[58]

- you are not a citizen of a Commonwealth country or an EU/EEA national; *and*
- you are aged 16 years or over and awarded a period of limited leave for more than six months in certain specified circumstances or, for employment purposes which require a work permit, for longer than three months.

To register you must notify your local police station of your name, address, employment and marital status and of any changes to those details as they occur.[59]

5. LEAVE, CONDITIONS AND SETTLEMENT

People who do not have the right of abode in the UK and who are therefore subject to immigration control require **leave to enter** (on arrival) and **leave to remain** (after entry).[60] (Special rules apply to certain special groups, see p7). Leave is of two kinds:[61]

- **limited leave** to enter or remain;
- **indefinite leave** to enter or remain.

Leave is a specific permission to remain. It must be distinguished from, for example, a period of grace in order to allow time to make a voluntary departure from the UK.[62]

For charts listing the types of status and conditions attached to leave, see pp39-43 and Appendix 5.

Limited leave

If you have a limited leave, you can only remain in the UK for a limited period of time. In order lawfully to remain in the UK after the time permitted, you must obtain further leave to remain and the application must be made before the existing leave ends (see p27). Certain conditions can be attached to a limited leave to enter or remain which may:[63]

- restrict or prohibit the employment or occupation you can take in the UK;
- require you to maintain and accommodate yourself and any dependants without recourse to public funds;[64]
- require you to register with the police if you are not a citizen of a Commonwealth country or an EU/EEA national;

- require you to report to a medical officer at a specified time and date.

The immigration rules set out the length of limited leave normally granted to a successful applicant in any category and the conditions that may be imposed upon that leave.

Limited leave may be varied if you apply directly to the Secretary of State. The Secretary of State can act unilaterally under the immigration rules. When leave is varied it may be extended, restricted, the time-limit removed or the conditions attached to it may be revoked or varied[65] (for chart of categories of people with limited leave, see pp39-43 and Appendix 5).

Employment conditions

The rules distinguish between:

- a **prohibition** upon employment (eg, visitors are usually prohibited from working[66]); *and*
- a **restriction** upon the freedom to take employment (given, for example, to students[67]).

While you can apply to the Department for Education and Employment to get working *restrictions* lifted in order to work legally, if you have a *prohibition* on working you must apply to the Home Office for the terms of your leave to be varied.

Overstaying leave and breaching conditions of leave

The consequences of overstaying your leave or otherwise breaching the conditions of your leave are that:

- you may be deported from the UK;[68]
- you are liable to be prosecuted for a criminal offence (although prosecutions are rare);[69]
- your existing leave to enter or remain in the UK may be curtailed;[70]
- any future applications under the immigration rules for entry clearance, leave to enter and leave to remain may be less likely to succeed.[71]

Indefinite leave

Indefinite leave to enter or remain in the UK (known as ILE and ILR) is leave without a time restriction. No conditions relating to employment, public funds etc can be attached to an indefinite leave.[72] Therefore, indefinite leave amounts to a right of permanent residence in the UK. However, a person who has indefinite leave is still a person who is subject to immigration control. Such people may, therefore, be deported on grounds that their presence is not conducive to the public good or following a recommendation made by the criminal court.[73] When they leave the common travel area (see p3) their leave lapses. They must then satisfy the provisions of the immigration rules in order to re-enter the UK.

If you had indefinite leave when you left the UK you can seek to re-enter as a returning resident[74] if you:

- can show that your re-entry is for the purpose of settlement;
- have been away from the UK for no more than two years (unless there are special circumstances – eg, previous long residence);
- did not receive assistance from public funds towards the cost of leaving the UK. 'Public funds' are restrictively defined[75] – for further details, see Chapter 5.

Settlement

A person who has indefinite leave is usually also settled in the UK. To be settled, you have to be lawfully 'ordinarily resident' (see p99) in the UK without your stay being time limited.[76] In practice, therefore, the terms 'indefinite leave to remain' and 'settlement' are often used interchangeability. People who are not subject to immigration controls are normally accepted as being settled as well. A person who is settled *and* subject to control may:

- come and go as a returning resident;
- have no conditions or limitations imposed on their leave; *but*
- be liable to deportation in the same circumstances described above.

You must be settled in order:

- to naturalise or register as a British citizen;[77]
- for your children born in the UK to become British citizens by birth[78] (see Chapter 2);
- to bring members of your family to the UK *under the immigration rules* (not just your spouse and children under 18 years) with a view to their living permanently in the UK with you.[79]

The following are the most important routes to settlement:

- Certain categories of admission under the immigration rules lead to the obtaining of indefinite leave to remain and settled status (usually after a period of limited leave in that capacity). Other more temporary categories do not lead to settlement (see below under categories of admission).
- Members of the family of a person (the sponsor) settled in the UK are also admitted with a view to settlement under the rules.

- Admission in other capacities leads to settlement even though there is no provision in the rules dealing with such settlement:
  - if you are a refugee you will normally be granted indefinite leave after four years;
  - if you are refused full refugee status but are nevertheless allowed to remain exceptionally because you are thought to be in need of some form of protection you may be granted indefinite leave after seven years leave (see p52);
  - if you have lived in the UK for a long period of time, you *may* be eligible to be granted indefinite leave to remain outside the immigration rules. In order to qualify, you need to show that you have remained in the UK either lawfully for ten years or otherwise for fourteen years. Indefinite leave on the basis of long residence is wholly discretionary and all of your circumstances – in particular, the nature of your immigration history – will be taken into account;
  - if you are liable for deportation or other forms of enforcement but the Secretary of State decides not to proceed against you or you are successful on appeal, then in order to regularise your position you would normally be granted indefinite leave even though you cannot fit into one of the categories under the rules.

6. CATEGORIES OF ADMISSION AND SWITCHING CATEGORY

Purpose of entering or staying in the UK

An application for leave is generally made for a particular purpose. If you do not state a purpose, the immigration authorities will ask you to say why you wish to enter the UK. The new forms which *must* be used for applications for leave to *remain*[80] will mean that the nature of the application will be taken from the form used. For example, when applying to *enter*:

- a Colombian man says that he wishes to enter 'in order to see his terminally ill mother in the UK before she dies';
- an Australian woman applies to come to the UK 'solely for a business meeting'.

Both these applications would be treated as applications for a visit and, if the requirements of the rules were found to be satisfied, the person would be admitted in the category of a visitor.

The immigration rules divide people into different categories according to the reason they are seeking leave to stay in the UK. In order to succeed in an application for entry clearance, leave to enter or an extension of leave you have to satisfy the appropriate requirements. It is not within the scope of this book to set out the requirements of the rules for the different categories or to attempt to explain what those different requirements actually mean. See Appendix 3 for sources of more detailed information. Details are only given in this book as to the common 'maintenance and accommodation' requirements which are explained in Chapter 5. The following examples illustrate the different requirements for those seeking leave to enter as students or as refugees.

Example I: students

To obtain leave to enter the UK as a student, the rules state you must:[81]

- be accepted for a course of study at either a publicly funded institution of further or higher education or a recognised private education institution or an independent fee-paying school; *and*
- be able and intend to follow *either* a recognised full-time degree course at a publicly funded institution of further or higher education *or* a weekday full-time course at a further or higher education college including at least 15 hours supervised study or a full-time course of study at an independent school; *and*
- be enrolled at an independent school for recognised full-time study; *and*
- intend to leave the UK at the end of your studies; *and*
- not intend to engage in business or take employment, except officially agreed part-time or vacation work; *and*
- be able to meet the cost of your course, accommodation and maintenance of yourself and any dependants without taking employment, engaging in business or having recourse to public funds (see p59).

To satisfy the immigration officer you will therefore need to provide details of your school/college/means/previous academic record. You may be admitted to the UK for a period appropriate to your course. You could still be refused leave even if you meet the above criteria if the 'general grounds' of refusal apply (see p45).[82] If you do not meet the rules for students you will not usually be given leave to enter.[83] In exceptional circumstances, the immigration authorities could waive the rules and admit you to the UK exceptionally (see Chapter 4).

Under the rules two conditions will probably be attached to your leave:

- you will not be allowed to take employment without permission;[84] *and*
- you maintain and accommodate yourself without recourse to public funds.[85]

Many foreign students are allowed to take vacation work to assist them with their maintenance during their studies. In order to get such permission, they must apply to the Department for Education and Employment at a JobCentre.

Example 2: refugees

To obtain leave to enter the UK as a refugee, you must:[86]

- be in the UK or have arrived at a port of entry in the UK; *and*
- be a refugee. A refugee is defined as a person who 'owing to a well-founded fear of being persecuted for reasons of race, religion, nationality, membership of a particular social group or political opinion, is outside his country of nationality and is unable or, owing to such fear, is unwilling to avail himself of the protection of that country; or who, not having a nationality and being outside the country of his former habitual residence…is unable or, owing to such fear, is unwilling to return to it'.[87]

You can still be refused asylum and leave to enter or remain in the UK as a refugee if you can be sent to another ('third') country of which you are not a national or citizen, in which your life or liberty would not be threatened for a Convention reason. The third country must be one:

- in which the government of that country would not send you on to the country in which you have a well-founded fear of persecution; *and*
- through which you travelled in order to come to the UK *and* you had the opportunity there to make contact with the authorities of that country and claim asylum there; *or*
- to which there is clear evidence that you would be admitted.

The onus is on applicants to show they satisfy the rules. Obtaining the necessary evidence and ensuring there are no misunderstandings, errors or discrepancies in the application is of the utmost importance. The credibility of the case presented is particularly important in refugee cases.

Dependants and family members

Family members can apply to join a relative (the sponsor) who is present and settled/or is being admitted for settlement in the UK. Such applications are, in themselves, a category under the rules. These family members include a spouse, a child under 18, and also elderly parents, grandparents, sisters, brothers, aunts and uncles. In certain circumstances, a child can be admitted to join a step-parent or adoptive parent. A sponsor almost always counts as settled if s/he has indefinite leave to enter or remain or if s/he is not subject to immigration controls (see p33).

You may also be admitted as a family member to join a person in the UK who is not here in a settled capacity. The conditions you must satisfy vary according to the status of the person you are joining. For example, a child joining a working holidaymaker must be under five, not under eighteen.[88] If the person you are joining is required not to have recourse to public funds, this will generally apply to you as well.

To count as a spouse under the immigration rules, you and your partner must be 16 years or over. If you are a woman you cannot qualify as a spouse if your marriage is polygamous and there is another wife alive who has:[89]

- *either* been in the UK since her marriage to your husband;
- *or* has been given (by the issue of a certificate of entitlement) the right of abode or has been granted entry clearance to enter the UK as the wife of your husband.

However, if another wife was here as a visitor or entered illegally or did not disembark from the ship or aircraft this will not affect your rights as the spouse. You will also still qualify as the spouse if you: [90]

- were in the UK before 1 August 1988 having been admitted for settlement as the wife of your husband; *or*
- have, since your marriage, been in the UK at any time since your husband's other wife or wives died.

Temporary and permanent/settled purposes

Some people are only admitted for temporary purposes which do not lead to settlement. In these cases, the leave granted is always time limited and applicants are expected to leave the UK when the purpose for which leave was granted has been fulfilled. Other people are admitted for longer term or permanent purposes which lead to indefinite leave and 'settlement' in the UK (both these terms amount to the right to live permanently in the UK – see p32 on indefinite leave and p33 on settlement). For some permanent/settled purposes, indefinite leave can be granted immediately, whereas in others, indefinite leave is usually only granted after a period of limited leave in the UK.

About the tables

The following tables set out separately the temporary categories and the categories leading to settlement together with a reference to the appropriate paragraphs in the current immigration rules.[91] It is important to identify whether you are in a category leading to settlement and, if so, whether you have to wait one or more years with limited leave before becoming settled or whether you may be settled immediately. Settled status is advantageous as it gives you increased rights to benefits, see Part 2. The tables also list:

- maintenance and accommodation/public funds requirements relating to the applicant and any dependants in each category; *and*
- employment conditions on limited leave granted in each category; *and*
- any requirements that relate to employment that you need to satisfy in order to obtain leave in that category; *and*
- whether an entrance clearance is required for entry of non-visa nationals; *and*
- at what point an applicant may become settled.

The employment factors are relevant to the 'available for and actively seeking work' test which affects access to JSA (for details of entitlement, see pp188-91). A condition 'restricting the freedom' of an applicant to take employment means that the s/he must apply to the Secretary of State for Education and Employment for permission to take or to change em - ployment of a particular kind with a particular employer. Provided you obtain permission, then you will not be in breach of your conditions of leave by taking the employment where such a restriction is imposed.

The tables give the maintenance and accommodation *requirements* for each category. This includes whether, in order to get leave in the first place, you are required not to have recourse to pubic funds. The rules do not currently state when a *condition* (as distinct from a requirement) that you are not to have recourse will also be imposed as part of your leave to remain. However, in practice, this condition is likely to be imposed if your leave is under a category which requires you not to have recourse to public funds. If your leave is under one of these categories, the benefit rules normally prevent entitlement to public funds. There are exceptions, so some people may be entitled. For details, see the chapter relevant to your immigration status in Part 2.

The tables state for each category whether an entry clearance is re- quired for entry to the UK *in that capacity*. When it is required everyone including non visa-nationals requires an entry clearance.

Finally, the table dealing with the 'non-temporary' categories states, in relation to each category, at what point it is possible to obtain indefinite leave to remain (normally after one or four years depending on the cate- gory, but sometimes immediately).

Switching categories

There are basically two types of category:

- temporary – see Appendix 5;
- permanent or 'leading to settlement' – see pp39-43.

Purposes leading to settlement		A=Applicant			
Category	Rule (HC395)	Employment conditions	Additional employment requirements	Requirements that applicant and dependants are adequately maintained and accommodated without recourse to public funds	Entry clearance required for non-visa nationals
Returning residents (immediate settlement)	18-20	None	None	None (but must show that A did not receive assistance from public funds towards cost of leaving the UK previously)	No
Work permit employment (leads to settlement after four years)	128-135	Freedom to take employment restricted to the approved employment	Must not intend to take employment other than that specified in the work permit	Yes, A must be 'able' to so maintain and accommodate	No, but work permit is required
Permit-free employment – ie, representatives of overseas media or businesses, diplomatic private servants, overseas government employees, ministers of religion, overseas airline ground crews (leads to settlement after four years)	136-185	None for which admitted	Must intend to work only in the occupation	Yes, A must show s/he 'can' so maintain and accommodate government employee'	Yes, although those in the category of 'overseas may, as an alternative, present any satisfactory evidence of their status
Commonwealth citizens with United Kingdom ancestry (leads to settlement after four years)	186-193	None	Must intend to take or seek employment	Yes, A must show that s/he 'will be able' to so maintain and accommodate	Yes, for leave to enter but not for leave to remain
Spouse and children of person with limited leave as work permit holder, permit-free employment, Commonwealth citizen with United Kingdom ancestry (leads to settlement in line with spouse/parent)	194-199	None	None	Yes, parties must show that they are 'able' to so maintain and that there will be such accommodation which they own or occupy exclusively. Child must show s/he 'can and will' be so maintained and accommodated in accommodation owned exclusively by her/his parents	Yes

Persons establishing themselves in business (leads to settlement after four years)	200-210	Freedom to take employment restricted	A must show that s/he will be actively involved full-time in the business and that s/he does not intend to take or seek employment in the UK other than work for the business	Yes, A must show that s/he has 'sufficient additional' funds to so maintain and accommodate until such time as the business provides A with an income and, thereafter, that A's share of the profits from the business will be sufficient for such maintenance and accommodation. A must show that this is the case without A's recourse to employment other than work for the business	Yes
Persons intending to establish themselves in business under the provision of an EC Association Agreement (leads to settlement after four years)	211-223	Freedom to take employment restricted	A must show that s/he will be actively involved in promoting/ managing the company or (if self employed or partnership) that s/he will be actively involved in trading or providing services and must not intend to supplement business activities by taking or seeking employment in the UK other than work for the business	Yes, A must show that s/he has 'sufficient additional' funds to so maintain and accommodate until such time as the business provides A with an income and, thereafter, that A's share of the profits from the business will be sufficient for such maintenance and accommodation. A must show that this is the case without A's recourse to employment other than work for the business	Yes, for entry but not in order to seek leave to remain
Investors (leads to settlement after four years)	224-231	Freedom to take employment restricted	None	Yes, A must be 'able' to so maintain and accommodate without taking employment (other than self employment or business)	Yes

Category	Ref	Freedom to take employment restricted	Must not intend to work other than as...	Maintenance and accommodation	
Writers/composers/artists (leads to settlement after four years)	232–239	Freedom to take employment restricted	Must not intend to work other than as related to self employment as a writer, composer, artist	Yes, A must show that s/he has previously been so maintained and accommodated and from A's own resources without working except as a writer/composer/artist. A must show that s/he 'will be able' to so maintain and accommodate from her/his own resources without working except as a writer/composer/artist	Yes
Spouse and children of person with limited leave as a person establishing themselves in business (under the provisions of an EC Association Agreement or not), investor/writer/composer/artist (leads to settlement in line with spouse/parent concerned)	240–245	None	None	Yes, the parties to the marriage must show that they 'will be able' to so maintain and that there will be such accommodation owned or occupied by themselves exclusively. Child must show s/he 'can and will' be so maintained and accommodated in accommodation which her/his parents own or occupy exclusively	Yes
Holder of Special Voucher (indefinite leave granted on admission)	249–254	None	None	None	Yes, *or be in possession of a special voucher issued by the British overseas post (High Commission/Embassy)*
Spouse and/or child of special voucher holder (indefinite leave granted on admission)	252–254	None	None	Yes, A must show that s/he 'can and will' be so maintained and accommodated	Yes

Retired person of independent means (leads to settlement after four years) and their spouse and children (leads to settlement in line with spouse/parent)	263-276	Employment prohibited	None	Yes, A must be 'able and willing' to so maintain and accommodate indefinitely from her/his own resources with no assistance from any other person and without taking employment. If the spouse is admitted, the parties must show that they 'will be able' to so maintain and accommodate in accommodation which they own or occupy exclusively. A child must show s/he 'can and will' be so maintained and accommodated in accommodation owned or occupied exclusively by her/his parent(s)	Yes
Spouse of settled person in UK (leave granted for twelve months initially, thereafter indefinite leave granted)	281-289	None	None	Yes, the parties must show that they 'will be able' to so maintain and that there will be such accommodation owned or occupied by themselves exclusively	Yes, required on entry but not for leave to remain
Fiance of settled person in UK (granted limited leave initially; with a view to marriage and settlement)	290-295	Employment prohibited	None	Yes, A must show that there will be adequate maintenance and accommodation available to her/him until the date of the marriage and that, after the marriage, the parties to the marriage 'will be able' to so maintain and that there will be such accommodation owned or occupied by themselves exclusively	Yes
Child of settled parent(s) or relatives in UK (indefinite leave granted on admission)	297-300	None	None	Yes, A must show that s/he 'can and will' be so maintained and accommodated in accommodation which the parent(s) or relatives own or occupy exclusively	Yes, on entry but not always in order to obtain leave to remain – eg, if the child was under 18

Child of parent(s) given limited leave to enter or remain in UK with a view to settlement (given limited leave initially with a view to eventual settlement)	301-303	None	None	Yes, A must show that s/he 'can and will' be so maintained and accommodated in accommodation owned or occupied exclusively by parent(s)	Yes
Parents, grandparents and other dependent relatives of persons settled in the UK (admitted with indefinite leave)	317-319	None	None	Yes, A must show that s/he 'can and will' be so maintained and accommodated in accommodation owned or occupied exclusively by the sponsor	Yes, on entry but not in order to remain
Refugee and spouse and child of refugee (limited leave granted initially, settlement usually follows after four years) and spouse and children	327-352	None	None	No	No

Note: For the requirements relating to non-British citizen children born in the UK to parent(s) given leave to enter or remain, see paras 304-309 HC 395 and for adopted children, see paras 310-316 HC 395.

Switching between categories and acquiring more rights while in the UK has been made more difficult by changes in the immigration rules.

In general, it is not possible to switch from purely temporary categories to permanent categories, or between permanent categories. You can switch from temporary to temporary or from permanent to temporary (although this would often remove benefit rights), provided you satisfy the requirements of the rules – in particular, the intention to leave requirement relevant to most categories of temporary leave. The immigration rules achieve this by generally imposing a requirement that the applicant entered the UK with a valid entry clearance in the capacity of the permanent category in which leave to remain is sought

In many permanent categories, the rules require you to remain in the UK with limited leave in the same capacity for a period of continuous years before applying for settlement (see pp39-43 and Appendix 5). It is often possible to ask for further leave in the *same* capacity. However, some categories (eg, a visitor) have a maximum period it is permitted to spend in *total* before you are required to leave.

The following are the *exceptions* to the general rules above:

i) It is possible to switch into any of the following categories if you are in any permanent or temporary category:

- a Commonwealth citizen with UK ancestry seeking to work in the UK (but not the spouse or child of such a person);[92]
- a person intending to establish her/himself in business under the provisions of an EC Association Agreement (but not the spouse or child of such a person);[93]
- the spouse of a person present and settled in the UK;[94]
- the parent, grandparent or other dependent relative of a person present and settled in the UK;[95]
- a refugee or accompanying spouse or child.[96]

ii) It is not possible to switch from a temporary or a permanent category into a temporary category for which an entry clearance or similar documentation is generally required (unless such entry clearance was obtained prior to entry). In other words, it is not possible to switch to:

- working holidaymaker or child of such a person;[97]
- seasonal worker at an agricultural camp;[98]
- teacher or language assistant under an approved scheme or spouse/child of such a person;[99]
- a person undertaking approved training or work experience (unless you were admitted or allowed to remain as a student) or the spouse/child of such a person.[100]

iii) It is not possible for **visa nationals** to switch from a temporary or a

iii) It is not possible for **visa nationals** to switch from a temporary or a permanent category into the following temporary categories *even though a visa is not mandatory for non-visa nationals*:

- student[101] (*unless* you are a national of any of the countries added to the visa national list from 4 April 1996[102] *and* your current leave to enter or remain was granted before 4 April 1996);[103]
- student nurse;[104]
- prospective student.[105]

In addition, it is not possible to switch to being an au pair. In order to obtain an extension in this capacity you need to have been granted leave to enter the UK as an au pair.[106] Also, you may not switch into the category of a person exercising rights of access to a child[107] as the rules only provide for leave to enter in that category and not leave to remain. The same is true of holders of special vouchers under the special voucher scheme.[108]

Whatever your new category, you must show that you satisfy the requirements of the immigration rules for being here in that capacity. The Home Office can treat an application to switch as evidence that you did not genuinely enter for the purpose for which you were granted leave. Under these circumstances, you may be refused leave to remain or even declared an illegal entrant (see p46 and 73).

You should always seek professional advice before making your application to remain or to change status.

Remember, even if you may not switch under the immigration rules, you may ask, exceptionally, for the no switching requirement to be waived.

7. REASONS FOR REFUSING AND CURTAILING LEAVE

Even if you satisfy the immigration rules which relate to the category in which you have applied, there is no guarantee that you will be granted leave. The rules say that where certain requirements are satisfied, leave (or entry clearance)[109] 'may' be granted for a particular period if particular conditions are satisfied.

There are general grounds on which you may be refused leave or have your leave curtailed. These general grounds do not apply to those applying for or granted leave as **refugees**.[110] It is not possible here to set out all of these rules. Most are self-explanatory and they are contained together in Part IX of the immigration rules.[111]

Some grounds for refusal are mandatory – ie, if such a reason applies to you, then your application *must* be refused under the immigration rules. For example, if you apply for leave to enter and you fail to produce a valid national passport or other satisfactory identity document you must be refused.[112] However, if you fail to observe the time-limit or conditions on a previous leave or that leave was obtained by deception, then the entry clearance officer or immigration officer *should normally* refuse your application, although there is still a discretion to allow your application.[113] Again discretion exists to allow your application for leave to remain where a sponsor refuses to give a written undertaking to be responsible for your maintenance and accommodation in the UK or fails to honour that undertaking[114] – see Chapter 5.

The discretion to grant leave by not applying the strict letter of the immigration rules is often referred to as 'exceptional leave' – see Chapter 5.

8. HOW TO DETERMINE YOUR IMMIGRATION STATUS

Note: See JCWI's Immigration, Nationality and Refugee Law Handbook, *Chapter 13, for examples of stamps and endorsements in passports.*

Entry clearance and certificates of entitlement

Both entry clearances and certificates of entitlement to the right of abode are endorsed in the passport in the form of a sticker together with the stamp of the issuing post. The entry clearance sticker should state for how long the entry clearance is valid and it should also contain details of the purpose for which entry clearance is granted. For example, if you get an entry clearance to come to the UK as a visitor, the purpose of 'visit' will be endorsed on the entry clearance sticker.

Leave to enter

If leave to enter is granted, the immigration officer should place a rectangular date stamp in your passport together with a statement of the length of the leave (if there is any limitation) and any conditions attached to the leave. For example, if employment is prohibited the endorsement will state this or will state that leave is granted 'on condition that the holder does not enter employment (etc)'. Unlike entry clearances, the stamp is unlikely to state the purpose for which leave is granted. Comparing the immigration rules with the time limitation of the leave and the conditions attached to it may give you an idea of the capacity in which leave was granted. There may also be work permits or other correspondence or notices which will indicate the nature of the leave granted. If the endorsements and correspondence make no reference to conditions, then there are no conditions attached to the leave. You can stay in the UK for the length of time indicated by the stamp and the period in question begins from the date of the stamp itself.

An indefinite leave to enter may be stated in the passport or may be signified by a rectangular date stamp with no statement as to any time-limit. Depending on the facts of your case, this occasionally may not be enough to amount to an indefinite leave if, for example, the immigration officer did not intend to give you indefinite leave.[115]

If the stamp in your passport is unclear or illegible, you will be treated as having leave to enter for six months with a condition prohibiting you from taking employment.[116] If you entered the UK before 10 July 1988 and were given a defective stamp in your passport, you are treated as having indefinite leave to enter the UK.[117] If you are a person who needs leave to enter the UK and there is no stamp in your passport because, for example, you are simply waved through by the immigration officer, you unfortunately and through no fault of your own, become an 'illegal entrant'[118] (see Chapter 6).

If you are re-admitted to the UK[119] to complete a previous leave and on the same conditions, the endorsement in the passport will state that the holder is given leave to enter to a certain date and the words 'section 3(3)(b)' are stamped in the passport.

A refusal of leave to enter is indicated by a cross being placed across the ordinary leave to enter date stamp.

Leave to remain

Where a person has been granted leave to remain or leave to remain is varied, you should receive a large rectangular stamp in your passport which states the revised leave and any conditions attached to the leave. That stamp should in turn be endorsed with a five-sided Home Office date stamp.

Where the date of expiry of the previous leave is underlined in the passport this indicates a refusal of an application for leave to remain. When no leave is stamped on the passport, the Home Office reference number of the applicant, written on the inside back cover of the passport, is underlined when an application is refused.

Departing from the UK

When you leave the UK, the immigration officer will place a triangular embarkation date stamp in your passport signifying the date of your departure. You will not get a stamp in your passport if you are not subject to immigration control.

Indefinite leave/settled status

- When you are granted indefinite leave to remain in the UK, this will be indicated by a sticker (previously a stamp) in your passport stating that leave is granted for an indefinite period. Confirmations in renewed passports or travel documents may simply indicate that there is no time-limit on the holder's leave.
- When you are granted indefinite leave to enter, this is likely to be stated in a much smaller stamp along with the immigration officer's ordinary on-entry date stamp.
- When indefinite leave to remain has previously been granted and you re-enter the UK, you may just receive the immigration officer's date stamp.

Most people who have indefinite leave to remain may also be regarded as settled in the UK (see p33).

Refugees

People accepted as refugees in the UK are issued with a notice by the Home Office stating this and setting out their rights as refugees. The notice should be endorsed with a Home Office stamp indicating the length of their leave. Refugees are also entitled to travel documentation.[120] These blue travel documents issued by the Home Office under the Convention should also be endorsed with the length of leave.

Asylum-seekers

People who have applied for refugee status in the UK, but whose claims have not yet been determined by the Secretary of State, are issued with an identity document called a 'standard acknowledgement letter' or 'SAL' for short. This is numbered '1' if issued at a port of entry or '2' if issued by the Home Office after entry. SALs issued before 24 October 1995 are not numbered. Asylum-seekers who have not yet been issued with a SAL may have a GEN 32 issued by the Asylum Screening Unit at the Home Office.

Exceptional leave to enter or remain

People who have applied for asylum who have exceptional leave to enter or remain (see p52) usually have a letter from the Home Office stating that, although their application for refugee status has been refused, the Home Office has considered it appropriate to grant leave exceptionally. Where such leave is renewed, the Home Office will usually write to inform the person of the renewal. The leave itself may be endorsed on the

Home Office correspondence, or on a valid national passport or on a special Home Office brown travel document issued to people with this status.

Policy on when people with exceptional leave to remain (who previously sought asylum) may be issued with travel documents is complex and has changed over time. There have also been delays obtaining travel documents from the relevant section in the Home Office. Broadly speaking, people who were first granted exceptional leave to remain after July 1993 (the time when the 1993 asylum legislation came into force), should automatically be able to obtain their travel documents. People who were first granted exceptional leave to remain prior to July 1993 will usually have to show that it would be unreasonable to expect them to approach their own national authorities to ask for documentation or that they had been unreasonably refused such documentation by their own national authorities.

People granted exceptional leave for other reasons may be difficult to identify other than by examining correspondence between the individual (or their representatives) and the Home Office. There are no specific endorsements in the passports. Determining whether someone has been granted leave exceptionally is important for benefit purposes – see Part 2.

Temporary admission or release

People granted temporary admission or release subject to conditions are given written notice to that effect along with the terms and conditions of their stay. Their passports are not stamped.

Deportation, illegal entry and removal

A decision to deport and the reasons for it are notified in writing together with notice of any appeal rights which exist. When a **deportation order** is actually made, the order, signed by the Secretary of State, is also served on the person concerned. A deportation order can be signed and 'served on the file' if that person cannot be found. If this happens the person concerned may have no documentation to indicate that s/he is actually subject to a deportation order.

An immigration officer will give a written notice of a decision that a person is an illegal entrant. Removal directions are given in writing where a person:

- is to be removed from the UK after a deportation order has been signed; *or*
- has been refused leave to enter; *or*
- has been determined to be an illegal entrant.

Such documents usually state the time and place that the person concerned must report to an immigration officer for removal from the UK.

Variation of leave order

People who are granted leave to remain on the basis of VOLO (see p28) do not receive any endorsement of leave in their passport. The leave is granted automatically when an application for leave to remain in the UK is made 'in time' – ie, within the period of the last grant of leave.

Protection from removal

People who have no leave but are protected from removal because they are asylum-seekers or have rights of appeal against a decision while they are in the UK, do not have endorsements saying this in their passports or travel documents and advisers should look at correspondence to and from the Home Office and/or the appellate authority (see glossary) in order to decide the person's position (see p80).

Requirement to register

People required to register with the police should have a notice to that effect stamped on their passport. For who may have to register, see p31.

CHAPTER FOUR

What is exceptional leave

This chapter covers:

1. The meaning of exceptional leave (below)
2. Importance of exceptional leave (below)
3. Narrow meaning of exceptional leave (p52)
4. Other circumstances when exceptional leave may be granted (p53)

I. THE MEANING OF EXCEPTIONAL LEAVE

When applicants are treated more beneficially or favourably than the immigration rules permit, they are said to be treated 'exceptionally'. People often talk of the Home Office discretion to 'depart from' the rules or 'waive' the rules or 'act outside' the rules. These distinctions can be important for the purposes of immigration appeals but are not important for benefit purposes. However, immigration officers and entry clearance officers are bound to apply the rules unless directed otherwise by the Secretary of State.[1] When the Home Office acts outside the rules the applicant is granted leave 'exceptionally' – ie, granted exceptional leave to enter or remain (abbreviated to ELE and ELR). Whenever the Secretary of State decides not to deport or remove someone who has no valid claim to enter or remain under the rules and thus to allow them to stay in the UK on a long-term basis, the likelihood is that the person will be granted leave so as to regularise their position in the UK.

2. IMPORTANCE OF EXCEPTIONAL LEAVE

It is important to determine whether you can argue that you have been granted exceptional leave because this may give you greater rights to benefit (see Chapter 14). It may be that simple waiver of a requirement of the rules that the Home Office knows you cannot satisfy is enough to establish that you have been granted leave exceptionally. The explanations in the remainder of this chapter indicate the circumstances to look out for. If you are granted leave as a recognised refugee, it does not matter if you are also treated under a practice outside the rules (see below) as your access to benefit is unaffected. In all cases you should seek specialist advice.

3. NARROW MEANING OF EXCEPTIONAL LEAVE

There is a narrower and more common use of the term 'exceptional leave' (ELR) which refers to the immigration status of a person who has applied for and been refused refugee status but whom the Secretary of State nonetheless believes is in need of some sort of protection.

Whenever the Home Office refuses an application for asylum as a refugee, it will always consider whether to grant ELR instead.[2] When ELR is granted for these reasons, it is a way of granting 'asylum' (meaning 'protection') to people who would be in danger if they were to be returned to the country from which they came although the government believes the individual cannot satisfy the criteria for being a 'refugee'.[3] The circumstances are best illustrated by official statements:

> There is also a significant number of applicants who while not satisfying the criteria for the grant of asylum are not required to return to their own countries, at least for the time being, either because of their individual circumstances, or more generally on account of the current political situation in their countries of origin. This policy of granting leave to remain on an exceptional basis will continue.[4]

> (ELR)...is by definition outside the immigration rules...we use exceptional leave to remain to respond to cases that are outside the Convention but within the terms of our other obligations, including the European Convention on Human Rights and UN Convention on torture.[5]

It is often the case that the Secretary of State will adopt a particular policy in relation to nationals of countries undergoing severe upheavals or periods of instability. For example, at different times this has applied to nationals of Afghanistan, Iran, Lebanon, Poland, Uganda, El Salvador, Bosnia, Sri Lanka and Somalia. Recent case law, however, has made it more likely that many people in this situation will be entitled to refugee status.[6]

People granted ELR are normally granted indefinite leave to remain (ILR) after seven years of exceptional leave. Although not 'settled' (see p33), spouses and children can join them in the UK after four years *if* they can satisfy the other provisions of the immigration rules. In fact the

Home Office may waive the maintenance and accommodation provisions if there are exceptional compassionate circumstances.[7]

4. OTHER CIRCUMSTANCES WHEN EXCEPTIONAL LEAVE MAY BE GRANTED

The immigration rules do not cover every circumstance and therefore the Home Office is often asked to pay regard to the particular circumstance of a case and act outside the rules. As a matter of fairness it has been recognised that immigrants in similar circumstances should be treated similarly.[8] Therefore, when the Secretary of State acts outside the rules, s/he must have regard to established policies or practices operated by the Home Office. These may:

- relate to persons in particular circumstances or to nationals of particular countries;
- become known in the form of guidance or instructions, letters or statements; *and*
- be changed at any time without the public or anyone else being informed.

For example, on 22 February 1996[9] the Home Office Minister Timothy Kirkhope announced amid much protest that the concessions relating to 'common law' spouses would be withdrawn. The Secretary of State is under no duty to announce her/his policy changes in Parliament as s/he must with the immigration rules which may be disapproved by either House of Parliament.[10]

It is unclear why *at least* the well known and published policies are not now contained within the immigration rules, particularly as the courts have made it clear that the appellate authorities may have regard to well known and published policies when deciding immigration appeals.[11]

In cases for which there is no established practice or policy, the Secretary of State may still consider treating you exceptionally on the basis of your particular circumstances.

The following is a non-exhaustive list of circumstances where the Secretary of State commonly acts outside the immigration rules.

Settlement and family reunion of refugees

The rules provide for the grant of leave to a person who is granted asylum by the Secretary of State.[12] The *practice* is to grant leave for one year in the first instance and subsequently for a further three years. Four years after having been granted leave as a refugee, that person becomes eligible for ILR.[13] Those people accepted as refugees are entitled to be joined in the UK immediately by their spouse and minor children. Despite the fact that the refugee is not settled, the maintenance and accommodation requirements are waived.[14] In the case of Somali nationals, the family reunion provision has been extended to other family members if they had been 'dependent members' of the sponsor's family unit before the sponsor came to the UK.[15]

Refugees for whom the UK is the most appropriate country of refuge

Although the UK has no obligations under the 1951 Geneva Convention relating to refugees who are not actually in the UK and therefore the immigration rules make no provision for such refugees, it has long been the policy of the Home Office to allow such people to come to the UK where, for example, they have particularly strong ties with the UK.[16] Refugees and asylum-seekers who arrive in the UK but who would normally and under the rules be the responsibility of another 'safe' third country (see p36) may be allowed to remain in the UK as refugees or to apply for refugee status if they have strong family links here as defined by the Home Office.[17]

Long residence concessions

In deciding whether to enforce departure from the UK, the Home Office will have regard to the length of continuous residence in the UK. If you have remained lawfully within the UK for a continuous period of 10 years (you are allowed sporadic short absences of up to six months abroad), you may expect your application for indefinite leave to remain in the UK to be considered sympathetically even if you do not meet any of the requirements for settlement under the rules. If you can show that you have remained continuously in the UK lawfully or unlawfully for a period of 14 years or more, then, provided there are no very strong 'countervailing factors' (such as a blatant disregard for the immigration law), you may expect to be granted indefinite leave.[18]

Deportation or illegal entry action involving family and children

Where the Home Office is considering deportation or illegal entry enforcement action, there may be prevailing compassionate family reasons why people should be allowed to remain in the UK. In March 1993, it came to light that the Home Office had issued internal guidance to its officers detailing the circumstances involving marriage or children where it would not be correct to proceed to enforce departure.[19] The instructions were changed with effect from March 1996.[20] The purpose of these instructions is to ensure that immigration decisions are in line with the UK's obligations under article 8 of the European Convention on Human Rights, namely the right to respect for private and family life.[21] The documents also give guidance on the approach to children who are on their own in the UK or who have been in the UK for 10 years or more.

Indefinite leave for elderly dependent relatives

Dependent relatives aged 65 or over of sponsors with settled status in the UK, are generally to be granted indefinite leave to *remain* even if the requirements of the rules are not satisfied.[22] Note that this will not affect elderly people applying for leave to enter or entry clearance.

People who are HIV positive or who have AIDS

The Home Office has issued at least two policy documents dealing with those people in the UK who are subject to control and who are HIV positive or who have developed AIDS.[23] The policy is not generous although concessions are made for those applying for leave to remain in the UK as opposed to those applying for admission.[24]

Domestic servants and overseas domestic workers

Domestic servants/overseas domestic workers who are over 18 are able to accompany their employers to the UK in order to continue to work for their employer in this country without having to comply with the work permit scheme. The worker must have worked for the employer overseas for at least 12 months where the employer comes to the UK as a visitor, and 24 months where the employer comes for any other purpose.[25] The Home Office has introduced measures at the entry clearance stage so as to ensure that such workers are provided with proper maintenance and accommodation by their employers and are not otherwise exploited.[26]

Deportation of students

A person who has failed to comply with a condition imposed upon their leave would normally be deported under the rules.[27] However, 'genuine' students who breach their conditions of leave by working without the consent of the Department for Education and Employment will 'not normally' be deported unless their offences are 'serious or persistent'.[28]

Carers

Special concessions are made for people subject to immigration control, present in the UK in a temporary capacity who seek to remain in the UK to care for a friend or relative who is suffering from a terminal illness or is mentally ill or disabled.[29]

Other groups

Help outside the rules has also been given to adoptive children, unmarried and overage siblings, children under 12 seeking to join a single parent settled in the UK and British Overseas Citizens (see Chapter 2) who are liable to deportation in circumstances where they are not admissible to any other country.[30]

Not all Home Office policies and practices relate to the grant of leave itself. For example, dependants of students are generally prohibited from working if they are granted less than 12 months' leave.[31] However, where a student would have qualified for more than 12 months' leave at the date of the application but, because of delays in dealing with the application, less than 12 months was granted, the minister has said that discretion can be exercised not to impose an employment prohibition on the leave.[32]

CHAPTER FIVE

Recourse to public funds

This chapter covers:

1. The importance of the public funds requirements (below)
2. What are public funds? (p59)
3. Maintenance and accommodation without recourse to public funds: the general tests (p59)
4. Application of maintenance and accommodation tests (p65)
5. Sponsorship and undertakings (p68)

1. THE IMPORTANCE OF THE PUBLIC FUNDS REQUIREMENTS

Requirements under the rules

In the majority of cases, in order to obtain entry clearance or leave under the immigration rules you will need to show that you and your dependants will be *adequately maintained and accommodated without recourse to public funds* (see p54). The government's reason for the predominance of this requirement in the immigration rules is that the taxpayer must be protected against those who are believed to be here to take advantage of the social security system or who might become a burden on it at some stage in the future. The categories of leave to which these requirements are applied are set out in the tables in Chapter 3 and Appendix 5. The only categories to which these requirements do not apply are:

- visitors in transit;[1]
- holders of special vouchers;[2]
- non-British citizen children born in the UK to parents given leave to enter or remain;[3]
- refugees and their dependants.[4]

Returning residents (who will have had indefinite leave to remain)[5] also do not have to satisfy these requirements, but they have to show that they did not receive assistance from public funds towards the cost of their previous departure from the UK. Changes in the rules from 1 November 1996 added post-graduate doctors and dentists, au pairs and seasonal workers at agricultural camps to the list of categories for which the public funds requirements are applied.[6]

If you are not in the above groups, in order to obtain entry clearance, leave to enter or leave to remain, you will have to *show* that you can satisfy the public funds requirements. Note: The immigration rules about public funds do not entirely match the social security rules relating to entitlement to 'public funds' benefits. You could, therefore, be entitled under the social security rules but damage your immigration position by claiming (see below). If you are in doubt, you should seek further advice.

Conditions of leave

From 1 November 1996, not having recourse to public funds in order to maintain and accommodate yourself and your dependants may also be a condition attached to your limited leave.[7] If you do subsequently have recourse to public funds this may be in breach of your conditions of leave. The possible consequences of this are severe (see Chapter 3), since you:

- are liable to deportation (see pp71-73);[8]
- are liable to be prosecuted for committing a criminal offence;[9]
- may be refused entry clearance, leave to enter or leave to remain in the UK on any future application (see p45);[10]
- may have your leave curtailed (see p45).[11] This is an 'exceptional' course only to be used where a person is likely to be a continuing and significant burden on public funds.[12]

The rules also provide that you may be refused further leave to remain in the UK and/or have any existing leave curtailed if you have recourse to public funds even if there is no public funds condition attached to your leave.[13] Although the wording of the rules does not make it clear, these steps would not be taken in the absence of a public funds condition unless it was a requirement of the rules by which you obtained leave that you would not have recourse to public funds.

A public funds condition can also be added to your existing leave.[14] This is likely to happen to people originally admitted subject to the public funds requirement when they obtain an extension to their leave. The Asylum and Immigration Act 1996 also denies a right of appeal to an adjudicator where a public funds condition is added or there is a refusal to remove it (see p76).[15]

2. WHAT ARE PUBLIC FUNDS?

Both social security law and housing legislation increasingly relate entitlement to public funds to immigration status. This is apparent in recent changes to housing legislation, in the 1996 Asylum and Immigration Act and amendments to social security regulations.[16] Not all benefits and services count as public funds, although what can constitute public funds has been expanded recently. The NHS and education services are *not* public funds.[17] Public funds are presently defined by immigration law as:[18]

- housing provided by local authorities;[19]
- attendance allowance (AA);[20]
- severe disablement allowance (SDA);[21]
- invalid care allowance (ICA);[22]
- disability living allowance (DLA);[23]
- income support (IS);[24]
- family credit (FC);[25]
- council tax benefit (CTB);[26]
- disability working allowance (DWA);[27]
- housing benefit (HB);[28]
- income-based jobseeker's allowance (JSA);[29]
- child benefit (CB).[30]

AA, SDA, ICA, DLA and DWA were added to the list of public funds from 4 April 1996.[31] Housing provided by local authorities (in addition to provision for the homeless), CB and income-based JSA were added to the list of public funds from 1 November 1996.[32]

3. MAINTENANCE AND ACCOMMODATION WITHOUT RECOURSE TO PUBLIC FUNDS: THE GENERAL TESTS

The specific requirements for each category are set out in the immigration rules (see tables on pp39-43 and in Appendix 5). It is also useful to consider statements made by Home Office ministers on the operation of the rules. These statements are often made to MPs or concerned organisations.

Adequate maintenance without recourse to public funds

There is no guidance on how much income will be sufficient for adequate maintenance for an applicant together with any dependants. Determining 'adequate maintenance' in any one case is, therefore, not a simple question of calculation. You should, however, try to work out your outgoings and income and regular commitments such as rent, bills, travel and tax so that an approximate figure for disposable income is available. The increasing complexity of the public funds requirements together with the broadening definition of what constitutes public funds means that decision makers and the appellate authorities must establish precisely:[33]

- what assets/resources are available for maintenance;
- what accommodation can be provided; *and*
- the level of resources that will be required.

For example, immigration appeal tribunals have taken the view[34] that it is not sufficient to demonstrate that an amount equal to the personal amount of IS would be available. The reasoning is that that amount would not be sufficient to meet outgoings such as rent and other housing costs which a person entitled to means-tested public funds would be able to meet with the assistance of further benefit. A tribunal has therefore concluded that a figure 'somewhat higher' than IS (or now, income-based JSA) levels would be appropriate.

An applicant could be indirectly reliant upon the public funds claimed by a third party (eg, a settled spouse who can get FC/HB) even if no extra benefit is claimed (see p61). Where this happens, there may still be a question of whether the means for maintaining the applicant will be *adequate*. It will also not be possible for an applicant to rely upon the proceeds of illegal or fraudulent activities for maintenance because their income would then be inherently insecure and therefore the applicant would not satisfy the test.[35]

If the leave which is sought by an applicant would entitle her/him to work, then reliance for maintenance might be placed on the income to be obtained from employment in the UK. Evidence of job offers and formal skills will be important, but a person's general resourcefulness and good character are also relevant.[36] The expression of a mere hope of obtaining employment is unlikely to be sufficient unless, of course, as happened in one case before the appellate authorities[37] the grounds for the hope are not challenged by the Home Office.

Adequate accommodation without recourse to public funds

In order to be 'adequate' for the needs of the applicant, the appellate authorities have adopted tests used in housing legislation – ie, the accommodation available must:[38]

- comply with the environmental health provisions so that it must not be statutorily unfit;

- be capable of accommodating the sponsor and the applicant(s) without 'overcrowding'.

'Overcrowding' is decided in accordance with housing legislation.[39] Two tests are applied – the 'room' standard and the 'space' standard.

- **The room standard** is not satisfied if two people of the opposite sex who are not a cohabiting couple have to sleep in one room. Children under the age of 10 years do not qualify as 'people' for these purposes.
- **The space standard** is not satisfied if there are too many people sharing accommodation of a given number of rooms or a given room floor area. In practice, it is the number of rooms that counts.[40] A room for this purpose must be 50 square feet or more. Living rooms count but bathrooms, kitchens etc do not. Children between one and ten years old only count as half a person; children under one year do not count at all. The number of persons per room is as follows:[41]

Rooms	Permitted number of persons
1 room	2 persons
2 rooms	3 persons
3 rooms	5 persons
4 rooms	7 and a half persons
5 rooms	10 persons, with an additional 2 persons for each room in excess of 5

The provider of the accommodation – whether it be the sponsor (see p68), friend, relative or applicant – must have some form of interest in the property. They do not need to own the freehold or leasehold as long as they have a tenancy or a licence to occupy.[42] As far as the common requirements of the rules are concerned, there is no objection to the sharing of communal facilities.[43]

Additional reliance on public funds

In some cases, an applicant may wish to rely on public funds claimed by another person. Whether this is acceptable has been considered twice in the High Court[44] and in both instances the rules were construed strictly against the applicant. In one case,[45] the sponsor proposed to support two applicant sons seeking entry as dependent children out of savings of £3,000 accrued from supplementary benefit (which was a public fund). The court said that if such a sponsor did manage to save a little money out of supplementary benefit, what 'he has saved should be available for use by him and his wife in a future time of their need and can hardly be regarded within the confines of the supplementary benefit legislation and the Immigration Act as being available to supply the means of others who arrive in this country'.

In some cases, the immigration appellate authorities have followed this strict interpretation of the law.[46] In other cases the opposite view has been expressed, requiring there to be *additional* recourse to public funds caused by the applicant's admission to or remaining in the UK before the rules are contravened.[47] The debate about what constitutes recourse to public funds and whether it includes public funds claimed by the sponsor is not completely resolved. It is an issue which has arisen particularly in the context of foreign spouses/fiancé(e)s applying for leave to join partners in the UK where the immigration rules require both parties to maintain and accommodate themselves without recourse to public funds. In other categories (eg, visitors) the 'no *additional* dependence' interpretation has been more readily adopted.[48] In some cases, the appellate authorities appear to have applied an *extremely* strict interpretation and effectively found that the maintenance and accommodation requirements are not satisfied in any case where, on the applicant's admission, *either* the applicant *or* the sponsor would be in receipt of public funds.[49] But this reasoning seems at odds with common sense as it would require an applicant, as was observed in one case,[50] not only to show that s/he would not become a burden on public funds, but also that s/he would remove her/his sponsor from such reliance.

Despite the view taken by some courts, the Home Office view is that the proper application of the maintenance and accommodation requirements is that indirect reliance upon funds claimed by others is perfectly permissible provided that there is no *additional* recourse to public funds. This view has been expressed regularly in correspondence from ministers responsible for immigration.[51] For example, in October 1994, Nicholas Baker MP (the responsible minister) wrote to Sir Giles Shaw MP stating:[52]

> The question is whether additional recourse to public funds would be necessary on the applicant's arrival here. The sponsor's means, including any public funds to which they are entitled in their own right, must therefore be sufficient to provide adequate maintenance and accommodation for the applicant and their dependants.

The Home Office consciously follows this policy contrary to the High Court decisions. This Home Office interpretation appears never to have been referred to in the High Court in the decisions referred to above and the most recent tribunal decisions on this issue are therefore in the applicant's favour.[53]

Recent tribunals have determined that they must apply the Home Office's stated interpretation/application of the rules or put more bluntly 'ignore the rules, and apply the less stringent dictate of government policy'.[54]

The key question is: will the **admission** of the applicant or **extension** of leave to remain granted to the applicant **cause** an extra demand upon public funds? The answer will not always be straightforward.

Example

In one case,[55] the sponsor's father, after giving a capital asset (a house) to his daughter became entitled to IS. The house was to be the matrimonial home of his daughter (the sponsor) and son-in-law (the applicant) on the latter's arrival in the UK. However, the motive for the gift existed independently of the applicant's admission. It was also to reward the sponsor for her efforts on behalf of the family over the years, and the sponsor's father did not foresee any increase in his terms of benefit at the time the gift was made. The tribunal held that there would be no 'recourse' caused by the admission of the applicant, the link between the extra benefit obtained and the admission of the applicant to the UK was simply not sufficiently direct. It could not be said that simply because a third party gives away capital and is then awarded income support, the beneficiary of the gift has recourse to public funds. The tribunal stated 'there is need for a direct link between the grant of support and the beneficiary'. In the same case, the tribunal determined that the dependence of the sponsor on her father for meals at a time when the father was in receipt of public funds was also insufficient to demonstrate any sufficient 'recourse' to public funds as, given the size of the sponsor's family and the relatively small proportion of IS (public funds) in relation to the overall income being drawn upon (£31.28 of £261.43 weekly), it could not be sensibly said that the meals were being provided through the small part attributable to income support.

If an applicant seeks to live in accommodation without making a contribution to the costs of the accommodation or paying rent and the owner or occupier receives benefit which includes an element of housing costs, tribunals have held that there will be a recourse to public funds.[56] In one case, the reasoning was that, if the sponsor's father charged rent or board and lodging and declared this income to the DSS, his own weekly IS would be reduced. By allowing the couple to live rent free, the sponsor's father was securing a higher weekly benefit and was, in turn, subsidising the couple who were living rent free.[57] Note that where this is the situation, advisers should be ready to point out the likely reduction in the amount paid in HB due to non-dependant deductions (see CPAG's *National Welfare Benefits Handbook*) and to question whether there is in fact any *additional* demand on public funds created in these circumstances.

When the test has to be satisfied

Maintenance and accommodation can become an issue overseas when applications for entry clearance are made. The means to maintain and accommodate do not have to exist at the time the decision on the application is made but only when the applicant expects to arrive in the UK.[58] However, only resources that are 'reasonably foreseeable' at the date of the decision can count. Where a sponsor is in receipt of public funds at the date of the decision, this will not *necessarily* damage the application.[59] In practice, the test will be whether the means will be in place six months after the decision on the application as:[60]

- entry clearances are usually valid for six months; *and*
- there is unlikely to be an actual date for when the applicant will arrive in the UK so it is assumed they will arrive at any date within six months of the decision.

If financial arrangements are put in place at a later date, the applicant will not be able to argue that means are available at the time when the application is made.[61] However, it is possible for the appellate authorities to take account of evidence that comes to light after the decision itself in order to determine whether the existence of the means relied upon was foreseeable at the date of the decision.[62] If not, the availability of further resources at a later date could form the basis of a request to an adjudicator to make a recommendation that entry clearance or leave be granted or could, alternatively, be put forward in a fresh application.

In one case,[63] a tribunal took into account an offer of accommodation made after a refusal of entry clearance, because:

- the offer was made contingent on any difficulties arising over the couple's accommodation; *and*
- the house was made available as soon as the difficulties were made known.

In the same case, which involved a wife seeking to join her student husband (the sponsor), the tribunal took account of the husband's industrious nature and the fact that his family also had the means to assist when assessing the ability of the couple to maintain themselves once the wife had arrived in the UK.[64]

Where the partner in the UK is living in her/his own accommodation and is in employment, the maintenance and accommodation test is likely to be satisfied unless there is evidence that the circumstances are likely to change.[65]

4. APPLICATION OF MAINTENANCE AND ACCOMMODATION TESTS

Are the requirements the same?

Where maintenance and accommodation without recourse to public funds is a requirement of the rules, there are a number of ways in which the rules vary in relation to the different categories of applicant. There are three main ways in which the requirements appear to differ.

1. Resources which must be left out of account

In many categories, the maintenance and accommodation requirements must be met not only without recourse to public funds but *also* without income from working or business activities in the UK. This stipulation is added where the rules for leave in a particular category require that the person does not intend to engage in economic activity *other than* that which is consistent with the purpose for which leave is granted. Indeed a condition is likely to be imposed upon the leave prohibiting any other economic activity. The maintenance and accommodation requirements closely reflect the rules for granting leave in each category. The following are examples of these rules.

Writers, composers and artists

A writer, composer or artist[66] must show that s/he will be able adequately to maintain and accommodate her/himself and any dependants without recourse to public funds from her/his own resources **without working except as a writer, composer or as an artist**. This stipulation reflects the fact that:[67]

- it is a requirement of getting leave in those capacities that the applicant does not intend to do work except in the occupation for which they are admitted; *and*
- a condition will normally be attached to their leave to the same effect.

Work permit holders/working holidaymakers

The same pattern is not followed for each category. Work permit holders, for example, can apparently rely on income from work other than that specified in the work permit.[68] *However*, in practice if it is clear you will be relying on funds from economic activities from which you are prohibited (or must show that you will not undertake), then you are likely to be refused leave. Even if you were not refused on maintenance and accommodation grounds, you could legitimately be refused because you are likely to enter such economic activity in order to maintain and accommodate yourself. The maintenance and accommodation requirements for a working holidaymaker[69] are not expressly qualified by the words 'without taking any employment other than that which *is incidental to a holiday*' – ie, the requirement in the working holidaymaker rules. However, if it is clear that, in order to maintain and accommodate themselves and their dependants, an applicant would have to spend more than 50 per cent of their time in the UK in full-time employment (which is the Home Office's rule of thumb as to whether the work is only 'incidental' to the holiday), then s/he would be likely to be refused. The ground for refusal, if they were not refused under the maintenance and accommodation rules, is the rule requiring applicants not to *intend* to take such employment. This would also apply to a teacher or language assistant under an approved scheme[70] or a person undertaking Department for Education and Employment approved training or work experience.[71]

Students and visitors

Another example is the difference between the maintenance and accommodation requirements for students and visitors. Students must be able to meet the requirements without having to take account of any earnings from employment or business in the UK.[72] However, after entry to the UK students may get permission to do part-time or vacation work,[73] and a common sense interpretation of the rules suggests that their reliance on this income would not mean students should be counted as failing the maintenance and accommodation requirements. In contrast to students, visitors are able to transact business (although not to produce goods or provide services or to take employment) in the UK. They can rely on the proceeds of business undertaken during visits, but not from the activities from which they are debarred.[74]

2. Reliance on third party support for maintenance and accommodation

The rules across the different categories also suggest that there may be differences about when it is permissable to rely on resources provided by a third party. In some categories, the rules state that:

- a person must be 'able to meet' the costs of her/his maintenance and accommodation;
- in others it is necessary to show that you 'can and will'; *and*
- in others you must be 'able and willing' or have 'sufficient funds available' or 'resources available [to you]' to be so maintained and accommodated without recourse to public funds.

Again, the differences reflect the different purposes and nature of the leave being sought (see following examples). In general terms, the Home

Office interpretation of the rules (see above) is consistent with a construction that would *allow* reliance on third parties.

Visitors

For example, visitors should maintain and accommodate themselves:

- out of resources available to them;[75] *or*
- through the support of relatives (the words 'and friends' are added for visitors seeking medical treatment).[76]

Clearly, it is reasonable to expect that a short-term visitor to the country may be maintained or accommodated over a limited period by a sponsoring relative or a friend.

Children

The dependent characteristic of children dictates that the maintenance and accommodation requirements in relation to children are usually to the effect that the child 'can and will' be maintained and accommodated without recourse to public funds.

Fiancé(e)s and spouses

There is a difference of view in the Immigration Appeal Tribunal as to how the rules about fiancé(e)s and spouses should be interpreted – in particular, whether the wording of the fiancé and marriage rules require a couple to be self-supporting. One leading commentator has referred to the fact that the rules are expressed in terms of the parties being able to 'maintain themselves and their dependants' but not necessarily be maintained '*by* themselves'.[77] This view is supported by several tribunal cases.[78] The other interpretation also expressed in the tribunal places emphasis on self-support,[79] or stresses the view that third-party support may only be sufficient in the short term.[80] The prevailing view is that third-party support is sufficient, but that it may be more difficult to demonstrate that there will be *lasting* third-party support. In cases where the applicant is seeking indefinite leave to remain, the evidence of the *lasting* nature of third-party support needs to be particularly precise and cogent compared to when an applicant proposes to maintain and accommodate her/himself out of their own resources or those generated by their own industry.[81]

Retired people of independent means and persons intending to establish themselves in business and writers/composers/artists

In order to obtain leave, retired people of independent means must have an income of £25,000 a year which is under their control and is disposable in the UK. They must also be able and willing to maintain and accommodate themselves and any dependants indefinitely in the UK:[82]

- from their own resources with no assistance from any other person; *and*
- without taking employment; *or*
- having recourse to public funds.

Although there are similarly phrased rules for people establishing themselves in business,[83] people intending to establish themselves in business under the provisions of an EC Association Agreement[84] and writers/composers/artists[85] are not explicitly prohibited from relying on resources from other people.

3. Accommodation 'owned or occupied exclusively'

For certain permanent categories of leave – in particular, spouses and fiancé(e)s – the maintenance and accommodation requirements specify that the accommodation must be 'owned or occupied *exclusively*' by the parties (to a marriage), the sponsor, parent or relative.[86] 'Exclusive' occupation does not mean occupation of the entire premises in which you reside. Provided the relevant person occupies a bedroom within those premises, the remainder of the facilities on the premises (eg, kitchen, living room, toilet, bathroom, halls etc) can be shared with other people.[87]

5. SPONSORSHIP AND UNDERTAKINGS

The sponsor (relative or friend) of any person seeking leave to enter or to remain in the UK may be asked to give a written undertaking to be responsible for that person's maintenance and accommodation for the period of leave granted **and** any further period of leave to remain that that person may be granted while in the UK.[88] The rules are drafted very widely, so it is possible that such an undertaking could be required of a sponsor even if the requirements of the rules do not specify maintenance and accommodation requirements for the category under which leave is sought. However, in practice it is very unlikely that an undertaking would be required in such a case. Examples of cases where undertakings may be requested relate to:

- dependent relatives (although not for children under 12 years coming for settlement); *or*
- students relying upon a private individual in the UK;

where there is insufficient or barely sufficient evidence to reassure the authorities that there will indeed be the means adequately to maintain and accommodate an applicant.

If you are asked to give an undertaking you must be aware that, depending on the circumstances of the case, this commitment could last a lifetime. If the person sponsored subsequently claims IS while in the UK, the DSS may ask you to pay back any IS claimed (see p157).[89] Court action may be initiated to enforce payment if it is not forthcoming. However, it is government policy to do this only where the sponsor, although financially able, refuses to honour the undertaking without good reasons.[90] The rules regarding entitlement to means-tested benefits for sponsored immigrants were changed on 5 February 1996. People in this situation may not be entitled to benefit even if their sponsor does not maintain them (see pp153-57). Persons who *are* granted leave to enter or remain on the basis of such written undertakings *may* also be dis-entitled to receive HB/CTB (for details see Part 2).

Often sponsors voluntarily make declarations as to maintenance and accommodation without being asked to provide an undertaking. Because of the possible consequences, it is advisable not to make such declarations of sponsorship unless specifically asked to make such a promise. However, a person making a voluntary declaration cannot be required to repay a benefit paid to the sponsored person; this only applies if the undertaking is legally required. Where the sponsor of a person declines to give an undertaking to be responsible for an applicant's maintenance and accommodation in the UK after being requested to do so, the normal course under the immigration rules is for that applicant to be denied entry clearance, leave to enter or remain.[91]

CHAPTER SIX

Enforcement and appeals

This chapter covers:

1. Deportation, illegal entry and removal (below)
2. Refusals and appeals (p75)

This chapter does not explain all the ways in which people can be forced out of the UK, or all the ways in which you may be able to contest decisions made against you. What it provides is:

- a summary of the main problems people may face under immigration law;
- how advisers can determine your status and take the appropriate emergency action, including referring you on for specialist immigration help and advice; *and*
- how to see how you may fit into benefit eligibility regulations.

I. DEPORTATION, ILLEGAL ENTRY AND REMOVAL

You may face criminal and administrative penalties if you are in breach of immigration control. You may be dealt with either by the Home Office administrative powers, which may lead to deportation or removal, or by being charged with a criminal offence in the courts. Court cases are rare. Under the 1971 Immigration Act, wide powers of detention are given to the immigration authorities to assist with regulating control and enforcement. These powers may be used against individuals whether or not they are charged with any offence, either immigration or otherwise. Much criticism has been directed at the widespread and apparently arbitrary use of such powers. There is also the suspicion that powers of detention have been used for the wider purpose of punishment and deterrence rather than for the narrow purposes of enforcement for which they are strictly provided.

Deportation means sending people away from the UK under an order signed by the Home Secretary and forbidding their re-entry. This process is used when you have entered the UK legally and have been granted leave to enter or remain but you then break a condition which has been imposed on your stay. In the past, this has most commonly been overstaying your permission to remain. If a person is convicted of a serious non-immigration criminal offence, the court may recommend deportation as part of the sentence. If the court does not, the Home Office may make its own decision to deport. If you return and enter the UK without the deportation order being revoked, you have re-entered illegally.

Illegal entry means entering the UK without permission from an immigration officer. All non-EU/EEA nationals who do not have the right of abode in the UK and who are not exempt (see p6) from control have to get permission to enter. You may be treated as an illegal entrant if you:

• avoid the immigration officers altogether; *or*
• enter while a deportation order is still current against you; *or*
• deceive an immigration officer about your identity or your reasons for coming to the UK.

The last is the most common ground for being considered an illegal entrant. The way the Home Office and the courts interpret illegal entry has been extended over recent years. The word used for the process of making an illegal entrant leave the UK is **removal**. This is also the word used when you are refused entry to the UK at a port, and never allowed into the country at all, and your departure is enforced.

You normally have the right to apply for bail, but sureties are usually set at a very high level – ie, £2,000-£5,000.[1]

The deportation process

Most people who are not British citizens and do not have the right of abode can be deported. Other people exempt from deportation *include*:

• diplomats;[2]
• Commonwealth country citizens and citizens of the Republic of Ireland *in certain circumstances*[3]; *and*
• people who become British citizens after the deportation process has commenced.[4]

EU/EEA nationals can only be deported in very restricted circumstances (see p74).

If you are not exempt, you may be deported because:[5]

• you were allowed in for a certain length of time and have overstayed without applying for further permission from the Home Office, or have remained after being refused permission to do so, or after you have lost appeals against refusals;

- you have broken a condition put on your stay – eg, you have worked when prohibited from doing so, or you have claimed a 'public funds' benefit when you had a condition stating that you must maintain and accommodate yourself without recourse to public funds. After leave has expired, there can no longer be any question of any conditions applying because the conditions can only be attached to the leave itself (although after leave has expired, you will become an overstayer);[6]
- you have been convicted of an imprisonable offence and a criminal court makes a recommendation that you are deported;[7]
- the Home Secretary deems your deportation is 'conducive to the public good';[8]
- you obtained leave to remain in the UK 'by deception'. This is a new ground for deportation introduced 1 October 1996;[9]
- you are the spouse, or the child under 18, of a person who is to be deported and do not have your own independent right to remain.[10]

It is up to the Home Office to prove that there are grounds to deport you.[11] If the reasons for deportation relate to:

- overstaying – the stamps in your passport will be evidence to prove the dates;
- working without permission – the evidence will be from your employer;
- claiming benefits – the evidence will be from the Benefits Agency.

The immigration rules[12] state that when the Home Office considers whether to deport people it must take into account 'all relevant factors known', including:

- age;
- length of residence in the UK;
- strength of connections with the UK;
- personal history, including character, conduct and employment record;
- domestic circumstances;
- the nature of any offence of which the person was convicted;
- previous criminal record;
- compassionate circumstances;
- any representations received on the person's behalf.

If you are to be deported as a member of the family of someone else who is to be deported, the Home Office must also consider whether you are able to maintain and accommodate yourself, and in the case of children, the effect on their education and the practicality of their care abroad.[13] If you already have permission to stay indefinitely, or were living apart from the person to be deported, your deportation would not normally be considered.[14]

The first step in the deportation process is for the Home Office to make a decision in principle to deport you. When the Home Office makes this decision it must inform you in writing, normally on a standard letter, reference APP 104. There is a right of appeal (see below). If the appeal is lost, the Home Secretary can then sign a deportation order and force you to leave.[15] If you are deported, you cannot return unless the deportation order is revoked. Usually you have to be outside the UK for at least three years before the Home Office will consider this. After the order has been revoked, you would once again need to satisfy the ordinary requirements of the immigration rules in order to re-enter.[16]

When you are in the UK without permission and before the Home Office has made a decision in principle to deport you, *because* you do not have leave to remain, the Home Office cannot impose any other conditions on what you can do here. You are therefore not restricted from working. If you have been allowed to work before, and have a national insurance (NI) number, you can continue to work legally.

From 27 January 1997, it is an offence for an employer to employ someone who is not permitted to work in the UK.[17] Employers will not be legally liable if, before the employment started, they saw and kept a copy of one of a number of specified documents relating to the employee. Such documents include an official document containing the person's NI number (eg, a P45), as well as passports and Home Office letters. The offence only relates to people who started jobs from 27 January 1997.

Illegal entry

The Home Office most commonly treats people as illegal entrants because it alleges they entered by deception.[18] They will often have stamps on their passports which state they have been granted leave to enter and will not understand how they can be 'illegal'. The Home Office or the immigration service may say that they told lies when applying for permission to enter. There is often no evidence to support the Home Office view, so it relies heavily on questioning people about their entry and using their answers against them. If you are treated as an illegal entrant you will be informed in writing on form IS 151A.

Because there is normally no right of appeal until after you have been sent back, the Home Office has powers to remove illegal entrants very quickly. It is necessary for you or your advisers to act promptly in making representations on your behalf and ensuring that specialist advice is sought. The Home Office may delay removing you while the case is being considered, particularly if your MP has agreed to take it up. You may also be able to apply for judicial review of the decision. While representations are being considered, or a judicial review is pending, arrangements for your removal will be delayed. If you are released on temporary admission while your case is considered, you will be told the terms and conditions of your release on form IS 96.

When there are strong compassionate or family reasons why you should be allowed to stay in the UK, representations can be made to the Home Office to treat you exceptionally and grant leave to enter or remain, even if there is no way of contesting the illegal entry decision. Similar considerations as for deportation will apply (see p72).

Benefit/working implications

When the Home Office has already decided that you are in the UK without permission, you may be a 'person from abroad' under benefits regulations and may not be eligible for income support (IS), housing benefit (HB) or council tax benefit (CTB). Unless the terms of your temporary admission prohibit you from working (and they often do) there is nothing to stop you working as you do not have leave to enter or remain in the UK. If you have applied for asylum you may be given permission to work if no decision is made on your case for more than six months.

Other enforcement procedures

There are various other procedures which may be invoked in order to enforce the departure of individuals in certain circumstances:

- EU/EEA nationals may be removed from the UK if they cease to exercise free movement rights or if their removal is justified on grounds of public policy, public security or public health;[19]
- people who are members of the armed forces of various 'friendly' states may be arrested, detained and removed from the UK if a request is made by the country concerned;[20]
- certain people who are receiving in-patient treatment for mental illness may also be removed from the UK with the approval of the Mental Health Review Tribunal provided that proper arrangements have been made for their treatment and it is in the interests of the person to be so removed.[21]
- people whose return is requested by foreign authorities in respect of criminal offences may be removed from the UK in a procedure known as 'extradition'. This is a large subject with rules of its own. It is not a common occurrence.[22]

2. REFUSALS AND APPEALS

When you apply to come to, or remain in, the UK, the immigration authorities may grant or refuse your application. If the Home Office considers that you satisfy the requirements of the immigration rules in the particular category in which you are applying, you should be granted permission to come or to stay here (see Chapter 3). If you do not fit into the rules, but if the Home Office believes there are good reasons, usually of a compassionate or family nature, to make an exception to the rules, you may be granted permission to enter or remain exceptionally (see Chapter 4). Otherwise, your application will be refused. Depending on the nature of the application and whether or not it was validly made while you had permission to be in the UK, there may be a formal right of appeal against a refusal.

When there is no right of appeal

Invalid applications

From 27 November 1996, all applications to the Home Office for leave to remain other than asylum applications, work permit applications and certain EEA applications must be made on the appropriate Home Office application form. All the documents requested on the form, or explanations of why the documents are not there and when they will be supplied, must be sent to the Home Office with the form. If this is not done, your application is not valid[23] and you could, therefore, lose your right of appeal against an adverse decision (for further explanation of VOLO, see p24). There is a special Application Forms Unit at the Home Office, tel: 0181 760 2233, which will send out forms on request.

Late applications

If you applied to the Home Office for permission to *remain* after your previous permission had run out you have no formal right of appeal against any refusal. It does not matter for how short a time you had overstayed, or whether you knew that the application was late, the right of appeal has still been lost.[24]

Visitors, prospective students and short-term students

Visitors, prospective students and students coming for courses of six months or less have no right of appeal against being refused entry clearance abroad or against being refused entry at a port if they have no entry clearance for these purposes.[25]

Mandatory refusals

When a refusal is 'mandatory under the immigration rules' there is no right of appeal.[26] A mandatory refusal relates to people who:

- do not have a document specified under the rules – ie, entry clearance, passport or other identity document, or work permit;
- do not meet a requirement of the rules such as age, nationality or citizenship. For example, a working holidaymaker must be a Commonwealth country citizen aged between 17 and 27. A 29-year-old Romanian who applied for entry as a working holidaymaker would have no right of appeal against refusal;
- apply to remain longer than permitted under the rules – eg, a visitor applying to stay longer than six months.

When the Home Office refuses these applications, it will inform you in writing stating that the application has been refused, there is no right of appeal, and you should leave the country within 28 days. If you do not leave within that time, the Home Office may make a decision to deport you. It may be possible to contest the refusal by applying for judicial review in the courts.

Decisions based on national security grounds

You may not appeal against an immigration decision where the Secretary of State has determined that your exclusion from the UK is justified on national security grounds.[27] However, the law on this question may be different for you in the future if you are a EU/EEA national.[28]

Maintenance and accommodation conditions

You are not entitled to appeal against a variation of leave which adds the condition (or refuses to revoke a condition) that you are required to maintain and accommodate yourself and any dependants without recourse to public funds.[29]

When people can appeal

There are rights to appeal against many immigration decisions and against most asylum refusals. When such decisions are concluded, you should be given:[30]

- notice of that decision and the reasons for it; *and*
- essential information concerning your rights of appeal – eg, the time-limit for appealing and the place to which the notice of appeal should be sent;
- the form on which to submit your appeal.

There are very strict time-limits laid down in special procedure rules[31] with regard to lodging appeals. **These time limits are important because the right of appeal may be lost if the forms are not received in time.** Thus when you have been refused and have a right of appeal, the first thing to check is the date of refusal. This is to ensure that any appeal is still in time. In order to ensure that there is proof the forms have been sent back, they should be posted by recorded delivery to addresses in the UK and by registered post abroad.

Because the time-limits are vital, you or a benefits adviser may need to lodge appeals to make sure they get in in time. It is not necessary to give full details of the reasons for the appeal; the grounds of appeal may be a bald statement such as, 'the decision is not in accordance with the immigration law and rules applicable', or 'discretion ought to have been exercised differently', or 'the appellant qualifies as a refugee under the terms of the UN Convention'. However you should immediately seek further specialist advice and help in preparing for the appeal. The Immigration Advisory Service and the Refugee Legal Centre are funded by the Home Office to provide free appeal representation; law centres and other specialist advice centres may be able to help (see Appendix 1).

Situations where people have appeal rights

Outside the UK
When entry clearance is refused at a British Embassy or High Commission abroad, there may be a right of appeal from abroad against that decision.[32] In addition there is an appeal right from abroad against some refusals of leave to enter where you have no current entry clearance or work permit. You may also appeal from abroad against a refusal to revoke a deportation order[33] and against certain asylum refusals (see p81).

At the port
When you are refused entry at a British port there may be a right of appeal. If you obtained entry clearance you may remain in the UK while the appeal is under consideration. If you did not have entry clearance, you can only appeal after you have been sent back.[34]

In the UK
When the Home Office refuses you permission to stay longer in the UK, or alters or refuses to alter your conditions of stay, there may be a right of appeal against the decision.[35] However, a valid application must have been made in time, on the correct Home Office official application form, before your leave ran out, to trigger an appeal right.[36]

When the Home Office makes a decision to deport you, there is a right

of appeal.[37] If you were last granted leave to enter the UK less than seven years before the date of the decision, the appeal is only on the legal facts of the case.[38] For example, if you are being deported because you have overstayed you can only argue at the appeal that you did not overstay and the Home Office had granted you leave to be here. The appeal cannot consider any family or compassionate reasons why you should not be deported.

Example

An Indian woman was last given leave to enter the UK for six months as a visitor on 21 December 1994 and then overstayed her leave beyond the time that it ran out on 21 June 1995 and made no further application to remain in the UK. On 2 October 1996, the Secretary of State made a decision to deport her on the grounds of overstaying. In the notice of the decision to deport, the Secretary of State briefly correctly related the facts as above. The grounds of appeal were restricted to whether there was a 'power in law' to deport because the woman last entered the UK less than seven years before 2 October 1996. The appeal was doomed to failure because there is a power to deport someone where that person has overstayed their leave and the Secretary of State had not committed any technical error in drawing up the notice of decision.

Although the appeal must ultimately fail, there is still the right to bring the appeal and that has some value. On the day of the appeal, the woman may accept that the appeal has to be dismissed but ask the adjudicator to make an extra-statutory recommendation to the Secretary of State that she be able to remain for a certain time upon compassionate or other grounds exceptionally outside the rules.

When you are alleged to be an illegal entrant, there is a right of appeal only after you have been removed. Again, the only grounds of appeal are on the legal facts of the case.[39]

Asylum refusals

Regardless of immigration status, when a person in the UK is refused asylum there is generally a right of appeal.[40] Some appeals must be lodged within *two days* of receipt of the refusal, but most within *seven days*.[41] However, where the Home Office issues a certificate that you may be safely sent to another European country to pursue your claim to asylum there, you are only entitled to appeal after you have left the UK.[42] If this is the case, you should seek specialist help to see if you can bring a judicial review against the Home Office decision *before* you leave the UK.

The appeal process

When the Home Office receives the completed appeal forms, it sends an acknowledgement letter to you, as the person appealing. When your appeal is against:

- a refusal to allow you to remain longer; *or*
- a decision to deport you; *or*
- most asylum refusals;

this letter confirms that you may remain in the UK and the Home Office will not take any action to make you leave until the appeal has been decided. There are no restrictions on you working during this period, but if you had not been allowed to work before the refusal your employer may be committing an offence by employing you.

The next stage is when the Home Office prepares an 'explanatory statement' explaining the reasons for the immigration refusal.[43] This will be sent together with any documentary evidence to the immigration appellate authorities, who will fix a date for hearing the appeal. The main hearing centre is at Thanet House in The Strand, London, but there are other hearing centres in London and throughout the country.

In asylum cases, there is usually no explanatory statement, but the Home Office provides its notes of interview with the asylum-seeker, a note of her/his immigration history and often other background information about the country from which s/he fled. In addition, the Home Office will already have supplied a letter which sets out in full the reasons for refusing asylum.

Apart from certain 'fast-track' asylum appeals,[44] appeals are very slow processes, particularly those in London. During 1996, people frequently waited more than a year for a hearing date.

For most appeals, there is a two-stage appeal hearing process. Appeals are first heard by a single **adjudicator**. When the case is a refusal of asylum, it is heard by a **special adjudicator**, who deals only with asylum cases. The losing side then has the right to apply for leave to appeal to the **Immigration Appeal Tribunal** to review the case. Some appeals go direct to the Tribunal. This is when the appeal is against a decision to deport made:[45]

- on grounds that the person's presence in the UK is not conducive to the public good – usually after a criminal conviction; *or*
- because you are the family member of another person being deported.

For some asylum refusals, there is no right for the applicant to appeal to the Tribunal.[46] The tribunal is a three-person panel, and will grant leave to appeal when it believes that there is a legal point at issue, or if there are other special circumstances which it believes justify a further appeal. When you are in the UK, immigration applications to the Tribunal must be received within *14 days* of the date of the adjudicator's decision and asylum applications within *five days* of receipt of the special adjudicator's decision.[47]

If the Tribunal refuses leave to appeal, the only remedy is to apply for for a judicial review of its decision. Specialist advice is necessary.

If the Tribunal dismisses the appeal after hearing it in full, there may be grounds for applying to the Tribunal for leave to appeal to the Court of Appeal and direct to the Court if the Tribunal refuses leave.[48]

Protection from removal while appeal is pending

Non-asylum cases

Although, in many cases while you have an appeal pending, you may no longer have any leave to stay in the UK, you are generally still protected from being removed from the UK:

- Where you have an in-country appeal pending against a refusal of leave to enter the UK, no directions for your removal from the UK may be given and any directions already given will have no effect.[49]
- Where you have an appeal pending against any variation of leave or refusal to vary it, you cannot be required to leave the UK.[50]
- Where you may appeal or where you have an appeal pending against a decision to make a deportation order, no deportation order may be made.[51]
- Where you appeal against the validity of directions for removal as a person entering in breach of a deportation order on the grounds that you are not the person named in that order or against removal on the basis of an objection to the destination, you may not be removed while the appeal is pending.[52]

In relation to appeals against refusal of leave to enter and removal, if the adjudicator dismisses the appeal the appeal will no longer be considered to be pending, and as a result, you will become liable to be removed *unless:*[53]

- you immediately ask the adjudicator for and obtain leave to appeal to the Immigration Appeal Tribunal; *or*
- if it is a case for which leave is not required, you give notice of appeal.

For other appeals, the appeal is pending and so you may not be removed for the whole appeal period:

- beginning when notice of appeal is duly given; *and*

- ending when the appeal is finally determined or withdrawn or (from 1 October 1996) is abandoned by reason of your having left the UK[54]

and includes any appeal which may be brought to the Immigration Appeal Tribunal from adjudicator level and to the Court of Appeal from the Tribunal.

Asylum cases

- In asylum cases, you may not be removed from, or required in any way to leave the UK during the period beginning when you make a claim for asylum till the time the Secretary of State gives you notice of the decision in your case.[55]
- If you bring an appeal under section 8 of the Asylum and Immigration Appeals Act 1993 (ie, against any of the particular immigration decisions or actions named there upon asylum grounds) then you are protected against removal (see above). You cannot be removed until there has been a final determination. This includes any further appeals to the Tribunal or Court of Appeal.[56]
- An exception to this protection for asylum-seekers, is where the Secretary of State issues a certificate[57] after the asylum claim to the effect that you may be sent to a safe third country which is a 'member state of the EU' or has been designated for such purpose by the Secretary of State. In such a case, you may be removed to the safe third country without being able to bring an appeal under section 8 or on any other basis. You may only appeal against the certificate once you are outside the UK.[58]

Disputes as to whether you can appeal in-country

The common sense approach must also be that the powers given to protect your removal from the UK pending an appeal can only apply where there is a valid in-country right of appeal against a particular decision. But what happens if there is a dispute about whether the right of appeal is in-country or not? For example, what happens if there is a dispute between you and the Secretary of State as to whether you held a 'current entry clearance' at the time you were refused leave to enter at the port entitling you to an in-country right of appeal against the refusal of leave to enter and you give notice of appeal.[59] There may then be a dispute as to whether you are entitled to the protection from removal pending the appeal.[60] It is probably the case that you may only be removed after the issue has been determined against you by the appellate authorities because it is they who must decide whether there is a right of appeal and while that matter has not been determined, the appeal is, *prima facie*, pending.[61]

Immigration and benefits

CHAPTER SEVEN

Immigration and benefits

This chapter covers:

1. Social security and immigration control (below)
2. Home Office links with benefits authorities (p85)
3. National insurance contributions (p89)
4. Proving identity, age and relationships (p92)

Not only do special benefit rules apply to migrants, but the interaction of social security and immigration control may cause problems. Migrants may also have special difficulties proving age or relationships. Advisers should also note that migrants whose first language is not English may have difficulties in claiming benefits and be more likely to make mistakes when claiming.

I. SOCIAL SECURITY AND IMMIGRATION CONTROL

Social security rules and administration are an increasingly important part of government immigration policies. Migrants' access to welfare has long been a political issue,[1] but until recently social security rules and practices directed at migrants had developed in a piecemeal fashion. There had been no real attempt at complete co-ordination of social security and immigration policy. However, in recent years social security has become perhaps the most important tool of internal immigration control.

The government uses social security rules and administration to:

- restrict benefits for legal non-EEA immigrants, despite their liability for taxes and contributions which pay for those benefits;
- help the Home Office find and catch those who are here illegally;
- force EU/EEA nationals to leave the UK without deportation being properly considered, denying rights of appeal guaranteed by EC law;[2]
- discourage *all* asylum-seekers from claiming asylum in the UK;

- impose a means-test on family unity;
- prevent *all* asylum-seekers from using rights of appeal provided by Parliament.

These are blunt tools and affect a much wider group than their supposed targets. As a result:

- confusion and ignorance amongst benefits and Home Office staff about the complicated rules of their own and each other's departments lead to wrong decisions and advice about the rights of migrants to benefits;
- confusion and ignorance amongst migrants lead to failure to take up rights to benefits;
- Black British citizens become the subject of official suspicion and enquiries about immigration status;
- asylum-seekers are demonised by the media;
- British citizens returning from abroad are denied means-tested benefits;[3]
- fear amongst migrants about the effects of contact with benefits authorities and/or the Home Office, and even advisers, makes many migrants vulnerable to exploitation by employers.

There remains a fundamental clash of cultures. The basic purpose of benefits authorities and their staff is to ensure payment of benefits to members of the community who cannot support themselves or who require special support. While the rules may restrict rights, the basic culture is broadly sympathetic to claimants. However, a key element of Home Office culture is to exclude those who seek to settle in the UK and to limit settlement of those already here, especially migrants from African and Asian countries. This clash has meant that many benefits staff are unhappy at their increasing role as immigration controllers.

2. HOME OFFICE LINKS WITH BENEFITS AUTHORITIES

Benefits are administered by several different government bodies, some of which are divided into different agencies (see below). All of these have links with the Home Office which administers immigration control in the UK.

The benefits authorities

The main benefits authority is the Benefits Agency. This is an 'executive', or 'Next Step', agency of the Department of Social Security (DSS). It employs adjudication officers (AOs) who decide on claims and staff who act on behalf of the Secretary of State for Social Security. It administers all social security benefits, except housing benefit (HB) and council tax benefit (CTB). Local offices administer most benefits including income support (IS), incapacity benefit (ICB) and severe disablement allowance (SDA). However, your local office may be split between a local counter service and an office in Glasgow or Belfast, where some of the staff are based. There are special national centres for each of disability living allowance (DLA)/attendance allowance (AA), child benefit (CB), family credit (FC)/disability working allowance (DWA) and pensions. Job-seeker's allowance (JSA) is administered at JobCentres, at which Benefits Agency staff work alongside Employment Service staff.

The other benefits authorities are:

- **Employment Service** – this is part of the Department for Employment and Education and administers JSA in JobCentres, alongside Benefits Agency staff;
- **Contributions Agency** – a DSS executive agency for National Insurance (NI) contributions (except Class 4 contributions which are collected by the Inland Revenue). It has a central office in Newcastle and a few staff based locally at Benefits Agency offices;
- **local authorities** – these administer HB and CTB, though these are almost entirely subsidised by central government.

Benefits authorities staff are expected to understand immigration law as well as the complicated benefits rules. In practice, they are not fully aware of the rules because there has been little training given to staff. For example, benefits staff confuse 'indefinite leave to remain' with 'exceptional leave to remain'. Benefits staff justify their decisions about immigration status with reference to informal remarks by Home Office staff, who themselves often misunderstand immigration law and practice.

Even though the benefits rules which apply to migrants may be different from those for other people, benefits decisions are made in the same way and by the same authorities and staff, regardless of the immigration status of the claimant. All claimants have the same rights of review and appeal. For details of how benefits decisions are taken and how to appeal see CPAG's *National Welfare Benefits Handbook, Rights Guide to Non-Means-Tested Benefits* and *Jobseeker's Allowance Handbook*.

Immigration checks by benefits authorities

All benefits authorities have links to the Home Office. Until the 1996 benefits changes, the most important of these links was with IS sections of local offices. However, as the rules have changed, other parts of the Benefits Agency have set up procedures for information exchange.

One purpose of the links is for benefits authorities to make enquiries of the Home Office about your immigration status. This is mainly to check whether your immigration status affects your rights to benefit.

Immigration checks are usually triggered if a benefits authority believes you may not be British. In the case of IS and income-based JSA claimants, the claim form asks 'Have you, your partner, or any of the children you are claiming for, come to live or returned to live in the UK in the last five years?' If you answer 'Yes' you are asked for the nationality of any person who has come in the last five years, the date you last came, whether you came to work or live in the UK and details of any limits on your stay in the UK. Claim forms for other benefits have similar questions. Immigration checks may also be triggered if:

- the Home Office gives the Benefits Agency information about a claimant as part of a Home Office query about benefit claims or simply 'information-sharing';
- you do not have an NI number or your IS reference number is not an NI number (see p91). At the end of 1996 some child benefit (CB) claimants were asked for their NI number, supposedly to streamline CB, but possibly to identify migrant claimants;
- you have a foreign-sounding name;
- you speak to a benefits officer but are not fluent in English;
- an allegation that you are not British is made to a benefits authority, either by another benefits authority or government agency, or by an individual.

If you are being paid IS/income-based JSA, a local authority dealing with a claim by you for HB/CTB should not make immigration checks.[4]

If you give your nationality as other than British, you will normally be asked to show the Benefits Agency a passport or for EU/EEA nationals, an identity card. The benefits authority may take your immigration status from your passport or from any letter sent to you by the Home Office. Otherwise, the benefits authority is likely to contact the Home Office to establish your immigration status. This may still be done even if your passport shows your status. Contact is made to a Home Office section (called the Immigration Status Enquiry Unit), except that straightforward queries about an asylum-seeker may be made to the Asylum Screening Unit (see Appendix 2).[5] If you have a British passport but are not a British citizen (eg, a British overseas citizen) the benefits authority may do this or may wrongly think that you are a British citizen (see p13).

If you are an EU/EEA national who has claimed or is receiving IS or income-based JSA, the JobCentre or the local Benefits Agency office may notify the Home Office of this fact. This may lead to the Home Office sending you a 'requirement to leave' letter. This does not mean that you will actually be required to leave, but it will stop your IS/income-based JSA. For details, see Chapter 27.

Links with entry clearance officers abroad

There are also links between the Benefits Agency Overseas Directorate (see Appendix 2) and entry clearance officers abroad. These are most likely to affect Asian widows who applied for a visa to join their late husbands in the UK, but were refused on the basis that they were not married as claimed. If you are a non-British citizen living abroad and you claim a retirement pension or widow's benefit on the basis of your spouse's contributions, the Overseas Directorate may contact an entry clearance officer in your country to see whether you have ever been refused a UK visa. Extracts from the entry clearance officer's file may be sent to the Benefits Agency. If there was an appeal against a refusal, the entry clearance officer's explanatory statement for that appeal will usually be passed to the Benefits Agency but other documents, including those which were sent in to support your visa request, *may* not be passed on. The entry clearance officer's papers are most important if the visa was refused because you were not accepted as married. The adjudication officer may agree with the entry clearance officer and refuse benefit. If this happens, you should appeal and get advice. The vast majority of visa refusals made before DNA tests in disputed relationship cases were wrong, as proved later by these tests.[6]

Home Office use of benefits information

The Home Office uses its links with benefits authorities to check on immigrants and to locate those not here legally with whom it is has lost contact. The Home Office gets information from benefits authorities in the following circumstances:

- when a benefits authority asks the Home Office about your immigration status for a benefit claim, the Home Office may keep a note of your address and other details and the fact that you have claimed benefit. If you are not here legally and the Home Office has lost contact with you, the Home Office may start removal action against you (see Chapter 6). If you are here legally, the fact that you have claimed benefits may be used against you when any application for further leave is considered. This could possibly be considered if you sponsor a person who applies for a visa or for leave to remain, but that is unlikely;
- if you apply for further leave to remain in the UK, the application form[7] asks whether you are receiving benefits which count as public funds.[8] If you are asking for leave as the spouse of a settled person, you are also asked whether your spouse is receiving public funds. The

Home Office may check the answers you give with the benefits authorities. The Home Office may also use benefits records to see how long
you have been in the UK;
- if you apply for a visa to come to the UK, the entry clearance officer
  may contact the benefits authorities in the UK to see whether your
  sponsor is claiming benefits or even whether you have claimed benefits
  on a previous visit.

3. NATIONAL INSURANCE CONTRIBUTIONS

Many benefits are paid out of the National Insurance (NI) fund, which is
funded by social security contributions of employees, employers, the
self-employed and other people who choose to make them. In this book
we only cover the rules that particularly affect migrants.

There are five types of contribution:

- Class 1 – payable by employed earners and their employers;
- Class 1A – payable by employers of employed earners;
- Class 2 – payable by self-employed earners;
- Class 3 – payable by voluntary contributors;
- Class 4 – payable by self-employed earners.

Contributions (except Class 4) are collected and recorded by the
Contributions Agency, a DSS executive agency. Class 4 contributions are
collected with income tax by the Inland Revenue: they do not affect entitlement to benefits. Contact with the Contributions Agency may lead to
information about you being passed to the Home Office (see p486).

For full details of the NI scheme and contribution conditions for benefits, see CPAG's *Rights Guide to Non-Means-Tested Benefits*.

Residence and presence

If your earnings are high enough for you/your employer to have to pay
contributions, those contributions only have to be paid if the residence
and presence rules apply. If contributions are not compulsory, you can
pay voluntary Class 2 or 3 contributions to help you meet the contribution conditions for benefits. If you wish to pay contributions while
abroad, the application form is in DSS leaflet NI38. For presence, residence and ordinary residence, see Chapter 8.

Contributions paid in Northern Ireland or the Isle of Man count
towards British benefits. You may also be able to use special rules if you
have lived in another EU/EEA member state (see Part 4) or a country
with which the UK has a reciprocal agreement (see Part 5) even if you are
not a national of that country.

Class 1 contributions

You are liable for Class 1 contributions in any week in which you are:

- employed in GB[9] and:
  - *either* resident and present in GB;
  - *or* ordinarily resident in GB;[10]
- employed by an overseas employer, even though you are not working in the UK.[11] You are only liable once you have been resident in the UK for one year. This also applies to some foreign students and apprentices;[12] *or*
- employed abroad, but only for the first year of that employment (after that you can voluntarily pay Class 3 contributions – see below)[13] if:[14]
  - your employer has a place of business in GB; *and*
  - you were resident in GB before your employment started; *and*
  - you are ordinarily resident in GB.

Class 2 contributions

You are liable for Class 2 contributions in any week in which you are self-employed in GB and *either* :[15]

- ordinarily resident in GB; *or*
- have been resident in GB for at least 26 weeks in the last year.

You can voluntarily pay Class 2 contributions for any other week in which you are present in GB.[16]

If you are self-employed abroad, you can voluntarily pay Class 2 contributions if you were self-employed or self-employed immediately before you left GB and *either*:

- you have been resident in GB for a continuous period of at least three years at some time before that; *or*
- you have paid sufficient GB contributions for three past contribution years (for details see CPAG's *Rights Guide to Non-Means-Tested Benefits*).

If you are a volunteer development worker employed abroad but resident in GB, you can voluntarily pay Class 2 contributions.[17] These are paid at a special rate and (unlike normal Class 2 contributions) count for contribution-based JSA. They are only payable if the Secretary of State certifies that it would be consistent with the proper administration of the law to allow you to do so.

Class 3 contributions

Class 3 contributions are always voluntary. You can pay them:[18]

- for any year during which you were resident in GB at some time;
- if you meet either of the conditions for voluntary payment of Class 2

contributions (see above) you do not need to have been employed or self-employed before you left GB; *or*

- if you have been paying Class 1 contributions from abroad.

Class 4 contributions
You are liable for Class 4 contributions in any week in which you are resident in GB for income tax purposes.[19]

Credits and home responsibilities protection
You may be credited for Class 1 or 2 contributions in certain weeks, including if you are incapable for work, or unemployed and actively seeking and available for work. Credits help meet the contribution conditions for benefits. The residence conditions for credits are the same as for actual contributions.[20] For details of credits, see CPAG's *Rights Guide to Non-Means-Tested Benefits*.

National Insurance numbers

The Contributions Agency refers to your NI record by an NI number which looks like this : MN 42 56 93 D. This number is also used as a reference for tax and for contribution-based benefits. If you do not have or know your number, benefits authorities, employers and the Inland Revenue are likely to want to check your immigration status.

NI numbers are now allocated automatically to children shortly before their 16th birthday, but only if CB is being claimed for the child.[21] If CB was being claimed for you at that time, you should have an NI number. The number you are given is based on the CB reference number.

Some IS/income-based JSA claimants who do not have an NI number (and are not given one when they claim benefit) are given a temporary IS/income-based JSA reference number which looks like an NI number. This is not an NI number.

If you do not have an NI number, you can apply for one. Having an NI number is important because:

- an employer should accept it as showing that there is no bar under immigration law on you taking work;
- it means any contributions you or your employer make should be correctly allocated to your name;
- it means any contributions for which you are credited should be correctly allocated to your name;
- you can deal more easily with other official bodies, such as the Inland Revenue.

If you claim IS/income-based JSA you may be given an NI number. If you are not claiming benefits, or are not given one, you can apply for a number at your local Benefits Agency office. You will usually be interviewed to establish identity and immigration status. If you are already employed a number is usually issued without difficulty. If you are not employed, you may be told by Benefits Agency staff that a number will only be issued once you have found work. That is wrong. You should insist on completing the NI application form and take advice if a number is not issued.

Making the most of your contribution record

Your benefits entitlement may depend upon your contribution record. In particular, your right to a state retirement pension and the amount of that pension is set by the number of contributions you have made. A small shortfall in your record may make a big difference to your benefits. A shortfall may be made up by voluntary contributions or by allocating to your name contributions already made.

If you have returned from abroad you should ask the Contributions Agency for a copy of your contribution record. You can then check they have allocated any contributions made while you were abroad. You may also be able to make up any shortfall in your record by voluntary contributions.

You may have used another person's number or a false number while in GB because you did not wish to come to Home Office attention. If you have since been given leave to remain in the UK, you should apply for an NI number in your own name. You may wish to ask the Contributions Agency to transfer contributions allocated to the number you used in the past to the number issued in your name. This would mean that the contributions paid for your work would be allocated to you. You may need to provide evidence that the contributions were paid because of your work. However, you may have committed a criminal offence by using a number which was not allocated to you – eg, if you used that number to get work you may have committed the offence of obtaining property (your wages) by deception (pretending that the number was allocated to you). Because of this, you should take independent advice before asking the Contributions Agency to transfer contributions to your name.

4. PROVING IDENTITY, AGE AND RELATIONSHIPS

For most people, proving identity, age and their relationships to others (eg, marriage or parentage) is straightforward. However, some people may have problems and migrants are most likely to be affected.

Identity

Identity is important in two different ways.

Some benefit rights depend on your showing that you are a certain named person. For example, in the case of an award of benefit, you must be the person named in the award, and in a claim for a contributory benefit, you must be the person who paid the contributions.

Some benefit rights do *not* depend upon showing that you are a certain named person. Even so a benefits authority may refuse benefit because you have not produced satisfactory evidence of your identity. Cases where this has happened are not limited to migrants and include:[22]

- a mentally ill man who did not know his name and about whom there was no documentary evidence;[23]
- a man claiming to be British against whom a deportation order had been signed as a non-British citizen.[24]

This second approach is wrong. Proof that you have a particular name which links with other records is not necessary for entitlement to benefit. That is because the conditions for benefit apply to your situation, regardless of your name, and even if you have more than one name. For example, if you are an 'on-arrival' asylum-seeker with no income, you are entitled to IS regardless of whether you are really the person in whose *name* the asylum claim was registered. What matters is whether you are the *person* who made the asylum claim. Therefore, if you have a genuine standard acknowledgement letter (SAL) with your photograph on it, the fact that you also have a passport in a different name does not prevent entitlement to IS. This does not mean that the benefits authority cannot investigate. In particular, the authority may wish to check that you are the same person who made the asylum claim and that you have not made a claim for the same benefit under the name on the passport. But benefit cannot be refused on the ground that you have not proved your name or identity.

This also applies to people with no documentary evidence. It is not necessary for you to show that the name you give is the name on your birth certificate or on any other official document.

Age

Your age or the age of members of your family may affect your rights to benefit or the amount of that benefit. This most commonly arises in claims for retirement pension, but the amount of other benefits (eg, IS) can also be affected by your age or the age of any children.

The most common situation in which the benefits authorities dispute age is where you were born abroad at a time when your place of birth did not have accurate records of date of birth. However, it can still apply to children born recently – eg, those born in a country during a protracted war, or while their parents were displaced persons.

Benefits authority officials are generally more willing than the Home Office to accept foreign records as accurate. If you have a birth certificate, that will usually be accepted as proof of your birth date. Other evidence which can show your birth date includes:

- passport or identity card;
- school or health records;
- army records;
- statements from people who know you or your family;
- astrological charts made for a baby at the time of the birth (especially in India) can be used to calculate the birth date.

You may be able to show your birth date by reference to the accepted birth dates of other relatives. For example, if you are recorded as the eldest child and your sister has been accepted as born on a date in 1927, you must have been born before that date.

Medical assessments are sometimes used as evidence of age. This involves a doctor examining you and guessing how old you are. Some doctors use X-rays as part of this assessment. In adults this method is only accurate to within a few years at best.

A common problem is conflicting evidence. Your birth date may have been wrongly recorded in your passport when it was issued – eg, because you gave the wrong date or because of an administrative error. The date in the passport may then have been used in many other official documents. It may be difficult to persuade the benefits authorities that all these dates are wrong. You should explain that all these dates come from one document, so the only real evidence for the date is the passport. If there is other evidence showing that date is not right, the passport is not conclusive evidence.

While each piece of evidence has to be considered, the oldest documents may be more reliable, since they were made nearer to the time of the events to which they refer.

If there is no documentary evidence, the benefits authorities should accept your own statements unless they are contradictory or improbable.

Your birth date may be given in the document(s) as a year or a month rather than an actual date. If this applies, the Benefits Agency will assume your birth date is the date least favourable to you. If you claim retirement pension, this will be the last day of the year/month. However, this date should then be used for all other benefit decisions, even if that is more favourable to you.

If a benefits authority refuses to accept your evidence about your age and so refuses benefit or pays it at a lower rate, you should appeal and take independent advice.

Marriages

You may need to show that you are/were married to your partner. This is most likely to apply to claims for widows' benefits. It may also apply where there is a question of the validity of the marriage (see p118).

A marriage certificate is the best evidence that you are or were married. However, if one is not available, other evidence can count. Your own statement that you were married should be enough. This is because, unlike date of birth, you can be expected to remember that you were married and to whom. If there is contradictory evidence, or if you are claiming benefit as an appointee for a person whose mental state prevents them from making such a statement or for a person who has died, you may need to show by other ways that there was a marriage.

The most important of these is the **co-habitation presumption**. If a couple live together as if they were husband and wife, it is presumed that they are married to each other, unless there is clear contradictory evidence to which the benefits authority can point.[25] Evidence of living together will usually be easier to get than evidence of the wedding, which may have happened a long time ago. This presumption is even stronger where there are children of the couple, because the effect of a decision that there was no wedding would be that the children were illegitimate. This presumption is different from benefit rules which treat unmarried couples as if they were married. You must still show that you were/are married, but showing that you were/are living together as husband and wife is enough, unless there is contradictory evidence.

Parentage

In rare cases you may need to show that you are (or your late husband was) the parent of a child. This could apply where CB is claimed for a child by you and one or more other people, none of whom is living with the child. In this situation, a parent has priority over other claimants.[26] It may also arise if you are refused widowed mother's allowance (or awarded it at a reduced rate) because it is disputed that your child or children are children of your late husband.[27]

DNA testing may be able accurately to establish whether the person is/was the parent of the child concerned. If this is not possible, the parent may be able to use the **presumption of legitimacy**. If the child was conceived by or born to a married woman, there is a legal presumption that her husband is the father.[28] If you were married to the mother, you are presumed to be the father. In the case of widowed mother's allowance, your late husband is therefore presumed to be the father of any child conceived or born during the marriage. The presumption applies even if the child was born after the wedding but obviously conceived before.[29]

The presumption can be overridden by evidence that the husband was not the father.[30] For the benefits authorities to do this, there must be evidence that shows the child was probably not legitimate.[31] If you are the claimed father but the mother was married to another man, he rather than you is presumed to be the father.

If the mother was not married at the time of conception or birth, there is no presumption.

Presence and residence

This chapter covers:

While presence and absence are quite straightforward, 'ordinary' and 'habitual' residence can cause problems.[1]

These problems most often arise with the habitual residence test for income support (IS) and income-based jobseeker's allowance (JSA), but they can arise with ordinary residence. Benefit rules are usually precise, even if they are complicated. However, the residence conditions are simple but very vague. They need judgment and weighing up of many different factors. Two different decision-makers can legally reach different opinions about the residence of a particular person. The vagueness of the residence conditions also allows for extremely restrictive interpretation, deliberate or accidental use of personal bias and assumptions about how people do or should lead their lives. This is most obvious when the decision-maker lacks knowledge of or ignores the claimant's own culture.

Guidance to benefits staff states that a decision must be made on all the facts, but sets out certain factors which may be relevant. Because staff are used to applying precise rules, they tend to change these factors into checklists. This often leads to far too much weight being given to certain factors and to decisions which are obviously wrong from a common-sense point of view.

Example

One tribunal decision[2] concerned a British citizen born abroad who lived and worked in the UK for two years and who then made an overseas visit of one month to her estranged husband who was very ill. The tribunal decided that on her return she was not habitually resident in the UK because: her husband and children lived abroad and she was unlikely to be able to afford ever to bring them to the UK, even if they were permitted to enter and she may have owned property abroad. That decision was clearly wrong on any understanding of habitual residence. The length of time the claimant had lived here, renting her own flat with her own permanent job (from which she had been made redundant), meant she became habitually resident, regardless of the whereabouts of her estranged husband and children, any property or her prospects of finding work. Her visit abroad did not break that residence. The tribunal went wrong because it focused on her family ties and prospects of employment.

Case law gives examples of how residence conditions have been considered and the factors which were important in those cases. However, it is important that these factors do not become *conditions* which the claimant has to meet. Each case is different and a factor which is crucial in one case may not be crucial in another. The residence tests (ordinary and habitual) are, it seems, slightly different (although this is being appealed – see p104). However, ordinary residence only has one meaning.[3] This means that a case on ordinary residence in one area of law applies to ordinary residence in a different area of law. Because habitual residence only has one meaning, a case on one area of law also applies in another. The only exception to this is where a court decides that, because of the legal context, ordinary (or habitual) residence has a special meaning in that area of law. Cases from that area of law will then not apply outside that area.

Sometimes you can use the facts of another case on residence (ordinary or habitual) to support your argument that you are resident. There are two sorts of residence case. First, where the court or tribunal is making a decision on residence itself – eg, family court cases. Here the facts of the case being considered may be a useful example. The second sort is where the court or tribunal is considering whether another body (eg, Inland Revenue Commissioners) was legally justified in deciding that, on the evidence before it, a person was (or was not) ordinarily resident. The facts of the second sort must be used more carefully because the court has only considered whether a person in that situation *can* be considered as resident, not whether the person *is* resident.

1. PRESENCE AND ABSENCE

Presence means physical presence. Great Britain (GB) is Wales, Scotland, England and adjacent islands (but not the Isle of Man or Channel Islands). The United Kingdom (UK) is GB plus Northern Ireland.

The UK includes UK territorial waters and GB includes UK territorial waters adjacent to GB.[4] Territorial waters are those 12 miles from the shore, except off Dover and near the Isle of Man where they stop mid-point.[5] This means that if you travel to GB by plane, you arrive when the plane lands. If you travel by boat you arrive when the boat enters adjacent territorial waters.

If you have to be present in GB to be entitled to the benefits, you must show that you were in GB from midnight to midnight.[6] If a benefits authority wants to disqualify you from benefit because you were absent from GB, it must show you were absent throughout that day. This means that on the day you leave GB and the day you arrive in GB you count as neither present nor absent.

The rules for child benefit (CB) are different. When working out whether a person was present or absent in the UK on a particular day, it is the situation at midnight at the beginning of the day that counts.[7] A week runs from Monday.[8] When working out whether a person is in a particular situation in any week, it is the situation at midnight at the beginning of that Monday that counts for the whole of the following week.[9] This means that, if you arrive in GB at 11.50 pm on Sunday, you count as present for the whole of the following week, but if you arrive at 12.10 am on Monday, you count as absent for that week.

2. ORDINARY RESIDENCE

A person must be ordinarily resident in GB to be entitled to:

- family credit (FC);
- disability working allowance (DWA);
- disability living allowance (DLA);
- attendance allowance (AA);
- invalid care allowance (ICA);
- severe disablement allowance (SDA);
- Category D retirement pension.

If a person stops being ordinarily resident in GB, the amount of her/his retirement pension (of any category) is frozen (see p141). In practice it is rare for a person in GB to be refused a benefit on ordinary residence grounds. However, because ordinary residence is closely connected with habitual residence (see p104), we explain it in some detail.

There is no definition in the benefits regulations of ordinary residence. This means ordinary residence is given its ordinary and natural meaning.[10] The most important case on ordinary residence is *Shah*.[11] In that case the House of Lords decided that ordinary residence means:[12]

> a person's 'abode in a particular place or country which he has adopted voluntarily and for settled purposes as part of the regular order of his life for the time being, whether of short or long duration.'

It should usually be clear whether residence is voluntary or for a settled purpose.[13]

The case law on ordinary residence shows that:

- ordinary residence can start on arrival in GB, or it can start before (see below);
- a person in GB for a temporary purpose can be ordinarily resident in GB (see below);
- a person who lives in GB but has no fixed abode can be ordinarily resident;[14]
- ordinary residence can continue during absences from the UK, but leaving GB to settle abroad will normally end ordinary residence (see p101);
- a person who spends most of the time (or even almost all of the time) outside GB can be ordinarily resident;[15]
- a person can be ordinarily resident in more than one place or country;[16]
- ordinary residence is different from the concept of 'domicile'.[17]

Special rules apply to children (see p102) and other people whose place of residence is beyond their control (see p102).

Ordinary residence on arrival

Ordinary residence can begin immediately on arrival in the UK.[18] In *Macrae* v *Macrae*[19] a man who separated from his wife in England (where he had lived and worked for three years) and went to live at his parent's house in Scotland, immediately became ordinarily resident there.[20] The Court of Appeal said that, where there is evidence that the person intends to make that place his home for an indefinite period, he is ordinarily resident when he arrives there. In another case, a court decided that a woman returning from Australia after some months there had never lost her ordinary residence in England, but, if she had, she became ordinarily resident again when the boat embarked from Australia.[21] The students in *Shah* had to show that they were ordinarily resident within a few weeks of first arriving in the UK, but nobody argued that they could not be ordinarily resident because they had only just moved to GB.[22]

Temporary purpose

To be ordinarily resident in GB you do not have to intend or be able to live here permanently.[23] The purpose can be for a limited period and Lord Scarman said that 'education, business or profession, employment, health, family, or merely love of the place spring to mind as common reasons for a choice of regular abode'.[24] You may have several different reasons for a single stay – eg, to visit relatives, get medical advice, attend religious ceremonies and sort out personal affairs.[25]

The reason must be a settled one. This does not mean that the reason has to be long-standing,[26] but there must be evidence of it. In most of the cases on ordinary residence, the court was looking back to see whether a person had been ordinarily resident months or years before.[27] This is much easier than deciding whether a person has recently become ordinarily resident. There is no minimum period of residence before you are ordinarily resident. If, for example, you have arrived in the UK and started work, the benefits authorities should consider how long you are likely to reside in the UK. If you intend to live here for the time being, the benefits authorities should accept your intention as sufficient, unless it is clearly unlikely that you are going to be able to stay. The benefits authorities should not make a deep examination of your long-term intentions.[28] The type of accommodation you occupy may be relevant.[29]

Absence from the UK

Once you are ordinarily resident in GB, you can lose that status if you go abroad. This depends upon:

- why you go abroad;
- how long you stay abroad;
- what connections you keep with GB – eg, accommodation, furniture and other possessions.[30]

If you decide to move abroad for the foreseeable future, then you will normally stop being ordinarily resident in GB on the day you leave.[31] A possible exception to this is where your plans are clearly impractical and you return to GB very quickly.

If your absence abroad is part of your normal pattern of life, your ordinary residence in GB will not be affected.[32] This applies even if you are out of GB for most of the year.[33] For example, if you spend each summer in GB but all winter abroad, you may be ordinarily resident in GB.[34]

If your absence abroad is extraordinary or temporary, and you intend to return to GB, your ordinary residence will not be affected.[35] A British woman who spent 15 months in Germany with her husband over a period of three years kept her ordinary residence in England. She had always intended to return here.[36]

However, if you are away for a long time and do not keep strong connections with GB you may lose your ordinary residence, even if you intend to return to GB. A Citizen of UK and Colonies (see p12) lived in the UK for over four years, and then returned to Kenya for two years and five months, because her business here failed and there was a business opportunity in Kenya. She intended to make enough money to support herself on her return to the UK. Her parents and parents-in-law remained in the UK. She lost her ordinary residence during her absence.[37]

Involuntary residence

A person who is held in a place against their will may not become ordinarily resident. These cases are very rare. Examples given by the courts are kidnap victims and being stranded on a desert island.[38] The courts have recognised that circumstances sometimes limit or remove a person's choice, but do not stop them from being ordinarily resident where they reside.[39] A woman who became mentally ill on a visit to England and remained in an asylum until she died over 50 years later, was ordinarily resident by the time she died, even though she never decided to stay here.[40] Deportation to GB does not prevent you becoming ordinarily resident here.[41] We consider that the issue is whether the person's residence is part of their settled purpose. If you have decided to live in GB, it does not matter that you have made that decision because you have been deported here.

Children

Where a benefit claimant or partner is aged 16-17, ordinary residence is in practice decided using the same rules as for adults.[42]

The only benefit for children under 16 with an ordinary residence test is DLA. A child's ordinary residence depends upon where the parent or person(s) with parental responsibility[43] live(s). Where there is only one person with parental responsibility, the child has the same ordinary residence as that person.

Where there are two such people who live apart, one should get the consent of the other to a change of residence of the child, otherwise the child may be treated as abducted. A child who is abducted is considered still to have the same ordinary residence as the person(s) with parental responsibility.[44] Agreement to a change of residence may be assumed if the other person takes no action.[45]

3. HABITUAL RESIDENCE

A habitual residence test was imposed for IS, HB and CTB on 1 August 1994.[46] This was the first use of habitual residence for British benefits rules, though it is part of some EC rules (see p105). It now also applies to income-based JSA. For examples, see the chapter relevant to your immigration status.

The government's reason for bringing in a habitual residence test was the supposed problem of 'benefit tourism' from other EU/EEA member states. Ministers accused young Europeans of coming to Britain for a holiday on means-tested benefits.[47] It was not explained why the availability for work rules do not deal with such a problem.

Rather than targeting 'benefit tourism', the habitual residence test has become an arbitrary barrier to benefits for some of the most vulnerable people in Britain.[48] In its first year, over 25,000 claimants failed the habitual residence test, more than five times the number the government had predicted. Only one fifth were EEA nationals. Black British citizens and their families have been badly affected by the test, but anyone who travels abroad may be caught.

The Benefits Agency and local authorities do not apply the habitual residence test properly or even consistently (see p97). In practice, the test usually means that a claimant is denied benefits at first, but not indefinitely. Local offices may have a rule of thumb, such as three months, after which a person will pass the test. However, practice varies between and within offices, so a person who passes the test at one office could have failed it at another. In practice, once you are accepted as habitually resident, you are very unlikely to fail the test at a later date, even if your benefit claim stops or you change benefit offices.

The habitual residence test for IS, income-based JSA, HB and CTB applies to residence anywhere in the UK, Ireland, Channel Islands or Isle of Man.[49] This means that any connections or residence in any of those places counts as if it were in the UK.

Habitual residence test and international law

Refusal of IS/income-based JSA/HB/CTB to nationals of EU/EEA member states and Cyprus, Malta and Turkey who fail the habitual residence test may break the UK's international obligations. Under the 1953 European Convention on Social and Medical Assistance[50] and the 1961 European Social Charter[51] the UK must not discriminate in provision of these benefits to nationals of those countries.[52] The habitual residence test discriminates between Irish nationals and nationals of those countries because habitual residence in Ireland counts, but not habitual residence in, say, Turkey.[53] Because these two treaties are not part of British law, breaches of the UK's obligations do not make the benefit refusal unlawful.[54] UK compliance with these treaties is supervised by the Council of Europe Committee of Experts and a complaint may lead the UK government to change the law. If this applies to you, consider a complaint. CPAG wants to hear from agencies and lawyers representing those interested in complaining.

The meaning of habitual residence

There is no definition in the benefits regulations of habitual residence. This means habitual residence is given its ordinary and natural meaning.[55] A person is habitually resident if s/he is ordinarily resident (see p99) and has been resident for an appreciable period of time (see below).[56] A commissioner has rejected an argument that an appreciable period of time is not always necessary.[57]

Benefits Agency guidance suggests that habitual residence is very different from ordinary residence, but the case law of the courts and commissioners shows that they are very similar concepts.[58]

Because the benefits habitual residence test is new, the case law is not yet certain and may change (see p98 for how to use court cases on residence). In particular, the Court of Appeal is to be asked to decide that habitual residence has the same meaning as ordinary residence.[59] Under the present case law:[60]

- if there is doubt about any of the facts in your case, you are entitled to the benefit of that doubt. This is because the benefits authority has to show that you are not habitually resident;[61]
- you must be seen to be making a home here, but it does not have to be your only home or a permanent one.[62] The resources available to you should be taken into account. This means that, if you have no money to get settled accommodation, any steps you take so that you will be able to get such a home (eg, approaching housing associations, trying to find work) are evidence that you are making a home here;
- there must be an appreciable period of residence here.[63] This is not defined in case law. It will vary from case to case. The period only needs to be long enough for residence to be habitual. Periods of two or three months are sometimes referred to,[64] but a commissioner has said that it is wrong to use these examples as minimum periods.[65] There is no minimum period laid down in the case law.[66] This means that in some cases it might be a matter of days or as soon as you arrive if you have been resident in GB previously. It can include visits to prepare for settled residence made before that residence is actually taken up;[67]
- the practicality or viability of your arrangements for residence may be relevant to deciding whether you are resident and the length of the appreciable period.[68] This is not in the court cases and comes only from commissioners' cases. It is difficult to understand why this is relevant to residence. If a person has no money to support her/himself in GB, s/he is likely to be resident here for the foreseeable future, because s/he cannot afford to go anywhere else. So a person with no income will have a short appreciable period. Lack of viability can only make it

more difficult to show habitual residence if it means you are likely to leave the UK soon;

- events after the date of benefit claim may show that your intention was always to reside in the UK.[69] For example, if you are refused income-based JSA because the Benefits Agency does not accept you have a settled intention to stay in the UK, the fact that you are still here by the time of the appeal hearing may help to show that you always intended to stay.

Because establishing an appreciable period of residence is only a matter of time, if you fail the test, appeal and also make regular fresh claims. Some Benefits Agency offices tell claimants the period of time they will need to be present to be accepted as habitually resident.

Habitual residence under EC law

Under the EC co-ordination rules (see Chapter 26) residence means habitual residence.[70] Habitual residence itself is not defined. The case law of the European Court of Justice explains what habitual residence means, but only in the situation where a person wishes to claim an unemployment benefit in a country other than the one where s/he last worked.[71] The Court explains that because this is a special situation, there must be a very restrictive approach to who can qualify. A person can only qualify under this rule if the country where the benefit is claimed is the country of habitual residence *and* the centre of that person's interests.[72] This means that the case law on this special provision[73] is not useful guidance on habitual residence in other situations under British or EC law.[74]

A commissioner has decided that the meaning of habitual residence for refugees seeking equal treatment for benefits under EC law is the same as that under British law.[75]

CHAPTER NINE

Special rules for family members

This chapter covers the special rules which apply to:

1. Couples where one partner is abroad (below)
2. Families where a dependent adult is abroad (p114)
3. Families where a child is abroad (p114)
4. Polygamous marriages (p116)
5. Children born in the UK without the right of abode (p118)

For the rules where the whole family is abroad, see Part 3.

There are special rules to stop you losing benefit if you move between GB and Northern Ireland.[1] You may also be able to use special rules if you have lived in another EU/EEA member state (see Part 4) or a country with which the UK has a reciprocal agreement (see Part 5) even if you are not a national of that country.

I. COUPLES WHERE ONE PARTNER IS ABROAD

Some benefits are paid at a higher rate if you have a partner (see p108). Some benefits are paid at a lower rate. If you are in GB but your partner (see glossary) is abroad, your benefit entitlement may be affected. For example, if your partner is working full time, you may be refused income support/income-based jobseeker's allowance – see Chapter 11.

If you are entitled to maternity allowance (MA), incapacity benefit (ICB), a retirement pension, severe disablement allowance (SDA) or invalid care allowance (ICA), you may get an increase for your spouse, even though s/he is abroad. For the rules on increases for adult dependants other than spouses, see p114.

Household

Under the rules for:

- income support (IS)
- income-based jobseeker's allowance (JSA)

- housing benefit (HB)
- council tax benefit (CTB)
- family credit (FC)
- disability working allowance (DWA)

a person can only count as your partner if you share the same household. This applies if you are a married couple[2] or an unmarried couple.[3] The usual rules about 'household' are that it is something abstract, not something physical like a home. It is made up of either a single person or a group of people held together by social ties.[4] A person cannot be a member of two households at the same time.[5] A person can be temporarily absent from the home but still be a member of the household.[6] If it is not obvious whether people share a household, the important factors are:

- whether they share the same physical space – eg, a house or flat;
- whether they carry out chores for the benefit of all of them – eg, cooking, shopping, cleaning.

There are special rules for each benefit which mean that certain temporary absences of one partner from other members of the family are ignored when considering whether there is a common household. These special rules do not override *all* the normal rules above about what is a household.[7] This means that, even if the temporary absence is ignored, your general situation may have changed enough for your partner to no longer be in your household. This is most likely to apply if your partner is now a member of a different household abroad.

Income support/income-based JSA

If a person abroad counts as your partner for IS/income-based JSA then:

- if your partner is in full-time employment (for details of what this means, see CPAG's *National Welfare Benefits Handbook*) you are not entitled to IS/income-based JSA.[8] This applies even if your partner is employed abroad and her/his earnings are very low in British terms or cannot be exchanged for pounds sterling;
- your partner's income and capital is taken into account as if they were your income or capital.[9] There are special rules about calculating capital abroad (see CPAG's *National Welfare Benefits Handbook*);
- your applicable amount (see glossary) includes an amount for your partner, but only in certain cases and then only for up to eight weeks (see p114).

If a person abroad counts as your partner, these rules mean that you will usually be paid less IS/income-based JSA than if s/he were living with you, or none at all. If this applies you can use the following rules to argue that the person should not count as your partner. If you receive any income from that person while s/he does not count as your partner, that will count as maintenance and so might be disregarded as your income (see CPAG's *National Welfare Benefits Handbook*).

When does a person count as your partner

A person of the opposite sex can count as your partner even though you are not married to them. This only applies if you are living with that person as if they were your spouse. In practice, if your unmarried partner is abroad, the Benefits Agency will *not* treat you as a couple for benefit purposes (but see p110 for when you may want to argue against this decision).

A person only counts as your partner if you are members of the same household (see p107). Some absences of your partner from you are ignored when considering whether you remain members of the same household. These rules do not apply if you have never actually shared a household with your partner.[10]

Example
Rifat marries Amjad in Pakistan. They have a week-long honeymoon. Rifat then returns to her home in the UK. Amjad intends to apply for a visa to join her in the UK. He works full time but earns the equivalent of £10 per week. Rifat loses her job and has to claim income-based JSA. The honeymoon was too short to count as sharing a household. Because they have never shared a household, the rules about ignoring temporary absences do not apply.

Temporary absences from other family members

If your partner is temporarily living away from you (for the meaning of temporary, see p242), that absence is ignored when considering whether you share a household with your partner *unless*:[11]

- your partner and/or you do not intend to resume living in the same household as each other.[12] You may intend to resume living together, but your intentions depend upon something beyond your control, such as getting a visa (see p109) or a job. If this applies, you may be able to argue that your intention does not count because it depends on these things;[13]
- your absence from each other is likely to exceed 52 weeks, but not if:
  - there are exceptional circumstances. The rules give examples of your partner having no control over the length of the absence, which would include delays caused by immigration; *and*

- the absence is unlikely to be substantially more than 52 weeks;
- your partner is serving a sentence imposed by a court or is detained pending trial or sentence;
- your partner is permanently in residential accommodation; *or*
- your partner is in residential care or a residential nursing home.

Any of these can apply where your partner is abroad.

The absence is from you, not from the family home, so these rules can apply even if your partner has never lived in your current home.[14] The length of the absence is worked out from when it started to when it is likely to finish. If circumstances change so that the likely total absence gets longer (or shorter) – eg, a family member falls ill – then the absence may become too long (or short enough) to count as temporary under these rules.

Example

Rifat joins Amjad in Pakistan for three months. She then returns home to the UK but, because of sickness, claims IS. Amjad applies for a visa and, because his absence is likely to substantially exceed 52 weeks, Rifat is treated as a single person and is entitled to IS. Three months later, Amjad is refused a visa on maintenance and accommodation grounds (see Chapter 5) and he appeals. One year later he wins his appeal and a visa is issued. Before he can travel to the UK his mother falls ill and he stays in Pakistan to care for her. Her illness is only expected to last a short time so Amjad expects to travel to the UK within a month. However, because his total absence from Rifat is now substantially more than a year, he is not treated as her partner even though the absence is expected to end soon.

If a couple is separated because one partner has to apply for a visa to come to the UK, there may be delay:

- to meet the immigration rules before applying for a visa, for example:
  - trying to get a job (or a job offer for the partner) so that the maintenance and accommodation rules are met;
  - waiting for recognition as a refugee, or four years' exceptional leave to remain, or indefinite leave to remain;
- waiting for a decision on a visa application. This takes around three to ten months;
- waiting for an appeal against a visa refusal. This takes at least six months from bringing the appeal until a visa is issued, if successful, and would normally be at least a year.

The likely length of your separation depends upon how likely you are to be refused a visa. Refusal rates are very high in African and Asian countries. If the absence is likely substantially to exceed 52 weeks, your absence from each other will not count as temporary (see above).

Getting IS/income-based JSA for a partner abroad

If your partner is temporarily absent (see p242) from GB but you are in GB, then as long as your partner meets the rules for a temporary absence of up to four/eight weeks (see p247):

- your 'applicable amount' (see glossary) stays the same;[15] *and*
- your partner counts as a member of your household, so her/his income and capital is taken into account in the usual way.[16]

If your partner stops meeting the temporary absence rules, or is absent for more than four/eight weeks, your applicable amount is reduced to that for a single person, even though any income or capital of your partner is still taken into account.[17] You may then want to argue that s/he no longer counts as your partner (see p108).

Housing benefit and council tax benefit

If you are being paid IS/income-based JSA (including urgent cases rate) your partner's absence from the UK does not affect the amount of your HB, and will only affect CTB in exceptional circumstances (see p112). This is because you are treated as having no income or capital, so you are entitled to maximum HB/CTB regardless of whether your applicable amount is for a single person or a couple.[18] The local authority which deals with your HB/CTB claim should not make enquiries about your partner's absence. If you are not being paid IS/income-based JSA the following rules apply.

If a person abroad counts as your partner (see below) for HB/CTB then your partner's income and capital is taken into account as if they were your income and capital.[19] There are special rules about calculating capital abroad (see CPAG's *National Welfare Benefits Handbook*):

- your applicable amount (see glossary) includes an amount for your partner; *and*
- for HB, your partner's absence does not affect the fact that you normally occupy your accommodation as your home.[20]

These rules mean that your HB/CTB will usually be the same as if your partner were living with you. This is different from the IS/income-based JSA rules which usually make you worse off.

If a person abroad does *not* count as your partner, your applicable amount will be for a single person, not a couple, so your HB/CTB may be paid at a lower rate.

In very unusual cases your partner or ex-partner may still be liable for current council tax, even though s/he no longer counts as your partner under CTB rules.[21] If this happens, your CTB will be worked on the basis of your 'share' (ie, half the council tax) even though you are legally liable to pay all the council tax.[22] If this applies, the local authority can top up your CTB, but only to the amount of your share. You should ask the authority to do this and also try to get your partner's name removed from the list of liable people. For more details, see CPAG's *Council Tax Handbook*.

The HB/CTB rules about who counts as your partner and temporary absences are the same as for IS, except:[23]

- there are no special rules for partners in prison or residential accommodation/care/homes;
- for CTB, there are no rules setting out the exceptions to the general rule that a temporary absence is ignored. However, absences which are likely to be more than 52 weeks may not count as temporary anyway. In practice, local authorities are likely to deal with CTB in the same way as HB.

For more information about HB/CTB temporary absences, see p251.

Family credit and disability working allowance

If your partner is in another EU/EEA member state, different rules may apply (see p353).

If a person abroad counts as your partner for FC/DWA then:

- if s/he is working full time abroad and has no earnings from the UK, you are not entitled to FC/DWA, even if you are employed full time in GB (but see below);[24]
- if s/he is not ordinarily resident (see p99) in GB, you are not entitled to FC/DWA;[25]
- your partner's income and capital are taken into account as if they were your income or capital.[26] There are special rules about calculating capital abroad (see CPAG's *National Welfare Benefits Handbook*);
- your FC applicable amount (see glossary) is the same as it would be for a couple (it is always the same);[27]
- your DWA applicable amount is for a couple, which is higher than it would be for a single person.[28]

These rules mean that you may not be entitled to FC/DWA, even though you would be if no one counted as your partner. If this applies you can use the following rules to argue that the person should not count as your partner. If you receive any income from that person while s/he does not count as your partner, that will count as maintenance and so might be disregarded as your income (see CPAG's *National Welfare Benefits Handbook*).

If you are a national of a country which is a party to the Fourth ACP (Africa, Caribbean, Pacific) – EEC Convention (see p380), some of the above rules may breach EC law. This can only apply if you are lawfully working in the UK. If you are, EC law may override the rules that your partner must be ordinarily resident in GB and must not receive all her/his earnings from full-time employment abroad.[29] If this may apply to you, ask an advice agency to contact CPAG.

When does a person count as your partner

A person only counts as your partner if you are members of the same household (see p106). If you are living apart, but both of you intend to live together again, you are treated as being members of the same household.[30] This does not apply if you have never actually shared a household with your partner (see example on p108).[31] You may be able to argue that your intention only counts if it is unqualified and does not depend upon something beyond your (or your partner's) control, such as getting a visa (see p109) or a job.[32]

A person abroad is treated as if s/he were not in your household (and so does not count as your partner) if s/he:[33]

- has been a hospital in-patient for 52 weeks or more;
- is detained in custody serving a court sentence of 52 weeks or more.

Child benefit

If you are a lone parent, you are not entitled to the higher single parent rate if a person abroad counts as your partner. These rules are less generous that the rules for lone parent rate family premium so you may still be entitled to this premium for IS/income-based JSA/HB/CTB.[34]

Married couple

If you have a spouse abroad you are not entitled to the higher lone parent rate if you are residing together.[35] You count as residing together even while you are apart unless:[36]

- you have been separated from each other:
  - by court order or deed of separation; *or*
  - for 91 consecutive days; *and*
- this separation is likely to be permanent.

This rule will usually mean that you are not entitled to the higher rate if you and your spouse want to reside together, but are separated by immigration laws, war, persecution or simply finances. However, because you only need to show that the separation is *likely* to be permanent, if your partner will probably never be able to join you, you are entitled to the higher rate.[37]

Any separation only because one (or both) spouses is an in-patient in a hospital or similar institution does not count as separation under this rule, even if it may be permanent.[38]

Unmarried couples

If you live with a person of the opposite sex as if you were married to each other, you are not entitled to the higher lone parent rate.[39] You can still count as living together during a temporary separation, but all the other circumstances of your relationship must be taken into account.[40] For living together as husband and wife, see CPAG's *National Welfare Benefits Handbook*.

Spouse increase for contributory benefits and disability benefits

You may be entitled to an increase for your spouse (see CPAG's *Rights Guide to Non-Means-Tested Benefits*) if you are entitled to:

- incapacity benefit;
- maternity allowance;
- Category A or C retirement pension;
- severe disablement allowance;
- invalid care allowance.

This increase is still payable while your spouse is abroad, if you are residing together.[41] You are treated as residing together during any temporary absence (see p242) apart from each other.[42] Even if you both intend to be permanently absent from GB, as long as your absence *from each other* is only temporary, the increase for your spouse is not affected.[43]

Any separation only because one (or both) spouses is an in-patient in a hospital or similar institution does not count as separation under this rule, even if it may be permanent.[44]

There are special rules if your spouse is in another EU/EEA member state (see Part 4).

2. FAMILIES WHERE A DEPENDENT ADULT IS ABROAD

You may be entitled to an increase for a dependent adult (for spouses see p106). Most people who get an increase are living together as husband and wife. You can get an increase (see CPAG's *Rights Guide to Non-Means-Tested Benefits*) if you are entitled to:

- incapacity benefit;
- maternity allowance;
- Category A or C retirement pension;
- severe disablement allowance;
- invalid care allowance.

This increase is still payable while the adult is abroad, but only if you are residing together outside GB and you are not disqualified from receiving the benefit because of any absence from GB.[45] You are treated as residing together during any temporary absence (see p242) from each other.[46] Even if you both intend to be permanently absent from GB, as long as your absence *from each other* is only temporary, the increase is not affected.[47]

There are special rules if the adult is in another EU/EEA member state (see Part 4).

3. FAMILIES WHERE A CHILD IS ABROAD

Some benefits are paid at a higher rate if you are responsible for a child. If that child goes abroad, your benefit entitlement may be affected.

Income support/income-based JSA

Your IS/income-based JSA applicable amount (see glossary) includes an amount for each child for whom you are responsible.[48] This only applies to a child who is in your household (see p106).[49] You will also get a family premium which may be paid at the lone parent rate and/or disabled child premium.

Only the following temporary absences (see p242) from your household of a child are ignored when considering whether the child remains a member of the household:

- up to eight weeks absence from the UK if you and/or your partner meet the temporary absence rules for IS/income-based JSA due to treatment of a child abroad (see p247);[50] *otherwise*
- up to four weeks absence from the UK.[51]

If you claimed either IS or income-based JSA after the child went abroad and you were not entitled to the other benefit immediately before claiming, these periods run from the date of claim.[52]

If the child is abroad for longer than these periods, your IS/income-based JSA is worked out ignoring the child.

Housing benefit and council tax benefit

If you are being paid IS/income-based JSA (including urgent cases rate) a child's absence from the UK does not affect the amount of your HB/CTB (see above). If you are *not* being paid IS/income-based JSA, then you may lose money if a child is treated as not being in your household. The following rules apply.

Your HB/CTB applicable amount includes an amount for each child for whom you are responsible.[53] This only applies to a child who is in your household (see p106).[54]

For HB/CTB, temporary absences (see p242) from your household of a child are ignored when considering whether the child remains a member of the household. For HB, the exceptions to this rule are:[55]

- the child and/or you do not intend to resume living in the same household as each other;[56]
- your absence from each other is likely to exceed 52 weeks, *unless*:
  - there are exceptional circumstances. The rules give examples of you having no control over the length of the absence; *and*
  - the absence is unlikely to be substantially more than 52 weeks.

For CTB, there are no rules setting out the exceptions to the general rule that a temporary absence is ignored. However, absences which are likely to be more than 52 weeks may not count as temporary anyway. In practice, local authorities are likely to deal with CTB in the same way as HB.

Child benefit and guardian's allowance

For the rules which apply when a child is abroad, see p134.

Family credit and disability working allowance

You are only entitled to FC if you or your partner is responsible for a child.[57] The child does not have to be present or ordinarily resident in the UK. For DWA, the applicable amount (see glossary) is higher for a lone parent than for a single person.

A person is responsible for a child under the FC/DWA rules if the child normally lives with her/him.[58] This applies if the child spends more time with that person than anyone else.[59] If the child spends equal time with one or more persons or there is no established pattern, then the person responsible for the child under FC/DWA rules is:[60]

- the person receiving CB for that child;
- if no one receives CB and only one person has claimed CB, that person; *otherwise*
- the person with primary responsibility for the child. Primary responsibility is not defined in the rules.

If a person counts as responsible for a child at the beginning of a FC/DWA award, that person counts as responsible for the rest of the 26-week period of that award.[61]

Child increase for contributory benefits and disability benefits

You may be entitled to an increase for a child (see CPAG's *Rights Guide to Non-Means-Tested Benefits*) if you are entitled to:

- incapacity benefit;
- Category A, B or C retirement pension;
- widowed mother's allowance;
- severe disablement allowance;
- invalid care allowance.

The increase is payable while the child is abroad, as long as you are entitled to CB.[62] If you are not entitled to CB, that does not affect payability of the increase if:[63]

- the only reason you are not entitled to CB is that the CB residence conditions (see p134) are not met; *and*
- no one else is entitled to CB for the child; *and*
- the absence from GB was throughout intended to be temporary.

If you are absent on the day of yearly up-rating of CB, your increase will continue to be paid at the same rate, even if the rules about overlapping benefits mean that it should be reduced.[66]

There are special rules if the child is in another EU/EEA member state (see Part 4).

4. POLYGAMOUS MARRIAGES

A polygamous marriage is a marriage in which one person is married to two or more people *and* the marriage took place under a law which allows polygamy.[65] Usually it is the husband who has more than one wife, but the rules work in the same way if a wife has more than one husband.[66] These rules only apply to people who are married and not to people who live with more than one person as if they were married.

Under British law a man and a woman do not usually count as legally married unless their marriage is a monogamous one – ie, not polygamous.[67] However, there are special rules for benefits.

For means-tested benefits, a polygamous marriage is treated very much like a monogamous marriage (see below). For non-means-tested benefits, parties to polygamous marriages are often not entitled to benefits which they would have been entitled to if the marriage was monogamous (see p118).

Means-tested benefits

For IS, income-based JSA, HB, CTB, FC and DWA all the spouses under a polygamous marriage count as your partners, but only if you share a household (see p106).[68] If you are not legally married or do not share a household, each person may claim benefit in their own right. The special rules for polygamous marriages are as follows.

For IS, income-based JSA, HB, CTB the applicable amount is worked out differently.[69] If you qualify for more than one premium based on different partners, you are entitled to the highest of those premiums. Instead of the couple personal allowance, you are entitled to a personal allowance of:

- the couple allowance based upon your oldest partner; *plus*
- an allowance for each extra partner equal to the allowance for a couple aged over 18 *minus* the allowance of a single person aged over 25.

For IS/income-based JSA, you only get this extra allowance for a partner who is:[70]

- aged 18 or over; *or*
- responsible for a child; *or*
- would be entitled to IS/income-based JSA in her/his own right.

For FC/DWA, the maximum FC/DWA includes an extra amount for each extra partner of:[71]

- if s/he is 18 or over, the amount for a person aged 18;
- if s/he is under 18, the amount for a person aged 16-17.

Income and capital of all your partners counts as your income/capital.[72] If any of your partners is working full time you are not entitled to IS/income-based JSA.

For how urgent cases IS/income-based JSA is worked out for polygamous marriages, see p124.

Non-means-tested benefits

For non-means-tested benefits a person does not count as a spouse on any day on which a marriage is actually polygamous.[73] A polygamous marriage is treated as monogamous on any day on which it is *potentially polygamous* (ie, neither husband nor wife has had more than one spouse) or when it is *formerly polygamous* (ie, the husband and/or wife has had other spouses in the past but now they have all died or been divorced).

You are not entitled to a widow's benefit if your marriage was actually polygamous on the day your husband died.[74] You are not entitled to an increase for a spouse for any day on which your marriage is actually polygamous.

If you have been refused benefits because your marriage is or was polygamous you should take advice. The rules about British recognition of foreign marriages and divorces are very complicated and are not dealt with here.[75] A marriage or divorce you think is legal may not be recognised in British law even if it was recognised in the country where it was carried out.

5. CHILDREN BORN IN THE UK WITHOUT THE RIGHT OF ABODE

Since 1 January 1983 not all children born in the UK are British citizens by birth (see p17). The child may have the nationality of its parents but have no immigration status in the UK. S/he is not an overstayer nor an illegal entrant, even if her/his parents were at the time of the birth. A deportation order can be made against the child if the parent(s) are to be deported or removed. The child may have a right to register as a British citizen (see p18).

The benefit rules which apply where a child does not have leave are covered below. A child may reach the age of 16 without an application for citizenship having been made and wish to apply for benefits in her/his own right. This is very unlikely, so we do not deal with it. Such a person should seek expert immigration advice to register.

Benefit rules for children with no right of abode

For almost all benefits the status of a child is irrelevant. The only effects are as follows.

IS/income-based JSA

The child's status only affects entitlement where the claimant's partner is a 'person from abroad' and it does *not* matter where:

- the claimant is a lone parent; *or*
- both members of the couple are 'persons from abroad'; *or*
- neither member of the couple is a 'person from abroad';

In particular, if both the couple are 'persons from abroad' any entitlement to urgent cases payment is not affected. For persons from abroad, see Chapter 10 and the chapter relevant to the parents' immigration status.

Where the claimant is *not* a person from abroad but the partner is a person from abroad, the claimant's applicable amount (see glossary) does not include an amount for a child who is a person from abroad. If the only child or all the children are persons from abroad, no family premium is payable.

A child born in the UK without the right of abode who has not been given leave to remain is *not* a person from abroad.[76] In particular, the child is *not* 'a person whose immigration status has not been determined by the Secretary of State'.[77] That is because the child's immigration status is clear: s/he is a person who requires leave to enter or remain in the UK but does not have that leave.

The only exception is where a deportation order has been made against the child.[78] This is unusual. In that case, the child would become a person from abroad when the order was made.

Housing benefit/council tax benefit

The status of the child is irrelevant.

CHAPTER TEN

Means-tested benefits

This chapter covers:

1. Income support (IS) (below)
2. Income-based jobseeker's allowance (JSA) (p127)
3. Housing benefit(HB) and council tax benefit (CTB) (p127)

This book is laid out so that, if you know your immigration status, you can work out which benefits you can get by using the chapter relevant to your immigration status. However, the rules for income support (IS), income-based jobseeker's allowance (JSA), housing benefit (HB) and council tax benefit (CTB) are much more complicated than for other benefits and entitlement to HB and CTB is also affected by entitlement to IS /income-based JSA. This chapter therefore explains the basic rules affecting migrants' entitlement to IS/income-based JSA/HB/CTB and how much benefit is paid. *You should use this chapter with the chapter relevant to your immigration status.* You can also use this chapter as an overview of how the rules apply to people with different immigration statuses.

The benefit rules treat some claimants differently from others by calling them 'persons from abroad'.[1] This is a legal definition and not a description. Not all people born abroad are 'persons from abroad' and a British citizen can count as a 'person from abroad'. You can be a 'person from abroad' because of your:

- immigration status; *and/or*
- lack of habitual residence in the UK.

The rules for the four benefits are similar, but there are differences between on the one hand IS/income-based JSA and on the other HB/CTB.

1. INCOME SUPPORT

If you are a person from abroad then:

- *either* you have an 'applicable amount' (see glossary) of nil;

- *or* you are entitled to IS at **urgent cases** rate which is less generous and worked out differently(see p122).

Your partner (if any) may be able to claim IS instead (see p123).

Persons from abroad – immigration status test

You are *not* a person from abroad *because of your immigration status* if you:[2]

- are a British citizen (unless your citizenship is disputed (see p132), in which case you may be a person from abroad). This does not include other British nationals (see p14);
- have the right of abode in the UK (see p13);
- are an EU/EEA national, *unless*:
  - you have been 'required to leave' the UK (see p365)
  - you are subject to a deportation order (see p70); *or*
  - your nationality is disputed (see p370);
- have indefinite leave to remain (unless you are a sponsored immigrant under the benefit rules – see p153);
- have been recognised as a refugee by the Home Office, even if you have not yet been given leave to enter or remain (see Chapter 13);
- have been given limited leave to remain, but *not* as a person who will not have recourse to public funds (see Chapter 15);
- have limited leave as a person who will not have recourse to public funds *and* you are a national of Cyprus, Malta or Turkey (see p184); *or*
- left Montserrat after 1 November 1995 because of a volcanic eruption.[3]

You *are* a person from abroad because of your immigration status if:[4]

- you have limited or indefinite leave *and* you are a sponsored immigrant (see pp153 or 182);
- you have limited leave as a person who should not have recourse to public funds (see p183) *unless* you are a national of Cyprus, Malta or Turkey (see p184);
- you had limited leave to remain in the UK and that leave has now ended (see p205) (for when leave is extended, see p28);
- a deportation order has been made against you (*not* a decision to deport – see p73);
- an immigration officer has decided in writing that you are an illegal entrant (see p73);
- you have exceptional leave to remain – see Chapter 14 (but this may not apply if this was on the understanding that you could not have recourse to public funds – see p175);

- an immigration officer has given you temporary admission to the UK (see pp24 and 49);
- you applied for asylum at a time when you were a person from abroad under these rules, and your asylum claim has not been finally determined (see Chapter 17); *or*
- your immigration status has not been determined by the Secretary of State. It is not clear to whom this applies (see also p210). We believe it only applies to you if the Home Office is considering a claim that you do not require leave to be in the UK because you claim that you:
  - are a British citizen (see Chapter 2);
  - are a national of an EU/EEA member state (see glossary); *or*
  - have the right of abode in the UK (see p13)

Persons from abroad – habitual residence test

If you are *not* a person from abroad because of your immigration status, you are still a person from abroad if you are:

- *neither* exempt from the habitual residence test;
- *nor* habitually resident (see p102).

You are exempt from the habitual residence test if you:

- are a refugee (see Chapter 13);
- have exceptional leave to remain in the UK (see Chapter 14); *or*
- have an EC right to be in the UK (see p358). This can apply to British citizens (p27) and nationals of non-EU/EEA member states (see p353); *or*
- left Montserrat after 1 November 1995 because of a volcanic eruption.[5]

The habitual residence test only applies to the claimant. The habitual residence of any partner or child does not affect the amount of benefit – they are not persons from abroad because of this.

Income support for persons from abroad

Urgent cases rate is the name for IS paid to some claimants who are persons from abroad. It is at a lower rate than normal IS and is worked out differently (see p124). It is paid in the same way as normal IS and it can be paid for years. If the claimant is not a person from abroad, but a member of their family has this status, then IS is not worked out at the urgent cases rate, even though it may be worked out differently (see below).

If you would be entitled to urgent cases IS as a person from abroad, you can claim IS even if you would normally have to claim income-based JSA instead.[6] This means that some asylum-seekers can choose to claim IS instead of income-based JSA (see p237).

If you are a person from abroad, you may be entitled to urgent cases IS if you:

- are an asylum-seeker (see Chapter 17); *or*
- are a sponsored immigrant (see p157); or
- have limited leave to enter or remain in the UK and money you are usually sent from abroad has stopped temporarily (see p186).

Single claimants and lone parents

If you are a person from abroad:

- who is not entitled to urgent cases IS, then you are not entitled to IS;[7]
- who would be entitled to urgent cases IS, then you are entitled to IS at the urgent cases rate (see p124).

If you are not a person from abroad any IS is worked out at the normal rate, even if one or more of your children are persons from abroad.

Couples

For polygamous marriages, see p124.

If you have a partner, you may be better off if your partner claims IS if:

- one partner is not a person from abroad, that partner should claim *unless* the other partner is a person from abroad who would be entitled to urgent cases rate *and* the couple have no or very little capital (see below);
- both partners are persons from abroad but only one would be entitled to urgent cases rate, that partner should claim.

If you are a person from abroad who is not entitled to urgent cases rate, then you are *not* entitled to IS even if your partner is *not* a person from abroad.[8]

If you are not a person from abroad but your partner is a person from abroad (whether or not s/he would be entitled to urgent cases rate) then, if you claim, you do not get urgent cases rate. However, your IS is worked out differently. The applicable amount (see glossary) used to work out your IS is the total of:[9]

- a personal allowance for you only as a single person/lone parent;
- a personal allowance for any children *except* any child who is a person from abroad;
- the family premium (at the lone parent rate if you are a lone parent) but only if there is a child who is *not* a person from abroad;
- other premiums, except those for which you would qualify only because of your partner or because of a child who is a person from abroad;[10]

- housing costs/residential allowance (for those in residential care/ nursing home), if any (see CPAG's *National Welfare Benefits Handbook*).[11]

There are no special rules for income or capital. If one partner is *not* a person from abroad, but the other is a person from abroad who is entitled to urgent cases rate, the couple may be better off on urgent cases. The applicable amount for urgent cases rate is always higher than under the above rule. However, the couple will only be better off on urgent cases if the difference in the applicable amounts outweighs the negative effect of the urgent cases income and capital rules (see p125).

If neither you nor your partner are a person from abroad, any IS is worked out at the normal rate, even if one or more of the children in your family is/are persons from abroad.[12]

If you are the claimant and are entitled to the urgent cases rate, you are paid at that rate even if your partner is not a person from abroad or is not entitled to urgent cases rate.

Polygamous marriages
The rules for polygamous marriages are the same as those for couples (see p123) where:

- the claimant is a person from abroad;[13] *or*
- the claimant is not a person from abroad, but one or more (but not all) of her/his spouses are persons from abroad.[14]

If you are not a person from abroad, but all of your spouses are, you are entitled to IS at the normal rate for polygamous marriages (see p117), except that you are not entitled to any premiums for which you would only qualify because of one or more of your spouses.[15]

How much is urgent cases rate

The basic rules for entitlement to IS apply to urgent cases IS, but with some important differences. For details of how normal IS is worked out, see CPAG's *National Welfare Benefits Handbook*.

If you are available and actively seeking work you may be able to get national insurance (NI) credits for unemployment (see CPAG's *Rights Guide to Non-Means-Tested Benefits*).[16]

If you are sick you can submit sickness certificates to get credited NI contributions for sickness (see CPAG's *Rights Guide to Non-Means-Tested Benefits*).[17] It may also mean that you get the disability premium once you have been incapable of work for 364 days (see CPAG's *National Welfare Benefits Handbook*).[18] This is important if you are excluded from disability living allowance (DLA), attendance allowance (AA) and severe disablement allowance (SDA) because of your immigration status.

Applicable amounts

The personal allowance is 90 per cent of the normal personal allowance.[19] Apart from that, the applicable amount (see glossary) is worked out in the ordinary way, including a personal allowance for all children (whether or not they are persons from abroad), any premiums, housing costs, residential allowance and any protected sum.[20]

If you are appealing against a decision that you fail the incapacity 'all-work' test, the usual rule that your IS is reduced by 20 per cent does *not* apply.[21]

Income

All income of every member of your family (see glossary) is taken into account, except for:[22]

- HB or any payment made by the DSS to compensate you for loss of entitlement to HB or housing benefit supplement;[23]
- payments (including payments in kind) made to you by the Macfarlane Trusts, Eileen Trust or the Fund, which help people who caught HIV through treatment for haemophilia, NHS operations, blood transfusions and transplants (see CPAG's *National Welfare Benefits Handbook* for details);[24]
- payments made to you by your partner out of money received by your partner from one of those Trusts or the Fund unless you are estranged or divorced from your partner.[25] The money must have been paid by or on behalf of your partner and does not include money from her/his estate;[26]
- payments made to you by your daughter or son (or step-daughter/son) or a child for whom you are a guardian out of money received by her/him from one of those Trusts or the Fund, but only where that child has no partner (an estranged or divorced partner does not count) and has no children who would count as family members for IS purposes. The payment will continue to be disregarded until two years after the person who made it dies;[27]
- payments made to (or for the benefit of) a child or young person who is a member of your family for IS purposes by a person who is or was a member of that child's family out of money received by that person from one of those Trusts or the Fund;[28]
- payments (including payments in kind) made to you by the Independent Living Funds (see CPAG's *National Welfare Benefits Handbook* for details);[29] *and*
- any backdated IS, HB or CTB paid to a member of your family because s/he has been recognised as a refugee (see p165 and 169).

The following types of income, part or all of which are usually treated as capital,[30] are instead treated as income:[31]

- charitable payments;
- holiday pay;
- income tax refunds;
- a lump-sum or 'bounty' paid to you as a part-time firefighter, part-time member of a lifeboat crew, auxiliary coastguard for coast rescue or member of the Territorial Army.

There is no earnings disregard. For the rules on working out weekly income, see CPAG's *National Welfare Benefits Handbook*.

Capital

There is no £3,000 capital exemption. There is no tariff income from capital.[32] If your capital is more than your applicable amount you are not entitled to IS. Your capital is calculated in the usual way but the following which are usually disregarded are instead taken into account:[33]

- arrears of the following benefits: AA, CTB, DLA, DWA, FC, IS, income-based JSA, earnings top-up, mobility supplement under the War Pensions scheme;[34]
- any concessionary payment to compensate for arrears of any of those benefits;
- business assets which you own and are liquid – ie, immediately available in cash;
- any tax refunds;
- any money from the sale of your home;
- money used as a deposit with a housing association which is now to be used to buy another home;
- any training bonus paid for Training at Work (see CPAG's *National Welfare Benefits Handbook*);
- any backdated IS or CTB (but not HB, which is disregarded instead) paid to a member of your family because s/he has been recognised as a refugee (see pp165 and 169).[35] You can argue that these count as income, not capital. If this applies, the backdated IS and CTB (along with any backdated HB) are disregarded and so are not taken into account when working out the amount of your IS (see p125).[36]

Following successful appeals, some asylum-seekers have been awarded arrears of urgent cases IS. When those arrears were paid, the Benefits Agency treated them as capital. This took the claimant's capital above their applicable amount and so stopped IS entitlement from the date the arrears were received. The claimants' appeals were allowed by a social security appeal tribunal, which decided that payment of IS arrears is not a change of circumstances for IS so there can be no review.[37] If this interpretation is wrong, the regulation seems to be so irrational as to be outside the Secretary of State's powers. If the regulation is irrational in that way, it is unlawful and arrears of IS would be disregarded as capital in the usual way.[38]

2. INCOME-BASED JOBSEEKER'S ALLOWANCE

If you count as a person from abroad under IS rules, you can always claim IS, even if you are looking for work (unless you are getting contribution-based JSA).[39]

The income-based JSA rules about who is a person from abroad are the same as for IS (see p121).[40] If you are a person from abroad, you are only entitled to income-based JSA if you are an asylum-seeker; *and*

- *either* you hold a work permit;
- or you have written permission from the Home Office to work in the UK.[41]

For details of these rules, see p212.

If you are a person from abroad entitled to income-based JSA, it is paid at the urgent cases rate.[42] This is worked out in the same way as for IS (see p124).[43]

The rules about the rate of income-based JSA you are entitled to if one or more members of your family are persons from abroad are the same as for IS (see p123).

3. HOUSING BENEFIT AND COUNCIL TAX BENEFIT

If you are being paid IS/income-based JSA (including urgent cases rate) you are not a person from abroad for HB/CTB.[44] The local authority which deals with your HB/CTB claim should not make enquiries about your immigration status or habitual residence.[45]

If you have been refused or have not claimed IS/income-based JSA, the local authority dealing with your HB/CTB claim can consider whether you are a person from abroad. This applies even if the Benefits Agency has decided that you *are* a person from abroad who is not entitled to urgent cases IS/income-based JSA. The local authority can disagree with the Benefits Agency opinion and decide that you are not a person from abroad.

If you are a person from abroad under HB/CTB rules, then the you are not entitled to HB/CTB.[46]

Differences from IS

The rules about persons from abroad for HB/CTB are similar to those for IS, with the following differences.

There is no urgent cases rate for HB/CTB. If a person is entitled to HB/CTB it is at the normal rate. The types of people entitled to urgent cases IS do not count as persons from abroad for HB/CTB purposes and are entitled to HB/CTB at the normal rate.

The persons from abroad rules apply only to the claimant. The status of any partner or children is irrelevant. However, if the amount of your HB/CTB depends on the inclusion in your family of your partner and/or children (because they give you a higher applicable amount – see glossary) *and* your partner/children have immigration leave on condition that they be maintained without recourse to public funds, their immigration status may be affected by your HB/CTB claim. This is because HB/CTB are public funds and the extra HB/CTB paid because of your partner/children is additional reliance on these public funds (see p62).

There are two situations in which the rules for HB/CTB are more generous than those for IS. Certain claimants who are not entitled to IS urgent cases are *not* persons from abroad for HB/CTB. You are *not* a person from abroad for HB/CTB if:

- an immigration officer has decided that you are an illegal entrant and you have not been given leave to remain *but* you have been allowed to remain in the UK with the written consent of the Home Office (see p215);[47] *or*
- a deportation order is made against you *but* your removal from the UK has been deferred in writing by the Home Office (see p215).[48]

If one of these applies you are also exempt from the HB/CTB habitual residence test.[49]

This is most likely to apply to:

- in-country asylum-seekers (see p219) who do not have or have lost transitional protection; *and*
- port applicant asylum-seekers (see p220) refused asylum and non-asylum-seekers who have used all rights of immigration appeal and are bringing a judicial review of the Home Office decision not to give leave to remain in the UK.

You are also *not* a person from abroad if you are a port applicant, regardless of whether you have temporary admission, bail or are detained. This is because the person from abroad definition does not apply to you. However, you must still pass the habitual residence test. The exemptions are the same as for IS (see p122).

Couples

If one partner is getting IS/income-based JSA (including urgent cases rate), s/he should claim HB/CTB.

If neither of you is getting IS/income-based JSA, and you may fail the immigration test or habitual residence test but your partner is more likely to pass, s/he could claim instead, though there may be disadvantages to this (see CPAG's *National Welfare Benefits Handbook*).

CHAPTER ELEVEN

British citizens and others with the right of abode

This chapter covers the benefit rules which affect migrants with the right of abode in the UK. The benefits covered are:

1. Income support (IS) (below)
2. Income-based jobseeker's allowance (JSA) (p132)
3. Housing benefit (HB) and council tax benefit (CTB) (p133)
4. Child benefit (CB) and guardian's allowance (p133)
5. Family credit (FC) and disability working allowance (DWA) (p138)
6. Short-term contributory benefits (p139)
7. Retirement pensions and widows' benefits (p140)
8. Industrial injuries benefits (p142)
9. Disability benefits (p145)
10. Statutory sick pay (SSP) and statutory maternity pay (SMP) (p147)
11. The social fund (p148)

Who has the right of abode?

British citizens (but not other types of British nationals) have the right of abode. A few Commonwealth citizens also have the right of abode. For full details of British citizenship and the right of abode, see Chapter 2.

If you are a British citizen or have the right of abode for other reasons you:

- are not subject to immigration control;
- do not need leave to enter or remain in the UK; *and*
- any leave you were given has no effect once you become a British citizen or get the right of abode.

Indefinite leave to remain is not the same as the right of abode.

I. INCOME SUPPORT

You are only entitled to IS if you are:

- in GB[1] (see p98) *or* temporarily absent from GB[2] (see p246); *and*

- *either* actually habitually resident (see p102) in the UK, Ireland, the Channel Islands or the Isle of Man *or* exempt from the habitual residence test (see below).

For the rules about the amount of IS if one or more members of your family are persons from abroad, see Chapter 10.

Habitual residence test

The habitual residence test applies only to the claimant.[3] It does not apply to any partner or child for whom IS is being claimed. If you might fail the test but have a partner who is more likely to pass, s/he can claim instead, though there may be disadvantages to this (see CPAG's *National Welfare Benefits Handbook*).

You pass the habitual residence test if you are habitually resident (see p102) in the UK, Ireland, the Channel Islands or the Isle of Man. If you are not habitually resident and you are not exempt (see below), you are a 'person from abroad'.[4] You cannot get urgent cases rate so you are not entitled to any IS (or income-based JSA – see p132).[5] If you have no means of support, you may be entitled to bed and board from a local authority under the National Assistance Act (see Appendix 6).

The Court of Appeal has decided that the IS habitual residence test is not outside the Secretary of State's powers under British law.[6] An argument that the test is unlawful under EC law was also rejected (see p357). If you are a national of Cyprus, Malta or Turkey (eg, as a dual national or otherwise with the right of abode) the habitual residence test may break the UK's international obligations.

Exemptions from habitual residence test

You are exempt from the habitual residence test if you left Montserrat after 1 November 1995 because of a volcanic eruption.[7]

You may be exempt from the habitual residence test under EC law (see p358). This can only apply to you if you or a member of your extended family is:

- a national of an EU/EEA member state (apart from the UK); *or*
- a British citizen who has travelled to another EU/EEA member state using the right of free movement under EC law.

Refugees and people with exceptional leave to remain (ELR) are exempt from the habitual residence test (see Chapters 13 and 14). It is not clear whether this exemption continues if that person is given British citizenship. The wording of the exemption do not seem to apply, because a British citizen cannot be a refugee and cannot have leave to remain. However, the principle behind the exceptions that the person has made the UK their permanent home because their own country is unsafe, continues to apply. If you were a refugee or had ELR before you got British citizenship and you have failed the habitual residence test, you should consider seeking specialist advice.

Disputed nationality or right of abode

Even if you have a passport which shows that you are a British citizen, the Home Office may refuse to accept that you are a citizen. This is very unusual. This may also happen if your claim to the right of abode is denied. If this happens:

- **at a port**, an immigration officer may:
  - *either* detain you;
  - *or* give you temporary admission to the UK (see p24); *or*
- **when you are already in the UK**, an immigration officer may:
  - *either* decide that you are an illegal entrant (see p73) and either detain you (see p70) or give you temporary admission to the UK;
  - *or* tell you that you will be investigated only.

If you are given temporary admission, you are not entitled to IS unless you count as an asylum-seeker under benefit rules (see Chapter 17).[8]

If you are not given temporary admission, but the Home Office is investigating whether you are a British citizen or have the right of abode, the Home Office may inform the Benefits Agency of this situation, though that is unlikely. If the Benefits Agency is aware that you are being investigated, they may decide to treat you as a person from abroad because your immigration status has not been determined by the Secretary of State.[9] If this happens, you are not entitled to IS unless you count as an asylum-seeker under benefit rules (see Chapter 17).

These rules do not affect your entitlement to IS if you left Montserrat after 1 November 1995 because of a volcanic eruption.[10]

If the Home Office later accepts that you are a British citizen or have the right of abode and you have lost benefit, seek expert advice.

2. INCOME-BASED JOBSEEKER'S ALLOWANCE

For contribution-based JSA, see p139.

The income-based JSA rules about who is a person from abroad are the same as for IS (see p131).[11] For the rules about the amount of income-based JSA if one or more members of your family are persons from abroad, see Chapter 10.

3. HOUSING BENEFIT AND COUNCIL TAX BENEFIT

If you are being paid IS/income-based JSA you are not a person from abroad for HB/CTB.[12] The local authority which deals with your HB/CTB claim should not make enquiries about your immigration status or habitual residence.[13] If you are *not* being paid IS/income-based JSA, the following rules apply.

You are only entitled to HB/CTB if you are *either* actually habitually resident in the UK, Ireland, the Channel Islands or the Isle of Man (see p102) or exempt from the habitual residence test (see below) *and*:[14]

- **for HB**, you have accommodation in GB which you normally occupy as your home (which may apply during a temporary absence – see p251);[15] *or*
- **for CTB**, you are liable to pay council tax for accommodation in which you reside (see p252).[16]

You are exempt from the habitual residence test if you left Montserrat after 1 November 1995 because of a volcanic eruption.[17]

You may be exempt from the habitual residence test because of your status under EC law or because you were a refugee or had exceptional leave to remain before you became a British citizen (see p131). If you are a national of Cyprus, Malta or Turkey with the right of abode, the habitual residence test may break the UK's international obligations (see p103).

If you are not actually habitually resident and you are not exempt, you are a 'person from abroad' and are not be entitled to HB/CTB.[18]

If your partner or children have immigration leave on condition that they will be maintained without recourse to public funds, their immigration status may be affected by your HB/CTB claim (see p187).

4. CHILD BENEFIT AND GUARDIAN'S ALLOWANCE

Child benefit

The nationality and immigration status of the child for whom you claim are irrelevant. British citizens and others with the right of abode do not require leave to be in the UK so cannot be denied CB as 'a person subject to immigration control'.[19] If you are responsible for a child and another person has been refused CB for that child because of that person's immigration status, you should claim CB instead. For details see CPAG's *Rights Guide to Non-Means-Tested Benefits*.

You are only entitled to CB for a child if:[20]

- you are in GB (claimant presence rule); *and*
- the child is in GB (child presence rule); *and*
- you have, *and* either the child or one of the parents of that child has, been in GB for more than 182 days in the last 52 weeks (182-day rule); *and*
- none of your earnings or those of your spouse are exempt from UK income tax (see p136).

There are exceptions to these rules and there are special rules for people working overseas, including civil servants and serving members of the armed forces (see p136). There are special rules to stop you losing benefit if you move between GB and Northern Ireland.[21] You may also be able to use special rules if you have lived in another EU/EEA member state (see Part 4) or a country with which the UK has a reciprocal agreement (see Part 5) even if you are not a national of that country.

If you often go abroad and may lose entitlement to CB under these rules, you should consider whether there is another person who could make a claim instead. For example, if your partner does not often go abroad, s/he could claim. For rules on who can claim, see CPAG's *Rights Guide to Non-Means-Tested Benefits*.

Exception to the claimant presence rule

For presence and absence, see p98. You are exempt from the rule while you are absent from GB **for up to eight weeks**, if the absence was throughout intended to be temporary *and either*:[22]

- you were entitled to CB for the week before the week in which you left; *or*
- you are the mother of the child the claim is for *and either*:[23]
  - you left GB after your child was born but in the week of the birth; *or*
  - the child was born outside the UK in the first eight weeks of your absence *and* you could have been entitled to CB for that child if s/he had been born on the Monday before you left GB.

If the claimant dies while exempt from the presence rule as a person entitled to CB for the week before the absence began, any person who then claims CB for that child is exempt for the remainder of the eight weeks.[24]

Exceptions to the child presence rule

You are exempt from this rule while the child is absent from GB if:[25]

- someone was entitled to CB for the week before the week in which the child left; *and*

- the absence has always been intended to be temporary; *and either*
  - the absence is eight weeks or less; *or*
  - the absence is three years or less *and* is for the child to attend a recognised educational establishment for full-time education;[26] *or*
  - the absence is for the child to receive treatment for an illness or disability which began before the absence *and* the Secretary of State has agreed to the absence.[27]

You are also exempt from this rule for any week in which you are exempt from the claimant presence rule as the mother of a child born abroad or taken abroad in the week of birth (see p134).[28]

Exceptions to the 182-day rule

For the 182-day rule:

- you are treated as present in GB on any day you are exempt from the claimant presence rule (see p134);[29] *and*
- a child is treated as present in GB on any day s/he is exempt from the child presence rule (see p134).[30]

There are three ways a claimant present in GB can be exempt from the 182-day rule.

The first claimant exception is if your stay in GB (including the days you have already stayed) is likely to be at least 183 consecutive days (ignoring up to 28 days of absence) and one of the following applies:

- you are employed or self-employed in the UK during that stay;[31] *or*
- you have been entitled to CB for any child in the last three years;[32] *or*
- you have a spouse who was entitled to CB for any child in the last three years and who *either* was living with you at that time *or* is now living with you.[33]

The second claimant exception is if you live with your spouse and s/he meets (or is exempt from) the 182-day rule.[34]

The third claimant exception is if:

- the child meets (or is exempt from) the child presence rule; *and*
- the child meets (or is exempt from) the 182 rule (unless that exemption is because the parents satisfy or are exempt from the rule: see below); *and*
- either of the following applies:
  - the child is living with you (or is treated as living with you – see CPAG's *Rights Guide to Non-Means-Tested Benefits*); *or*
  - you are contributing at least the weekly rate of CB to the cost of providing for the child (see CPAG's *Rights Guide to Non-Means-Tested Benefits*).[35]

A child is exempt from the 182-day rule if s/he is in GB *and either*:

- one of the parents satisfies or is exempt from the 182-day rule;[36] *or*
- the child lives with someone other than her/his parents *and* the child is likely to continue to live with that person permanently *and* unlikely to again live with either parent *and* the person with whom the child lives meets or is exempt from the 182-day rule;[37] *or*
- guardian's allowance would be payable if the child were exempt from the 182-day rule.[38]

Special rules for persons working abroad

You are also exempt from the claimant presence rule and the 182-day rule if you are:[39]

- a UK civil servant, unless you became a civil servant or were recruited outside the UK (except if that was when you were a serving member of the UK's armed forces); *or*
- a serving member of the UK's armed forces overseas; *or*
- employed outside GB *and* half or more of your income from that job will be liable to UK income tax in the current tax year[40] *and* you are only temporarily absent from GB because of that job; *or*
- the spouse of a person in one of the above situations; *or*
- the unmarried partner (see glossary) of a person in one of the above situations and you were the partner of that person when both of you were last in GB.

Any child living with you is also exempt from the child presence rule and the 182-day rule if s/he is:[41]

- *either* your son or daughter;
- or you have been entitled to CB for that child before.

You may also be exempt from the 'living with' rule, which is not covered here.[42] For details, see CPAG's *Rights Guide to Non-Means-Tested Benefits*.

If you cannot use these rules remember that you may be able to use EC rules (see Part 4) or a reciprocal agreement (see Part 5).

People exempt from UK income tax

If any of your earnings or your spouse's earnings (but only if you are residing with your spouse) is exempt from UK income tax because of a double taxation treaty or exemption for foreign officials, you are not entitled to CB.[43] This applies even if most of your earnings are not exempt. This is most likely to affect you if you are (or your spouse is) a member of a foreign armed service or a diplomat.

Guardian's allowance

Guardian's allowance is paid to a person entitled to CB for a child who is not her/his child where both of the child's parents are dead, or, in some situations, where only one parent is dead (for details of these situations, see CPAG's *Rights Guide to Non-Means-Tested Benefits*).[44] The nationality and immigration status of the child is irrelevant.

You may also be able to use special rules if the parent(s) lived in another EU/EEA member state (see Part 4) or a country with which the UK has a reciprocal agreement (see Part 5) even if s/he was not a national of that country. There are special rules to stop you losing benefit if the parent(s) moved between GB and Northern Ireland.[45]

The 182-day rule for CB is waived for a child where that would lead to entitlement to CB and guardian's allowance but no entitlement to CB.[46]

You are only entitled to guardian's allowance if:[47]

- one or both of the child's parents was born in the UK; *or*
- at the date of the parent's death which led to the claim, one or both of the child's parents had been in GB for at least 52 weeks out of any period of two years since that parent's 16th birthday. The 52-week period does not have to be continuous.

For the 52-week exception, an absence from GB is ignored if that parent was absent only because s/he was:[48]

- an offshore worker under GB NI contributions rules;[49]
- a serving member of the armed forces; *or*
- a mariner or air(wo)man under contributions rules.[50]

If you are or become not ordinarily resident (see p99) in GB, then the amount of guardian's allowance paid for any day you are absent from GB is frozen. It is frozen at the rate paid when you stopped being ordinarily resident or the rate it was first paid, if that was later.[51]

If one parent is dead, guardian's allowance is paid if the other parent is in prison.[52] Only serving prisoners (and those detained during Her Majesty's pleasure/pending Her Majesty's directions) are 'in prison' under guardian's allowance rules.[53] A person serving a sentence of five years or more in a prison abroad should count as a person 'in prison'. However, a person detained under Immigration Act powers of administrative detention (see p70) is not 'in prison'.

If a child is adopted, the adoptive parents become the parents under guardian's allowance rules, but only if the adoption is carried out in the UK or is a foreign adoption recognised under British law.[54] This means that a person can only get guardian's allowance if the adoptive parents are both dead or, in certain situations, one is dead.[55] An adoption carried out abroad which is not recognised under British law does not count for this purpose. In that situation, if both (or, in certain situations, one) of the child's natural parents are dead, the unofficial adoptive parents may be entitled to guardian's allowance.

5. FAMILY CREDIT AND DISABILITY WORKING ALLOWANCE

To be entitled to FC/DWA you must be treated as present in the UK.[56] You are only treated as present in the UK if:[57]

- you are present in GB; and
- you and any partner (see glossary) are ordinarily resident (see p99) in GB; *and*
- at least part of your earnings (or those of a partner) come from full-time work in the UK (for the definition of full-time work, see CPAG's *National Welfare Benefits Handbook*); *and*
- neither you nor your partner receives all your or their earnings from full-time work done outside the UK (see below); *and*
- for FC, you have a child who normally lives with you or is treated as living with you (see below).

If you do not meet these rules because you (or your partner or child) were present, resident or work in another EU/EEA member state you may be entitled because of EC law (see Chapter 25).

If you or your partner would qualify for FC/DWA in Northern Ireland you are not entitled to FC/DWA in GB.[58] You must claim in Northern Ireland instead.

The nationality and immigration status of your partner and children are irrelevant to FC/DWA entitlement because those rules only apply to the FC/DWA claimant.[59]

FC/DWA counts as public funds for immigration purposes.[60] An FC/DWA claim can affect the immigration status of your partner and any children. The Benefits Agency may pass information about you to the Home Office (see Chapter 7). If your partner or any child is covered by Chapters 15 or 16 of this book or is a non-EEA national abroad you should seek specialist advice before claiming or renewing a claim.

An FC claim must normally be made by the female partner, but the Benefits Agency can allow the male partner to claim if it would be reasonable to accept a claim from him.[61] If he would have a better chance of meeting the presence/residence conditions than the woman, the Benefits

Agency should consider it reasonable for him to be the claimant. If it refuses such a claim, you cannot appeal to a tribunal because it is a Secretary of State's decision. You should quickly take specialist advice.

A DWA claim for a couple must be made by the disabled partner.[62] If both partners are disabled workers, the couple can decide who makes the claim.[63] If one partner is responsible for a child *and* the disabled partner fails (or would fail) the immigration test (see p195) the other partner may be able to claim FC, but see above for possible effects on immigration status.

Where one member of a couple receives all her/his earnings from part-time work outside the UK, FC/DWA can still be paid, as long as the other member receives some earnings from full-time work in the UK. This is because the rule refers to 'remunerative work' which does not include part-time work.[64] For details of full-time and part-time work, see CPAG's *National Welfare Benefits Handbook*.

For couples where one partner lives abroad, see p111.

To be entitled to FC you (or your partner) must be responsible for at least one child, but that child does not need to be present or ordinarily resident in GB when you claim.[65] The amount of FC is increased for each child for which you (or your partner) are responsible.[66] For responsibility for a child, see p115.

When you must meet the conditions

FC/DWA is normally awarded for 26 weeks.[67] You only need to meet these conditions on the day your claim is made or treated as made.[68] If you stop meeting one or more of these conditions, that is not a change of circumstances allowing the Benefits Agency to review the award.[69] This means that your entitlement continues while you are absent from GB.

You must again meet all the conditions if you make a further claim. If you make a renewal FC/DWA claim within the time-limits or claim FC after a DWA award (or DWA after a FC award), it will normally be treated as made on the day after your last award ran out.[70] If you did not meet the conditions for entitlement on that day (for example, you were on holiday abroad) but did meet them on a later date, you should write on the renewal claim form that your claim is from that later date. The Benefits Agency must then deal with your renewal claim in that way.[71] For claims, see CPAG's *National Welfare Benefits Handbook*.

6. SHORT-TERM CONTRIBUTORY BENEFITS

These are **contribution-based JSA, incapacity benefit (ICB)** and **maternity allowance (MA)**.

You are only entitled to these benefits if you are:[72]

- present in GB (see p98); *or*
- treated as present in GB (see below); *or*
- temporarily absent from GB (for income-based JSA see p256, for ICB see p257, and for MA see p257).[73]

You are treated as in GB while you are absent if the reason for the absence is that you are a mariner or an offshore worker (see pp143 and 256).[74]

Because you must also meet the contribution conditions (see CPAG's *Rights Guide to Non-Means-Tested Benefits*), you are unlikely to qualify unless you have lived and worked in the UK for several years or unless you can use a reciprocal agreement (see below).

There are special rules to stop you losing benefit if you move between GB and Northern Ireland.[75] You may also be able to use special rules if you have lived in another EU/EEA member state (see Part 4) or a country with which the UK has a reciprocal agreement (see Part 5) even if you are not a national of that country.

Dependant additions

For adult and child dependant increases, see Chapter 9.

Contributory benefits (including dependant additions) do not *count as public funds for immigration purposes.*[76] *But, because of DSS-Home Office links (see Chapter 7), information about a dependant may be passed to the Home Office and it could affect their immigration status. If your partner or any child is covered by Chapters 15 or 16 or is a non-EU/EEA national abroad you should seek specialist advice before claiming or renewing a claim.*

7. RETIREMENT PENSIONS AND WIDOWS' BENEFITS

These benefits are Category A, B, C and D retirement pensions, widow's allowance, widowed mother's allowance and widow's pension.

If you are present in GB these benefits are calculated in the normal way, even if you are not ordinarily resident (see p99) in GB.[77]

There are no residence conditions imposed on the first claim for these benefits (except Category D pension).

Because you (or your late husband in the case of widows' benefits) must meet the contribution conditions (see CPAG's *Rights Guide to Non-Means-Tested Benefits*), you are unlikely to qualify unless you have (or your late husband had) lived in the UK for several years unless you can use a reciprocal agreement (see Part 5).

You may wish to de-retire to increase the amount of your pension (see CPAG's *Rights to Non-Means-Tested Benefits*). You can only do this if you are ordinarily resident (see p99) in GB.[78]

For adult and child dependant increases, see Chapter 9.

There are special rules to stop you losing benefit if you move between GB and Northern Ireland.[79] You may also be able to use special rules if you have lived in another EU/EEA member state (see Part 4) or a country with which the UK has a reciprocal agreement (see Part 5) even if you are not a national of that country.

Freezing the rate of payment

If you are not ordinarily resident (see p99) in GB, then the amount of benefit (except a widow's payment) paid for any day you are absent from GB is normally frozen. It is frozen at the rate paid when you stopped being ordinarily resident, or at the rate it was first paid, if that was later (except Category A and B pension for certain claimants – see below).[80] Freezing also applies to SERPS and any graduated retirement benefit.[81]

Your frozen benefit may be paid at a higher rate than it would be under current rules if it was frozen before 7 August 1991.[82] Those old rules are not covered in this book.

There are special rules (see below) for certain benefits.

Category A and B pensions

If your entitlement to part or all of a Category A or B pension depends on your husband's or former spouse's NI contributions, your annual up-rating of that pension is not frozen if your husband or former spouse whose contributions are used is ordinarily resident (see p99) in GB on the day before the date of that up-rating.[83]

You are still entitled to annual up-rating of your Category B pension even while you are not ordinarily resident in GB if:[84]

* the spouse on whose contributions the Category B pension is based has died or you are divorced from her/him; *and*
* you have married again; *and*
* your new spouse was not entitled to a Category A pension before the up-rating date; *and*
  - *either* you were still married to your new spouse on the day before the up-rating date;
  - *or* you married her/him on or after that date.

Category C pension

Category C pension is a non-contributory pension paid to some men born before 1884 (and/or their wives or ex-wives) and women born before 1889. Because so few people now qualify, the residence rules are not dealt with in this book.[85] For details, see *Ethnic Minorities Benefits Handbook* 1st edn, p206.

Category D pension

You are only entitled to a Category D pension if:[86]

- you were resident in GB for at least 10 years in any continuous period of 20 years ending on or after your 80th birthday; *and*
- you were ordinarily resident (see p99) in GB on:
  - *either* your 80th birthday;
  - *or* the later date on which you claimed Category D pension.

Age addition

You are only entitled to an age addition for any day you are absent from GB, if *either*:[87]

- you are ordinarily resident (see p99) in GB; *or*
- you were entitled to an age addition before you stopped being ordinarily resident in GB; *or*
- you are entitled to an increased rate of any category of retirement pension under a reciprocal agreement (see Part 5).

Widow's payment

You are only entitled to this lump-sum payment if *either*:[88]

- you or your late husband was in GB at the time of his death; *or*
- you returned to GB within four weeks of your late husband's death; *or*
- you meet the contribution conditions for widowed mother's allowance or widow's pension (see CPAG's *Rights Guide to Non-Means-Tested Benefits*).

8. INDUSTRIAL INJURIES BENEFITS

The benefits are disablement benefit, reduced earnings allowance, retirement allowance, constant attendance allowance and exceptionally severe disablement allowance.

Where did the accident happen/disease start?

You are entitled to industrial injuries benefit *for an accident*, only if that accident:

- 'arises out of and in the course of' employed earner's employment (see CPAG's *Rights Guide to Non-Means-Tested Benefits* for these rules); *and*
- you were in GB (which includes adjacent UK territorial waters – see p98)[89] when the accident happened.[90]

You are entitled to industrial injuries benefit *for a disease*, only if that disease:

- is 'prescribed in relation to' an employed earner's employment (see CPAG's *Rights Guide to Non-Means-Tested Benefits* for these rules); *and*
- you were engaged in GB in the employment which caused that disease (even if you have also been engaged outside GB in that employment).[91]

There are exceptions to these rules (see below).[92]

Mariners and air(wo)men

You are treated as in GB while you are:

- employed as a mariner or air(wo)man;[93]
- employed as an apprentice pilot on board a ship or vessel;[94]
- on board a test flight in the course of your employment.[95]

There are also more generous rules for accidents and for complying with time-limits under benefit rules.[96]

Volunteer development workers

You are treated as employed in GB if an accident happens or you contract a disease:[97]

- after 30 September 1986;
- while you are a volunteer development worker; *and*
- paying GB NI contributions as such a worker.

Benefit is not payable until your return to GB after the accident or contracting the disease.

Offshore workers

You count as an offshore worker if an accident happens or you contract a disease while you are:

- employed on a rig or boat at sea in connection with exploring or exploiting the seabed, subsoil or natural oil or gas in an area over which a EU state or Norway exercises sovereign rights but which was outside any country's territorial seas;[98] *and*
- in the territory of an EU state or in an area over which the sovereign rights are exercised *or* travelling between that area and an EU state or Norway.[99]

The accident/disease is treated as if it happened/arose in GB.[100]

Your employment also counts as employed earner's employment, but only if:[101]

- had it been in GB, it would have been employed earner's employment; *and*
- you did not sustain the accident or contract the disease in the territory of an EU state; *and*
- you are ordinarily resident (see p99) in GB; *and*
- you were resident (see p99) in GB immediately before the employment began; *and*
- your employer has a place of business in GB.

If this applies to you and you were refused benefit (or a declaration of industrial accident) before 6 April 1975, you can request a review but arrears are limited to one month from the request.[102]

These rules apply to accidents sustained or diseases contracted before 29 November 1964.[103]

Visiting forces and international bodies

You are treated as if you are *not* in employed earner's employment while you are:[104]

- a member of visiting armed forces; *or*
- a civilian employed by visiting armed forces, except if you are ordinarily resident (see p99) in the UK; *or*
- employed as a member of certain international organisations, *unless*:
  - there is liability for Class 1 NI contributions (see CPAG's *Rights Guide to Non-Means-Tested Benefits*); *and*
  - you are ordinarily resident (see p99) in the UK.

Entitlement

If you qualify under the rules above you do not have to be present or resident in GB to be entitled to **disablement** benefit or **retirement allowance**.[105] It is up-rated annually regardless of where you live.

You are not entitled to reduced **earnings allowance**, **constant attendance allowance** or **exceptionally severe disablement allowance** unless you are:[106]

- *either* present in GB;
- *or* temporarily absent from GB (see p261).

For **reduced earnings allowance**, you count as present in GB while you are employed as a mariner or air(wo)man.[107]

Decisions on entitlement to **constant attendance allowance** and **excep-**

tionally severe disablement allowance are made by the Secretary of State so there is no right of appeal to a tribunal, and any challenge must be in the High Court.[108]

There are special rules to stop you losing benefit if you move between GB and Northern Ireland.[109] You may also be able to use special rules if you have lived in another EU/EEA member state (see Part 4) or a country with which the UK has a reciprocal agreement (see Part 5) even if you are not a national of that country.

9. DISABILITY BENEFITS

These are disability living allowance (DLA), attendance allowance (AA), invalid care allowance (ICA) and severe disablement allowance (SDA).

There are special rules to stop you losing benefit if you move between GB and Northern Ireland.[110] You may also be able to use special rules if you have lived in another EU/EEA member state (see Part 4) or a country with which the UK has a reciprocal agreement (see Part 5) even if you are not a national of that country.

Disability living allowance/attendance allowance

You are not entitled to DLA/AA for a day, unless on that day:[111]

- you are ordinarily resident (see p99) in GB; *and*
- you are present in GB (but see also below); *and*
- you have been present in GB for a total of at least 26 weeks in the last 52 weeks.

You are treated as present in GB for these rules, including the 26-week rule, if you are abroad only because:[112]

- you are a serving member of the armed forces; *or*
- you live with a serving member of the armed forces and are the spouse, son, daughter, step-son, step-daughter, father, father-in-law, step-father, mother, mother-in-law or step-mother of that person; *or*
- you a mariner or air(wo)man;[113] *or*
- you are an offshore worker.[114]

You may also be treated as present in GB during a temporary absence (see p262). This may help you meet the 26-week presence rule.

If you are terminally ill, the 26-week presence rule is waived.[115]

For children aged less than six months, the 26-week period is reduced to 13 weeks.[116] Because presence does not start until birth,[117] a child born in GB must be 13 weeks old before being entitled to DLA, unless s/he is terminally ill (when the 13-week period is waived. If DLA entitlement begins before a child is six months old, the period of 26 weeks continues to be reduced to 13 weeks until the child's first birthday.[118]

People exempt from UK income tax

There is an extra residence condition if any of your earnings or your spouse's earnings are exempt from UK income tax because of a double taxation treaty or exemption for foreign officials. This is most likely to affect you if you are (or your spouse is) a member of a foreign armed service or a diplomat. This also applies to a child aged under 16 who is the daughter, step-daughter, son or step-son of a person receiving UK tax-free earnings.

If this applies, you (or the child if s/he is the disabled person) must have been actually present in GB for a total of 156 weeks in the last four years.[119] For this rule, you are not treated as present during any absence, but you may be able to use the special EC rules (see Part 4). This rule is not waived if you are terminally ill.

Invalid care allowance

The rules for ICA are the same as those for DLA/AA (see p145) except that:[120]

- the 26-week rule is *not* waived if the disabled person is terminally ill;
- people who receive (or whose spouse or parents receive) UK tax-exempt earnings are *not* treated differently.

For adult and child dependant increases (see Chapter 9). ICA is public funds under the immigration rules.[121] *If your dependant is covered by Chapters 15 or 16 of this book or is a non-EU/EEA national abroad you should seek specialist advice before claiming or renewing a claim.*

Severe disablement allowance

The rules for SDA are the same as those for DLA/AA (see p145) except that:[122]

- once you have been awarded SDA, you do *not* have to meet the ordinary residence rule or the 26-week presence rule again in the same period of incapacity (for period of incapacity, see CPAG's *Rights Guide to Non-Means-Tested Benefits*) – see example below.[123] Non-contributory invalidity pension (NCIP), which SDA replaced in 1984, counts as SDA for this purpose (see below also);
- there is *no* exemption from the 26-week rule for the armed forces and those working abroad (see p145) or for the terminally ill.

You may count as present in GB during a temporary absence (see p265).

For adult and child dependant increases see Chapter 9. SDA is public funds under the immigration rules.[124] *If your dependant is covered by Chapters 15 or 16 or is a non-EEA national abroad you should seek specialist advice before claiming or renewing a claim.*

Some women who do not meet the current disability or residence rules for SDA may still be entitled. You can use this argument if you should have been entitled to NCIP but did not meet the household chores test (see 16th edn of CPAG's *Rights Guide to Non-Means-Tested Benefits*). If you are a woman who was:[125]

- resident in the UK for 10 years in the 20 years up to 28 November 1984; *and*
- present in the UK for 24 weeks out of the 28 weeks up to 28 November 1984; *and*
- married or cohabiting on 28 November 1984; *and*
- incapable of work from 27 June 1984 to 28 November 1984;

argue that you are entitled to SDA for any day falling within the same period of incapacity (see CPAG's *Rights Guide to Non-Means-Tested Benefits*). This is because the 1984 NCIP rules for married and cohabiting woman were unlawfully discriminatory.[126] This may mean that you do not have to meet the ordinary residence or 26-week presence rules for SDA.[127]

Example

Jean, a British national, is entitled to SDA. She leaves GB intending to live permanently in Latvia. Her entitlement to SDA ends because her absence from GB is not temporary. Three years later Jean returns to live permanently in GB. She has certificates to show that she remained incapable of work while in Latvia. She meets the disability rules for SDA. She does not have to satisfy the ordinary residence or 26-week rule and is again entitled to SDA from the day she arrives in GB.

---

10. STATUTORY SICK PAY AND STATUTORY MATERNITY PAY

SSP/SMP are paid by employers to employees. You only count as an employee if you are:

- an employed earner for GB NI purposes (even if you work outside GB);[128] *or*
- you are employed in an EU country other than the UK *and* if that

employment were in GB you would be an employee under SSP/SMP rules *and* the UK is the appropriate country under EC rules (see p316);[129] *or*
- an offshore worker;[130]
- a mariner (but see below);[131] *or*
- for SSP only, an air(wo)man (but see below).[132]

Only mariners or air(wo)men who meet certain rules count as employees.[133] These are not dealt with here.

You are also an employee under SMP rules for any week you were employed in another EU country apart from the UK if:[134]

- that week was in the 26 weeks before the 15th week before your expected week of confinement (see CPAG's *Rights Guide to Non-Means-Tested Benefits*); *and*
- you were employed in GB by the same employer in that 15th week.

Your entitlement to SSP/SMP is not affected by any absence from GB, as long as you meet these rules.[135]

Your employer is not required to pay you SSP/SMP if:[136]

- your employer is not required by law to pay employer's Class 1 NI contributions (even if those contributions are in fact made) because at the time they become payable your employer is:[137]
  - not resident or present in GB; *nor*
  - has a place of business in GB; *or*
- because of an international treaty or convention your employer is exempt from the social security Acts or those Acts are not enforceable against your employer (for SMP, this appears to apply only if your employer is a woman).

If you have to give your employer notice about SSP/SMP (or the other way around) and that notice cannot be given because you are outside the UK, you (or your employer) is treated as having complied with the rules if the notice is given as soon as reasonably practicable.[138] For notices which must be given, see CPAG's *Rights Guide to Non-Means-Tested Benefits*.

11. THE SOCIAL FUND

The social fund is run by the Benefits Agency and is in two parts: regulated and discretionary. Regulated social fund decisions can be appealed to a tribunal in the same way as IS, but there is a separate review and appeal system for discretionary social fund decisions. For a full description of the fund, see CPAG's *National Welfare Benefits Handbook*.

Regulated social fund

There are three types of payments: maternity expenses, funeral expenses and cold weather payments.[139] There are no residence/presence conditions for the claimant in the rules covering these payments, but because you must be in receipt of certain benefits to get a payment (see below) you must meet the residence/presence rules for one of those benefits.

Maternity expenses payments

You are only entitled to a maternity expenses payment if, at the date you claim, you or your partner is entitled to IS/income-based JSA (including urgent cases rate), FC or DWA.[140]

Funeral expenses payments

You are only entitled to a funeral expenses payment if, at the date you claim, you or your partner is entitled to IS/income-based JSA (including urgent cases rate), HB, CTB, FC or DWA.[141]

The funeral (ie, the burial or cremation) must take place in the UK.[142] This rule is not unlawful under British rules against racial/national discrimination.[143] However, the European Court of Justice has decided that this rule breaches EC law.[144] A social security appeal tribunal has decided this means the rate does not apply to any claimant – advisers can contact CPAG for details.[145] If you are refused a payment because the funeral took place outside the UK, you should appeal and seek advice.

The deceased must have been ordinarily resident (see p99) in the UK at the time of death.[146] This only applies to claims made after 6 April 1997. This rule may also breach EC law.

Cold weather payments

You are not entitled to a cold weather payment unless, on a day within the cold weather period, you are entitled to IS/income-based JSA (including urgent cases rate).[147] Cold weather payments are normally paid without the need for a separate claim.[148]

Discretionary social fund

There are three types of payment: community care grants, budgeting loans and crisis loans.

These can only be paid to meet needs which occur in the UK.[149] That should not exclude a need which occurs in the UK because of expenditure abroad – eg, a need for a budgeting loan because the claimant has spent money helping relatives abroad. It is the place of the need which matters, not the ultimate reason for that need. This rule may breach EC law (see p356).

Community care grants

You cannot be given a community care grant unless, when you apply, you are in receipt of IS/income-based JSA (including urgent cases rate), with one exception.[150] This means that, while there are no residence/presence conditions in the community care grant rules, you must meet the residence/presence rules for IS/income-based JSA (see p130 or 132.

The exception is when:[151]

- the grant is to help you re-establish yourself in the community following a stay in institutional or residential care; *and*
- your discharge from that care is planned to be within six weeks; *and*
- you are likely to receive IS or income-based JSA upon that discharge.

If this applies to you, because you do not need to be entitled to IS or income-based JSA when you apply, you do not need to meet the residence/presence rules for either of those benefits when you apply. However, you must show that you are likely to meet those rules (and the other IS/income-based JSA rules) after you are discharged. The place providing your care does not have to be in the UK. This means that if you are being cared for abroad but intend to return to GB on your discharge, you may be considered for a grant.

This type of grant can only be paid to 're-establish' a person in the community. The community is GB. This means that the person must intend to live in GB and have previously lived in GB.[152] This rule may breach EC law (see p356).

Budgeting loans

You cannot be given a budgeting loan unless, when you apply, you are being paid IS/income-based JSA (including urgent cases rate).[153] This means that, while there are no residence/presence conditions in the budgeting loan rules, you must meet the residence/presence rules for IS/income-based JSA (see p130 and 132).

Crisis loans

You do not need to be receiving any benefits to be given a crisis loan.

If you are not entitled to IS/income-based JSA because you are a person from abroad (or would not be entitled if you claimed) you can only be given a crisis loan if you meet certain rules. This can only affect a British citizen or another person with the right of abode if you are not habitually resident in the UK, Ireland, the Channel Islands or the Isle of Man and are not exempt (see p131). The rules you must meet are that the loan is:[154]

- to meet expenses to alleviate the consequences of a disaster; *and*
- the only way to prevent serious damage or serious risk to your health or safety or to that of a member of your family.

A crisis loan will only be made if the Benefits Agency considers that you are likely to be able to repay it.[155] The overall maximum loan is £1000.[156] The maximum loan for living expenses is 75 per cent of the IS personal allowance plus £16.90 for each child.

There is no definition of 'disaster'. If you have been refused IS because the Benefits Agency has decided that you are not habitually resident, you could argue that this refusal is a 'disaster' in the ordinary meaning of that word. You should explain why the refusal is disastrous for you and your family, and the serious damage/risk that the refusal causes.

You will also need to explain how you would repay the loan. Since it is only a matter of time before you are treated as habitually resident and awarded benefit, you will then be able to repay the loan.

It is not clear whether the social fund officer (SFO) considering if you are a 'person from abroad' has to agree with the decision of the adjudication officer (AO) on your IS/income-based JSA claim.[157] The social fund directions do not refer to the IS/income-based JSA decision. We consider that the SFO has to reach her/his own opinion on this and does not have to agree with the AO. When applying for the loan always explain why you consider yourself to be habitually resident.

If you are refused a loan, you should apply for a review of that refusal and seek specialist advice.

CHAPTER TWELVE

Indefinite leave to remain

This chapter covers the benefit rules which affect people with indefinite leave to remain in the UK. The benefits covered are:

1. Income support (IS) (p153)
2. Income-based jobseeker's allowance (JSA) (p158)
3. Housing benefit (HB) and council tax benefit (CTB) (p159)
4. Child benefit and guardian's allowance (p160)
5. Family credit (FC) and disability working allowance (DWA) (p160)
6. Short-term contributory benefits (p160)
7. Retirement pensions and widows' benefits (p160)
8. Industrial injuries benefits (p161)
9. Disability benefits (p161)
10. Statutory sick pay (SSP) and statutory maternity pay (SMP) (p161)
11. The social fund (p161)

Who has indefinite leave to remain?

You have indefinite leave to remain if you have leave to be in the UK with no time-limit on that leave. This is also called 'settled' status.[1] It is sometimes known unofficially as 'permanent residence'. For full details, see pp39-43.

If you become a British citizen you no longer have leave to remain because you are no longer subject to immigration control (see p130). Instead, see the rules for British citizens, Chapter 11. Remember that British nationals who are not British citizens (see p14) can have indefinite leave to remain.

If you become a British citizen, the most important changes in your rights to benefits are:

- the sponsored immigrant rule (see p153) cannot apply; *and*
- you can use EC rules on benefits.

However, if you are a refugee or have exceptional leave to remain and you become a British citizen, this change may remove your exemption from the habitual residence test (see p131).

It is possible to be an EU/EEA national and have indefinite leave to remain (but not if you are a British citizen). If this applies, you can use either these rules or the rules for EU/EEA nationals (see Part 4) whichever one is more favourable. However, if you have indefinite leave to remain you will never be worse off under the rules for EU/EEA nationals.

I. INCOME SUPPORT

You are only entitled to IS if:

- you are in GB[2] (see p98) *or* temporarily absent from GB[3] (see p246); *and*
- you are *not* a 'sponsored immigrant' (if you are, then you may be entitled to urgent cases rate IS – see p157); *and*
- you are habitually resident in the UK, Ireland, the Channel Islands or the Isle of Man (see p102) *or* exempt from the habitual residence test (see p158).

You are exempt from the sponsored immigrant rule *and* the habitual residence test if you left Montserrat after 1 November 1995 because of a volcanic eruption.[4]

In practice, if everyone for whom you are claiming has been present in the UK for the five years before you sign the IS claim form, the Benefits Agency will normally assume that you meet those rules. This is because the claim form asks if the claimant, partner or children being claimed for have come to live or returned to live in the UK in the last five years. However, even if you answer no to this question, the Benefits Agency might ask you extra questions about your immigration history, particularly if you have recently been paid IS/income-based JSA at the urgent cases rate.

Sponsored immigrants

If you are a 'sponsored immigrant' you are not entitled to IS (or income-based JSA/HB/CTB), unless one of the exceptions below applies.[5] 'Sponsored immigrant' has a special meaning under benefit rules and does not apply to every migrant who has a sponsor (see below for details). This rule does not apply if you have been resident in the UK for five years (see p156).

If you are a sponsored immigrant, you should consider whether your partner, if you have one, should claim instead (see p131). For the rules when a member of your family is a sponsored immigrant, see Chapter 10.

You are only a sponsored immigrant for IS if:[6]

- the Secretary of State has given you leave to enter or remain in the UK; *and*
- that leave was given because someone else gave a written undertaking under the immigration rules[7] to be responsible for your maintenance and accommodation in the UK; *and*
- you have been resident in the UK for less than five years since the date you entered the UK or the date of the undertaking, if that is later.

Each of these rules is covered in more detail below. If any of these rules does not apply or no longer applies (see below), you are not a sponsored immigrant and you are entitled to IS in the same way as any other person with indefinite leave to remain. If you are treated as a sponsored immigrant you should appeal and take independent advice. CPAG would be interested to hear from advisers dealing with refusals.

A written undertaking

Only an undertaking on an official form in response to a request should count, because otherwise it is not 'given in pursuance of the immigration rules' as the benefit rules require. Any other type of undertaking or promise, even one in writing, does not count.

A written undertaking is made at the request of the Home Office or an entry clearance officer when an application for leave to remain or an entry clearance has been made. An undertaking is usually only requested for dependent elderly relatives or children and *not* for spouses. The sponsor will usually be the relative whom the applicant is to join. The undertaking is given on a RON 112 form (see Appendix 4).

The Benefits Agency appears to be confused about who is a sponsored immigrant under benefit rules. Even where the Home Office has told the Benefits Agency that an undertaking has not been signed, claimants have been treated as sponsored immigrants. The Benefits Agency does not seem to understand the difference between sponsorship arrangements with formal undertakings and those with informal undertakings. The Benefits Agency can only treat you as a sponsored immigrant if they can show that an undertaking has been given. If they cannot obtain the written undertaking on a RON 112 from the Home Office or entry clearance officer, you should not be treated as a sponsored immigrant.

Leave to enter or remain in the UK

You are only a sponsored immigrant if your leave was given by the Secretary of State.[8] Immigration officers give leave to enter.[9] The Secretary of State only gives leave to remain to people who already have leave to enter. The rules therefore appear to mean that, if your leave was given by an immigration officer you are not a sponsored immigrant under the benefit rules.

In some cases, the Home Office agrees to waive one of the immigration rules when granting leave. This means that your leave is not under the immigration rules, but is exceptional leave to remain (see Chapter 14). In this case, you may be able to argue that, because your leave was outside the immigration rules, the undertaking was also not given in pursuance of the immigration rules. *You should not use this argument unless you have a written record proving that the Home Office knew that you did not meet the requirements of the immigration rules. You must have this record because otherwise the Home Office may try to take your leave away on the ground that your leave was obtained by deception.* Proof includes a letter from the Home Office agreeing to waive one of the immigration rules, or a letter from you or your adviser, which you know the Home Office received, stating that you do not meet one of the rules. If this argument applies, you should also be exempt from the habitual residence test as a person with exceptional leave to remain (see p158).

Only a person with leave to enter or remain in the UK can be a sponsored immigrant under the benefit rules. This does not seem to apply if you also have an EC law right to remain in the UK (see p351):[10]

How you stop being a sponsored immigrant

If you stop being a sponsored immigrant under the benefit rules, the ordinary rules apply. You stop being a sponsored immigrant if:

- you are given indefinite leave to enter the UK as a returning resident after going outside the common travel area (see below);
- you have been resident in the UK for five years (see p156); *or*
- you get an EC law right to reside in the UK (see p351).

For the situation where your sponsor dies, see p157.

Returning residents

If you are given indefinite leave on an undertaking and later travel outside the common travel area (ie, outside the UK, Ireland, Channel Islands and the Isle of Man) that undertaking does not apply to any indefinite leave you are given when you return. This is because:

- the rules about public funds do not apply to returning residents;[11] *and*
- the undertaking is stated only to apply to 'the period of leave and any variation of it'. Leave given to a returning resident is new leave not a variation of your old leave.

You are no longer a sponsored immigrant under the immigration rules. This must mean that you are no longer a sponsored immigrant under benefit rules, especially since your sponsor is no longer liable in law to maintain you (see p157). The Benefits Agency may not accept this conclusion.

Five years residence

You stop being a sponsored immigrant for benefit purposes when you have been resident (see p99) in the UK for five years.[12] This does not have to be continuous residence. The Benefits Agency is instructed to work out the length of your residence starting with the date you first entered the UK or if it was later, the date of the undertaking.[13] The rule is that you must be resident *not* present, so time abroad may count for your period of residence in the UK (see p101). However, because a returning resident is not a sponsored immigrant (see p155) only absences in Ireland, Channel Islands and the Isle of Man matter. If the Benefits Agency decides that, because your absences abroad do not count, you are still a sponsored immigrant even though five years have passed as residence, you should seek independent advice.

Exception – transitional protection

Under the benefit rules sponsored immigrants are not entitled to IS. There are two exceptions. The first exception is transitional protection. It applies if, *before 5 February 1996*:[14]

- you were being paid or were entitled to IS; *and*
- an undertaking was given by someone else to be responsible for your maintenance and accommodation in the UK.

Benefits Agency guidance suggests that you only have transitional protection if you were entitled to IS on 4 February 1996 and that it only continues until the end of that IS award.[15] We believe this guidance is wrong. It is enough if, at any time before 5 February 1996, you were entitled to IS in your own name. That is because regulations giving transitional protection usually state that the claimant must have been entitled on a particular date.[16] The regulations giving transitional protection to sponsored immigrants apply if you were entitled 'before the coming into force of these regulations'. They do not require entitlement on a particular date or '*immediately* before the coming into force'.

Transitional protection continues even if there is a break in your entitlement to IS. It applies to every IS claim made after 4 February 1996. That is because the regulations do not state that the transitional protection ends at the end of the IS claim as transitional protection regulations usually do.[17]

Transitional protection does not apply to income-based JSA, even if your JSA entitlement would begin immediately after your IS entitlement ends (see p158).

Exception – sponsor has died

If you are a sponsored immigrant under the benefit rules who does not have transitional protection (see p156) and the sponsor who gave the undertaking has died, you are entitled to IS at the urgent cases rate.[18] If more than one sponsor gave an undertaking, each of them must have died for this to apply to you. To work out the urgent cases rate, see Chapter 10. If the sponsored immigrant rule stops applying to you (eg, you have been resident for five years) you get ordinary rate IS/income-based JSA.

Sponsor's liability to maintain and recovery of IS

Since 1980, the DSS has had the power to recover from a sponsor IS[19] paid to a sponsored immigrant.[20] The definition of sponsored immigrant for liability to maintain (see below) is different from that for the claimant's benefit entitlement. Recovery is through the magistrate's court (in Scotland, sheriff's court). There is also a power to prosecute for failure to maintain the claimant.[21] The DSS has used the threat of court action to persuade sponsors to provide some, often very little, financial support to the claimant concerned. If the sponsor could not support the claimant the DSS usually took no further steps. Court action was very rare.[22]

Under the liability to maintain rules, a sponsored immigrant is a person for whom there still applies a sponsorship undertaking given after 22 May 1980 on an official form (now a RON 112 (see Appendix 4)) on a request from the Home Office or entry clearance officer.[23] There is no five years rule.

These powers (or the threat of them) may still be used against sponsors of claimants on IS, especially where the claimant has transitional protection. If the Benefits Agency approaches you about an undertaking you have made, you should consider seeking advice. A liability to maintain should not delay an award of IS to which the claimant is entitled. Nor can any IS which is paid be recovered from the claimant.

Habitual residence test

The habitual residence test only applies to the IS claimant.[24] It does not apply to any partner or child for whom IS is being claimed. If you might fail the test but have a partner who is more likely to pass, s/he can claim instead, though there may be disadvantages to such a decision – see CPAG's *National Welfare Benefits Handbook*.

You pass the habitual residence test if you are habitually resident (see p104) in the UK, Ireland, the Channel Islands or the Isle of Man. If you are not habitually resident and you are not exempt (see below), you are a 'person from abroad'.[25] Unless you qualify for urgent cases rate (see p153) you will not be entitled to IS (or income-based JSA – see p158).[26]

The Court of Appeal has decided that the IS habitual residence test is not outside the Secretary of State's powers under British law.[27] An argument that the test is unlawful under EC law was also rejected (see p357). If you are a national of Cyprus, Malta or Turkey, the habitual residence test may break the UK's international obligations (see p103).

Exemptions from habitual residence test

You are exempt from the habitual residence test if you left Montserrat after 1 November 1995 because of a volcanic eruption.[28]

You may be exempt from the habitual residence test under EC law (see p358). This will not apply to you *unless* either you or a member of your extended family:

- is a national of an EU/EEA member state (apart from the UK); *or*
- is a British citizen who has travelled to another EU/EEA member state using the right of free movement under EC law.

You are also exempt from the habitual residence test if:

- you are a refugee (see Chapter 13).[29] You may count as a refugee for this rule even if the Home Office has not accepted that you are a refugee; *or*
- you have exceptional leave to remain in the UK (see Chapter 14).[30] This is not limited to people refused recognition as refugees but given leave, but covers anyone who did not qualify for leave to remain under the immigration rules, but was given leave anyway.

2. INCOME-BASED JOBSEEKER'S ALLOWANCE

For contribution-based JSA, see p160.

The income-based JSA rules about who is a person from abroad are the same as for IS (see p153) with the following exceptions if you are a sponsored immigrant under benefit rules (for sponsored immigrant see p153):[31]

- if you can claim urgent cases IS but only at urgent cases rate because your sponsor has died (see p157), you are *not* entitled to income-based JSA, even if you are available for work.[32] You should claim IS instead;
- IS transitional protection for sponsored immigrants does *not* apply to income-based JSA (for IS transitional protection see p156).[33] If you are a sponsored immigrant, you are a person from abroad under income-based JSA rules and so are not entitled to income-based JSA.[34]

The rules about liability to maintain (see p157) apply to income-based JSA as they do to IS, except that the Benefits Agency cannot recover from the sponsor any JSA paid to the claimant.[35]

3. HOUSING BENEFIT AND COUNCIL TAX BENEFIT

If you are being paid IS/income-based JSA (including urgent cases rate) you are not a person from abroad for HB/CTB.[36] The local authority which deals with your HB/CTB claim should not make enquiries about your immigration status or habitual residence.[37] If you are *not* being paid IS/income-based JSA the following rules apply.

You are only entitled to HB/CTB if:

- **for HB**, you have accommodation in GB which you normally occupy as your home (which may apply during a temporary absence – see p251)[38] or, **for CTB**, you are liable to pay council tax for accommodation in which you reside (see p252)[39]; *and*
- you are *not* a sponsored immigrant (see below); *and*
- you are *either* habitually resident in the UK, Ireland, the Channel Islands or the Isle of Man *or* exempt from the habitual residence test (see below).

If you do not meet these rules, you are not entitled to HB/CTB.[40]

You are exempt from the sponsored immigrant rule *and* the habitual residence test if you left Montserrat after 1 November 1995 because of a volcanic eruption.[41]

The rules for sponsored immigrants are the same as those for IS (see p153), except that if your sponsor has died (see p157) you are *not* a sponsored immigrant for HB/CTB rules.[42] The liability to maintain and recovery rules (see p157) do not apply to HB/CTB.

The habitual residence test and exemptions are the same as for IS (see p157).

If you claim HB/CTB soon after you are given leave under an immigration rule requiring there to be no recourse to public funds, there is a theoretical risk to your immigration status (see comments on FC/DWA on p160).

If your partner or children have immigration leave on condition that they will be maintained without recourse to public funds, their immigration status may be affected by your HB/CTB claim (see p187).

4. CHILD BENEFIT AND GUARDIAN'S ALLOWANCE

The rules for CB and guardian's allowance are the same as those for British citizens (see p133). The CB rules exempt people with indefinite leave to remain from the CB immigration condition.[43]

5. FAMILY CREDIT AND DISABILITY WORKING ALLOWANCE

The rules for FC/DWA are the same as those for British citizens (see p138). You meet the immigration condition for FC/DWA because indefinite leave cannot be subject to any condition or limitation.[44] This applies even if your leave was given on the basis that you would not claim public funds.

FC/DWA are public funds under the immigration rules.[45] However, because no conditions can be attached to indefinite leave, claiming FC/DWA does not break any immigration condition or put you at risk of prosecution. In theory, if your current indefinite leave was given under an immigration rule which requires no recourse to public funds (see p57), claiming FC/DWA soon after that leave was granted might allow the Home Office to say that your leave was obtained by deception. The Home Office would have to show that they relied on false information about your finances or those of any sponsor or that you lied when you said you did not intend to claim public funds. This could not be done where your leave was as a returning resident (see p33), because the immigration rules allow returning residents to claim public funds. In practice, the Home Office is not known ever to have done this and it is very unlikely to do so.

6. SHORT-TERM CONTRIBUTORY BENEFITS

The rules for contribution-based JSA, incapacity benefit and maternity allowance are the same as those for British citizens (see p139).

7. RETIREMENT PENSIONS AND WIDOWS' BENEFITS

The rules for Category A, B, C and D retirement pensions, widow's allowance, widowed mother's allowance and widow's pension are the same as those for British citizens (see p140). If you are not entitled to a full pension because part of your working life (or your spouse's working life) was spent abroad you may be able to use EC rules (see Part 4) or a reciprocal agreement (Part 5) to increase your pension.

8. INDUSTRIAL INJURIES BENEFITS

The rules for disablement benefit, reduced earnings allowance, retirement allowance, constant attendance allowance and exceptionally severe disablement allowance are the same as those for British citizens (see p142).

9. DISABILITY BENEFITS

The rules for DLA, AA, ICA and SDA are the same as those for British citizens (see p145). You meet the immigration condition for these benefits because indefinite leave to remain cannot be subject to any condition or limitation.[46] This applies even if your leave was given on the basis that you would not claim public funds.

DLA, AA, ICA and SDA are public funds under the immigration rules.[47] However, because there are no conditions on indefinite leave, claiming these benefits does not break any immigration condition. The possible effects on your immigration status are the same as those for FC/DWA (see p160).

The rules for sponsored immigrants only apply to IS, income-based JSA, HB and CTB. Even if you are a sponsored immigrant for those benefits, your rights to other benefits are not affected.

10. STATUTORY SICK PAY AND STATUTORY MATERNITY PAY

The rules for SSP and SMP are the same as for British citizens (see p147).

11. THE SOCIAL FUND

The social fund rules are the same as those for British citizens (see p148).

If a **crisis loan** is made to you and you are a sponsored immigrant under the liability to maintain rules (see p157 – this is different from a sponsored immigrant under the benefit entitlement rules) the Benefits

Agency can recover the amount of that crisis loan from your sponsor.[48] Social fund guidance states that this will be only be done if you are not entitled to IS: if you are entitled to IS the loan will be recovered from you in the usual way.[49] For recovery of crisis loans, see CPAG's *National Welfare Benefits Handbook*.

There are special rules for applications for a crisis loan (see p150) if:

- you are not entitled to IS/income-based JSA because you are not habitually resident or because you are a sponsored immigrant; *or*
- you are entitled to IS urgent cases rate as a sponsored immigrant whose sponsor has died.

CHAPTER THIRTEEN

Refugees

The benefits covered in this chapter are:

1. Income support (IS) (p165)
2. Income-based jobseeker's allowance (JSA) (p167)
3. Housing benefit (HB) and council tax benefit (CTB) (p168)
4. Child benefit and guardian's allowance (p169)
5. Family credit (FC) and disability working allowance (DWA) (p169)
6. Short-term contributory benefits (p171)
7. Retirement pensions and widows' benefits (p171)
8. Industrial injuries benefits (p171)
9. Disability benefits (p171)
10. Statutory sick pay (SSP) and statutory maternity pay (SMP) (p173)
11. The social fund (p173)

This chapter deals with refugees. Benefit rules often give favourable treatment to refugees. The rules for IS, income-based JSA, HB and CTB refer simply to refugees. This seems to include people who *are in fact* refugees even if the Home Office has not accepted them as such. The rules for other benefits refer only to refugees who have been recorded as such by the Home Office. For details, see below.

For dependants of refugees, see the chapter relevant to their status. Dependants given leave in line with the limited leave of a recognised refugee are exempt from the no recourse to public funds requirement (see p57).

Who is a refugee?

A refugee is a person who is outside the country of their nationality because of a well-founded fear of persecution for reasons of race, religion, nationality, membership of a particular social group or political opinion.[1] Once you meet this definition, you are a refugee even though the Home Office has not (yet) recognised that status.[2]

A person who seeks to remain in the UK (or in another country) because of their status as a refugee is said to claim asylum. In this book, a person claiming asylum who has not yet been given leave to remain is referred to as an **asylum-seeker**. Some of the rules below may apply to refugees who are asylum-seekers – ie, people who have not yet been recognised as refugees. For rules on asylum-seekers, see Chapter 17.

Not all refugees in the UK have claimed asylum. For example, they may be here as a student or as a British citizen's spouse. They may have been recognised as a refugee by another country or have never claimed asylum anywhere. For example, a person who has indefinite leave to remain in the UK because of long residence (see p132) does not need to claim asylum because s/he can stay here as long as s/he likes.

The Benefits Agency approach

It is very unlikely that the Benefits Agency will accept a person as a refugee unless that person has been recognised by the Home Office as a refugee – ie, **a recognised refugee**. If you have been recognised by the Home Office as a refugee and given leave to remain in the UK as a refugee, you will have been sent a letter confirming that status. The Benefits Agency will accept this letter as proof that you are a refugee. Your status as a refugee continues even if you have been given indefinite leave to remain in the UK. This means that you remain exempt from the habitual residence test (see p165).

You may count as a refugee under some benefit rules, even though the Home Office has not recognised you as a refugee – ie, an **unrecognised refugee**. You will also have an immigration status (eg, here with limited leave). Remember that unrecognised refugees and asylum-seekers always have an immigration status – being an asylum-seeker is not an immigration status on its own (see p219). *Claiming benefit and/or stating that you are a refugee may affect your immigration status. Unless you have indefinite leave to remain in the UK or have claimed asylum you should seek expert advice before claiming benefit or stating that you are a refugee.*

If you have been recognised by another country as a refugee, the Benefits Agency should accept that you are a refugee. If the Benefits Agency does not do this seek expert advice.

If you have not claimed asylum, but you have a well-founded fear of persecution in your own country, the Benefits Agency is very unlikely to accept that you are a refugee. You could claim asylum from the Home Office, but because that would have an effect on your immigration status you should seek expert advice before doing so. If you have indefinite leave to remain, the Home Office is very unlikely to consider a request for recognition as a refugee. Because the Benefits Agency has to decide your IS claim, it will have to decide whether you are a refugee, though it can ask for Home Office help.

I. INCOME SUPPORT

If you are a recognised refugee you are only entitled to IS if you are in GB[3] (see p98) *or* temporarily absent from GB[4] (see p246). Recognised refugees are exempt from the rules for persons from abroad, including the habitual residence test.[5]

If you are an unrecognised refugee (see p164) you are also exempt from the habitual residence test. This is because the IS habitual residence test exempts *refugees* and not only recognised refugees.[6] In practice, this is only likely to make a difference if you have indefinite leave to remain. This is because, if you do not have indefinite leave to remain, your immigration status is very likely to mean that you are a person from abroad anyway (even though you may in fact be a refugee) and therefore:

- *either* entitled only to urgent cases IS;
- *or* not entitled to IS at all (unless you have exceptional leave to remain, in which case you are exempt from the habitual residence test anyway – see p174).

If you have indefinite leave you could argue that you are exempt as a refugee. If you do not have indefinite leave, see the chapter relevant to your immigration status. In any case, the Benefits Agency is very unlikely to accept that you are a refugee for habitual residence purposes.

Backdating IS after recognition as a refugee

If you have been recognised by the Home Office as a refugee, you may be entitled to backdated IS (or extra IS) for the period before you were recognised. There are three different sets of rules, but you may be able to use any or all of them. The rules are:

- if you were not entitled to IS because you were
  - an in-country asylum applicant; *or*
  - refused asylum and only recognised as a refugee after appealing, you are entitled to backdated urgent cases IS (see below);
- if you were paid urgent cases IS as an asylum-seeker, you may be entitled to the backdated difference between urgent cases IS and ordinary IS (see p166);
- if either of the above rules apply and you can argue you were *not* a person from abroad before you were recognised as a refugee, you may be entitled to ordinary IS (see p209).

Backdated urgent cases IS under British law

This is under British regulations.

If you were refused IS (or did not claim) for a period between your asylum claim and the date you were recognised as a refugee by the Home Office, you can claim backdated urgent cases IS. You must make this claim within 28 days of receiving the Home Office written notification that you have been recognised as a refugee.[7] This time-limit cannot be extended. Your claim is treated as made on the date you claimed asylum or, if you claimed on arrival in the UK, on the date that claim was first refused by the Home Office.[8] You are entitled to urgent cases IS as if you had been an asylum-seeker under IS rules from that date. Any IS already paid to you or your partner for that period is offset against any extra IS to which you are entitled.

You may have been paid contribution-based JSA, but still lost out because this was less than urgent cases IS. Even if this applies, you cannot claim urgent cases IS for any period when you received contribution-based JSA.[9] This only applies to the JSA claimant so, if your partner has been recognised as a refugee and did not receive contribution-based JSA, s/he should make the claim for backdated IS instead. Your contribution-based JSA will be treated as income, so your partner will get the difference between that and urgent cases rate. If this is not possible you should ask the Benefits Agency to make an extra-statutory payment of the difference between contribution-based JSA and urgent cases IS and ask an adviser to contact CPAG about your case.

Backdated ordinary IS under EC law

Some refugees are entitled to equal treatment with British citizens under EC law.[10] The Benefits Agency does not accept that this can apply for a period before a person is recognised as a refugee. However, a social security commissioner has decided that under EC law some recognised refugees may be entitled to backdated ordinary IS for the period *before* recognition by the Home Office at the rate a British citizen would have been paid.[11] In the case before the commissioner, the claimants lost because neither of them had worked in the EU/EEA, but his ruling on the law may help people who have worked. You are only likely to be able to use this EC rule if:

- you have been recognised by the Home Office as a refugee;[12] *and*
- before you were recognised you were an 'employed or self-employed person' in the UK or elsewhere in the EU/EEA.[13] You need only have worked for a short period for this to apply. You cannot use this decision for a period before you first worked in the UK or elsewhere in the EU/EEA.

If you can use this rule, you are entitled to ordinary IS for any period:[14]

- after 30 May 1992;[15] *and*

- after you first became an 'employed or self-employed person' (see above); *and*
- during which you would have been paid ordinary IS if you had been a British citizen (eg, a period when you got urgent cases IS); *and*
- during which you were habitually resident under EC law (see p105) in the UK.[16]

You do not need to have been awarded urgent cases IS to use this rule. If you were paid urgent cases IS then the money you will gain by using this rule is the difference between urgent cases IS and ordinary IS, which is normally 10 per cent of the claimant's personal allowance.[17] For details, see Chapter 10.

If you can use this rule, you may also be entitled to backdated DLA/AA/SDA/ICA (see p171).

How to get backdated ordinary IS
Using this rule depends on whether or not you claimed IS before you were recognised as a refugee.

- If you claimed IS before you were recognised as a refugee and a decision was made to award or refuse urgent cases IS, you should immediately ask the Benefits Agency to review that decision on the ground that it was in breach of EC law. The usual limit on backdating does not apply.[18] However, you cannot do this if you were refused IS on the same basis as a British citizen – eg, you were working more than 16 hours a week. If this applies to you, you may be able to make a late claim for FC/DWA instead (see p169).
- If you did *not* claim IS before you were recognised as a refugee (eg, because you knew that you would be refused because of your immigration status), there is no decision to review. However, you can claim urgent cases IS under British law within the time limit (see p165). You should do this and ask for ordinary IS to be paid instead of urgent cases IS for the period over which you want to use the EC rule.

You should also seek urgent independent advice because this is a difficult point of EC law. The commissioner's decision is recent[19] and it is not clear how it will be applied by the Benefits Agency. CPAG would like to hear from advisers helping claimants under this rule.

2. INCOME-BASED JOBSEEKER'S ALLOWANCE

For contribution-based JSA, see p171.

Income-based JSA rules about who is a person from abroad are the same as those for IS (see p165).[20]

If you were paid urgent cases income-based JSA, under EC law you may be entitled to backdated income-based JSA at the ordinary rate. The same rules apply as those for IS (see p166).[21]

If you were not entitled to IS/income-based JSA before you were recognised as a refugee:

- you may be entitled to backdated urgent cases IS under British regulations (see p165). This is paid instead of backdated urgent cases income-based JSA;
- you may also be entitled under EC law to backdated IS at the ordinary rate (see p166). Instead of this, you can use EC law to seek backdated income-based JSA at the ordinary rate. The only advantage of doing this is that you will be credited NI contributions for that period. As well as meeting the EC rules, you must show that you were actively seeking and available (which may have required Home Office permission) for work.

3. HOUSING BENEFIT AND COUNCIL TAX BENEFIT

If you are being paid IS/income-based JSA you are not a person from abroad for HB/CTB.[22] The local authority which deals with your HB/CTB claim should not make enquiries about your immigration status or habitual residence.[23] If you are not being paid IS/income-based JSA the following rules apply.

If you are a recognised refugee you are only entitled:

- to **HB** if you have accommodation in GB which you normally occupy as your home (which may apply during a temporary absence – see p251);[24]
- to **CTB** if you are liable to pay council tax for accommodation in which you reside (see p252).

Recognised refugees are exempt from the rules for persons from abroad, including the habitual residence test.[24]

If you are an unrecognised refugee (see p164) you are also exempt from the habitual residence test. This is because the HB/CTB habitual residence rule exempts refugees not only recognised refugees. In practice, this is only likely to help you if you have indefinite leave to remain. This is because, if you do not have indefinite leave to remain, your immigration status is very likely to mean that you are a person from abroad anyway (even though you may in fact be a refugee) and:

- *either* not entitled to HB/CTB;

- *or*, if you are an on-arrival asylum-seeker (see Chapter 17) or have exceptional leave to remain (see Chapter 14), entitled to HB/CTB anyway.

If you have indefinite leave you could argue that you are exempt as a refugee. If you do not have indefinite leave, see the chapter relevant to your immigration status. In any case, the local authority which deals with your benefit claim may not accept that you are a refugee for habitual residence purposes.

Backdating HB/CTB after recognition as a refugee

If you have been recognised by the Home Office as a refugee, you may be entitled to backdated HB/CTB for the period before you were recognised. This is under British law. The rules are the same as for backdating urgent cases IS (see p165).[25]

4. CHILD BENEFIT AND GUARDIAN'S ALLOWANCE

If you are a recognised refugee, the rules for CB and guardian's allowance are the same as those for British citizens (see p133). Recognised refugees are exempt from the CB immigration condition.[26]

5. FAMILY CREDIT AND DISABILITY WORKING ALLOWANCE

If you are a recognised refugee, the rules for FC and DWA are the same as those for British citizens (see p138). Only *recognised refugees* are exempt from the immigration conditions for FC/DWA,[27] and unrecognised refugees should see the chapter relevant to their immigration status.

You may be able to use EC law to backdate FC/DWA for the period before you were recognised (see p170). There is no FC/DWA equivalent of the British regulations for backdating urgent cases IS for recognised refugees (for these IS regulations, see p165).

Backdating FC/DWA

If you have been recognised as a refugee, but before that you were not entitled to FC/DWA only because of your immigration status, you may under EC law be entitled to backdated FC/DWA for the period before recognition by the Home Office. This is because you are entitled to equal treatment with British citizens.[28] This will only apply for a period during which:

- you were habitually resident in the UK under EC law (see p105);[29] *and*
- you met all the usual rules for FC or DWA – eg, you or your partner were working more than 16 hours a week (for the usual rules see CPAG's *National Welfare Benefits Handbook*).

Using this rule depends upon whether you claimed FC/DWA before you were recognised as a refugee.

- If you claimed FC/DWA before you were recognised as a refugee and you were refused FC/DWA, you should immediately ask the Benefits Agency to review that decision because it was in breach of EC law. However, you cannot do this if you were refused FC/DWA on the same basis as a British citizen – eg, you were working less than 16 hours a week. If this applies you may be able to make a claim for backdated IS instead (see p166).
- If you did *not* claim FC/DWA before you were recognised as a refugee (eg, because you knew that you would be refused because of your immigration status), there is no decision to review. You should immediately make a late claim for FC/DWA for the period over which you want to use the EC rule. You should explain why you did not claim FC/DWA earlier. You can claim for up to three months before the date of claim, as long as you can show it was not reasonable to claim earlier because, for example, you were advised in writing by a solicitor that you could not claim (for details, see CPAG's *National Welfare Benefits Handbook*).[30] If all of the period covered by the EC rule is more than three months before the claim date, EC law may override the three-month time-limit.[31]

If you apply for a review or make a late claim you should seek urgent independent advice because this rule involves difficult issues of EC law. The commissioner's decision is recent[32] and it is not clear how it will be applied by the Benefits Agency. CPAG would like to hear from advisers helping claimants under this rule.

6. SHORT-TERM CONTRIBUTORY BENEFITS

If you are a recognised refugee, the rules for contribution-based JSA, incapacity benefit and maternity allowance are the same as for British citizens (see p139).

7. RETIREMENT PENSIONS AND WIDOWS' BENEFITS

If you are a recognised refugee, the rules for Category A, B, C and D retirement pensions, widow's allowance, widowed mother's allowance and widow's pension are the same as those for British citizens (see p140).

8. INDUSTRIAL INJURIES BENEFITS

If you are a recognised refugee, the rules for disablement benefit, reduced earnings allowance, retirement allowance, constant attendance allowance and exceptionally severe disablement allowance are the same as those for British citizens (see p142).

9. DISABILITY BENEFITS

If you are a recognised refugee, the rules for DLA, AA, ICA and SDA are the same as those for British citizens (see p145). Only *recognised refugees* are exempt from the immigration conditions,[33] and unrecognised refugees should see the chapter relevant to their immigration status. For the period of benefit awards to refugees, see below.

You may be able to use EC law to backdate a disability benefit for the period before you were recognised (see p172). There is no disability benefit equivalent of the British regulations for backdating urgent cases IS for recognised refugees (for these IS regulations, see p165).

If you have been recognised as a refugee, but before that you were not entitled to one of these benefits only because of your immigration status, you may be entitled under EC law to backdated benefit for the period *before* recognition by the Home Office. This is because you are entitled to equal treatment with British citizens.[34] This is under the same rules as those which apply to IS.[35] If you have never been an employed or self-employed person in the EU/EEA, but you are the dependant of someone who has been, you may still be able to use this rule.

How long benefit is awarded for

Benefits are awarded for an indefinite period or, where that is not appropriate, a limited period.[36] Where a medical condition is permanent, especially where a person is old, awards of DLA, AA and SDA are often made for life. Benefits Agency guidance suggests that refugees with limited leave to remain should not get life awards. We believe this is wrong.

When a person is recognised as a refugee, the Home Office normally gives four year's leave and states that, if an application is made shortly before that leave runs out, indefinite leave to remain will be given. Benefits Agency guidance states that any award of a disability benefit should be limited to the date your immigration leave is due to run out.[37] The reason seems to be that the Benefits Agency considers that you will stop being entitled to the benefit if your leave runs out. If your award is limited like this, you will need to claim that benefit again at the end of the award, and again show that you meet all the benefit conditions, including those about disability. This places you in a worse position than a British citizen who would have been given a life award, especially since her/his benefit could only be withdrawn if the Benefits Agency showed that the disability conditions were no longer satisfied.[38]

We believe the Benefits Agency approach is wrong because:

- for SDA, once the claimant satisfies the immigration condition, s/he is treated as satisfying it for the rest of that period of incapacity. In other words, even if leave does run out there is no relevant change of circumstances;[39]
- a recognised refugee remains exempt under disability benefit rules from the immigration conditions even if leave runs out.[40] This means that the end of the period of leave is not a potential relevant change of circumstances;
- even if this is wrong and the end of immigration leave is relevant to the benefit award, there will only be a relevant change of circumstances at the end of the leave if the person does not apply for an extension in time, which is very unlikely;
- it is discriminatory to make a limited award where a life award would have been made to a British citizen.

If a limited award is made because of your immigration leave, you should consider appealing that decision. You must not wait until the award runs out.

10. STATUTORY SICK PAY AND STATUTORY MATERNITY PAY

If you are a recognised refugee, the rules for SSP and SMP are the same as those for British citizens (see p147).

11. THE SOCIAL FUND

There is no special treatment for recognised refugees in the social fund rules. The rules are the same as those for British citizens (see p148).

CHAPTER FOURTEEN

Exceptional leave to remain

The benefits covered in this chapter are:

1. Income support (IS) (p176)
2. Income-based jobseeker's allowance (JSA) (p176)
3. Housing benefit (HB) and council tax benefit (CTB) (p176)
4. Child benefit and guardian's allowance (p177)
5. Family credit (FC) and disability working allowance (DWA) (p177)
6. Short-term contributory benefits (p177)
7. Retirement pensions and widows' benefits (p178)
8. Industrial injuries benefits (p178)
9. Disability benefits (p178)
10. Statutory sick pay (SSP) and statutory maternity pay (SMP) (p179)
11. The social fund (p179)

This chapter deals with benefits for people who have 'exceptional leave to remain' (ELR) – see Chapter 4. People in this situation are always given the same special treatment under UK benefit rules as that given to people recorded by the Home Office as refugees. ELR is not defined in the benefit rules. It is *not* limited to people who were refused refugee status.

People with ELR cannot use EC law to backdate certain benefits in the same way as a refugee.[1] However, you may be able to use these rules if you are not a national of any country – ie, stateless. If this applies, you should seek advice.

ELR includes leave to enter.[2] If you apply for further leave (of any kind) before your ELR runs out, your ELR is automatically extended until a decision is made on that application (this is called VOLO leave). If the application is refused, your ELR continues for a further 28 days. For details, see p28.

Example
Dogan has had ELR as a failed asylum-seeker for six years. His elderly mother, Sahnuz, arrives in the UK and is given leave to enter exceptionally as his dependant. Just before completing seven years' ELR, Dogan applies for and is given indefinite leave to remain. Sahnuz is given leave in line with

Dogan – ie, indefinite leave to remain. Neither Dogan nor Sahnuz are entitled to leave under the immigration rules so both still have ELR. This means that, even though she has been in the UK for less than one year, Sahnuz has indefinite leave to remain exceptionally outside the immigration rules.

Normally, ELR is given on the understanding that you can have recourse to public funds. *However, a benefit claim may affect the immigration status of some people with exceptional leave.* This applies if your leave was given on the understanding that you would not have recourse to public funds. For example, you are given leave to remain as an artist even though you entered on a student visa. Because the Home Office waived the rule that you should have an artist visa, your leave is exceptional. However, even though your leave is exceptional, it has been given on the understanding that you would maintain and accommodate yourself without recourse to public funds (unless that condition has also been waived). *A benefit claim could lead to a refusal to extend leave, or your current leave could be taken away, on the ground that your leave was obtained by deception.* If this could apply to you, take expert advice before claiming any public funds benefit.

Showing that you have exceptional leave to remain

If you have limited ELR as a failed asylum-seeker, the Home Office will have written to you stating that the Secretary of State has decided 'exceptionally to give you leave' or 'to give exceptional leave to remain'. This letter (Gen 19, see Appendix 4) should be enough. This should also be enough if you have been given indefinite leave to remain after completing seven years.

If you have ELR as the dependant of a failed asylum-seeker you may not have such a letter. The benefits authorities may be persuaded if you can show your relative's letter and show that your leave was granted in line with that of your relative.

If you have other sorts of ELR it may be difficult to persuade the benefits authorities. If the Home Office stated in writing when giving leave that it is exceptional, this should be enough for the benefits authorities. If the Home Office did not state that in writing, you should try to produce any correspondence with the Home Office before leave was granted showing that it knew that you did not meet the requirements of the rules, and thus that your leave must be exceptional. The Home Office could also be asked to state whether your leave was exceptional and, if not, under which part of the immigration rules it was granted. *If the Home Office has not already accepted in writing that your leave is exceptional, seek expert advice before approaching them or claiming to have ELR, because your immigration status may be affected.* If you have VOLO leave (see p28) you can show this by showing evidence of your most recent grant of ELR and of the date you applied for further leave.

The benefits authorities are often unclear about ELR. They can confuse it with 'indefinite leave to remain'. This is sometimes made worse by taking advice from Home Office staff who are rarely aware of all the different Home Office policies and practices about giving leave. Some Benefits Agency guidance suggests that only exceptional leave for failed asylum-seekers counts under the benefit rules.[3] This guidance is wrong because the benefit rules do not limit ELR in this way (see p174).

1. INCOME SUPPORT

You are only entitled to IS if you are in GB[4] (see p98) or temporarily absent from GB[5] (see p246).

People with ELR are exempt from the rules for persons from abroad, including the habitual residence test.[6]

The only possible exception to this exemption is where your leave was given on the understanding that you would not have recourse to public funds.[7] If this applies, you can argue that your leave was not given under the immigration rules, so you are not a person from abroad (see p175). However, if this applies to you a benefit claim may affect your immigration status (see p175).

2. INCOME-BASED JOBSEEKER'S ALLOWANCE

For contribution-based JSA, see p177.

Income-based JSA rules about who is a person from abroad are the same as those for IS (see above).[8]

3. HOUSING BENEFIT AND COUNCIL TAX BENEFIT

You are only entitled:

- to **HB** if you have accommodation in GB which you normally occupy as your home (which can include certain temporary absences) (see p251);[9]
- to **CTB** if you are liable to pay council tax for accommodation in which you reside (see p252).[10]

If you are being paid IS/income-based JSA you are not a person from abroad for HB/CTB.[11] The local authority which deals with your HB/CTB claim should not make enquiries about your immigration status or habitual residence.[12] If you are not being paid IS/income-based JSA the following rules apply.

People with ELR are exempt from the rules for persons from abroad, including the habitual residence test.[13]

The only possible exception to this exemption is where your ELR was given on the understanding that you would not have recourse to public funds.[14] If this applies, you can argue that your leave was not given under the immigration rules, so you are not a person from abroad (see p175). However, if this applies to you a benefit claim may affect your immigration status (see p175).

4. CHILD BENEFIT AND GUARDIAN'S ALLOWANCE

The rules for CB and guardian's allowance are the same as those for British citizens (see p133). You are exempt from the CB immigration condition.[15]

If your ELR was given on the understanding that you would not have recourse to public funds, your immigration status may be affected by your claim (see p175).

5. FAMILY CREDIT AND DISABILITY WORKING ALLOWANCE

If you have exceptional leave to remain, the rules for FC and DWA are the same as those for British citizens (see p138). You are exempt from the immigration conditions for FC/DWA.[16]

If your ELR was given on the understanding that you would not have recourse to public funds, your immigration status may be affected by your claim (see p175).

6. SHORT-TERM CONTRIBUTORY BENEFITS

The rules for contribution-based JSA, incapacity benefit and maternity allowance are the same as those for British citizens (see p139). The JSA immigration condition only applies to income-based JSA.[17]

7. RETIREMENT PENSIONS AND WIDOWS' BENEFITS

The rules for Category A, B, C and D retirement pensions, widow's allowance, widowed mother's allowance and widow's pension are the same as those for British citizens (see p140).

8. INDUSTRIAL INJURIES BENEFITS

The rules for disablement benefit, reduced earnings allowance, retirement allowance, constant attendance allowance and exceptionally severe disablement allowance are the same as those for British citizens (see p142).

9. DISABILITY BENEFITS

The rules for DLA, AA, ICA and SDA are the same as those for British citizens (see p145). You are exempt from the immigration conditions for those benefits.[18]

If your ELR was given on the understanding that you would not have recourse to public funds, your immigration status may be affected by your claim (see p175).

How long benefit is awarded for

Benefits are awarded for an indefinite period or, where that is not appropriate, a limited period.[19] Where a medical condition is permanent, awards of DLA, AA and SDA are often made for life. Benefits Agency guidance suggests that people with limited ELR should not get life awards. We believe this may be wrong in the cases of people who are granted exceptional leave to remain under the failed asylum-seeker policy (see below). In other cases, unless the Home Office has stated in writing the circumstances in which leave will be extended, it will be difficult to argue that the award should not be limited, except for SDA (see below).

When a person is given ELR under the failed asylum-seekers policy, s/he is normally given leave in stages of one year, three years, and then indefinite leave to remain (see p52). Benefits Agency guidance states that any award of DLA/AA/ICA/SDA should be limited to the date your current immigration leave is due to run out.[20] If your award is limited in this manner, you will need to claim that benefit again at the end of the award, and again show that you meet all the benefit conditions, including those about disability. This places you in a worse position than a British citizen who would have been given a life award (or one longer than your period of leave), especially since her/his benefit could only be withdrawn if the Benefits Agency showed that the disability conditions were no longer satisfied.

We believe the Benefits Agency approach is wrong because:

- for **SDA**, once the claimant satisfies the immigration condition, s/he is treated as satisfying it for the rest of that period of incapacity, so there is no change of circumstances if leave does run out;[21]
- for **other benefits**, there will only be a change of circumstance at the end of the leave if the person does not apply for an extension in time, which is unlikely, or if an extension is refused. Otherwise you will continue to have ELR. Home Office practice in the case of failed asylum-seekers is almost always to extend exceptional leave. In the very rare cases where extensions have been refused the person had visited their own country or had claimed and been refused asylum again. Unless this applies to you, the end of your present period of leave is not a future change of circumstances because your leave will in practice be extended;
- the Benefits Agency can easily review your award if leave is not extended, so there is no good reason to limit the award to the end of your existing leave.

If a limited award is made because of your limited leave, consider appealing that decision. You should not wait until the award runs out.

10. STATUTORY SICK PAY AND STATUTORY MATERNITY PAY

The rules for SSP and SMP are the same as for British citizens (see p147).

11. THE SOCIAL FUND

There is no special treatment for people with exceptional leave to remain in the social fund rules. The rules are the same as those for British citizens (see p148).

CHAPTER FIFTEEN

Limited leave to remain

The benefits covered in this chapter are:

1. Income support (IS) (p181)
2. Income-based jobseeker's allowance (JSA) (p187)
3. Housing benefit (HB) and council tax benefit (CTB) (p192)
4. Child benefit and guardian's allowance (p193)
5. Family credit (FC) and disability working allowance (DWA) (p195)
6. Short-term contributory benefits (p197)
7. Retirement pensions and widows' benefits (p198)
8. Industrial injuries benefits (p199)
9. Disability benefits (p199)
10. Statutory sick pay (SSP) and statutory maternity pay (SMP) (p201)
11. The social fund (p201)

This chapter deals with people who have limited leave to remain in the UK. The most common types of leave to remain are for spouses of people settled here, students and visitors. There are special rules if:

- you are a **refugee**, even if your leave to remain is not because the Home Office recognises you as a refugee (see Chapter 13); *or*
- you have **exceptional leave to remain**, even if your leave was not described as exceptional by the Home Office (see Chapter 14).

Who has limited leave to remain?

You have limited leave to remain if you are in the UK and you have been given leave to enter by an immigration officer or leave to remain by the Home Office and there is a time limit on that leave. This is usually done by a stamp on your passport or a letter. For details, see p25 and 28.

Temporary admission is *not* leave to remain. Temporary admission is given by a letter. If you have temporary admission you are not in the UK with limited leave to remain (see Chapter 16).

In this chapter, limited leave includes **VOLO leave** (for full details see p28). Even if your leave stamp has expired, you still have limited leave to remain if an application for extension of leave was made before or on the date of that stamp. This leave continues until 28 days after your leave application is refused or withdrawn. If the application is granted and you are given further leave, that leave is effective from the date it is given. Any conditions of your leave continue to apply as long as you have VOLO leave.[1]

If your application for an extension was made after the date your leave expired, then you do *not* have leave to remain. You are an **overstayer,** see Chapter 16).

If the time-limit on your leave to remain has been removed in writing, you have **indefinite leave to remain** (see Chapter 12).

If you are an **EU/EEA national** you are very unlikely to have leave to remain. That is because EU/EEA nationals arriving in the UK normally have an EC right to enter the UK and do not need leave to enter or remain,[2] so the Home Office never gives EU/EEA nationals leave to enter.[3] For the rules for EU/EEA nationals, see Part 4.

When **you leave the UK** your leave ends.[4] This does not apply if you remain in the 'common travel area' – Republic of Ireland, Channel Islands, Isle of Man and UK or travelling between those places (see p3).[5]

I. INCOME SUPPORT

Most people with limited leave are not entitled to IS (or to income-based JSA) because of the persons from abroad rules *or* because the conditions of their leave to remain mean that they cannot meet the JSA rules about availability for work.

However, some people with limited leave may be entitled to one of the following:

* **ordinary rate IS** if:
  – you are *not* a person from abroad (see p182) *and*
  – you fall into one of the groups who can claim IS (see p182); *or*
* **income-based JSA** if:
  – you are *not* a person from abroad (see p182); *and*
  – there is no condition on employment as part of your leave (see p189); *or*
* **urgent cases IS/income-based JSA.** This is paid at a lower rate than ordinary IS/income-based JSA. If you are entitled you can always claim IS instead of JSA; *or*
* **income-based JSA hardship payments,** but only for special groups (see p190) who are not persons from abroad. Hardship payments are less than urgent cases IS/income-based JSA.

Who can claim IS?

You can claim IS if you are:

- a single parent of a child aged 16 or under; *or*
- incapable of work; *or*
- aged 60 or over; *or*
- temporarily looking after
  - a child because the person who normally looks after the child is either ill or is temporarily absent from home; *or*
  - your partner or child who is ill; *or*
- regularly or substantially engaged in caring for a person who:
  - receives AA or higher/middle rate DLA; *or*
  - has claimed AA/DLA but that claim has not been determined.

Other people can also claim. For full details, see CPAG's *National Welfare Benefits Handbook*.[6]

Deciding what to claim

You could end up with *less benefit* by arguing that you are *not* a person from abroad. However, in some cases you may be able to increase your entitlement this way.

If the only reason you are not entitled to urgent cases IS is that your income or capital is too high, you should consider arguing that you are not a person from abroad. This is only worth it if you would be entitled to ordinary rate IS/income-based JSA. You should always take advice first.

If you are entitled to urgent cases IS and have no income or capital, you should *only* argue that you are not a person from abroad if you are confident that you are entitled to ordinary IS/income-based JSA instead. If you argue successfully that you are not a person from abroad, but fail the normal conditions for IS/income-based JSA, you will be left without either benefit.

If you are not entitled to IS, your partner may be able to claim instead (see p131).

Persons from abroad

You are a person from abroad if:

- your leave was given under an immigration rule which requires no recourse to public funds (see p183); *or*
- you are a sponsored immigrant under the benefit rules (see p153); *or*
- you are not habitually resident in the UK, Ireland, the Channel Islands or the Isle of Man (see pp131).

There are exceptions to these three rules (see pp184-86).

You are *not* a person from abroad if you left Montserrat after 1

November 1995 because of a volcanic eruption.[7] You do *not* have to be a national of Montserrat to use this rule. If you are exempt from the person from abroad rules because of this rule, you may have to claim income-based JSA instead of IS.

Even if you are a person from abroad, you may be entitled to urgent cases IS (see p186).

No recourse to public funds

You are a person from abroad for IS purposes if your leave was given under an immigration rule which requires you not to have recourse to public funds (see below) *and* none of the exceptions to that rule apply (see p184).[8]

When deciding whether your leave is 'no recourse to public funds leave', it is the type of leave that you were given that counts, *not* what the Home Office or the Benefits Agency now says about your status.

Limited leave given to adults normally requires that there be no recourse to public funds. The most important exception is family members of a recognised refugee who are given leave in line with her/him. This may not apply if the refugee had indefinite leave at the time the family member is granted leave. For full details of all exceptions, see p57. If your leave is one of the exceptions, your limited leave does *not* mean that you are a person from abroad. This remains the case if you apply for an extension before this leave runs out (see VOLO leave – p28). However, you will still count as a person from abroad if you do not pass the habitual residence test (see p185).

Even if you are not a person from abroad, claiming IS may still affect your immigration status (see p187). In particular, if the leave stamp states that you must not have recourse to public funds (which is only possible for leave granted or changed after 1 November 1996 – see p58) *you will break the terms of your leave and commit a criminal offence even if that condition could not be attached to your leave.*[9] If this condition has been attached, you may want to ask the Home Office to remove that condition, but you should seek expert advice before making such a request.

Arguing that your leave was not given under the immigration rules

If you do not have leave under one of the exceptions (see p57), you are a person from abroad unless you can argue that you were not given leave under the immigration rules. Because of the wording of the IS rules, even if you seem to have 'no recourse to public funds leave', this may not apply for IS purposes. If you did not meet one of the requirements of the relevant immigration rules at the time leave was given, your leave does not qualify as 'no recourse to public funds leave' *under IS rules*. This is because the IS rules refer to leave *given in accordance* with the immigration rules. If you did not meet the requirements of the relevant rules, your leave is not in accordance with them. This applies even if the immigration stamp refers to public funds. You should also be exempt from the habitual residence test as a person with exceptional leave to remain (see p176) and from the sponsored immigrant rule (see p155).

If you use this argument, the Benefits Agency is almost certain to tell the Home Office that you are claiming public funds (see Chapter 7). The Home Office may try to take your leave away on the ground that it was obtained by deception (see p29). Because of this, *you should not use this argument unless you have a written record proving that the Home Office/entry clearance officer knew that you did not meet the requirements of the immigration rules.* Proof includes a letter from the Home Office agreeing to waive one of the immigration rules, and a letter from you or your adviser, which you know the Home Office received before granting leave, stating that you do not meet one of the rules.

Claiming IS may affect your immigration position in other ways, see p187.

Exceptions to no recourse to public funds
Even if you have 'no recourse to public funds leave', you are *not* a person from abroad because of that leave if:[10]

- you are a national of Cyprus,[11] Malta or Turkey; *and*
- you have limited leave, including VOLO leave (see p180).

Despite this exception, some nationals of Malta or Turkey with VOLO leave may count as persons from abroad.[12] This rule is unclear, but we believe you cannot use this exception if the reason that you have VOLO leave is that you applied to change the conditions of your leave.[13] You can still use this exception if you have only asked for an extension of your leave on the same conditions as your old leave. This is because the Immigration Act 1971 makes a distinction between conditions (eg, not to take employment) and limitation (ie, how long the leave is for).[14]

Even though you are entitled to claim IS, it may affect your immigration position (see p187).

Even if you are *not* a person from abroad because of this rule, you may still be a person from abroad because of the habitual residence test (see p185).

If you are not a person from abroad you may have to claim income-based JSA (see p187).

Sponsored immigrants and exceptions

For who is a sponsored immigrant under the benefit rules, see p153.

You are exempt from the sponsored immigrant rule if you have transitional protection. This transitional protection applies to more people than the definition of sponsored immigrant under the benefit rules (see p207). If you still count as a person from abroad because of your limited leave, you may be able to use this transitional protection to get urgent cases IS (see p156). If the rule about 'no recourse to public funds' does not apply to you because a requirement of the immigration rules was waived (see p183), then you can use the same argument to show that you are not a sponsored immigrant under the benefit rules (see p153).

Even if you are *not* a person from abroad because of this rule, you may still be a person from abroad under the habitual residence test (see below).

You may be entitled to urgent cases IS, see p157.

Habitual residence test

You are a person from abroad if you fail the habitual residence test (see below).[15] This means that you may still count as a person from abroad even if you have 'no recourse to public funds' leave nor are you a sponsored immigrant under the benefit rules.

The habitual residence test only applies to the IS claimant.[16] It does not apply to any partner or child for whom IS is being claimed. If you might fail the test but have a partner who is more likely to pass, s/he could claim instead, though there may be disadvantages to this (see CPAG's *National Welfare Benefits Handbook*).

You pass the habitual residence test if you are habitually resident (see p102) in the UK, Ireland, the Channel Islands or Isle of Man. If you are not habitually resident and you are not exempt (see below), you are a person from abroad.[17]

The Court of Appeal has decided that the IS habitual residence test is not outside the Secretary of State's powers under British law.[18] If you are a national of Cyprus, Malta or Turkey, the habitual residence test may break the UK's international obligations (see p103).

Exemptions from habitual residence test

You are exempt from the habitual residence test if you left Montserrat after 1 November 1995 because of a volcanic eruption.[19]

You may be exempt from the habitual residence test under EC law (see p358). This will not apply to you *unless* either you or a member of your extended family is:

- a national of an EU/EEA member state (apart from the UK); *or*
- a British citizen who has travelled to another EU/EEA member state using the right of free movement under EC law.

You are also exempt from the habitual residence test if you are a refugee (see Chapter 13) or have exceptional leave to remain (see Chapter 14).

Urgent cases rate

If you are a person from abroad, you are entitled to urgent cases IS if:[20]

- you are an asylum-seeker and other rules are met (see Chapter 17); *or*
- you are a sponsored immigrant under the benefit rules and your spon-sor(s) has/have died (see p156); *or*
- money you are usually sent from abroad has been disrupted (see below).

You are entitled to urgent cases IS even if you are a person from abroad for more than one reason. For example, if your leave is 'no recourse to public funds leave' *and* you are a sponsored immigrant, you are entitled to urgent cases IS if your sponsor dies, even though you still have the same leave.

Urgent cases IS is paid at a different rate from ordinary IS and other rules apply. For details, see p124.

Temporary disruption of funds

If you are a person from abroad with limited leave, you are entitled to urgent cases IS if:[21]

- you were expecting to be sent money from abroad but that has not happened; *and*
- there is a reasonable expectation that money will be sent in the future; *and*
- since you were last given leave to remain in the UK you have sup-ported yourself without receiving public funds (see p59) *except* where those public funds were paid because of this rule.

The maximum period during which IS can be paid under this rule is 42 days in any one period of leave.[22] This does not have to be a continuous claim, but could, for example, be for seven separate weeks. Each period of leave runs from the last grant of leave to remain (or leave to enter if this is your first period since entering the UK). It ends with the grant of the next period of leave to remain, or with the end of any VOLO leave (see p180).[23]

Examples of situations when this rule may apply are:

- disruption to the banking system in your home country;
- a collapse in exchange rates which means that your sponsor abroad

cannot immediately buy hard currency; *or*
* your sponsor abroad has financial difficulties.

You can only use this rule if you were expecting to receive money from abroad, so if your only sponsor or potential sponsor is in the UK, you cannot use this rule if their support stops. However, the rule does not say that the money which you *now* expect to receive in the future also has to be from abroad, so you could qualify because a person in the UK will give you financial support in the future.

Home Office policy is that reliance on public funds for a short period through no fault of the person concerned will not be used to refuse further leave.[24] However, even a claim for IS for a short period may mean that the Home Office will look much more closely at any application for an extension of leave and, in particular, your ability to support yourself.

Effect of public funds (including IS) on immigration status

IS is public funds under the immigration rules.[25] If you have claimed asylum, then claiming any public funds is very unlikely to affect your immigration position. In other situations, whether or not you are a person from abroad for IS purposes, *claiming public funds may mean that*:

* *The Home Office may refuse you further leave to remain, if that leave would require 'no recourse to public funds'*. Home Office policy is that short periods of reliance on public funds will not normally lead to refusal of further leave. However, it may affect the Home Office's treatment of you. For example, if you claim public funds during your one year's leave as the spouse of a person settled in the UK, at the end of that year you may be given a further year's leave before indefinite leave is considered, instead of immediate indefinite leave.
* *If your leave was given after 1 November 1996 and the stamp states that you must not have recourse to public funds, you break the terms of your leave and commit a criminal offence by claiming IS. Any action is very unlikely, especially if your claim is covered by the Home Office policy.*[26]

Because of these problems, you should weigh up the risks and advantages of claiming public funds before you make a claim. If possible, take expert advice before claiming.

2. INCOME-BASED JOBSEEKER'S ALLOWANCE

For contribution-based JSA, see p197.

It is difficult for people with limited leave to meet the normal rules for income-based JSA, so you should always check to see if you may be entitled to IS instead (see p181).

Income-based JSA is public funds under the immigration rules.[27] *The possible effects of claiming income-based JSA on your immigration position are the same as those for IS (see p187).*

The rules about who is a person from abroad are the same as for IS (see p182).[28] If you are a person from abroad with limited leave you are not entitled to income-based JSA. This is because the only persons from abroad who can get income-based JSA are asylum-seekers under the benefit rules, and if you have limited leave to remain you will not count unless you claimed asylum after a fundamental change declaration (see p227).

If you are *not* a person from abroad, your entitlement to income-based JSA depends on whether or not your leave has a prohibition/restriction on employment (an employment condition).

Leave with an employment condition

Your limited leave may have a prohibition or restriction on working (see below). This may have been overridden by the Home Office (see p212).

If you have a prohibition or restriction on working which has not been overridden, you cannot meet the usual JSA condition that you are immediately able to work as an employed earner.[29] This means that you can *only* be entitled to JSA if:

- you are treated as available for work (see p189). This is very unlikely to be useful for people with an employment condition; *or*
- you are entitled to hardship payments (see p190). This is different from urgent cases rate.

Who has leave with an employment condition?

Conditions of your immigration leave can only be imposed in writing.[30] If you do not have a written employment condition as part of your current leave (or your last leave if you have VOLO leave – see p28), then there is no employment condition on your leave. This applies even if an employment condition is normally imposed with the type of leave which you have. The only exceptions to these rules are:

- you were given an unreadable leave stamp by an immigration officer. If this applies, you are treated as having been given leave to enter for six months with a prohibition on taking employment (see p25);[31]
- you entered the UK from another part of the common travel area (Ireland, the Channel Islands or Isle of Man) without being given written leave (see p3). If this applies, you *may be* treated as having been given limited leave to enter for a limited period with a prohibition on taking employment.[32]

There are two types of employment condition:

- **prohibition** – the stamp reads 'employment prohibited' or 'condition that holder does not enter employment paid or unpaid'. This is usually imposed on visitors (including visitors in transit) and prospective students (for full list, see pp39-43 and Appendix 5); *and*
- **restriction** – the stamp reads 'condition that holder does not enter or change employment paid or unpaid without the consent of the Secretary of State for Employment'. There are two groups affected:
  - people who have a work permit or permit for training/work experience from the Overseas Labour Service who have permission to work in the job referred to in the permit; *and*
  - students, *au pairs*, seasonal workers, working holiday-makers and others (for full list, see pp39-43 and Appendix 5) who must approach the JobCentre for permission to take any and each job (for details of this procedure, see JCWI *Handbook*, 1997 edn, p169).

Treated as available for work

Under JSA rules, certain people are treated as available for work for short periods. In theory, you can use these rules even though your immigration leave means that you cannot take employment. In practice, because a jobseeker's agreement is normally required, these rules are very unlikely to help anyone who has a condition on employment. It may be possible to be entitled for a few weeks before the agreement interview by using the rules which treat some people as available for work, actively seeking work and as exempt from needing an agreement.[33] For details of these rules, see CPAG's *Jobseeker's Allowance Handbook*.

Leave with no employment condition

For employment conditions, see p32. The most important types of leave with *no* condition on employment are:

- spouse of a person settled in the UK;
- spouse of a person with limited leave (eg, student, work permit holder);
- private servant in a diplomatic household; *and*
- Commonwealth citizen with UK ancestry.

For full details of the types of leave with no conditions on employment, see p39-43.

If you are *not* a person from abroad (see p188) and your leave has no condition on employment, you are entitled to income-based JSA as long as you meet the normal rules for entitlement. The most important of these are that you:[34]

- are not in full-time employment;
- are available for and actively seeking employment; *and*
- have made a jobseeker's agreement.

For full details of these and the other rules, see CPAG's *Jobseeker's Allowance Handbook*.

Claiming JSA may break the conditions of your immigration leave and have other effects on your immigration status (see p187).

Hardship payments

Hardship payments of JSA are different from urgent cases income-based JSA. They are intended for people who are not available for work, where a vulnerable person will suffer hardship if JSA is not paid. If you are entitled to a hardship payment, you do not have to be available for and actively seeking work *or* have signed a jobseeker's agreement.[35] This means that someone who has limited leave with an employment condition, but is *not* a person from abroad, can be entitled to a hardship payment of JSA. For details of hardship payments and how to claim them, see CPAG's *Jobseeker's Allowance Handbook*.

The hardship payment rules apply to people who are just outside the rules for IS. You are a person in hardship if:[36]

- you are pregnant or your partner is pregnant (claim IS if you are more than 29 weeks pregnant); *or*
- you are a lone parent of a child aged 17-18 (claim IS if you care for a child aged 16 or under); *or*
- you have limited capacity because of a chronic medical condition and that condition has lasted for at least 26 weeks (claim IS if you are incapable of work); *or*
- you or your partner devotes a considerable portion of the week to caring for a person who:
  - receives AA or higher/middle rate DLA; *or*
  - has claimed AA/DLA but that claim has not been determined
  (claim IS if you are regularly or substantially engaged in caring for such a person).

Unless JSA is paid, you are *only* a person in hardship if:

- in the case of a person who has claimed or is receiving AA/DLA, the carer would not be able to continue caring; *or*
- the vulnerable person will suffer hardship.[37] The vulnerable person is the pregnant woman, child or chronically sick person mentioned in the rule above. If you want to use the above rules, you must *also* show that as a chronically sick person, your health would decline further within two weeks.

When considering whether a person would suffer hardship, the rules require the adjudication officer to take into account:

- yours or any partner's potential entitlement to the disability premium if the other conditions for JSA were met (for disability premium, see CPAG's *Jobseeker's Allowance Handbook*);
- your potential entitlement to a disabled child premium for a child living with you if the other conditions for JSA were met (for disabled child premium, see CPAG's *Jobseeker's Allowance Handbook*);
- the resources available to you or any partner, including resources available to (either of) you from other members of the household;
- the short-fall of those resources below the amount of any hardship payment which would be made;
- any substantial risk that essential items, including food, clothing, heating and accommodation, will cease to be available (or will only be available at considerably reduced levels) to you or any partner or children living with you;
- the length of time the situation will continue.

If you have applied for asylum and are awaiting a Home Office decision, you should ask the adjudication officer to take into account:

- your fear of going back to your own country and the reasons for that fear;
- that you need money to telephone and write to the Home Office and/or your advisers and to attend appointments with them;
- any need for money to telephone and write to your family and others abroad to get information for your case and to keep in contact;
- that the Home Office can take years to make a decision on an asylum claim.

Claiming JSA may break the conditions of your immigration leave and have other effects on your immigration status (see p187).

Amount of hardship payments

Hardship payments are worked out in the same way as normal income-based JSA (see CPAG's *Jobseeker's Allowance Handbook*) except that the applicable amount is reduced by:[38]

- 20 per cent of the appropriate personal allowance for a person of your age, if you, any partner or any child you are responsible for is pregnant or seriously ill; *or*
- otherwise, 40 per cent of that allowance.

3. HOUSING BENEFIT AND COUNCIL TAX BENEFIT

HB/CTB are public funds under the immigration rules.[39] *The possible effects of claiming HB/CTB on your immigration position are the same as those for IS (see p187).*

The HB/CTB rules are very like the IS rules, but with some differences. There is no urgent cases rate for HB/CTB – the categories of people covered by urgent cases rate get normal HB/CTB.

If you are being paid IS/income-based JSA you are not a person from abroad for HB/CTB.[40] The local authority which deals with your HB/CTB claim should not make enquiries about your immigration status or habitual residence.[41] If you are not being paid IS/income-based JSA the following rules apply.

You are *only* entitled to HB/CTB if:

- you are *not* a person from abroad (see below); *and*
- for **HB**, you have accommodation in GB which you normally occupy as your home (which can include temporary absences – see p251),[42] or for **CTB**, you are liable to pay council tax for accommodation in which you reside (see p252).[43]

If you do not meet these rules, you are not entitled to HB/CTB.[44]

Persons from abroad

You are a person from abroad if:

- your leave was given under an immigration rule which requires no recourse to public funds (see p183)[45] *unless:*[46]
  - you are a national of Cyprus,[47] Malta or Turkey with limited leave (which includes VOLO leave, see p28);[48] *or*
  - you have a temporary disruption of funds (see p186); *or*
- you are a sponsored immigrant under the benefit rules[49] (see p153) *unless* your sponsor has died (see p159);[50] *or*
- you are not habitually resident (see p102) in the UK, Ireland, the Channel Islands or Isle of Man *unless:*[51]
  - you have a temporary disruption of funds (see p186); *or*
  - one of the habitual residence exemptions applies (see p185).

You are exempt from all these rules if:

- you are an asylum-seeker and other rules are met (see Chapter 17); *or*
- you left Montserrat after 1 November 1995 because of a volcanic eruption.[52] You do *not* have to be a national of Montserrat to use this rule.

4. CHILD BENEFIT AND GUARDIAN'S ALLOWANCE

CB is public funds under the immigration rules.[53] *If your leave requires you to have no recourse to public funds (see Chapter 5), claiming or receiving CB can affect your immigration position (see p187).* Guardian's allowance is not public funds, but cannot be paid without a current award of CB (see p137).

Child benefit

People with limited leave to remain are not entitled to CB (but see below for exemptions and transitional protection). This is because you need leave to remain in the UK.[54] People with indefinite leave to remain are exempt from this rule (see Chapter 12).

If you are exempt or have transitional protection, you must still meet the other residence rules to be entitled to CB (see p133).

Exemptions from the immigration condition

You are exempt from the CB immigration condition if:[55]

- you are an EU/EEA national (see glossary);
- you are the family member of an EU/EEA national, including a British citizen. This includes a partner and may also include adult children, parents and other relatives (see p355). This means that the parent of a British citizen child is exempt for CB claims for any child;
- you have been recognised as a refugee by the Home Office (see Chapter 13);
- you have exceptional leave to remain (Chapter 14). This is not limited to people given leave under the failed asylum-seeker policy, but covers anyone who did not qualify for leave to remain under the immigration rules, but was still given leave (see p174);
- you are a national of Algeria, Morocco, Slovenia or Tunisia (or possibly Turkey – see p380) *and* you are lawfully working in GB.[56] 'Lawfully working' is not defined in the benefit rules. We consider that you are working lawfully if your work is not in breach of a condition attached to your leave to remain;
- you are a family member (see p355) of a person who is
  - a national of Algeria, Morocco, Slovenia or Tunisia (or possibly Turkey – see p380); *and*
  - lawfully working (see above) in GB;
  and you are living with that person; *or*
- in the past you have lived in a country to which a reciprocal agreement

about CB applies (see Part 5). This can apply regardless of your nationality.

If you were being paid CB on 6 October 1996 *and*:

- one (or more) of the above exceptions applies to you; *and*
- that (or those) exception(s) stops applying to you; *and*
- the award of CB has *not* been reviewed since 6 October 1996 (eg, because of a new child or a child left school)

then you remain entitled to CB under the rules for existing claimants (see below).

Transitional protection for pre-October 1996 claimants

If none of the exceptions above applies to you, but you were being paid CB on 6 October 1996, the CB immigration condition does not apply to you and you remain entitled to CB.[57] Your entitlement continues until your CB is reviewed by an adjudication officer.[58] A review can only be carried out if there is a ground for review because:[59]

- your last award of CB was made in ignorance of a material fact, based on a mistake of material fact or there was a mistake of law; *or*
- there is a change of circumstances after your last award of CB.

Because the October 1996 changes do not come into effect for an existing claimant until a review is carried out, those changes are *not* a relevant change of circumstance enabling a review to be carried out. This practice may be the subject of a judicial review in 1997 (see also p200). If your award is reviewed in this way, you should ask an advice agency to contact CPAG.

You do not have to tell the Benefits Agency about your immigration status unless asked. A change in your immigration status (eg, your leave expires) is not a relevant change of circumstance.[60]

Transitional protection continues until the date any review is carried out, *not* the date of the change of circumstances which led to the review.

You have a duty to report any change of circumstances which could affect the amount of your benefit to the Benefits Agency.[61] If you sign the order book without disclosing a relevant change of circumstance about which you know, *you commit a criminal offence* (for details see CPAG's *Rights Guide to Non-Means-Tested Benefits*).[62]

There may be a delay in reporting a change of circumstance which would normally increase the amount of CB – eg, the birth of a new child. If this happens, your CB will only stop from the date on which the review is carried out. There is no overpayment of CB, unless for another reason you were not entitled to CB before the review. Your CB entitlement cannot be changed on the review for the period before the review date, because transitional protection from the October 1996 changes applies to the period up to the date on which the review is carried out.[63]

Guardian's allowance

You are not entitled to guardian's allowance unless you are entitled to CB, because entitlement to CB is a condition of entitlement to guardian's allowance.[64]

If you are entitled to CB only because you are a pre-October 1996 claimant (see p194), you can still claim guardian's allowance for the first time after 6 October 1996. A review of an award of guardian's allowance does not affect your entitlement to CB but, if the change of circumstances is relevant to both guardian's allowance and CB, you will lose both benefits from the date of the review.

5. FAMILY CREDIT AND DISABILITY WORKING ALLOWANCE

People with limited leave to remain are not entitled to FC/DWA because of the immigration condition for those benefits (but for exemption and transitional protection, see below). This is because your right to reside in the UK is subject to a limitation.[65] This does not apply to people with indefinite leave to remain (see Chapter 12).

Even if you are exempt or have transitional protection, you must still meet the other residence rules to be entitled to FC/DWA (see p138).

The FC/DWA claim form asks for your nationality. If you are not an EU/EEA national, the Benefits Agency is likely to ask you for further details of your immigration status (see Chapter 7). If you are entitled but a decision or payment is delayed because of these enquiries, you should ask an advice centre to contact CPAG.

FC/DWA are public funds under the immigration rules.[66] If your leave requires you to have no recourse to public funds (see Chapter 5), claiming or receiving FC/DWA can affect your immigration position. Because claiming FC/DWA means that you are working as well as claiming public funds, a claim is likely to lead to close Home Office attention to any request for further leave. For other effects of claiming public funds, see p187.

If the immigration status of your partner and any children for whom FC would be claimed would not be affected by an FC claim (eg, a person with indefinite leave to remain), your partner could claim instead. The amount of FC for a couple is the same as for a single parent, so your membership of the family does not lead to additional recourse to public funds. This means that your immigration status ought not to be affected by a claim (see p62).

Exemption from immigration condition

You are exempt from the immigration condition for FC/DWA if:[67]

- you are an EU/EEA national (see glossary);
- you are the family member of an EU/EEA national, including a British citizen. This includes a partner and may also include adult children, parents and other relatives (see p355). This means that the parent of a British citizen child is exempt for FC/DWA;
- you have been recognised as a refugee by the Home Office (see Chapter 13);
- you have exceptional leave to remain (see Chapter 14). This is not limited to people given leave under the failed asylum-seeker policy, but covers anyone who did not qualify for leave to remain under the immigration rules, but was still given leave (see p174);
- you are a national of Algeria, Morocco, Slovenia or Tunisia (or possibly Turkey – see p380) *and* you are lawfully working in GB.[68] 'Lawfully working' is not defined in the benefit rules. We consider that you are working lawfully if your work is not in breach of a condition attached to your leave to remain;
- you are a family member (see p355) of a person who is:
  - a national of Algeria, Morocco, Slovenia or Tunisia (or possibly Turkey – see p380); *and*
  - lawfully working (see above) in GB;

  and you are living with that person.

If you are a national of a country which is a party to the Fourth ACP (Africa, Caribbean, Pacific) EEC Convention (see p380) *and* you are lawfully working in the UK *and* none of these exemptions apply, you may be exempt from the immigration condition under EC law.[69] If this may apply to you, ask an advice agency to contact CPAG.

Transitional protection for pre-February 1996 claimants

If none of the exceptions above applies, but you were being paid FC before 5 February 1996, the immigration condition does not apply to you until your FC award is reviewed by an adjudication officer.[70] The same applies for DWA if you were being paid DWA.[71] You are not protected if you swap between FC and DWA (or the other way around).[72]

Benefits Agency guidance suggests that transitional protection only applies if FC/DWA was being paid on 4 February 1996 and that it continues only until the end of the 26-week period of the FC/DWA award.[73] We believe that the guidance may be wrong and that you do not have to be in receipt of FC on 4 February 1996 to have transitional protection. It is enough if, at any time before 5 February 1996, you were entitled to FC in your own name. This is because regulations giving transitional protection usually state that the claimant must have been entitled on a particular date.[74] The regulations giving transitional protection for FC/DWA apply if you were entitled 'before the coming into force of these regulations'. They do not require entitlement on a particular date or '*immediately* before the coming into force'.

The rules say that this protection continues 'until your entitlement to FC/DWA is reviewed'. The regulations do not state that the transitional protection ends at the end of the FC/DWA claim as transitional protection regulations usually do.[75] A renewal claim for FC/DWA does not cause a review, so protection does not end at the end of an award, but continues until an award is reviewed. The Benefits Agency approach would mean that the transitional protection makes no difference because FC/DWA limits on reviews[76] mean that the award current on 5 February 1996 is not affected anyway. The protection only has a point if it applies to subsequent renewal claims. Several tribunals have accepted this argument and allowed appeals.[77]

These rules mean that a person who was paid FC/DWA at any time before 5 February 1996 is protected from the new rules for any claim made after 4 February 1996, until an award of FC/DWA is reviewed.

6. SHORT-TERM CONTRIBUTORY BENEFITS

These benefits are contribution-based JSA, incapacity benefit and maternity allowance. The rules are the same as for British citizens (see p139), though the conditions of your leave may mean that you do not meet these rules for JSA (see p198). There are no special rules for people with limited leave. Claiming these benefits may affect your immigration status (see below).

Effect of claiming on immigration status

Contribution-based JSA, incapacity benefit and maternity allowance are *not* public funds under the immigration rules.[78] The Home Office application forms for extension of leave refer to JSA as public funds.[79] This is wrong because only income-based JSA is public funds.

However, to be entitled to these benefits you must have paid contributions as an employed or self-employed person (see CPAG's *Rights*

Guide to Non-Means-Tested Benefits). A claim for these benefits may lead to the Home Office being told that you have been working. If you worked in breach of your immigration conditions, there is a risk of prosecution for that breach.[80] *Even if you had permission to work, a claim may cause problems if the Home Office is informed. Any request for further leave may be looked at more closely to see if you can support yourself without recourse to public funds. If you were a student when you worked, the Home Office may check that your work was only vacation or part-time work. If it was not, further leave as a student could be refused.*

Meeting the usual rules for contribution-based JSA

The 'person from abroad' rules for income-based JSA do *not* apply to contribution-based JSA.[81] However, because of the normal rules for JSA, your entitlement to contribution-based JSA depends on which of the three groups below you fall into. The rules for these groups are the same as for income-based JSA. The three groups are:

- you have limited leave of some sort (the conditions do not matter) and the Home Office has given you written permission to take any type of work (see p212); *or*
- you have limited leave with a prohibition or restriction on employment (an employment condition) (see p188); *or*
- you have limited leave with no prohibition or restriction on employment (no employment condition) (see p189).

7. RETIREMENT PENSIONS AND WIDOWS' BENEFITS

The rules for Category A, B, C and D retirement pensions, widow's allowance, widowed mother's allowance and widow's pension are the same as those for British citizens (see p140). There are no special rules for people with limited leave.

These benefits are *not* public funds under the immigration rules.[82] However, to be entitled to these benefits you (or your spouse) must have paid contributions as an employed or self-employed person (for details, see CPAG's *Rights Guide to Non-Means-Tested Benefits*). If this means that you have worked in the UK, a claim may affect your immigration status, in the same way as a claim for a short-term contributory benefit (see p197).

8. INDUSTRIAL INJURIES BENEFITS

The rules for disablement benefit, reduced earnings allowance, retirement allowance, constant attendance allowance and exceptionally severe disablement allowance are the same as those for British citizens (see p142). There are no special rules for people with limited leave.

These benefits are *not* public funds under the immigration rules.[83] However, to be entitled to these benefits you must normally have worked in the UK. This means a claim may affect your immigration status, in the same way as a claim for a short-term contributory benefit (see p197).

9. DISABILITY BENEFITS

These benefits are DLA, AA, ICA and SDA. People with limited leave to remain are not entitled to these benefits because of the immigration condition for them (but see below for exemption and existing claimants). That is because the right to reside in the UK is subject to a limitation.[84] This does not apply to people with indefinite leave to remain (see Chapter 12).

Even if you are exempt or have transitional protection, you must still meet the other residence rules (see p145) for DLA, AA, ICA or SDA.

DLA, AA, ICA and SDA are public funds under the immigration rules.[85] *If your leave requires you to have no recourse to public funds (see p183, claiming or receiving these benefits can affect your immigration position, in the same way as a claim for IS (see p187).*

Exceptions to immigration condition

You are exempt from the immigration condition for DLA/AA/SDA/ICA if:[86]

- you are an EU/EEA national (see glossary);
- you are the family member of an EU/EEA national, including a British citizen. This includes a partner and may also include adult children, parents and other relatives (see p355). This means that the parent of a British citizen child is exempt;
- you have been recognised as a refugee by the Home Office (see Chapter 13);
- you have exceptional leave to remain (see Chapter 14). This is not limited to people given leave under the failed asylum-seeker policy, but covers anyone who did not qualify for leave to remain under the immigration rules, but was given leave anyway;
- you are a national of Algeria, Morocco, Slovenia or Tunisia (or

possibly Turkey – see p380) *and* you are lawfully working (see p193) in GB;[87]
- you are a family member (see p355) of a person who is:
  - a national of Algeria, Morocco, Slovenia or Tunisia (or possibly Turkey – see p380); *and*
  - lawfully working (see p190) in GB;

  and you are living with that person;
- for DLA/AA, in the past you have lived in the Isle of Man, Jersey or Guernsey (or, for AA only, Norway) and a reciprocal agreement about DLA/AA applies to you (see Part 5). This can apply regardless of your nationality.

Transitional protection for pre-February 1996 claimants

If none of the above exceptions applies, but you were being paid one of these benefits before 5 February 1996, the immigration condition does not apply to you for that benefit until that award is reviewed by an adjudication officer.[88]

Benefits Agency guidance suggests that this protection only applies if the benefit was being paid on 4 February 1996, and only continues until the end of the benefit award.[89] We believe that the guidance may be wrong and that you do not have to be in receipt of the benefit on 4 February 1996 to have transitional protection. It is enough if, at any time before 5 February 1996, you were entitled to that benefit in your own name. We consider that protection continues after the end of any award to any renewal or further claims you may make, unless and until a review is carried out. For details see the equivalent FC/DWA rule on p196.

Transitional protection ends when a review is carried out. The Benefits Agency has now applied for reviews in many DLA/AA cases, on the ground that the February 1996 change in the law counts as a change of circumstances. We consider that this is wrong because:

- the February 1996 changes do not come into effect for an existing claimant until a review is carried out; *so*
- those changes are *not* a relevant change of circumstance enabling a review to be carried out.

A social security tribunal has accepted this argument and allowed an appeal against a review.[90] A judicial review is also being brought.[91] If your award is reviewed in this way, you should ask an advice agency to contact CPAG *before you or anyone on your behalf corresponds with the Benefits Agency*. This is because any letter you send could be treated as an application for a review, which may allow the Benefits Agency to override your transitional protection.

A request for a higher rate of one of the components of DLA/AA will allow a review to be carried out which will end transitional protection. If you do ask for a review and you are not exempt (see p199), you will lose all that benefit. As a result, you should not ask for a review unless you are confident that you are exempt from the immigration condition.

10. STATUTORY SICK PAY AND STATUTORY MATERNITY PAY

The rules for SSP and SMP are the same as those for British citizens (see p147). There are no special rules for people with limited leave.

These are not social security benefits, but minimum rates of pay made by your employer. They are *not* public funds under the immigration rules.[92] Because these benefits are paid by your employer, it is very unlikely that a request for them or payment of them will come to the attention of the Home Office. The Benefits Agency will only become involved if there is a dispute about entitlement, but even then, because your immigration status is irrelevant, it is very unlikely that the Home Office will be advised.

11. THE SOCIAL FUND

The social fund rules are the same as those for British citizens (see p148).

You cannot normally get social fund payments unless you are in receipt of a means-tested benefit (see p149). These rules mean that if you are not entitled to these benefits because of your immigration status, you cannot be given a social fund payment.

The exception is a *crisis loan*. There are special rules for a crisis loan (see p150) if:

- you are not entitled to IS/income-based JSA because you are a person from abroad; *or*
- you are entitled to IS/income-based JSA at the urgent cases rate.

CHAPTER SIXTEEN

No leave to remain

The benefits covered in this chapter are:

This chapter deals with people who need leave to enter or remain in the UK, but do not have that leave. If you do not *need* leave to enter or remain in the UK because you are a person with the right of abode (which includes British citizens) or an EU/EEA national or family member, see the chapter relevant to your immigration status.

Most benefit rules are based solely on immigration status and do not treat asylum-seekers differently from people with the same immigration status; but special rules apply to some asylum-seekers for IS, income-based JSA, HB and CTB (see Chapter 17). However, even asylum-seekers should check this chapter first, because you may be better off without using the special rules for asylum-seekers. In particular, not all asylum-seekers are persons from abroad.

The benefit rules covered by this chapter can be confusing. In particular, many people – including Benefits Agency and Home Office staff – mix up terms like 'deportation' and 'removal', or 'decision to deport' and 'deportation order'. Each term used in this book has a special meaning and only applies to that situation. You should make sure you understand the terms that are being used (see Part 1).

Effect of claiming benefit on immigration position

The Benefits Agency, JobCentre or local authority may notify the Home Office of any benefit claim you make (see Chapter 7). This is more likely for IS/JSA/HB/CTB than other benefits, but is possible for any benefit. Because of this *you should always seek immigration advice before approaching the Benefits Agency.* The only exception is if you are an asylum-seeker whose claim has not been decided or who has an outstanding appeal *and* the Home Office knows your address. The possible effects of a benefit claim are:

- if the Home Office has lost touch with you, information about a benefit claim, including your address and details of family members may be passed to the Immigration Service. This may lead to deportation or removal action being taken against you, including the possibility that you may be detained; *or*
- if the Home Office knows your address but has taken no action for a long time on your case, a benefit claim may lead to your file being acted on by the Home Office, which may lead to an unfavourable decision more quickly than if you do not claim; *or*
- if you have asked for leave to remain in the UK on the basis that you are self-supporting, a benefit claim may harm the chances of you being given leave.

WHO DOES NOT HAVE LEAVE TO REMAIN?

This chapter covers:

- port applicants (see p204). This is not the same as on-arrival asylum applicants;
- overstayers (see p205);
- people who had leave to remain until a deportation order was made (see p205); *and*
- illegal entrants (see p206).

Your entitlement to IS, income-based JSA, HB and CTB may depend upon which of these groups you are in. This is because not all people who have no leave to remain are 'persons from abroad' under the rules for these benefits. It is also wise to check that you fall into one of these groups to make sure that you have not made a mistake about your immigration status. You can only be in *one* of these groups.

Port applicants

We describe you as a **port applicant** if you applied at a port of entry for leave to enter the UK and you have not yet been given leave. The only exception to this is if your leave application was made after you had entered the UK illegally (see below). A port applicant is not the same as an 'on-arrival applicant', which applies to some asylum-seekers (see p220). However, the Benefits Agency does use 'port applicant' to mean 'on-arrival asylum-seekers'.

You can be a port applicant even if your application was made after you were refused leave to enter at a port.

An asylum-seeker can be a port applicant. This is because when you claim asylum you are applying for leave to enter the UK as a refugee. You are also a port applicant if you have a valid UK visa (see p21) but have been refused leave to enter and are appealing that decision.

A port applicant has never had leave to enter the UK since arriving at a port. However, as long as you comply with the terms of your temporary admission or bail (see below) you are in the UK legally. You are *not* an overstayer, nor are you subject to a deportation order, nor are you an illegal entrant.

If you are given leave, your immigration status changes and you should see the chapter relevant to your status. If you are refused leave, the rules covered by this chapter continue to apply to you until:

- *either* you are given leave to enter by an immigration officer;
- *or* you leave the UK

regardless of the results of any appeals. If an immigration officer decides that you are an illegal entrant, then different rules apply (see below).

If you applied at a port you *must* be:

- given temporary admission by an immigration officer (see p24) – this covers almost everyone (form IS 96, see Appendix 4); *or*
- detained under the Immigration Act (see p70); *or*
- given bail under the Immigration Act (see p71) – this is unusual and is almost always given by an adjudicator; *or*
- released by the High Court or Court of Appeal on bail or after an application for *habeas corpus* – this is very unusual.

If none of these applies to you, you did not apply for leave to enter at a port. However, because one of these applies do not assume you must be a port applicant. These conditions can also apply to people who no longer have leave and to illegal entrants.

If you break the terms of your temporary admission or bail, or escape from immigration detention, an immigration officer may decide that you are an illegal entrant. If this happens, different rules apply – see p206.

Overstayers

You are an overstayer if you had limited leave to enter or remain in the UK, but have overstayed that leave.

You become an overstayer on the day after your leave runs out. However, if you applied for leave to remain before your leave runs out, you may still have limited leave to remain, even if there is no stamp in your passport. This is called VOLO leave, see p28.

Under the benefit rules, once you are an overstayer, you remain an overstayer until *either* you are given leave to enter or remain (see relevant chapter) *or* you leave the UK. Your status does not change if a decision to deport is made or if a deportation order is signed.

You can tell if you are an overstayer if:

- your last leave stamp has run out and you did not apply for an extension before the date on the stamp; *or*
- the Home Office has made a decision to deport for the reason that you have remained in the UK without leave.

Before a decision to deport is made an overstayer can only be detained by the police. This is usually only for long enough for an immigration officer to interview you.

In *some* cases, where a decision to deport has been made, an overstayer is:

- given temporary admission by an immigration officer (see p24 for full details and form IS 96, Appendix 4); *or*
- detained under the Immigration Act (see p70); *or*
- given bail under the Immigration Act (see p71) – this is almost always by an adjudicator; *or*
- released by the High Court or Court of Appeal on bail or after an application for *habeas corpus* – this is very unusual.

In most cases none of these are done: the overstayer simply remains at liberty. If you break the terms of your temporary admission or bail, or if you escape from immigration detention, you remain an overstayer, you do not become an illegal entrant under benefit rules.

If you do not appeal the decision to deport or you lose your appeal and a deportation order is made, a restriction order may be made. You cannot be given temporary admission or bail.

Deportation order made while in UK with leave

Most deportation orders are made against overstayers. However, a deportation order may be made even though you have leave to remain in the UK. This has the effect of ending your leave from the date the deportation order is signed. If you have leave to remain, a decision to make a deportation order (this is different from the deportation order itself) does not affect your benefit entitlement. For details about deportation orders and when they can be made, see Chapter 6.

Once a deportation order is signed, removal directions (see p49) are usually made straight away or as soon as your whereabouts are known to the Home Office. If you are not going to be removed immediately, the Home Office will normally notify you in writing that your removal has been deferred. This is usually done by making a restriction order.

Illegal entrants

You are only an illegal entrant for benefit purposes if an immigration officer has told you in writing that you are an illegal entrant.[1]

You remain an illegal entrant for benefit purposes until you are given leave to enter or remain in the UK. If you lose benefit because of an immigration officer's decision that you are an illegal entrant and the High Court or Court of Appeal overrules that decision,[2] you may be able to argue that the benefit decisions were wrong because they relied on an invalid decision. If this applies you should take expert advice.

Before any illegal entry decision is made

Until an immigration officer decides that you are an illegal entrant, you are not one for benefit purposes, even if you obviously entered the UK illegally. The benefit rules treat you as if you were not an illegal entrant. Until an immigration officer decides that you are an illegal entrant, the following rules apply:

- *either* you were given leave to enter the UK – eg, as a visitor;
- *or* you entered the UK without leave. This happens when:
  – *either* you were not seen by an immigration officer – eg, you were hidden in a lorry;
  – *or* you presented a travel document which the immigration officer did not stamp – eg, a passport issued to a British Citizen or EU/EEA national.

If you were given leave, that leave counts under the benefit rules (see Chapter 15) until it runs out. If it runs out, you become an overstayer (see p205). If an immigration officer decides that you are an illegal entrant, your leave ends on the date of the decision.[3]

If you were not given leave, none of these rules should apply to you, but see each benefit for details.

1. INCOME SUPPORT

Claiming IS may seriously affect your immigration position (see p203).
If you are covered by this chapter, you are entitled to IS if:

- *either* you are a person from abroad entitled to urgent cases IS (see below);
- *or* you are *not* a person from abroad (see p209).

If you lose benefits under these rules and you are later recognised as a refugee, you may be able to claim backdated benefit (see Chapter 13).

If you are not entitled to IS, your partner may be able to claim instead (see p131).

Persons from abroad

You are a person from abroad if:

- you are a port applicant (see p204) *and* an immigration officer has given you temporary admission (see p24);[4]
- you are an overstayer (see p205);[5]
- a deportation order has been made against you (see p205);[6] *or*
- an immigration officer has decided that you are an illegal entrant (see p206).[7]

You are not a person from abroad if you left Montserrat after 1 November 1995 because of a volcanic eruption.[8] If this applies you are also exempt from the habitual residence test.

If you are a person from abroad, you are only entitled to IS if you meet the urgent cases rules (see below).

For a list of people who are *not* persons from abroad, see p209.

Urgent cases rate

If you are a person from abroad you are entitled to urgent cases IS if:[9]

- you are an asylum-seeker and other rules are met (see Chapter 16); *or*
- you can use the transitional protection where a sponsorship undertaking was given (see below).

Transitional protection where a sponsorship undertaking was given

The benefit rules have transitional protection where a sponsorship undertaking was given. This may apply to you, even though you are not a sponsored immigrant under benefit rules (see p153) – eg, there was no written undertaking. You are protected if:[10]

- you were entitled to IS for a period before 5 February 1996. Your entitlement to IS counts under this rule even if it did not continue to 4 February 1996, and even if you were only entitled because of a late claim made after 5 February 1996;[11] *and*
- before 5 February 1996 someone gave an undertaking to the Home Office, an immigration officer or an entry clearance officer to be responsible for your maintenance and accommodation (see below).

This transitional protection rule is worded more widely than the rule denying benefit to sponsored immigrants (see p153). This means that the following may count as an undertaking under this rule:

- a written undertaking which is not on a RON 112 form (see Appendix 4);
- a verbal undertaking – eg, a promise to an entry clearance officer by your sponsor that s/he would maintain you.

If transitional protection applies, you can use the much more generous urgent cases rules which applied before 5 February 1996 to get urgent cases IS for any period after 4 February 1996 during which:[12]

- you have temporary admission (see p24);[13]
- a deportation order has been made against you, but your removal from the UK has been deferred in writing by the Home Office or an immigration officer (see p215);[14] *or*
- an immigration officer has told you in writing that you are an illegal entrant but you have been allowed to remain by the Home Office or an immigration officer (see p215);[15] *or*
- your status has not been determined by the Secretary of State (see pp122 and 210);[16] *or*
- you have claimed asylum but that claim has not yet been finally determined;[17] *or*
- you are appealing under the Immigration Act 1971 (for details see p75) to:[18]
  – an adjudicator; *or*
  – the Immigration Appeal Tribunal; *or*
  – the Court of Appeal or House of Lords from a decision of the Immigration Appeal Tribunal (this does not include a judicial review); *or*
- a deportation order has been made against a member of your family *and* their removal from the UK has been deferred in writing by the Home Office or an immigration officer (see p215) *and* you have been allowed to stay in the UK until that person is removed;[19] *or*
- you have no (or no further) rights of appeal under the Immigration Act 1971 but you have been allowed to stay in the UK while the Home Office is considering a request that you should not be removed.[20]

Even if there is a break in your claim, transitional protection continues as long as one of the old urgent cases rules applies to you. It also continues if your immigration status changes (but you still count as a person from abroad) – eg, if you were an overstayer and then an immigration officer decides that you are an illegal entrant. You remain protected if your sponsor dies.

Because you are entitled to urgent cases IS, you do not have to claim income-based JSA so you do not have to be available for work.[21] Urgent cases IS is paid at a different rate from ordinary IS (see p124).

People who are not persons from abroad

Some people covered by this chapter are not persons from abroad (see below). The Benefits Agency is very unlikely to accept this conclusion because it assumes that anyone who does not have leave to remain must be a person from abroad. This is wrong. The definition of persons from abroad in the IS rules is specific and the Benefits Agency must be able to say which part applies to you. However, even if the definition does not apply, you will still have to pass the habitual residence test (see p210).

You could end up with *less benefit* by arguing that you are *not* a person from abroad. However, in some cases you may be able to increase your entitlement in this way.

If the only reason you are not entitled to urgent cases IS is that your income or capital is too high, you should consider arguing that you are not a person from abroad. This is only worth considering if you would be entitled to IS/income-based JSA. You should always take advice first.

If you have no income or capital and you are entitled to urgent cases IS, you should only argue that you are not a person from abroad if you are confident that you are entitled to ordinary IS/income-based JSA instead. If you argue successfully that you are not a person from abroad, but fail the normal conditions for IS/income-based JSA, you will be left without either benefit.

Who is not a person from abroad?

You are *not* a person from abroad if:

- you are a port applicant (see p204) *and either*:
  – you have been given bail (see p71); *or*
  – you were released by a court (see p204); *or*
  – you are detained under the Immigration Act (see p70).
  This is because under benefit rules only port applicants with tempo-rary admission count as persons from abroad, not other port appli-cants.[22] However, if you claimed asylum while you had temporary admission, you remain a person from abroad until the asylum claim is

finally determined, even if your temporary admission ends and you are detained or on bail.[23] A person detained under the Immigration Act 1971 is *not* a 'prisoner' under IS rules;[24]

- you entered the UK without being given leave to enter, but an immigration officer has not yet decided that you are an illegal entrant (see p206). This is because you only become a person from abroad under IS rules when an immigration officer decides that you are an illegal entrant.[25] For those who were given leave to enter illegally, see p206.

If you use these arguments, the Benefits Agency may claim that you are a person whose 'immigration status has not been determined by the Secretary of State' and are therefore a person from abroad.[26] We believe that such a conclusion may be wrong. In this context, 'immigration status' means whether or not you are someone who requires leave to enter the UK. This would cover, for example, a person whose claim to be a British citizen is being investigated by the Home Office. The 'determination of immigration status' cannot apply just because an application for leave to enter has been made – eg, as a refugee. In this particular situation, your status is clear and the Secretary of State has been asked to grant leave, *not* to determine your status. The Benefits Agency interpretation is wrong because it would mean that anyone who asked for leave or an extension of leave would automatically become a person from abroad. This would extend the persons from abroad rules in such a way that the other parts of the definition covering people with leave applying for extensions would become meaningless.[27]

Getting over the habitual residence test

If you are not a person from abroad because of your immigration status, you must still pass the habitual residence test. If you are not habitually resident (see p102), you may be exempt from the habitual residence test if:

- you are the family member of an EU/EEA national (see p355); *or*
- you are a refugee (see Chapter 13). It can be argued that all refugees are exempt from the habitual residence test, not only those the Home Office recognises as refugees (see below).

If you have claimed asylum but no decision has been made on that claim, the benefits authorities may have to decide whether or not you are a refugee. The Benefits Agency will not make such a decision, so you would have to appeal to a social security appeal tribunal and argue your case. If you want to take this route, you should get expert advice. This is because the way your case is presented at a tribunal hearing may affect your chances of the Home Office accepting that you are a refugee. For example, if your evidence to the tribunal hearing is less detailed than in a later Home Office interview, it may then be suggested that you have changed your account.

If the Home Office has decided that you are not a refugee, a social security tribunal is very unlikely to decide that you are a refugee unless there is now evidence available which the Home Office did not have, or you have won your asylum appeal against the Home Office decision on asylum but the Home Office are appealing against that decision.[28] You should take expert advice.

If the Home Office has decided that you are a refugee, the Benefits Agency ought to accept that you were a refugee when you claimed asylum, unless there was a subsequent change of circumstances. This is because you become a refugee as soon as you are outside your own country and you have a well-founded fear of persecution (see Chapter 13).[29] If this applies in your case, then you were exempt from the habitual residence test from the date you became a refugee, *not* the date on which the Home Office decision was made. You can use this argument to get back-dated ordinary rate IS for a period when you were *not* a person from abroad which was:

- before 7 October 1996 (the introduction of JSA) if you were *either*:
  - in a group which was exempt from the requirement to be available for work; *or*
  - available for work; *or*
- after 6 October 1996 if you were in one of the groups which can claim IS (see p182).

This is different from the rule for recognised refugees to get backdated benefit at the urgent cases rate (see p165). It is also different from the EC law argument about backdating benefit at the full rate (see p166).

2. INCOME-BASED JOBSEEKER'S ALLOWANCE

For contribution-based JSA, see p216.

It is difficult for people with no leave to meet the normal rules for income-based JSA, so you should always check to see if you may be entitled to IS instead (see p207).

Claiming income-based JSA may seriously affect your immigration position (see p203).

The rules about who is a person from abroad are the same as for IS (see p207).[30] You are only entitled to income-based JSA if you are:

- a person from abroad *and* you are an on-arrival asylum-seeker (see p220) entitled to urgent cases income-based JSA; *or*

- *not* a person from abroad (see above) *and* there is no written prohibition on taking work (see p188) *and* you are *either*:
  – available for work – then you are entitled to full rate income-based JSA; *or*
  – not available for work and qualify for hardship rate JSA (see p190) – then you are entitled to hardship rate income-based JSA.

Written permission to work

Under British law no one needs government permission to work. Only if you have written permission to be at liberty in the UK, can a prohibition on taking work be attached to that permission. If you have no permission to be at liberty in the UK, no prohibition can be attached. If you have overstayed your leave to remain, or that leave has been ended by a deportation order, any work condition attached to that leave ended when the leave ended. In practice, Home Office and Department for Education and Employment staff do not understand this and wrongly assume that anyone without leave cannot work without permission to work.

An employer may commit a criminal offence by employing a person in the UK without leave who does not have Home Office permission to work.[31]

If you claim asylum, after six months the Home Office will normally give you permission to take work if you ask for it. This is done by stamping your Standard Acknowledgement Letter (SAL) with the words 'there are no restrictions on the person named above taking employment and s/he does not need to get permission from the Department for Education and Employment before taking work,' or something similar. This overrides any restriction or prohibition on working which is part of your temporary admission. Sometimes this permission is refused or withdrawn, particularly if you have been refused asylum.

In theory, this kind of permission to work may be given to other people who have applied to stay for exceptional reasons – eg, statelessness, but we are not aware of any such case.

Even if you can work legally without permission, you may need written permission to work from the Home Office to get urgent cases JSA. This is very unusual for an on-arrival asylum-seeker and applies if you:

- have bail (see p71) with no prohibition on taking work; *or*
- have been released by a court after an application for *habeas corpus*.

If this applies, the Home Office may be prepared to give you written permission to work, even though you do not need it. You should seek expert advice before approaching the Home Office. Some of the people in this situation will not be persons from abroad (see below).

People who are not persons from abroad

Some people covered by this chapter are not persons from abroad under the benefit rules. The attitude of JobCentres to these people is the same as the Benefits Agency (see p209). However, even if the definition does not apply, you will still have to pass the habitual residence test (see below).

You may get *less benefit* by arguing that you are *not* a person from abroad (see p209).

You are *not* a person from abroad if:

- you are a port applicant *and either*:
  – you have been given bail; *or*
  – you were released by a court; *or*
  – you are detained under the Immigration Act 1971 (see p70); *or*
- you entered the UK without being given leave to enter, but an immigration officer has *not* yet decided that you are an illegal entrant (see p206).

For a possible argument the JobCentre may use against this conclusion, see p210.

If you are not a person from abroad because of your immigration status, you must still pass the habitual residence test. If you are not habitually resident (see p102), you may be exempt from the habitual residence test (see p210).

Availability for work

If you pass the habitual residence test, you will only be entitled to full rate income-based JSA if you are available for work (for details of the relationship between this rule and immigration restrictions, see pp188-90). You can only meet that rule if:

- you are a port applicant *and either*:
  – you have been given bail with no prohibition on taking work; *or*
  – you were released by a court following an application for *habeas corpus*; *or*
- you entered the UK without being given leave to enter, but an immigration officer has *not* yet decided that you are an illegal entrant (see p206).

You do *not* need Home Office permission to work to be available for work. This is different from getting urgent cases JSA (see p212).

Hardship payments

Hardship payments of JSA are different from urgent cases income-based JSA. They are intended for people who are not available for work, but where a vulnerable person will suffer hardship if JSA is not paid. For details, see p190.

3. HOUSING BENEFIT AND COUNCIL TAX BENEFIT

Claiming HB/CTB may seriously affect your immigration position (see p203).

The HB/CTB rules are very like the IS rules, but some claimants who are persons from abroad for IS are *not* persons from abroad for HB/CTB. There is no urgent cases rate for HB/CTB: the types of cases covered by urgent cases rate get normal HB/CTB.

If you are being paid IS/income-based JSA (including urgent cases rate) you are not a person from abroad for HB/CTB.[32] The local authority which deals with your HB/CTB claim should not make enquiries about your immigration status or habitual residence.[33]

You are only entitled to HB/CTB if:

- you are not a person from abroad (see below); *and*
- for **HB**, you have accommodation in GB which you normally occupy as your home (which can include certain temporary absences) (see p251);[34] *or* for **CTB**, you are liable to pay council tax for accommodation in which you reside (see p252).

If you do not meet these rules, you are not entitled to HB/CTB.[35]

Persons from abroad

You are a person from abroad if:[36]

- you are an overstayer (see p205);
- a deportation order has been made against you (see p205) *unless* the Home Office has deferred removal in writing (see p215);
- an immigration officer has decided that you are an illegal entrant (see p206) *unless* the Home Office has allowed you to remain in writing (see p215).

People who are not persons from abroad

Some people covered by this chapter are not persons from abroad. Local authorities are unlikely to accept this conclusion because they may assume that anyone who does not have leave to remain must be a person from abroad. This is wrong. The definition of persons from abroad in the HB/CTB rules is specific and the local authority must be able to say which part applies to you.

You are *not* a person from abroad if:

- you left Montserrat after 1 November 1995 because of a volcanic eruption; *or*
- you are an asylum-seeker and other rules are met (see Chapter 17); *or*
- a deportation order has been made against you (see p205) *but* the Home Office has deferred removal in writing.[37] Once a deportation order is signed, removal directions can be made. If the Home Office or an immigration officer has written to you or your advisers stating that removal directions have been deferred, you are not a person from abroad. If you need to get such a letter for HB/CTB you should seek immigration advice first; *or*
- an immigration officer has decided that you are an illegal entrant (see p206) *but* the Home Office has allowed you to remain in writing.[38] If you are not detained you will be given a Form IS 96 (see Appendix 4) which shows that you are allowed to remain in the UK for the time being. This means that you are not a person from abroad; *or*
- you can use the transitional protection for sponsored immigrants.[39] This is the same as for IS (see p207), except that HB/CTB protection does not include the first four groups listed there.

If any of these applies to you, you are exempt from the HB/CTB habitual residence test.[40]

You are also *not* a person from abroad if you are a port applicant, regardless of whether you have temporary admission, bail or are detained. This is because the person from abroad definition does not apply to you. However, you must still pass the habitual residence test. The exemptions from the test are the same as for IS (see p210).

The argument that you are a person from abroad because your 'immigration status has not been determined by the Secretary of State' (see p210) cannot be used for HB/CTB because that is not part of the person from abroad definition under HB/CTB rules.

4. CHILD BENEFIT AND GUARDIAN'S ALLOWANCE

Claiming CB or guardian's allowance may seriously affect your immigration position (see p203).

The rules are the same as for people with limited leave (see p193).

5. FAMILY CREDIT AND DISABILITY WORKING ALLOWANCE

Claiming FC or DWA may seriously affect your immigration position (see p203).

To be entitled to these benefits you must be working. A claim for these benefits may lead to the Home Office being told that you are working. If you have written permission to work, this will not affect you. If you are prohibited from working by the conditions of your temporary admission or bail, there is a risk that you will be arrested for breach of those conditions.[41] You may be refused further temporary admission or bail, and it is possible that you will be prosecuted for the breach.[42] If there were bail sureties it is possible that those sureties will be forfeited.[43]

The rules are the same as for people with limited leave (see p195).

6. SHORT-TERM CONTRIBUTORY BENEFITS

These benefits are contribution-based JSA, incapacity benefit and maternity allowance. *Claiming may seriously affect your immigration position* (see p203 and below).

There are no special rules for people with no leave to remain. The rules are the same as for British citizens (see p139), though the conditions of any temporary admission, bail or detention may mean that you do not meet those rules for contribution-based JSA (see below).

To be entitled to these benefits you must have paid NI contributions as an employed or self-employed person (see CPAG's *Rights Guide to Non-Means-Tested Benefits*). A claim for these benefits may lead to the Home Office being told that you have been working. For possible effects if you worked in breach of the conditions of your temporary admission or bail immigration, see above.

Special rules for contribution-based JSA

The 'person from abroad' rules for income-based JSA do not apply to contribution-based JSA.[44] However, because of the normal rules for JSA:

- you are only entitled to full-rate contribution-based JSA if there is no written prohibition on taking work (see p188) *and* you are available for work;
- *otherwise*, check whether you qualify for income-based JSA, paid at the hardship rate (see p211).

7. RETIREMENT PENSIONS AND WIDOWS' BENEFITS

These are Category A, B, C and D retirement pensions, widow's allowance, widowed mother's allowance and widow's pension. *Claiming may seriously affect your immigration position* (see pp203 and 216).

The rules for entitlement are the same as those for British citizens (see p140). There are no special rules for people with no leave.

8. INDUSTRIAL INJURIES BENEFITS

These are disablement benefit, reduced earnings allowance, retirement allowance, constant attendance allowance and exceptionally severe disablement allowance. *Claiming may seriously affect your immigration position* (see pp203 and 216).

The rules for entitlement are the same as those for British citizens (see p142). There are no special rules for people with no leave.

9. DISABILITY BENEFITS

These benefits are DLA, AA, ICA and SDA. *Claiming may seriously affect your immigration position* (see p203).

From 5 February 1996, people with no leave to remain are not normally entitled to these benefits because of the immigration condition for them. The rules for these benefits and the exceptions are the same as for people here with limited leave (see p199).

10. STATUTORY SICK PAY AND STATUTORY MATERNITY PAY

The rules for SSP and SMP are the same as those for British citizens (see p147). There are no special rules for people with limited leave.

These are not social security benefits, but minimum rates of pay to be paid by your employer. They are *not* public funds under the immigration rules.[45] Because these benefits are paid by your employer, it is very unlikely that a request for them or payment of them will come to the attention of the Home Office. The Benefits Agency will only be involved if there is a dispute about entitlement, but even then, because your immigration status is irrelevant, it is very unlikely that the Home office will be advised. If the Home Office is informed your immigration position may be affected (see p203) and if you have worked in breach of conditions that may have effects (see p216).

11. THE SOCIAL FUND

The social fund rules are the same as those for British citizens (see p148).

You cannot normally get social fund payments unless you are in receipt of a means-tested benefit (see p149). These rules mean that if you are not entitled to these benefits because of your immigration status, you cannot be given a social fund payment.

The exception is a *crisis loan*. There are special rules for a crisis loan (see p150) if:

- you are not entitled to IS/income-based JSA because you are a person from abroad; *or*
- you are entitled to IS/income-based JSA at the urgent cases rate.

CHAPTER SEVENTEEN

Asylum-seekers

This chapter deals with people who have claimed asylum in the UK but who have not yet been recognised as refugees or given exceptional leave to remain. 'Asylum-seeker' is not an immigration status. Asylum-seekers may have leave to enter or remain in the UK: they may be port applicants or illegal entrants. The starting point for all benefit rules is immigration status and not whether an asylum claim has been made. This chapter covers:

1. Who becomes an asylum-seeker for benefit purposes? (below)
2. When you stop being an asylum-seeker (p231)
3. Income support (IS) (p236)
4. Income-based jobseeker's allowance (JSA) (p237)
5. Housing benefit (HB) and council tax benefit (CTB) (p237)

Only for these benefits can an asylum-seeker be treated differently from other people with the same immigration status. This chapter only covers those special rules for asylum-seekers. The immigration status of some asylum-seekers may affect entitlement to benefit, so always read this chapter with the chapter on your immigration status.

For refugees given asylum, including how to backdate benefits for the period during which you were claiming asylum, see Chapter 13. For people given exceptional leave to remain, see Chapter 14.

For benefit purposes, asylum-seeker is defined in the benefit rules. It is not the same as the various definitions for immigration purposes.[1]

Some persons from abroad, including asylum-seekers, may not be entitled to any means-tested benefits.

I. WHO BECOMES AN ASYLUM-SEEKER FOR BENEFIT PURPOSES?

Until **4 February 1996** under the **old rules** a person became an asylum-seeker when:[2]

- s/he claimed asylum; *and*
- the Home Office recorded that claim as having been made.

Since **5 February 1996** under the **new rules** a person becomes an asylum-seeker when:[3]

- s/he claims asylum on arrival in the UK; *and*
- the Home Office records that claim as having been made.

The new benefit rules treat 'on-arrival' applicants differently from 'in-country' applicants. This rule was declared unlawful by the Court of Appeal on 21 June 1996.[4] The court's reason was that removal of benefits did such harm to asylum-seekers and to their ability to appeal a refusal of asylum that the Secretary of State did not have the power to make such a change.

The effect of that judgment was reversed on 24 July 1996 by Parliament through the Asylum and Immigration Act 1996.[5] The old benefit rules applied to asylum-seekers from 5 February 1996 to 23 July 1996 (see p236 for this period).[6] This means that the new rules for asylum-seekers only came into effect on 24 July 1996.

The new benefit rules apply from 24 July 1996, but the transitional provisions only apply to those who had entitlement before 5 February 1996 (see p228).

There are special rules that apply when the Home Secretary makes a declaration that a country is subject to a fundamental change of circumstances (see p227).

Asylum claimed on arrival in the UK

From 5 February 1996 a person becomes an asylum-seeker when:[7]

> '*he submits on his arrival (other than on his re-entry) in the UK from a country outside the common travel area a claim for asylum to the Secretary of State...and that claim is recorded by the Secretary of State as having been made.*'

To qualify under this rule you must have:

- made a claim for asylum (see p224); *and*
- made that claim to the Secretary of State (see p224); *and*
- made that claim on your arrival in the UK (see p222); *and*
- be arriving from a country outside the common travel area (see p225); *and*
- *not* be re-entering the UK when you arrive in the UK (see p226); *and*
- that asylum claim must be recorded by the Secretary of State (see p225).

The Home Office and Benefits Agency refer to on-arrival applicants as 'port applicants' and to others as 'in-country applicants'. This is confusing because it assumes that claiming asylum at port and claiming 'on arrival' are always the same. We use the term 'on-arrival applicant' for a person who claimed asylum 'on-arrival'. We use the term 'port applicant' for a person who claimed asylum at a port.

In practice

It is important that advisers helping asylum-seekers are aware that practice at ports varies widely and that both benefits authorities and the Home Office are unreliable sources of information about what happens in practice. In particular, Immigration Service records are sometimes poor and conversations with asylum-seekers are not always recorded. The Immigration Service can be particularly careless when providing information to the Benefits Agency.

There are three main sorts of asylum-seekers. These are those who:

- arrived in the usual way at a port of entry intending to claim asylum as soon as possible;
- arrived in the usual way at a port of entry who *either* did not want to claim asylum at port *or* did not realise that they could do so;
- arrived secretly *either* hidden at a port of entry *or* not at a port of entry – eg, on a beach.

Some asylum-seekers did not claim asylum at port because they did not come to the UK for asylum. They may have come here a long time ago and only recently become at risk of persecution. There are no special rules relating to people for whom the risk of persecution arose after arrival. These people are still in-country applicants (see p220) unless they come from a 'fundamental change' country (see p227).

The most important document for asylum-seekers is the Standard Acknowledgment Letter (SAL). Until October 1995 there was only one type of SAL which was issued by the Asylum Screening Unit at Lunar House. Since 12 October 1995, there have been two sorts of SAL with different colours:

- SAL1 (blue/orange) is for on-arrival applicants. These are issued by immigration officers at ports;
- SAL2 (red/grey) is for in-country applicants. These are issued by the Asylum Screening Unit and by immigration officers who are not based at ports.

Benefits Agency and local authority staff are instructed to treat a person with a SAL1 as an on-arrival applicant and a person with a SAL 2 as an in-country applicant.[8]

In practice, the SAL is not always a good guide to whether a claim was made on arrival. For example, a claimant attending the Asylum Screening Unit to add dependants to his asylum claim had his SAL1 taken away and replaced with a SAL2.

Deciding whether the claim was 'on arrival'

The decision about whether the claim was on arrival is for the benefits authorities. It is *not* made by the Home Office. It is no different from any other decision about benefit, though it may be based upon information from the Home Office. This means that, even though the Home Office issued a SAL2 to you, you may be an 'on-arrival' applicant.

'On arrival'

'On arrival' is not defined in the benefit rules. As a result, the words have their ordinary meaning, and not any special meaning. While many cases will be clear, until guidance comes from the Commissioners or the courts, the meaning may not be clear for many cases.

Because of the practical context in which asylum claims are made, we consider that the basic question for considering 'on arrival' is 'was the claim made at the first realistic opportunity after the person became physically present in the UK?' This is because:

- the claim does not have to be made 'immediately on arrival' – the benefit rules do not use the words 'on arrival';
- in many cases accepted as 'on arrival', the asylum-seeker was physically present in the UK for hours before the asylum claim was made – eg, because of landing, collecting baggage and queuing. This shows that the time that has passed since becoming physically present in the UK is not important;
- asylum-seekers claim 'on arrival' if the first person who is told about the asylum claim is an immigration officer. It is not necessary to tell other officials (eg, airline staff) even though this may have led to an immigration officer being called for the asylum claim to be made more quickly. This shows that a claim is made on arrival if it is made at the first *realistic* opportunity;
- Benefits Agency guidance accepts that a person who is 'prevented' from claiming asylum, for example, because there is no interpreter present, claims asylum on arrival if when an interpreter is first available s/he claims asylum.[9] We consider that this is one example of the principle that a person claims on arrival if s/he claims at the first *realistic* opportunity to do so;
- this Benefits Agency guidance also shows that a person's own circumstances may affect whether a claim was made 'on arrival'. For

example, a person whose physical or mental health, language or ignorance means that s/he does not recognise or does not use an opportunity to claim asylum, makes an asylum claim which counts as 'on
arrival' if s/he does so at the first *realistic* opportunity;
* 'arrival' is not the same as 'entry', which is a term used in immigration
  law.[10]

Some asylum-seekers arrive in the UK via the Channel Tunnel, without
having claimed asylum at immigration control on the train. They then
claim asylum – eg, at Waterloo Station Immigration Service office. Immigration control on the train often takes place *before* the train arrives in
the UK. If this applies, it can be argued that the claim at Waterloo is
made on arrival in the UK, because a claim at train immigration control
would have been physically outside the UK, therefore that would have
been before *arrival*, not *on* arrival. This argument is possible because,
even though you 'enter' the UK when passing through train immigration
control, you do not 'arrive' in the UK until you are physically present.

Asylum-seekers who entered the UK secretly are usually treated as 'in-
country' asylum-seekers. However, many will have claimed at the first
realistic opportunity to do so (see examples below).

Example 1

Riza is a Kurd who was tortured by the Turkish police because he refused to
join the village guard system. He paid an agent to take him to a safe country.
He flew to the Ukraine and then travelled by lorry to a Belgian beach. He
was taken by boat to Margate, Kent and left at the harbour where there is no
immigration officer. He speaks no English and had only a few English coins.

  He telephones his cousin in London. His cousin drives to Margate and
takes Riza to the local police station where an officer is informed that he
wishes to claim asylum. An immigration officer is called and issues Riza with
a SAL2.

  Riza cannot claim asylum at the harbour because there is no official with
whom to lodge a claim. He claims asylum as soon as he can. He can argue
that he claimed on arrival in the UK.

Example 2[11]

Irina entered at Ramsgate on a coach of Ukrainian tourists. She spoke no
English and her passport was held by the tour operator. The party were
taken straight to London. The following morning was a Saturday and Irina
approached a policeman and asked for asylum. He directed her to the
Asylum Division at Lunar House and she claimed asylum there on Monday.
The tribunal decided she intended to claim but could not do so at port.
Since Irina took the next best possible step, she was found to have claimed
on arrival. Her appeal was allowed.

What counts as an asylum claim

There is no definition in the benefit rules of an asylum claim. The clearest claim is when a person says to an immigration officer 'I want asylum' or 'I am a refugee'. However, this is not required for a claim to be made:

- a claim can be spoken or written – a person who hands a letter to an immigration officer asking for asylum, even if it is not in English, has claimed asylum;
- the words 'asylum' or 'refugee' do *not* have to be used. It is enough if you tell the immigration officer that you may suffer harm if you are sent away from the UK or if you say that you want to stay in the UK because it is a safe place;
- the claim can be made by another person on your behalf – eg, if you do not speak English.

To whom the asylum claim must be made

The benefit rules say that the asylum claim must be made to the Secretary of State. In practice, even though immigration officers are legally differ-ent from the Secretary of State,[12] a claim made to an immigration officer counts as a claim to the Secretary of State (but see below for immigration officers who refuse to accept claims).

Problems may arise where a person has entered the UK secretly and then claims asylum from an official who is not authorised by the Home Office to receive asylum claims – eg, to a police officer or the DSS. If our understanding of the meaning of 'on arrival' is right (see p222), this will not usually matter because that will not count as a realistic opportunity to claim asylum. However, there may be cases where a person claims asy-lum (but not from the Home Office) as soon as possible, but then delays going to the Home Office. Where this happens, it may be necessary to argue that the first asylum claim was 'to the Secretary of State'. The bene-fit rules do not say that the claim must be made to the Secretary of State for the Home Department, that is, the Home Office. Other benefit rules do make a distinction between different Secretaries of State,[13] so the 'on arrival' rule appears to refer to all Secretaries of State.[14] This may mean that an asylum claim can be made to any officer of a Secretary of State, including a DSS officer. A claim made to another official (eg, a police offi-cer) would only seem to count if that police officer had actual or appar-ent authority from a Secretary of State to receive an asylum claim. This would include a police officer who agrees to inform the Secretary of State that a person has claimed asylum.

Some immigration officers now refuse to acknowledge asylum claims – eg, those at Becket House in south London and Waterloo Station. Asylum-seekers are told to approach another section of the Home Office directly, usually Lunar House. If a claim is made to a port immigration officer, it must be referred to the Home Office, so an immigration officer cannot refuse to accept it.[15] In other cases, it can be argued that an Immigration Service office is an office of the Secretary of State, so an asylum claim made there always counts for the benefit rules, even if internal Home Office rules mean that you must also go to another office.

Recording asylum claims

You only become an asylum-seeker under the benefit rules when your asylum claim is recorded by the Secretary of State as having been made. Even though your claim must be made 'on arrival', the record of it does not have to be made 'on arrival'. This means that, even if no record of your claim is made (eg, because you claim at Waterloo Station) as long as that claim is later recorded as made, you become an asylum-seeker from the date of that record.

In practice, almost all port asylum claims are recorded within a few hours of being made, so it will only be unusual cases where there is any difference between the date of claim and the date of record.

There are no published rules about how the Secretary of State records asylum claims. If the claim is verbal, a brief note of the person's name and the fact that a claim is made qualifies as a record of the claim. If the claim is made in writing, by filing that letter the Secretary of State records the claim.

The decision on whether a claim qualifies as an asylum claim is made by the benefits authorities. For example, if on arrival you said to an immigration officer that you were afraid to go back to your own country but did not give any reasons for that statement, the Home Office may have recorded that request but not treated it as an asylum claim. It is up to the benefits authorities to decide whether it was an asylum claim. If it was, your asylum claim was 'on arrival'.

Arriving from outside the Common Travel Area

The common travel area is the UK, Republic of Ireland, Channel Islands and the Isle of Man (for details, see p3). A very few asylum-seekers arrive in the UK from Ireland and are usually removed back to Ireland on safe 'third country' (see p81) grounds. In practice, asylum-seekers do not arrive in the UK from elsewhere in the common travel area, but anyone doing so would probably have come via Ireland or France and so would also be likely to be removed to that country on third country grounds.[16]

The only person who sought asylum in the Channel Islands in recent years was taken to the UK for his claim to be considered here. If that happens again in a case where the person claimed asylum on arrival in the Channel Islands or Isle of Man, s/he will not be an asylum-seeker for benefit purposes and the Secretary of State should be asked to make extra statutory payments as if the asylum claim had been made on arrival in the UK.

Claiming when re-entering the UK

This exception seems to be intended to stop people who did not claim asylum on arrival in the UK from going abroad for a short period and then claiming on the second arrival.[17]

The benefit rules state that the asylum claim must be made 'other than on his re-entry'. This is different from stating that the claim must be made 'on first arriving in the UK'. 'Entry' has a special meaning under immigration law.[18] We consider that this meaning also applies to the word 'entry' used in the benefit rules.[19] Only people given leave to enter the UK or who enter illegally have 'entered' the UK. A person who is detained on arrival and/or given temporary admission does not 'enter' the UK, even though s/he is physically present in the UK (see p24). If on your previous stay(s) in the UK you did not 'enter' the UK and you subsequently claim asylum on arrival, you are not 're-entering' and thus you are an 'on arrival' asylum-seeker. This is most likely to apply to people who were refused asylum in the UK on 'safe third country' grounds (see p81) and removed to that safe third country but 'bounced back' to the UK by that country, claiming asylum in the UK again.

Where a person has previously *entered* the UK, the effect of the re-entry rule is not clear. This rule cannot sensibly apply to every person who has previously entered the UK. For example, a visit may have taken place many years ago when the person was a child or when the situation in that person's country was very different to the one which has lead to the claim for asylum. If it had been intended to exclude all such people it would have been easy for the rules to state 'except where he has previously entered the UK', but they do not.

Our view is that the re-entry rule only applies to people who enter or seek to enter the UK before the date on which their previous leave would have run out if they had remained in the UK (see example below).[20] This is the meaning given to 're-entry' under immigration law.[21]

Previous entry to a part of the common travel area (see p3) other than the UK does not count as entry. A previous visit to, for example, Ireland, will not prevent an 'on arrival' claim, as long as you do not arrive in the UK directly from Ireland.

Example

Elizabeth and Mary, who are Nigerian, are given leave to enter the UK for six months. After three months Elizabeth goes on a day trip to France. On her return to the UK she claims asylum at port. Mary returns to Nigeria after five months in the UK. She discovers that her mother has been arrested for political activity. Three months later she has enough money to fly to the UK. She does so and claims asylum on arrival.

Elizabeth is not an asylum-seeker under benefit rules, because she claimed before her six-month leave would have run out – therefore, on her re-entry to the UK. Mary is an asylum-seeker under benefit rules because she claimed asylum after her earlier six-month leave would have expired – therefore, not on her re-entry to the UK.

Fundamental change countries

If neither the 'on arrival' rule (see p220) nor transitional protection (see p228) applies, the only way to become an asylum-seeker under the benefit rules after 5 February 1996 is if the Secretary of State makes a declaration that a country is subject to such a fundamental change in circumstances that s/he would not normally order the return of a person to that country.[22] This is also known as an 'upheaval declaration'.

At the time of writing, a declaration has been made about former Zaire (see p228).

If a declaration is made about a country, you become an asylum-seeker for benefit purposes:

• if you are a national of that country when the declaration is made; *and*
• if you claim asylum within three months of the date of the declaration;

from the date the Home Office records that claim as having been made.

If you have an asylum claim or appeal outstanding when the declaration is made *and* you are not an asylum-seeker under benefit rules, you will need to make a fresh asylum claim to become an asylum-seeker under the declaration. Even if you are not entitled to benefits because you are working or because of your income or capital, you can consider making a fresh claim so that you would be able to claim benefits if, for example, you lost your job.

You should take immigration advice before you make a fresh asylum claim. This is because the rules about making fresh claims are complex and the Home Office may refuse to accept a fresh claim from you.[23] It is best if any fresh claim is prepared by an immigration adviser. However, if there is not time to take advice before the three month limit runs out, you can claim asylum again by writing to Lunar House (for address, see Appendix 2) giving details about the recent developments in your country.

You can only use this rule if you are a national of the country for which the declaration has been made. If you have no nationality – ie, you are stateless (see p17) – you can be a refugee from your country of former habitual residence, but even though that country is named in a declaration, an asylum claim will not make you an asylum-seeker under benefit rules. You should seek advice about asking for an extra-statutory payment.

If the Home Secretary refuses to make a declaration naming a country, the only way to challenge that refusal is by judicial review.

A declaration was made on 16 May 1997 that former Zaire (now known as Democratic Republic of Congo) is subject to a fundamental change.[24] This means, unless it is extended, only asylum claims made on or before 16 August 1997 count for the benefit rules.

Disputed nationality

In some cases, the Home Office disputes that you are a national of the country you say you are from. This is common where there is a policy of granting exceptional leave to remain to people from that country.[25] If a declaration is made but the Home Office disputes that you are a national of that country, the benefits authorities may refuse to treat you as an asylum-seeker under this rule. The decision on your nationality is made by the benefits authority and you can appeal in the usual way. The Home Office opinion on your nationality is only an opinion: the benefits authorities do not have to follow it.

Transitional protection for existing asylum-seekers

Under the old rules before 5 February 1996, asylum-seekers remain asylum-seekers for benefit purposes from that date under transitional protection rules.[26] This applies even if your asylum claim was refused before 5 February 1996. The Court of Appeal has decided that the date for transitional protection is *not* 24 July 1996 even though the new rules only came into force on that date.[27]

Transitional protection continues until the new rules about when a person stops being an asylum-seeker apply (see p231). There is no transitional protection from those rules.

It is not clear whether transitional protection is limited to the benefits you were entitled to before 5 February 1996, or whether entitlement to, say, only HB, also gives transitional protection for IS and CTB.

The old rules

Until 4 February 1996, a person *became* an asylum-seeker when:[28]

- s/he claimed asylum; *and*
- the Home Office recorded that claim as having been made;

and only *stopped* being an asylum-seeker when:[29]

- the asylum claim was finally determined, including any appeal or further appeal, *or* was abandoned; *and*

- the Home Office recorded that final determination or abandonment.

You only have protection if your asylum claim was made *and* recorded by the Home Office before 5 February 1996. Remember, there are no rules about how an asylum claim is made: a verbal request or a letter may be enough. It is for the benefits authority, not the Home Office, to decide whether an asylum claim was made and whether a record of it was made by the Home Office.

DSS guidance

DSS guidance to the Benefits Agency and to local authorities states that a person is an asylum-seeker from 5 February 1996 if on 4 February 1996 the person was entitled to benefit under the rules for asylum-seekers.[30]

You do not have to be in receipt of benefit on 4 February 1996. You are protected if you are awarded benefit for that date, even if the award is made after 5 February 1996. This means that a successful late claim for benefit for a period before 5 February 1996 will give you protection. You must show good cause for the delay in claiming.[31] The restriction on late benefit claims in the Asylum and Immigration Act 1996 (see p220) does not apply to claims for periods before 5 February 1996.

Broken claims

According to DSS guidance, transitional protection stops if there is a break in the benefit claim. Local authorities are advised that an HB or CTB claim counts as unbroken if a renewal or repeat claim is made which means there is no day without entitlement.

We consider the DSS guidance on broken claims to be wrong. You do not have to be entitled to benefit on 4 February 1996 to have transitional protection. It is enough if, *at any time* before 5 February 1996, you were entitled to benefit in your own name (for family members, see p230). This is because regulations giving transitional protection usually state that the claimant must have been entitled on a particular date.[32] However, the regulations giving transitional protection for asylum-seekers apply if 'before the coming into force of these regulations' (ie, 5 February 1996) you were entitled to benefit. They do not require entitlement on a particular date or '*immediately* before the coming into force'.

The rules do not say when transitional protection stops. They do not state that protection stops at the end of the benefit claim as transitional protection regulations usually do.[33] This means that, if your benefit entitlement ends after 5 February 1996 because, for example, you get a job, the transitional protection does not end. The protection continues until you stop being an asylum-seeker, so if you need to claim benefit again you are still an asylum-seeker under benefit rules.

Family members of asylum-seekers

The transitional protection for asylum-seekers also applies to members of an asylum-seeker's family.[34] These rules were brought in on 26 July 1996, but the DSS accepts that they apply from 5 February 1996.[35] You are protected if *on 5 February 1996*:

- *either*:
  - you were included as a dependant of an asylum-seeker on her/his asylum claim;[36] *or*
  - you had claimed asylum in your own right and were a family member of an asylum-seeker;[37] *and*
- that asylum-seeker has transitional protection (see p228).

This applies not only to members of the family for benefit purposes, but also dependent relatives who can only claim benefits in their own name. This means that where a couple separate or a child leaves school, the family member can claim benefit in their own name and will be treated as an asylum-seeker.

Such protection lasts as long as the asylum-seeker whose family member you are or were has protection, and also continues if you then claim asylum in your own right (see example on p231). This is most likely to happen where the Home Office stops treating you as a dependant of the asylum-seeker whose family member you were (eg, where you were one of a couple who have separated) so that you then have to claim asylum in your own right.

If a family member claims asylum in her/his own right after 4 February 1996, transitional protection as a family member does not stop. This is because the protection applies to people who were family members of an asylum-seeker on 4 February 1996. The rules do not state that protection stops if you cease to be a family member or make an asylum claim in your own right.[38] If you claim asylum in your own right, transitional protection continues until you (or, if later, the person whose dependant you were/are) stop being an asylum-seeker for benefit purposes (see p23). This applies even though your asylum claim was not made 'on arrival'. This is because your transitional protection means that the old rules (see p228) apply to your asylum claim and, because that claim would have counted as an asylum claim under the old rules, it counts as long as you have transitional protection.

In some cases, it may be possible to argue that, even though you were recorded as a dependant, you in fact made a claim for asylum. This may be important for your immigration appeal rights.[39] You should seek immigration advice, if possible, before telling the Home Office that you want to be treated as an asylum-seeker in your own right.

Example

Metin and Hanim are a married couple from Turkish Kurdistan who were both active there in an illegal left-wing organisation. They enter the UK illegally in 1989 and Metin claims asylum asking for Hanim, his wife, to be recorded as his dependant. Metin is awarded IS urgent cases rate for the couple. On 5 February 1996, Metin qualifies for protection because he was entitled before that date to IS as an asylum-seeker. Hanim also qualifies for protection because she is a member of Metin's family, but it does not matter at this time because she is not claiming benefit in her own right.

In August 1996 the couple separate. Because Hanim is protected and Metin's asylum claim has not been decided, she is entitled to urgent cases IS. In September 1996 Hanim claims asylum in her own right. She remains protected under two separate rules: because she was a member of Metin's family on 4 February 1996 *and also* because she has now become an asylum-seeker for benefit purposes. In November 1996 the Home Office refuses Metin's asylum claim. Hanim remains protected until her claim is decided because she is still an asylum-seeker.

2. WHEN YOU STOP BEING AN ASYLUM-SEEKER

Until 4 February 1996 a person stopped being an asylum-seeker for benefit purposes when their claim was finally determined.[40] A claim was not finally determined while on appeal or the judicial review was pending.

From 5 February 1996 a person stops being an asylum-seeker for benefit purposes when the *next decision* after that date is taken on the asylum claim (even if you have transitional protection):[41]

- if you claimed asylum after 5 February 1996, the next decision will be the Home Office decision on your asylum claim;
- if you claimed asylum before 5 February 1996 but the Home Office was still considering that claim on 5 February 1996, the next decision will be the Home Office decision on your asylum claim;
- if you were refused asylum before 5 February 1996 and an appeal is pending on that date, DSS guidance says that the next decision is that made at the end of that stage of the appeal process, even if you succeed at this stage. For details of this rule, see p233.

There is no transitional protection against these rules: the only protection is that you remain an asylum-seeker until the next decision on your asylum claim. If the next decision on the asylum claim was taken between 5 February 1996 and 24 July 1996, you stopped being an asylum-seeker on 24 July 1996 when the new rules came into effect (see p236).

The date of the Home Office refusal

Under the benefit rules, the date of the Home Office refusal is the date on which the asylum claim is recorded as having been determined.

At first, DSS guidance stated that the refusal is made on the date it is received by the asylum-seeker.[42] Practice was often different and many asylum-seekers had their first indication that asylum had been refused from the DSS. Guidance was changed so that the Asylum Division now notifies the Benefits Agency and the asylum-seeker that asylum has been refused, but the asylum-seeker is given no reasons for the refusal. The Benefits Agency treats that notice as the date of refusal. The file is sent to the immigration officer who then arranges the refusal interview at which the asylum-seeker is given the reasons for refusal.

The High Court has now decided that the date of refusal is the date a proper record of refusal is made by the Home Office, even if this is not notified to the claimant.[43] In the two cases considered, the internal Home Office memo was so unclear that only the letter to the claimant (in one case) or to the Benefits Agency (in the other) were clear enough to be a proper record.

This case means that the Home Office notification of refusal to the claimant is the latest date for the refusal even if no reasons are given at the time. If the Benefits Agency wants to withdraw benefit from an earlier date, it must provide a clear refusal made on that date.

Where the Home Office agrees to reconsider

In some cases, the Home Office agrees to reconsider a refusal of asylum. In the past it was not usually important that the earlier refusal was withdrawn. Because of the new benefit rules, it can now be important to get the Home Office to withdraw the earlier refusal and accept that the original claim for asylum is still outstanding and has not been determined. If this is done, there will be no date of determination for benefit purposes and you will become an asylum-seeker again backdated to the date of the earlier refusal of asylum.

The Home Office is very unlikely to withdraw an earlier refusal willingly and will certainly refuse to do so if reconsideration is only because further evidence has been provided or where an adjudicator has heard an appeal (unless that appeal was on 'third country' grounds – see p81). However, because of the effect of a refusal decision under the new benefit rules the Home Office should agree to withdraw a refusal of asylum in certain cases and particularly where asylum was refused:

- on safe third country grounds and the Home Office has now agreed to consider the substance of the asylum claim; *or*
- without full information because of the Home Office's fault – eg,

documents given to an immigration officer were not passed to the Asylum Division or you were not told about an interview.

If the Home Office agrees to reconsider but refuses to withdraw the refusal of asylum, judicial review should be considered.

Pending asylum appeals

An appeal was pending on 5 February 1996 if an appeal has been made or can still be made.[44] This is only important if DSS guidance is right in stating that you stop being an asylum-seeker at the end of the current stage of the appeal process (see p231). An appeal was pending in the following situations:

- **A special adjudicator appeal was pending if** *on 5 February 1996 either:*
  - a notice of appeal (including a late appeal) to a special adjudicator had been received before that date by the appropriate office;[45] *or*
  - the time-limit for appealing to a special adjudicator had not run out (see p78); *or*
  - a late appeal from a decision made before 5 February 1996 is made after that date to a special adjudicator;

  and the adjudicator had neither determined that appeal nor refused to extend time for appealing before 5 February 1996.

- **An Immigration Appeal Tribunal appeal was pending if** *on 5 February 1996 either:*
  - an application for leave to appeal to the tribunal had been received before that date by the tribunal (there is no provision for late applications);[46] *or*
  - the time-limit for applying for leave to appeal to the tribunal had not run out (see p80);[47]

  and the tribunal has neither refused leave to appeal to the tribunal nor determined that appeal before 5 February 1996.

- **An appeal before the Court of Appeal was pending if** *on 5 February 1996 either:*
  - an application to the tribunal for leave to appeal to the Court of Appeal had been received before that date by the tribunal (there is no provision for late applications to the tribunal);[48] *or*
  - the time-limit for applying to the tribunal for leave to appeal to the Court of Appeal had not run out;[49] *or*
  - the tribunal has refused leave to appeal to the Court of Appeal and an application to the Court of Appeal for leave to appeal had been received before 5 February 1996 by the Court (including a late application) or the time-limit had not run out;[50] *or*

- the tribunal or the Court of Appeal has granted leave to appeal and a notice of appeal has been received before 5 February 1996 by the Court (including a late notice) or the time-limit had not run out;[51] *or*
- a late application or appeal from a tribunal decision made before 5 February 1996 is made after that date to the Court of Appeal,

and the Court has neither refused leave to appeal nor determined that appeal before 5 February 1996.

The rules for appeals to the House of Lords are the same as for the Court of Appeal, except the time-limits may be different.[52]

For the effect of judicial reviews of special adjudicator and tribunal decisions, see p235.

Asylum appeals pending from 1993

There are still asylum appeals pending from decisions made before 26 July 1993. Those appeals are made under the 1971 Act, not the 1993 Act.[53] The only differences which affect these benefit rules are:[54]

- an application for leave to appeal from an adjudicator can be made to the adjudicator immediately after the decision. This is unusual but, if leave is granted, a notice of appeal must be received by the adjudicator within 14 days of the decision being appealed;
- if the application for leave is made to the tribunal it must be received by the tribunal within 14 days of the decision being appealed.

When an asylum appeal is determined

An appeal is determined on the date the final decision is sent or given to the appellant. In the case of special adjudicator and tribunal decisions, this is the date of the covering letter sent with the decision. A preliminary ruling does not determine an appeal, unless that ruling includes the dismissal of the appeal. In the case of the Court of Appeal and House of Lords, the appeal is determined on the date the court order is sealed.

DSS guidance states that the appeal is determined when the next decision after 5 February 1996 is given on the appeal, even if there is then a further appeal.[55] This is only the right interpretation if the words 'that appeal' in the rules mean 'that stage of the appeal process'. The second, alternative, interpretation is that the words 'that appeal' mean the whole appeal process. The DSS interpretation causes unfairness – eg, if the adjudicator allows your appeal but the Home Office appeals to the tribunal.[56] In that case, your benefit entitlement would end when the adjudicator's decision was issued, even though the adjudicator decided that you are a refugee, and this would continue until any Home Office appeal was decided. The second interpretation avoids this unfairness. The DSS may argue that the second interpretation is wrong because it would be the same as the old rules before 5 February 1996, so the new wording would be pointless. However, the second interpretation is different from the old rules, because a person challenging a decision by judicial review would not be an asylum-seeker for benefit purposes, because s/he would not be making an asylum appeal, even though s/he would have been under the old rules (but see below for where a judicial review succeeds). If the second interpretation is right, you remain an asylum-seeker for benefit purposes while you have a right of appeal (except for judicial review).

Appeal decisions which are overturned
If the DSS guidance is right, there may be cases where the determination of a stage of the appeal process is undone by later events. This would mean that you become an asylum-seeker again even though the first asylum decision after 5 February 1996 went against you. In some cases a decision on appeal may be overturned by a later decision of the tribunal or a court. For example, the next decision after 5 February 1996 may be a decision of an adjudicator dismissing your appeal. The tribunal may allow your appeal against this decision and remit your appeal to a different adjudicator. If this happens in your case, you may be able to argue that your appeal from the Home Office decision is still outstanding because the tribunal's decision means that the original adjudicator's decision has no legal force. This means that you again become an asylum-seeker for benefit purposes. This is backdated to the date of the adjudicator's decision and continues until the date of the next adjudicator's decision. This argument can be used in the following situations:

- the next decision after 5 February 1996 was by an adjudicator and *either*:
  - you or the Home Office appeal(s) and the tribunal remits the case to an adjudicator (the same or a different one); *or*
  - the tribunal does not remit the appeal but there is a further appeal and the Court of Appeal or the House of Lords remits the case to an adjudicator; *or*
  - the adjudicator's decision is quashed on judicial review; *or*
- the next decision after 5 February 1996 was by the tribunal and *either*:
  - there is a further appeal to the Court of Appeal or House of Lords which remits the appeal to an adjudicator/the tribunal; *or*
  - the tribunal remits the appeal to an adjudicator but the tribunal's decision to do that is quashed on judicial review.

Rules for 5 February – 23 July 1996

Because the Court of Appeal decided that the 5 February 1996 changes to rules for asylum-seekers were unlawful,[57] the old rules (see p228) apply from 5 February-23 July 1996. On 24 July 1996 the Asylum and Immigration Act 1996 reversed the effect of the Court of Appeal ruling.[58]

This means that if you claimed benefit before 24 July 1996 the old rules apply to you until 23 July 1996. This only makes a difference if:

- the transitional protection rules (see p228) applied to you on 5 February but transitional protection would have ended before 24 July 1996 because you stopped being an asylum-seeker (see p23); or
- you claimed asylum before 5 February 1996 but do not have transitional protection because you were not entitled to benefit before 5 February 1996 (and the family member rules do not apply – see p230); or
- you made an in-country asylum claim (see p220) after 4 February 1996.

If one of these applies, you stop being an asylum-seeker under benefit rules on 24 July 1996.

The Asylum and Immigration Act 1996 also prevents a person to whom one of these rules applies from making a benefit claim or review request after 23 July 1996 for a period during 5 February-23 July 1996 when transitional protection would not have applied.[59] The date of a benefit claim is defined by regulations (for details, see CPAG's *National Welfare Benefits Handbook*).[60] Under these rules the date of claim can be earlier than the day a claim form was received by the benefits authority. This may mean that a claim made physically after 23 July 1996 is legally made before that date.

3. INCOME SUPPORT

Persons from abroad

If you are a person from abroad you can only get IS if you are entitled to urgent cases IS (see p207).

Some asylum-seekers are not persons from abroad for IS purposes. The most important groups who can argue this are:

- nationals of Cyprus, Malta or Turkey with limited leave to remain or who applied for asylum while in the UK with leave (see p184). This argument can be used to help people who made in-country asylum claims; *and*

- port applicants on bail (see p209). This can help on-arrival asylum-seekers who have been refused asylum.

This is *not* a complete list. You must check the chapter which deals with your immigration status to see if you are a person from abroad for IS purposes. Remember that the rules for HB/CTB are more generous.

If you are an asylum-seeker under benefit rules, you may be worse off by arguing that you are *not* a person from abroad – see the chapter relevant to your immigration status.

Urgent cases IS

Asylum-seekers are entitled to urgent cases IS if:

- you are an asylum-seeker for benefit purposes;[61] *or*
- a sponsorship undertaking (verbal or written) was given for you before 5 February 1996 and you were entitled to IS before that date (see p207). This can be used if your asylum claim is refused (after 5 February 1996) and as a result you are no longer an asylum-seeker for benefit purposes.

For how urgent cases IS is worked out, see Chapter 10.

4. INCOME-BASED JOBSEEKER'S ALLOWANCE

An asylum-seeker who would be entitled to urgent cases income-based JSA is always entitled to IS instead. The only advantage of claiming JSA is that your contribution record is maintained (see CPAG's *Jobseeker's Allowance Handbook*).

The rules for persons from abroad are the same as for IS (see p236). If you are not a person from abroad for JSA you may fail the usual rules for JSA – see the chapter relevant to your immigration status.

If you are a person from abroad you are entitled to urgent rate income-based JSA only if you:[62]

- are an asylum-seeker for benefit purposes; *and*
- have written permission from the Home Office to take work.

5. HOUSING BENEFIT AND COUNCIL TAX BENEFIT

The HB/CTB rules are very similar to the IS rules, but some claimants who are persons from abroad for IS are *not* persons from abroad for

HB/CTB. There is no urgent cases rate for HB/CTB – the types of cases covered by urgent cases rate get normal HB/CTB.

If you are being paid IS/income-based JSA (including urgent cases rate) you are not a person from abroad for HB/CTB.[63] The local authority which deals with your HB/CTB claim should not make enquiries about your immigration status or habitual residence.[64]

You are only entitled to HB/CTB if you are *not* a person from abroad (for other rules, see relevant chapter).

You are *not* a person from abroad for HB/CTB purposes if you are an asylum-seeker for benefit purposes.

If you are not an asylum-seeker for benefit purposes, you may still be able to argue that you are not a person from abroad. **In-country cases** (see p220) include:

- nationals of Cyprus, Malta or Turkey with limited leave to remain or who applied for asylum while in the UK with leave (see p184);
- when a deportation order has been made against you but the Home Office has deferred removal in writing (see p215); *or*
- when an immigration officer has decided that you are an illegal entrant but has allowed you to remain in writing (see p215).

On arrival cases (see p220) who have been refused asylum but who may be able to argue that they are not a person from abroad include:

- port applicants on bail (see p215); *or*
- where a sponsorship undertaking (verbal or written) was given for you before 5 February 1996 and you were entitled to IS before that date (see p207).

These are *not* complete. Check the chapter which deals with your immigration status to see if you are a person from abroad for HB/CTB.

PART THREE

Going abroad

CHAPTER EIGHTEEN

Introduction

This Part explains the effects on your benefit entitlement of going abroad from the UK and returning. The rules setting out who may come and go from the UK, under what conditions and the associated procedures are described in Part 1.

There are two main considerations which affect your benefit entitlement:

- **the ordinary UK rules** determining the effect of your absence on entitlement to the different benefits. There are important differences depending on whether your absence is 'temporary' or 'permanent' – see p242;
- **the reciprocal agreements** between the UK government and governments overseas under which you may qualify for benefits abroad – see Part 5.

If you are travelling to or from Europe and you are:

- a national of an EU member state;
- a national of a European Economic Area (EEA) state;
- a dependent family member of an EU or EEA national;
- a third country (see Part 5) national from a country which has an association agreement with the EU;

you may have further rights to certain benefits while in the UK. Such rights may be related to the social security system here or that of another member state and you may be able to take certain UK benefits abroad to another member state. These rights are dealt with in Part 4.

In describing the effect of going abroad on your benefit entitlement, we use several phrases which have a particular legal meaning. These phrases are:

- presence;
- absence;
- temporary absence;
- permanent absence;
- residence; *and*
- ordinary residence.

Generally, the meaning of these phrases is in keeping with their common sense meaning. However, for their precise meaning, see p98. For the meaning of temporary/permanent absence, see p242.

You should use this Part in conjunction with Part 2 which sets out the residence and presence conditions for the various benefits and also deals with the absence abroad of partners and children.

The following general factors should be borne in mind if you are considering an absence from the UK. In relation to:

- **contributory benefits** – where there are no specific residence requirements, the contributions system itself acts as a residence test, since the condition that certain contributions be made prior to entitlement requires periods of residence in the UK. For the contribution conditions, see CPAG's *Rights Guide to Non-Means-Tested Benefits*;
- **means-tested benefits** – going abroad may have an effect on whether or not you are able to continue to satisfy the 'habitual residence' test. Unless you fall into one of the exceptions to the rule, if you are not habitually resident in the UK you are defined as a 'person from abroad' for benefit purposes. This may have serious implications for your benefit entitlement. For details about habitual residence, see p131.
- **other benefits** – absences from the UK may affect your ability to satisfy the relevant ordinary residence and past presence rules for a particular benefit.

CHAPTER NINETEEN

Temporary absence

This chapter deals with the meaning of 'temporary absence'. This term is important in determining whether you can remain entitled to particular benefits when you go abroad.

For many benefits, the fact that your absence abroad is temporary is a precondition for retaining entitlement. However, for specific benefits there are additional requirements that relate primarily to the purpose and/or length of time you are away. For certain benefits, absences from Great Britain (GB) – temporary or otherwise – are of very little importance. For details, see Chapter 20.

WHAT IS TEMPORARY ABSENCE?

'Temporary absence' is not defined in the legislation and there are no clear rules determining whether your absence will be treated as being temporary. The only guidance available is the case law of the courts and the social security commissioners, which sets out the factors an adjudication officer (AO) must consider in determining whether the absence is temporary. It also provides examples of situations that will lead to a finding that your absence is not temporary. Every absence is unique and distinct, and accordingly, your case will be given individual consideration, so it is important that you provide full details of:

- why you wish to go abroad;
- how long you intend to be abroad; *and*
- what you intend to do while you are abroad.

It is your responsibility to demonstrate that your absence is a temporary one.[1]

In the case of *Javed Akbar*,[2] the High Court concluded that a temporary absence was the opposite of a permanent absence. In other words, an absence was temporary if it was 'not permanent'. In the past, social security commissioners had not always adopted the same view.[3]

However, the Court of Appeal overruled the view taken by the High

Court.[4] As a result, a temporary absence is not just an absence that can be described as being not permanent, although if an absence is permanent it will never be temporary.

Both the High Court and Court of Appeal agreed that a person can still be temporarily absent even though they have not fixed the date for their return. In addition, the Court of Appeal agreed that *in the particular* case of Javed Akbar, the overall conclusion that the claimant's absence was temporary was correct. That case, therefore, serves as a useful example.

Example

Javed Akbar advised his local office that he was going temporarily to visit Pakistan to try and clear his depression and that he would return after three months. The local office accepted that this was a temporary absence and continued to pay invalidity pension. However, he did not return after the three months but stated that, although he definitely intended to return, he could not be sure exactly when he would be back as it depended upon the medical treatment he was receiving. The AO treated the absence as temporary for a further seven months but, when Javed could still not give a date for his return, concluded that the following six weeks of absence was no longer temporary. Javed continued to submit sick notes for the whole period and, by the time of his appeal against the decision some few months later, he had in fact returned to GB. He had, therefore, been out of the country for about 15 months, had always very clearly stated his intention to return and there was a specific temporary purpose for the absence although he was unable to give an exact date for his return. It should be noted that the adjudicating authorities are entitled and should take into account circumstances arising after the date of the AO's decision. In this case, it was relevant that Javed did actually return to GB which confirmed the integrity of his intentions.[5]

As we have seen, the three most important factors in determining whether your absence is temporary are: [6]

- your intention when going abroad;
- the length of the absence;
- the purpose of the absence.

Intention will always be an important factor but will never be conclusive.[7] For example, a person may wish to return but there may be other obstacles (perhaps financial) which prevent her/him returning for the foreseeable future. This may mean that her/his absence ceases to be temporary.

There is no set period for a temporary or non-temporary absence, although commissioners have tended to treat a period of 12 months or more as demonstrating a non-temporary absence.[8] There is no reason in principle why an absence of several years could still not be temporary, but the circumstances would need to be exceptional.[9] The number and lengths of other absences (past and intended) may also be taken into account in determining whether the immediate absence is temporary.[10]

If the purpose of the trip abroad is obviously temporary (eg, for a holiday or to visit friends or relatives or for a particular course of treatment) and you buy a return ticket, then your absence will be viewed as temporary.

The nature of an absence can change over time. If an absence, after the factors above have been considered, is found to be temporary at the beginning of the period, that does not mean that it will always remain temporary.[11] If circumstances change while you are abroad (eg, you go abroad for one reason and decide to stay abroad for longer for a different purpose) then your absence may in time come to be regarded as no longer temporary.

Example

Zeinab is in receipt of long-term incapacity benefit, housing benefit and council tax benefit. She goes abroad for two months to visit her family. Her council flat remains empty while she is abroad and this absence is accepted as temporary by the Benefits Agency and her local authority. After two months abroad, she contacts them to say that she has decided to stay for a further four months as she is having medical treatment from a hospital which is assisting her condition. This further absence is also accepted as being temporary and benefit continues to be paid. After she has been abroad for six months, payment for incapacity benefit stops as she has had the maximum payment of 26 weeks benefit. A month later, Zeinab writes again, stating that her plans have changed and she will be remaining abroad for at least a further twelve months. This is because her new partner lives locally and is six months into a lucrative extendable work contract. She states that it is probable that she will return to live in the UK at some point later. At this point, the adjudication officer and the local authority decide that the absence has become non-temporary and decisions are issued to this effect. Payments of housing benefit and council tax benefit cease.

For more details about how the temporary absence rules apply to the benefits mentioned in this example, see Chapter 20.

Where the rules for the different benefits (see Chapter 20) refer to 'temporary absence' and 'temporarily absent', you should take care to note that the absence is often qualified by other subtle conditions which vary from benefit to benefit. For some benefits, you must 'intend' to return to GB within a specific period and for others you must 'intend' the absence to be temporary as well as it actually being temporary. In many cases, these differences should not affect the outcome.

Finally, it is important to note that in calculating the period over which you are temporarily absent from GB, the day you leave and the day you return are counted as days in GB.[12]

CHAPTER TWENTY

Entitlement to benefit and going abroad

This chapter deals with the effect of going abroad on your entitlement to benefits. The following benefits are covered:

1. Income support (IS) (below)
2. Income-based jobseeker's allowance (JSA) (p248)
3. Housing benefit (HB) and council tax benefit (CTB) (p251)
4. The Social fund (p253)
5. Family credit (FC) and disability working allowance (DWA) (p254)
6. Short-term contributory benefits (p256)
7. Retirement pensions and widows' benefits (p258)
8. Industrial injuries benefits (p261)
9. Disability and carers' benefits (p262)
10. Statutory sick pay (SSP) and statutory maternity pay (SMP) (p265)
11. Premiums and absence abroad (p265)

This chapter does not help you to determine if you are entitled to benefit in the first place. It deals with the *effect* of going abroad on your entitlement to benefits. For entitlement to means-tested benefits, see CPAG's *National Welfare Benefits Handbook*; for entitlement to non-means tested benefits, see CPAG's *Rights Guide to Non-Means-Tested Benefits*. To determine your immigration status, see Part 1 of this book. For the special effect of your immigration status on your right to claim benefit, see the appropriate chapter in Part 2.

For many benefits, an important consideration for entitlement is whether you are going abroad on a temporary or a permanent basis. For the meaning of 'temporary absence', see Chapter 19. For the meaning of other terms relating to absence and residence, see pp98-99.

I. INCOME SUPPORT

For people required to sign on as available for work, income support (IS) was replaced by income-based JSA on 7 October 1996.[1] To be entitled to IS you must be present in GB.[2] If you have become entitled to IS while in

GB, during a temporary absence you may remain entitled for a period of either four or eight weeks. It is not necessary for any IS payments to be *received* prior to any temporary absence, but you must have claimed and satisfied the conditions of entitlement.

Regardless of the other reasons for your absence from GB, you only remain entitled to IS if:[3]

- you leave temporarily; *and*
- the period of your absence is unlikely to exceed 52 weeks; *and*
- you continue to satisfy all other conditions of entitlement to IS (ie, you do not work, you remain in incapable of work etc).

HB and CTB may continue to be paid in addition to any IS you are paid during such an absence (see HB and CTB below).

You will remain entitled for a period of eight weeks if you satisfy the above three requirements *and*:[4]

- you are accompanying a child or young person who is a member of your family abroad solely in order for that person to be treated for a disease or physical or mental disablement; *and*
- those arrangements relate to treatment outside GB which is provided by or under the supervision of an appropriately qualified person while you are abroad.

You will remain entitled for a period of four weeks if you satisfy the above three requirements and:[5]

- the reason you are exempted from the requirement to be available for work is *not* one of the following:
  - you are incapable of work – but see below for qualification for benefit when you are incapable of work;
  - you are in education;
  - you are involved in a trade dispute or are within a period of 15 days of returning to work following a trade dispute;
  - you are a person from abroad who is entitled to urgent cases payments of IS (see Chapter 10);
  - you are a person who is appealing against a decision that you are not incapable of work; *or*
- you are incapable of work and the only reason you are absent from GB is to get treatment related to your incapacity from an appropriately qualified person; *or*
- you are in Northern Ireland; *or*
- you have a partner who is also absent from GB and who is entitled to a pensioner, enhanced pensioner, higher pensioner, disability or severe disability premium. It is only necessary for you to be entitled to the premium. It is not necessary for you to be being paid it; *or*

- on the day you leave GB you have been incapable of work for a period of:
  - 196 days (28 weeks) if you are either terminally ill or you are entitled to the highest rate of the care component of DLA; *or*
  - 364 days in any other case.

Breaks in periods of incapacity of eight weeks or less are disregarded in both instances.

2. INCOME-BASED JOBSEEKER'S ALLOWANCE

Jobseeker's allowance (JSA) was introduced on 7 October 1996 to replace unemployment benefit (UB) and (for people who have to look for work in order to qualify for benefit) IS. For full details, see CPAG's *Jobseeker's Allowance Handbook.*

Presence in Great Britain

To be entitled to JSA you must be present in GB.[6] If you have become entitled to JSA while in GB, during a temporary absence you may be treated as still in GB and therefore remain entitled for a period of up to one, four or eight weeks provided that your absence is unlikely to exceed 52 weeks.[7] It is necessary that you satisfy all the other conditions of entitlement for JSA,[8] the most important of which is that you are available for and actively seeking employment. Unless you go to Northern Ireland (in which case you may remain entitled for up to four weeks), there are certain other conditions you need to satisfy in order be treated as present in GB[9] and these overlap with the circumstances in which you can be treated as available for and actively seeking work despite your absence (see below).

Available for and actively seeking employment

To get JSA you must be available for and actively seeking employment.[10] You could cease to satisfy these conditions if you go abroad. However, when you go abroad you will still be treated as available for and actively seeking employment for:[11]

- **a maximum of one week** if you are temporarily absent from GB to attend a job interview (but you must notify an employment officer of your absence);[12] *or*
- **a maximum of four weeks** of your absence if you are part of a couple and you are getting the pensioner, enhanced pensioner, higher pensioner, disability or severe disability premium for your partner and both you *and* your partner are absent from GB; *or*

- **a maximum of eight weeks** temporary absence if you take your child abroad for medical treatment by an appropriately qualified person.

In addition, in order to be treated as actively seeking work in any of these three circumstances you (and in the case of the third condition, your partner) must be absent from GB for at least three days for each week you wish to be treated as available for work.[13] In all cases, in order to remain entitled to benefit, the temporary absence must be unlikely to exceed 52 weeks.[14]

Even if you satisfy the above requirements, you will not be treated as still present in GB unless:

- **if you are going abroad in order to attend an interview**, you:[15]
  - are not actually absent from GB for more than seven continuous days; *and*
  - can demonstrate to your employment officer on your return that you attended the interview;
- **if you are taking your child abroad for medical treatment**, the treatment is:[16]
  - for a disease or physical or mental disablement;
  - performed outside GB;
  - performed while you are temporarily absent from GB and is by or under the supervision of a suitably qualified person.

You are also treated as available for and actively seeking employment where someone else is abroad if you are:[17]

- part of a couple and you are looking after your child while your partner is temporarily absent from the UK;
- temporarily looking after a child on a full-time basis because the person who normally looks after the child is ill, temporarily absent from the home or is looking after another family member who is ill.

In both cases, entitlement will be for a maximum of eight weeks. In addition, you must look after the child at least three days in every week you wish to be treated as actively seeking employment.[18]

People in receipt of a training allowance

People in receipt of a training allowance from a Training and Enterprise Council (in England and Wales) or a Local Enterprise Company (in Scotland) but not receiving training can get income-based JSA without being available for or actively seeking employment and do not require a jobseeker's agreement.[19] In these circumstances, you can still get JSA for four weeks if you are temporarily absent from GB and entitled to a training allowance, without having to show that your absence is unlikely to exceed 52 weeks.[20]

Holidays from jobseeking
You can take a holiday from jobseeking and still remain entitled to JSA. You may spend a maximum of two weeks in any one period of 12 months (not calendar years) not actively seeking employment and living away from home.[21] You must:

- tell your employment officer about your holiday – in writing, if requested; *and*
- fill out a holiday form so you can be contacted if employment becomes available.

Although, you are exempt from *looking* for work during this period, you still have to be *available* and willing to return to start work during the holiday. In practice, therefore, absences abroad during this period are unlikely to be allowed.

Housing costs
During your four or eight-week temporary absence from GB, you remain entitled to any housing costs paid as part of income-based JSA, provided:[22]

- your home is not let or sub-let to anyone else;
- you intend to return to live in your home;
- the period of your absence is unlikely to exceed 13 weeks.

If you do not go abroad but:

- are absent from your home; *and*
- satisfy the above conditions; *and*
- continue to be entitled to some income-related JSA;

you remain entitled to your housing costs for a period of 13 weeks. In certain circumstances, you may remain entitled to your housing costs for a period of 52 weeks[23] – see CPAG's *Jobseeker's Allowance Handbook* for details and these circumstances. The rules are similar to those for HB and CTB – see p251.

Back to work Bonus
Back to work bonus can be paid whether you are in GB or abroad. So if you stop claiming JSA and are going abroad to start work, you should ensure that you make your claim.[24]

3. HOUSING BENEFIT AND COUNCIL TAX BENEFIT

For the basic rules about who can get HB and CTB, see Part 2.

Housing benefit (HB)

During a temporary absence abroad, you can remain entitled to HB for a period of either 13 or 52 weeks.

You remain entitled to HB for the first 13 weeks of any period of temporary absence from your home provided that:[25]

- the property is not let or sub-let while you are away; *and*
- you are unlikely to be away for in excess of 13 weeks; *and*
- you intend to return to occupy the dwelling as your home; *and*
- you meet the other conditions of entitlement to benefit.

You remain entitled to HB for the first 52 weeks of any period of temporary absence from your home provided:[26]

- you intend to return to occupy the property as your home; *and*
- the property is not let or sub-let while you are away; *and*
- you are unlikely to be absent from the property for longer than 52 weeks although, under exceptional circumstances, you are permitted to be away for a further short period[27] (DSS guidance[28] interprets this to be a further three months at most); and in *addition*

you fall into one of the following categories:[29]

- you are sick and in hospital; *or*
- you or your partner or child are undergoing medically approved treatment or convalescence in the UK or abroad; *or*
- you are on a training course in the UK or abroad approved by or on behalf of a government department, a local authority, any Secretary of State, the Scottish Enterprise or Highlands and Islands Enterprise or operated on their behalf by a local authority;[30] *or*
- you are caring for someone who is sick in the UK or abroad and the care you are providing is medically approved; *or*
- you are caring for a child whose parent or guardian is temporarily absent from their home because they are receiving medical treatment; *or*
- you are receiving medically approved care not in residential accommodation in the UK or abroad; *or*
- you are a student eligible for HB – see CPAG's *National Welfare Benefits Handbook*; *or*
- you left your home as a result of fear of violence and you are not entitled to HB for the accommodation you now occupy.[31]

In determining whether you intend to return home, account will be taken of whether you have left your personal belongings in the dwelling.[32]

With both durations of HB entitlement during a temporary absence, the entitlement period begins on the first day that you are absent from the home[33] and the period of temporary absence begins again each time you leave – even if you only return for a very short period.[34] However, you will not necessarily remain entitled by returning to your home for short periods and leaving again. You are only entitled to HB/CTB to help you pay for accommodation which you and your family (if any) *normally* occupy as your home.[35] If you have another home abroad which you or members of your family also occupy,[36] then your absences from the UK could affect your entitlement to benefit if your absences are long enough or regular enough to mean that your 'main' home ceases to be in the UK. However, you will not lose benefit on these grounds if members of your family normally occupy a home abroad, but are not part of your household.[37]

Council tax benefit (CTB)

To be able to claim CTB, you must first be liable to pay council tax for the accommodation in which you live.[38] If your main home is abroad, you may avoid liability for the council tax altogether.[39] However, demonstrating that your main home is abroad would adversely affect your HB entitlement (see above) and could have a negative effect on other benefits you wish to claim.

If you are temporarily absent from GB, you can continue to get CTB for a period of either 13 weeks or 52 weeks. The rules are almost the same as for HB (see p251).[40] The only variation relates to the transitional provision that applies to CTB and which is important. If you have been absent from your accommodation prior to 1 April 1995, you continue to be entitled to CTB for as long as that period of absence lasts (provided you satisfy the other entitlement conditions).[41]

You may also avoid liability for the council tax itself by showing that your dwelling is exempt.[42] Absences abroad may mean this is the case where the property is left unoccupied. The following are the most likely circumstances where this would apply:

- the property will be substantially unfurnished for a period of less than six months;
- the previous resident is either receiving personal care other than in a hospital or home *or* is providing someone else with personal care;
- the property is substantially unfurnished and requires or is undergoing major repairs or structural alterations to make it habitable or for six months after the repairs have been completed.

For more details, see CPAG's *Housing Benefit and Council Tax Benefit Legislation.*

4. THE SOCIAL FUND

The social fund is divided into two parts:

- **the regulated social fund** from which three benefits are payable:
  - payments for maternity expenses;
  - funeral expenses; *and*
  - cold weather payments;
- **the discretionary social fund** from which there are three types of payment:
  - budgeting loans;
  - community care grants; *and*
  - crisis loans.

For details of when you are entitled to payments from the social fund, see Part 2.

Regulated social fund

Maternity/funeral expenses

Entitlement to maternity expenses payments is restricted to claimants who have been awarded IS, income-based JSA, FC and DWA.[43] All such claimants and those people in receipt of HB, CTB and second adult rebate can also claim funeral expenses.[44]

Cold weather payments

Cold weather payments are payable only to people in receipt of IS or income-based JSA on at least one of the days during the period of cold weather.[45]

There are no additional presence and residence tests for the regulated social fund. The tests are dictated by the presence and residence conditions attached to the various means-tested benefits identified above. You should refer to the section in this Part dealing with the relevant benefit to identify the effect of absences from GB on your entitlement to benefits from the regulated social fund.

Deregulated social fund

Payments from the deregulated or discretionary social fund can only be paid to meet needs which occur in the UK.[46] It is only necessary, therefore, that you are in the UK for a sufficient period to allow your particular need to be established here.

Budgeting loans

In order to get a budgeting loan, you need to be receiving IS or income-based JSA when the decision is made on your application and you or your partner must have been receiving either qualifying benefit for 26 weeks before that date.[47] You should therefore check the rules relating to absence for the qualifying benefit – see p246 (IS) or p248 (JSA).

Community care grants

You can get a community care grant if when you make your application:[48]

- you are receiving IS or income-based JSA;
- you have been staying in institutional or residential care, and it is planned that you will be discharged within six weeks and it is likely that you will receive IS or income-based JSA when discharged.

If your claim is made on the basis that you are 're-establishing' yourself in the community,[49] the High Court has concluded that the 'community' is restricted to GB. As a result, you can only claim successfully on this basis if you lived in GB before the time you made your application.[50] If your claim is made on any other basis, providing you are in receipt of a qualifying benefit there is no other presence or residence test to satisfy.

Crisis loans

You do not need to be entitled to or receiving any other benefit in order to get a crisis loan.[51] Persons from abroad (see Chapter 10) who are not entitled to IS or income-based JSA are excluded from claiming a crisis loan, unless this is the only way of alleviating the consequences of a disaster.[52] Even in this situation, it will be necessary to show the social fund officer that you are able to repay the loan.[53]

5. FAMILY CREDIT AND DISABILITY WORKING ALLOWANCE

The rules relating to absences for FC and DWA are the same.

Both benefits are paid weekly for periods of 26 weeks. Benefit entitlement is determined by your circumstances at the start of the 26-week period. There are only certain special changes in your circumstances that can affect your benefit within the 26-week period.[54] None of these changes relate to absence abroad. For details, see CPAG's *National Welfare Benefits Handbook*.

Example
If a child or young person is provided for in your award of FC/DWA and:

* they leave your household; *and*
* are provided for in another award of FC, IS or DWA;

then your FC/DWA award is terminated with effect from the first date of the overlap between the two awards.[55]

In order to be entitled to FC[56] or DWA,[57] you must be 'in' GB. This means that you must be present and ordinarily resident in GB (and your partner, if you have one, must be ordinarily resident in GB) when you make your claim. If your partner is not ordinarily resident in GB and you previously lived together abroad, you can claim FC as a lone parent if you and your partner do not intend to resume living together. For details of these tests, see p98. For the other basic rules of presence and residence for FC and DWA, see p138. For further details about dependants, see Chapter 9.

So if you go abroad, there is no direct effect on your current award of benefit. However, in order to be entitled to FC/DWA on your return, you once again need to satisfy the presence and residence rules. Your absence from GB can affect whether or not you are ordinarily resident when you return. You may be refused benefit if you are regularly absent from GB and, as a result, the Benefits Agency believes that you no longer normally live in GB as part of the regular order of your life.[58] Under these circumstances, you would need to re-establish yourself in GB before becoming entitled to FC/DWA again.

For all claims of DWA, you also need to be in receipt of a qualifying benefit.[59] The qualifying benefits have presence and residence tests, so you may lose your entitlement following a temporary absence abroad. For more details, see Chapter 11. In addition, second and subsequent claims for DWA are linked either to entitlement to certain benefits or satisfying certain disability tests. Your absences may therefore affect your entitlement to these benefits and, in turn, your entitlement to DWA.

If you go abroad to work, then you may lose entitlement to FC/DWA on your return unless you are immediately re-employed in this country. This is because, in order to get FC/DWA:

* your earnings and those of any partner must derive at least in part from work in the UK and not wholly from work done outside the UK;[60] *and*
* you must be employed at the date of the claim;[61] *and*

- you must be employed in your 'normal' work which is likely to last for a period of five weeks or more beginning with the date of the claim;[62] *and*
- you must work for 16 or more hours in the week of your claim or in one of the two preceding weeks or, if you have been on holiday from work, be expected to work for 16 hours or more in the week after you return.[63]

You should get specialist advice in relation to FC/DWA if:

- you are intending to go abroad, other than during a period of holiday from your work; *or*
- your absences are likely to be prolonged or frequent; *or*
- you are giving up work to go abroad or intending to work while abroad.

6. SHORT-TERM CONTRIBUTORY BENEFITS

These benefits are contribution-based JSA, incapacity benefit (ICB) and maternity allowance (MA). For the details of the presence and residence conditions for these benefits, see Chapter 11.

Contribution-based JSA

The rules relating to absences for contribution-based JSA are the same as for income-based JSA[64] – see p248. Note that unemployment benefit, which has been replaced by contribution-based JSA, was not payable under the ordinary rules if the claimant left GB (see CPAG's *Ethnic Minorities Handbook*, 1st edn, p170).

However, like other contributory benefits, you need to satisfy the contribution conditions[65] which means that you are unlikely to qualify unless you have lived and worked in the UK for several years. For the contribution conditions, see CPAG's *Rights Guide to Non-Means-Tested-Benefits*.

For contribution-based JSA, you are still treated as present in GB if you are outside GB because you are an offshore worker[66] *or* because you are a mariner and you are left outside GB, provided you report to the consular officer or chief officer of customs within 14 days or as soon as reasonably practicable.[67] For what counts as an offshore worker for these purposes, see p143. If you fall into one of these categories, then you remain entitled to benefit despite your absence from GB provided you fulfil all other entitlement conditions.

Incapacity Benefit

If you are temporarily absent (see p242) from GB then you can remain entitled to benefit. Unless you are receiving either attendance allowance (AA) or disability living allowance (DLA) or you are a member of the family of a serving member of the forces and temporarily absent because you are living with that person,[68] then you only remain entitled to benefit for the first 26 weeks of any such absence[69] and unless either of these conditions apply to you, the Secretary of State must certify that it would be consistent with the proper administration of the benefits scheme for you to qualify for benefit despite your absence.[70] You *also* need to satisfy one of the following conditions:[71]

- you are going abroad for treatment for an incapacity which began before you go abroad. This must be the reason why you go abroad. You cannot simply decide to receive such treatment while you are abroad.[72] The treatment itself must be carried out by some other person[73] and must usually be of a medical nature. Convalescence or a trip abroad for a change in environment will not qualify;[74] *or*
- your incapacity. is the result of an industrial injury[75] (see CPAG's *Rights Guide to Non-Means-Tested Benefits*) and you go abroad in order to receive treatment which is appropriate to that injury; *or*
- at the time you go abroad, you have been continuously incapable of work for six months and you remain continuously incapable of work for the time that you are abroad and claiming benefit. In this case, it is not necessary for your absence to be for the purpose of receiving treatment.

You can also get benefit for the whole of the period of the temporary absence if one of the above three conditions applies to you and you have been continuously absent from GB since 8 March 1994.[76]

You are also treated as present in GB and entitled to benefit if you are outside GB because you are an offshore worker[77] *or* because you are a mariner.[78] For what counts as an offshore worker for these purposes, see p143. If you fall into this category, then you remain entitled to benefit despite your absence from GB provided you fulfil all other entitlement conditions.

Maternity Allowance

In order to get MA, you need to have been in employment either as an employed or a self-employed person for at least 26 weeks in the 66 weeks before the week in which your baby is due. You must also have paid Class 1 or Class 2 National Insurance (NI) contributions during each of these 26 weeks.[79] MA is payable for a period of 18 weeks starting at any time from the beginning of the 11th week before the week in which the baby is due to the week following the week in which you actually give birth to your baby.[80]

However, in order to satisfy the 'recent work' test you have to have been employed or self-employed in GB.[81] As a result, a lengthy recent absence abroad may mean that you fail to become entitled to MA. However, you may still be entitled to MA if you:[82]

- have been working abroad and you return to GB; *and*
- remained ordinarily resident in GB during your period of absence; *and*
- have paid class 1 NI contributions.

If you think this applies to you, then you should get help from your local advice centre.

The rules dealing with whether you remain entitled to MA when you are temporarily absent from GB are nearly the same as for ICB (see above). The only differences are first that the test of treatment for an incapacity arising as the result of an industrial injury does not apply and, secondly, MA is only payable for a period of 18 weeks.

Your pregnancy alone will not be sufficient for the purposes of remaining entitled to benefit during your period of temporary absence. You need to show a further specific incapacity.[83] It would be advisable to obtain backdated medical certificates before going abroad.

7. RETIREMENT PENSIONS AND WIDOWS' BENEFITS

These benefits are category A, B, C and D retirement pensions and widow's payment, widowed mother's allowance and widow's pension.

For the presence and residence requirements of these benefits and for further entitlement details, see p97. There are residence requirements for categories C and D retirement pension and widow's payment. Category C pension is not covered because you need to be well over 100 years to be entitled and so few people now qualify[84] – for details, see 15th edn of CPAG's *Rights Guide to Non-Means-Tested Benefits*.

Retirement pensions

Both category A and B retirement pensions are contributory benefits. Category A pensions depend on either your own or your spouse's contribution record and category B pensions depend upon your spouse's contribution record. For the contribution conditions, see CPAG's *Rights*

Guide to Non-Means-Tested Benefits. There are no residence or presence rules for either category, but you are unlikely to qualify unless you or your late spouse lived in GB for several years. It is possible to qualify for a reduced rate category A or B pension where insufficient NI contributions have been paid to satisfy the contribution conditions in full. Reduced rate pensions are frequently paid to people who have arrived in GB part of the way through their working lives and to people who have spent periods of their working lives abroad and have not paid contributions to maintain their pension entitlement.

So if you are relying on your spouse's contribution record, you may be entitled to a pension even if you have never worked in or been to the UK and you still remain abroad. You can also claim a retirement pension based on your own or your spouse's contributions even if you are not living in GB when you reach pensionable age.

Example

George came to Britain in 1965. He worked for 23 years until, at the age of 55, he decided to return permanently to Jamaica. He told the Benefits Agency Overseas Branch about his plans and provided an address in Jamaica for them to send his retirement pension claim forms in 10 years' time. While in Jamaica, he paid voluntary contributions to increase his pension entitlement. He is not yet 65, and so is waiting for his retirement pension claim forms, which should arrive about four months before his 65th birthday. If they do not, he knows that he should contact the Overseas Benefits Directorate (for address, see Appendix 2).

Category D pensions are for those people who are aged over 80 years. You must satisfy the following residence and presence requirements:[85]

- you were resident in GB for at least 10 years in any continuous period of 20 years ending on or after your 80th birthday; *and*
- you were ordinarily resident in GB on:
  - *either* your 80th birthday;
  - *or* a later date on which you claimed category D pension.

A category D pension is generally worth less than a category A or B pension. The pensions 'overlap' which means that if you will be entitled to a category A or B pension, the above residence and presence conditions are not important. Absences from GB during the 20-year period prior to your 80th birthday could therefore affect your entitlement to benefit as could absences around the time of your 80th birthday or the date of your claim. If you wish to spend time abroad or live abroad after you are 80, then it is important to carefully plan any such absences because you will be unlikely to qualify for any other benefit which you will be able to claim while you are abroad. Dependants' additions are not paid with a category D pension.

To be entitled to a category C pension, you also must have satisfied certain residence and presence conditions. This benefit is not dealt with in this book (see above).

After establishing entitlement to any retirement pension, you will continue to be entitled to it regardless of any absences from GB.[86] However, absences abroad can still have an effect on the *amount* of benefit you receive. If you spend a sufficient amount of time abroad so that you cease to be ordinarily resident (see p99) in GB, the amount of benefit you receive is frozen for any day on which you are absent. This means that benefit for those days will be paid at the rate when you stopped being ordinarily resident or the rate at which it was first paid if that was later.[87] Your benefit is not uprated along with everyone else's benefit.

However, you will still be entitled to an uprated benefit, even if you are not ordinarily resident if your entitlement is based upon the contributions of your spouse and that person is ordinarily resident in GB on the day before the benefit is uprated.[88]

You remain entitled to uprated category B pension even though you are not ordinarily resident in GB if:[89]

- the spouse on whose contributions the category B pension is based has died or you are divorced from him; *and*
- you have married again; *and*
- your new spouse was not entitled to a category A pension before the uprating date; *and*
  - *either* you were still married to your new spouse on the day before the uprating date;
  - *or* you married on or after that date.

In all cases, when you return after your absence, you will again be entitled to the uprated amount of benefit *provided* you are once again ordinarily resident. You should, therefore, try to time any permanent retirement abroad so that you can take the maximum benefit with you.

You are only entitled to the age addition of 25p payable with your pension when you are 80 for any day you are absent from GB if you:[90]

- are ordinarily resident in GB; *or*
- were entitled to the age addition before you stopped being ordinarily resident in GB; *or*
- are entitled to an increased rate of any category of retirement pension under a reciprocal agreement (see Part 5).

Widows' benefits

Widow's payment, widow's pension and widowed mother's allowance are all contributory benefits and the contribution conditions must be satisfied in relation to your late husband's contribution record – see CPAG's *Rights Guide to Non-Means-Tested Benefits*.[91]

The only presence and residence conditions that apply for these benefits are those which relate to widow's payment. You cannot become entitled to widow's payment unless:[92]

- you or your late husband were in GB at the time of his death; *or*
- you returned to GB within four weeks of your late husband's death; *or*
- you meet the contribution conditions for widowed mother's allowance or widow's pension.

Absences from GB are only significant for certain women who wish to claim the lump-sum widow's payment who, if they or their husband were not in GB at the time of his death, have to come to GB within four weeks of the death in order to claim the payment.

It is therefore important for widows whose late husbands have worked and made NI contributions in GB, but who themselves are living abroad, to check their benefit entitlement. Often, the widow's entitlement only comes to light when relatives in this country ask about their benefit rights because they are trying to support her when she is living abroad. The time limit for claiming widows' benefits is 12 months[93] and this can be extended when the widow was unaware of her husband's death.[94] Therefore, it is always worth checking for these benefits. Once entitlement to widow's pension or widowed mother's allowance has been established, the rules governing entitlement to benefit while abroad are as for retirement pension (see above).

8. INDUSTRIAL INJURIES BENEFITS

These benefits are disablement benefit, reduced earnings allowance, retirement allowance, constant attendance allowance and exceptionally severe disablement allowance.

You are only entitled to these benefits if you:

- have an accident which 'arises out of and in the course of' employed earner's employment or a disease which 'is prescribed in relation to' employed earner's employment[95] – for details, see CPAG's *Rights Guide to Non-Means-Tested Benefits*. An employed earner is defined as a person employed in GB;[96] *and*
- were in GB when the accident happened[97] or engaged in GB in the employment which caused the disease.

For details about when you may be treated as being in or employed in GB or your accident/disease may be treated as if it arose in GB and when your employment may count as employed earner's employment (including mariners, air(wo)men, volunteer development workers, offshore workers), see p43.

To get disablement benefit or retirement allowance, you do not have to satisfy any presence or residence conditions.[98] As a result, your absences from GB do not affect your entitlement to these benefits provided you are able to satisfy the requirements relating to your work and your accident or disease (see pp142-45). You will also be entitled to annual uprating of disability benefit while you are absent from GB.[99]

In order to get reduced earnings allowance, constant attendance allowance or exceptionally severe disablement allowance you must be present in GB when you claim.[100]

You remain entitled to constant attendance allowance and exceptionally severe disablement allowance for a period of six months (beginning with the first date on which you are absent) during which you are temporarily absent (see p242) from GB.[101] If your period of temporary absence is longer than six months, then the Secretary of State has a discretion to allow you to continue to receive benefit.[102]

You remain entitled to reduced earnings allowance for a period of three months (beginning with the first date on which you are absent) during which you are temporarily absent from GB.[103] If your period of temporary absence is longer than three months, then the Secretary of State has a discretion to allow you to continue to receive benefit.[104] Both for constant attendance allowance/exceptionally severe disablement allowance and reduced earnings allowance (REA), the Secretary of State in exercising this discretion will consider the reasons for your absence and any other relevant matters. To be entitled to REA:[105]

- your absence from GB *must* not be in order to take work or engage in any other economic activity; *and*
- your claim must have been made before you leave GB; *and*
- you must have been entitled to REA before going abroad.

You count as present in GB for the purposes of REA while you are employed as a mariner or an air(wo)man.[106]

9. DISABILITY AND CARERS' BENEFITS

These benefits are disability living allowance (DLA), attendance allowance (AA), invalid care allowance (ICA) and severe disablement allowance (SDA). For the details of the presence and residence conditions in relation to these benefits and for the circumstances in which you may be treated as present as the result of either your occupation or that of another member of your family, see Chapter 11. Your absences abroad are likely to affect your ability to satisfy these initial presence and past presence requirements for these benefits. The position for SDA, however, is slightly different (see p265).

Disability living allowance/attendance allowance

If you are coming to GB and are unable to satisfy the residence rule that you have been present in GB for a total of 26 weeks in the last 52 weeks (13 weeks for children under six months of age), you will only be able to get these benefits if you are terminally ill.[107] If you are terminally ill, you still need to be present and ordinarily resident in GB in order to be entitled to these benefits.[108] However, if your earnings or your spouse's earnings are exempt from UK income tax, you are subject to an extra test of having been present in GB for a total of at least 156 weeks in the last four years. This residence condition is not waived because you are terminally ill.[109]

If you have been abroad, it may be difficult for you to show that you satisfy the criteria for the mobility and/or the care component for the necessary three months prior to the claim. If you experience difficulties with this, you should seek advice.

If you go abroad, then you are still treated as present in GB and therefore entitled to benefit if you are:

- temporarily absent from GB and have not been absent for a period of more than 26 weeks and the absence was intended to be temporary at the outset;[110] *or*
- temporarily absent from GB for the purpose of being treated for an incapacity or a disabling condition which began before you left GB *and* the Secretary of State certifies that it is consistent with the proper administration of the system that you should continue to receive benefit;[111] *or*
- abroad as a serving member of the forces, an air(wo)man or mariner, or a continental shelf worker, or if you are living with a close relative (as defined, see p145) who is a serving member of the forces.[112]

If you satisfy any of the above requirements for any particular day, then you are also treated as present in GB for the purposes of the past presence requirement for DLA and AA. These requirements are that you have been present in GB for a period of 26 weeks in the last 52 weeks before your claim to benefit.[113]

Those who wish to go abroad and who have reached 66 years of age and are receiving the lower rate care component or the lower rate mobility component of DLA should be aware that if they break their claim by going abroad, they will not requalify for benefit when they return.[114] They will be too old to qualify for DLA and they may be unable to satisfy the stricter tests which apply to AA.

Invalid care allowance

The residence and presence conditions for invalid care allowance (ICA) are the same as for DLA/AA, *except* that:[115]

- there is no waiver of the 26-week rule for the terminally ill; *and*
- those who receive UK tax-exempt earnings are not treated differently from those who do not.

For the details of these rules, see Chapter 11.

If you go abroad, you will remain entitled to ICA (and you will still be treated as present in GB for the purposes of the 26-week rule) if you go abroad **temporarily**[116] *and*:

- the absence is for a continuous period that does not exceed four weeks and was always intended to be temporary (in practice, the disabled person would need to travel with you or you would fail to satisfy the ordinary conditions of entitlement, but see below); *or*
- the absence is for the specific purpose of caring for the disabled person who is also absent from GB and who remains entitled while absent to AA/DLA at the highest or middle rate or constant attendance allowance. 'Specific' here does not have to mean sole purpose but the major purpose of the absence.[117]

You will also remain entitled to benefit if you go abroad without the person who you care for provided:[118]

- the absence is for a continuous period that does not exceed four weeks and was always intended to be temporary; *and*
- you have only temporarily stopped providing care of at least 35 hours a week; *and*
- you have provided the necessary amount of care for at least 14 weeks in the period of 26 weeks before you go abroad *and* you would have provided that care for at least 22 weeks in that period but were unable to because either yourself or the person that you care for had to go into a hospital or a similar institution for medical treatment. However, you will lose your benefit if the person you care for loses their entitlement to AA/DLA after that person had been in hospital, residential or

nursing care for four weeks, or 12 weeks for those who are under 16 years and in receipt of DLA.

You are, therefore, able to take a four-week temporary holiday from caring every six months in which either you or the person you care for may go abroad and you will still be able to receive benefit for this period.

Severe disablement allowance

The rules dealing with whether you remain entitled to severe disablement allowance (SDA) when you are temporarily absent from GB are nearly the same as for ICB[119] (see p257). The only differences are:[120]

- the test of treatment for an incapacity arising as the result of an industrial injury does not apply; *and*
- if you are a member of the family of a serving member of the forces, then, unlike ICB and MA, you are still only entitled for the first 26 weeks of the period of your temporary absence.

The initial presence and residence rules are similar to DLA/AA (see p145) – ie, present, ordinarily resident and present for 26 weeks in the 52 weeks preceding the claim.[121] However, if you return from an absence abroad within the same period of incapacity (for period of incapacity, see CPAG's *Rights Guide to Non-Means-Tested Benefits*), then you do not have to satisfy the presence and residence requirements again when you return[122] (see example, p147).

10. STATUTORY SICK PAY AND STATUTORY MATERNITY PAY

From 6 April 1996, there are no longer any requirements of presence or residence for statutory sick pay (SSP) or statutory maternity pay (SMP). You remain entitled to these benefits wherever you are based, provided you meet the normal entitlement rules – see p147 for details.[123] However, for SMP if your baby was due in any week beginning before 18 August 1996, you will not be able to get SMP if you work for a UK employer outside the EU.[124]

11. PREMIUMS AND ABSENCE ABROAD

Premiums are paid as part of your weekly entitlement to IS, income-based JSA, HB and CTB. Many of these premiums are dependent on your receipt of another benefit – eg, DLA, AA or ICA. If your absence abroad means that you will lose entitlement to the qualifying benefit, you will also lose the relevant premium, although carer's premium continues to be paid for a further eight weeks (see above). You may not be entitled to the premium as soon as you return, since you may need to satisfy again the presence test for the qualifying benefit.

If you are receiving premiums, it is important to consider the full implications of your absence abroad on your benefit entitlement. It may be possible for you to time your absences in such a way that your premiums are not affected. For more information, consult your local advice agency.

CHAPTER TWENTY ONE

Getting paid while abroad

This chapter covers:

1. General rules (below)
2. Getting your benefit while abroad (p268)
3. Paying national insurance contributions while you are abroad (p271)

1. GENERAL RULES

This chapter deals with how to get your benefit paid to you when you go abroad. Because some benefits require National Insurance (NI) contributions, the chapter also covers how to make voluntary NI contributions in GB when you are abroad. For further details about NI contributions, see CPAG's *Rights Guide to Non-Means-Tested Benefits*.

In order to find out whether you are entitled to benefit, see the chapter relevant to your immigration status in Part 2 of this book. In order to find out how your absence or absences abroad affects your benefit entitlement, see Chapter 20. If a number of benefits are paid, the temporary absence rules will affect each benefit separately.

For all benefits, if you delay for a year in cashing or collecting your benefit after it has been issued to you (perhaps because you have gone abroad), you will lose your right to have it paid to you even though you are strictly 'entitled' to the benefit.[1] The only exceptions to this rule are if:[2]

- you ask for the benefit to be paid over to you and you have good cause for not asking for the money earlier (for the meaning of 'good cause', see CPAG's *National Welfare Benefits Handbook*); *and*
- the Secretary of State certifies either that no payment was issued either by girocheque, order book or direct debit *or* payment was issued and returned and no duplicate payment has been issued.

2. GETTING YOUR BENEFIT WHILE ABROAD

If you go abroad and remain entitled to benefit, there are a number of ways in which you can be paid while you are abroad. You should tell your local office of your preference at the time you notify them of your absence. You can:

- keep your order book and simply cash the orders when you return to the UK; *or*
- authorise a person in the UK to cash your order book; *or*
- ask for your benefits to be paid directly into a bank or building society account in the UK;[3] *or*
- ask the Benefits Agency to pay your benefits directly into a bank account abroad, although in some countries you will have to open an account with a specific bank in order to be paid in this way.

Contact your local office to get more details about the procedures. In addition, you can contact: the Benefits Agency Overseas Directorate, DSS, Tyneview Park, Whitley Road, Benton, Newcastle-upon-Tyne, NE98 1BA, tel: (0191) 218 7777.

There are specific considerations relating to particular benefits which are described below.

Income support/income-based JSA

If you are going abroad, you should contact your local office to let them know. If you are claiming income-based JSA and you are going abroad in order to attend a job interview (see p249), you should notify your employment officer (EO) who may also ask you to explain your absence in writing. Similarly, if you are taking a two-week holiday from jobseeking (see p250) you must notify your EO in writing and you will be asked to fill out a holiday form so you can be contacted if a job becomes available.

It is normal practice for the Benefits Agency to ask you to return your order book when you go abroad for a temporary absence, even if you retain your benefit entitlement. If this happens, you should contact the Agency as soon as you return and ask them to pay you the arrears you are owed. If you are paid by giro, you will normally be told to claim after you have returned.

If you remain abroad longer than the period for which you are entitled to benefit, or if you are not entitled to these benefits while abroad, you will need to make fresh claims for housing benefit and council tax benefit – see below.

Family credit/disability working allowance

If you are in receipt of either of these benefits and are going abroad for up to three months, you can cash your order book up to the date of your departure and then cash the remaining orders upon your return. This is because each order is valid for three months. If you are going abroad for more than three months, you will need to arrange another method of payment for the FC or DWA due while you are abroad. You should contact either the FC Unit (DSS, Family Credit Unit, Government Buildings, Cop, Penwortham, Preston PR1 0BR or telephone 01253 500 050) or the Disability Working Allowance Unit (you can send a freepost letter to this unit at DSS, Freepost (PR 1211), Preston, PR2 2TF or telephone on 01772 883300).

Housing benefit/council tax benefit

If you are going abroad, you should tell your local authority about your absence and notify them of any reduction in income that may occur. This is because such a reduction may affect the amount of benefit to which you are entitled. HB is awarded for a maximum 'benefit period' of 60 weeks but your benefit could be awarded for a shorter period. Your claim will still be treated as continuous if you re-apply for benefit either 13 weeks before your claim runs out or four weeks afterwards.[4] So before going abroad, check when your benefit period is due to end and, if necessary, re-apply before you leave or immediately after you come back. If your claim on your return will be more than four weeks late, you will need to argue that you have good cause for a late claim.[5] If you have any difficulties getting such a claim accepted, you should contact your local advice centre.

In some circumstances (eg, where you will lose most of your benefits when going abroad) you may become entitled to HB or CTB while abroad, even if you were not entitled while in the UK. If you are in this situation, you should try to work out the date from which you will become entitled. You should then make a claim before you go abroad, covering you from the date in question and providing details of the anticipated reduction in income. If there will be no one checking your post who can provide any further details that might be requested while you are away, you should authorise the local authority to check the details directly with the relevant Benefits Agency office and/or your employer.

If you are going abroad for longer than you will be able to claim HB/CTB, and there is someone living in your home while you are away, then, depending on this person's circumstances, it might be possible for this person to argue that they are responsible for paying the housing costs and so claim HB/CTB in their own right.

If you are a private or housing association tenant and your HB is paid directly to you, while you are away you may need to make arrangements with your local authority to request that the benefit is paid directly to your landlord.

ICB/SDA/MA/contribution-based JSA

Incapacity benefit (ICB), severe disablement allowance (SDA) and maternity allowance (MA) can be paid to you while you are abroad. Before going abroad, you should inform your local office of your trip and the reasons for it. You will be asked to fill out form BF 5 which asks questions about the reasons for your absence and when you intend to return to the UK. You should tell your office well in advance of your trip abroad otherwise it may not be possible to reach a decision on your claim before you go abroad.

If you have claimed ICB or SDA and you are due a medical examination when you go abroad, you should ask if this can be arranged abroad. If this is not resolved, you will run an increased risk of the Secretary of State refusing to pay these benefits during your absence.

Retirement pensions and widows' benefits

Both retirement pensions and widows' benefits can be paid to you while you are abroad. If the Benefits Agency thinks that you are entitled to retirement pensions and they have an address at which to contact you, they will write to you a few months before you reach state pension age to determine whether or not you wish to claim. If you do not receive a letter but you think that you may be entitled, you should contact the Benefits Agency yourself (for address, see Appendix 2).

If you are happy for your benefit to be paid in the UK or to cash your order book on return, you do not need to tell your local office that you are going abroad if you will not be away for more than three months. If, however, you are going abroad for more than three months, then you should tell your local office so that arrangements can be made to pay your benefit to you abroad. If benefit is paid to your address abroad, it will be paid every four or thirteen weeks. If you are going abroad and you are going to return within two years, you can choose to have the benefit paid as a lump sum when you return. If you will need to get your benefit paid into a bank account while you are abroad, you should give the Benefits Agency as much notice as possible as it is often very slow in making these arrangements. If you have not resolved this before you leave, you should ask a friend, relative or advice agency in the UK to complete the arrangements.

Attendance allowance/disability living allowance

If you are going abroad and you are in receipt of AA/DLA, you should write and tell either the Attendance Allowance Unit (AA Unit, Norcross, Blackpool, FY5 3TA) or the Disability Living Allowance Unit (DLA Unit, Warbreck House, Warbreck Hill, Blackpool, FY2 OYJ). If you are in receipt of severe disablement allowance or extra premiums paid on your HB/CTB, remember that you may lose these allowances if your absence means that you will lose entitlement to DLA or AA. It may be possible for you to time your absence to avoid this situation and to ensure that you can continue to claim on your return (see p263).

Invalid care allowance

If you are going abroad and are in receipt of ICA, you should return your order book to the Invalid Care Allowance Unit at: Fylde Benefits and War Pensions Directorate, Invalid Care Allowance Unit, Palatine House, Lancaster Road, Preston, PR1 1HB.

If you lose your entitlement to ICA, you continue to have entitlement to carer's premium for a further period of eight weeks to be paid with your IS/income-base JSA/HB or CTB, provided you are entitled to these benefits while you are away.[6] If you will lose your entitlement to ICA while you are abroad and the disabled person you care for is staying in GB, they may be entitled to a severe disability premium during your absence. For further information, see CPAG's *National Welfare Benefits Handbook*.

3. PAYING NATIONAL INSURANCE CONTRIBUTIONS WHILE YOU ARE ABROAD

Entitlement to many benefits (called 'contributory benefits') depends on the NI contributions you have made. When you go abroad you can generally decide whether or not to continue to voluntarily pay NI contributions here in order to protect your entitlement to certain benefits. The contribution rates if you pay abroad are the same as if you pay in the UK.

For pensions, you can obtain a 'pension forecast' from the Benefits Agency by returning form BR 19 (available from your local office) which may help you to decide whether to make voluntary contributions or not. If your pension will be so low that you will always need to claim a means-tested benefit to top it up and you are planning to stay in this country when you retire, it is probably not worthwhile making voluntary contributions (for further details, see CPAG's *Rights Guide to Non-Means-Tested Benefits*).

Payments may be made in any of the following ways:

- by direct debit every month in arrears;
- once a year at the end of the year for which the contributions are due;
- by a person you nominate to make the payments for you in the UK in either of the above two ways.

For further information about whether or not to make voluntary contributions and how to make them, you can contact the Benefits Agency Overseas Directorate (see p268) and obtain leaflet NI 38. With this leaflet you will also be sent Form CF 83 which you should fill in and return if you decide to make contributions while you are abroad.

PART FOUR

Europe

CHAPTER TWENTY TWO

The European Community's legal system

This chapter covers:

1. Foundations of the European Union (below)
2. EC institutions (p275)
3. European legislative instruments and methods (p276)

Since 1972, when the UK joined the European Community, the EC's legal system has had an important effect on English law. EC law is given direct effect in the UK by virtue of section 2 of the European Communities Act 1972. The European legal system and its terminology are somewhat different to domestic law. It is helpful to have a basic understanding of European terms and institutions to understand the effects of EC law on your rights and benefits.

The following is a very basic outline of EC law. You can find more detailed explanations in some of the books listed in Appendix 3.

I. FOUNDATIONS OF THE EUROPEAN UNION

The European Union (EU) is the product of a number of international treaties. The ones which relate to this book are the Treaty of Rome (the EC Treaty), as amended by the Single European Act 1986, and the Treaty of European Union ('Maastricht') 1993.[1]

The objects of the EC Treaty as amended include:

- the promotion of economic and social cohesion through the creation of an area without frontiers;
- the prohibition of discrimination on grounds of nationality; *and*
- the introduction of a concept of European citizenship.[2]

2. EC INSTITUTIONS

The most important EC institutions are the Commission, the Council, the European Parliament and the European Court of Justice.

The Commission,[3] which is based in Brussels, is effectively the EU's civil service. There are 17 commissioners in charge of the various 'Directorates', and they are European officials, not representatives of their states of origin. But, unlike the British civil service, it is the Commission which makes proposals for European legislation.

The Council[4] consists of the representative minister from each member state who has domestic responsibility for a particular policy area. So, in the field of social security, the Council consists of the Minister for Social Security from each member state; and in the field of free movement of persons the Council consists of all the Ministers for Home Affairs.

Most Community measures require the Council to vote unanimously to pass them before they become law. Others require only a single majority or a qualified majority to be passed. Both the social security provisions made under Article 51 of the EC Treaty and the free movement provisions made under Article 48 (described in later chapters) were passed unanimously.

The Council decides whether or not to pass community legislation, following consultation with the European Parliament.[5]

The European Parliament is an advisory and supervisory body. Unlike the British Parliament, it cannot pass laws itself, although it can require the Council to consider its representations. Members of the European Parliament are directly elected by people of the member states and sit in political groups reflecting their political opinions rather than their nationalities.

The European Court of Justice (ECJ)[6] consists of 13 judges, assisted by six advocates-general. It is the task of the ECJ to ensure that EC law is observed and applied in the same way throughout the EU. In every case, an advocate-general writes an opinion to assist the ECJ before it reaches its conclusion. Although the advocate-general's opinion is not binding, it is often followed by the ECJ, and thus reading the advocate-general's opinion often illuminates the reasoning of the Court.

Actions in the ECJ refer to questions on the interpretation or validity of EC law. Some are direct actions – eg, an action brought by the Commission against a member state for failure to fulfil a Treaty obligation[7] or an action brought by one member state against another.[8] The other way in which cases reach the ECJ is on a reference from a national court under Article 177 of the EC Treaty. Where a question of interpretation of EC law arises in any court or tribunal of a member state, that court or tribunal may request a ruling on that question if it considers that a decision on the question is necessary to enable it to give judgment. Any court or tribunal (including an SSAT or a social security commissioner) can make a reference to the ECJ, and the domestic proceedings are then adjourned pending the outcome of the reference. A final Court of Appeal must make a reference in relation to a question of EC law. In the UK, this means the House of Lords, or the Court of Appeal if leave to appeal to the House of Lords is refused. Once judgment has been given by the ECJ, the member state must act to give effect to it.[9]

3. EUROPEAN LEGISLATIVE INSTRUMENTS AND METHODS

The relationship between EC law and the domestic law of member states is complex. There are two important principles to bear in mind. The first is the supremacy of EC law over domestic law. The second is that EC law may have direct effect in domestic courts. Therefore, if a member state has passed a domestic law measure which is inconsistent with EC law, a Court or Tribunal should not apply it.[10]

Interpreting European law and British law requires two different approaches. European law is 'purposive', that is you interpret a legal instrument by establishing its objective. It is therefore important to interpret any EC provisions in the light of the objectives of EC law as a whole. In contrast, in British law the emphasis is on taking a literal meaning of the words and phrases, and only if the meaning is ambiguous would you then examine the purpose of the legislation.

The Articles of the EC Treaty are its primary legislation. The early articles of the EC Treaty set out the general principles upon which it is based, and the later ones set out the EC's fields of competence and the extent of its powers – eg, Articles 48 and 51.

Some Treaty articles have 'direct effect' and can be relied upon directly by individuals in domestic law proceedings. An article can only be relied upon in this way if it is clear, unconditional and does not depend upon further action being taken by Community or national authorities to implement it. So Article 48 is probably directly effective,[11] but Article 51 is not.

Apart from Treaty Articles, there are four other forms of EC legislative instruments:

- Regulations
- Directives
- Decisions
- Recommendations

Regulations (cited as 'Council Regulations (EEC) – or (EC) No...') are of general application. They are binding in their entirety and are directly applicable by any person in the legal system of all Member States.[12] Where a Regulation is the legal instrument used, it lays down the content law itself: it is unnecessary (and impermissible) for a member state to seek to legislate in the same field as a Regulation. So Council Regulation (EEC) 1408/71 *is* the European law on portability of social security benefits. There are no transposing regulations in domestic law.

Unlike Regulations, **Directives** are addressed, not to every legal person in the Community, but only to member states. Although a Directive is binding upon the member state as to the result to be achieved, it leaves the state with a discretion as to how to achieve it.[13] Directives are transposed into domestic law via a statute or statutory instrument (confusingly also called 'a regulation').

Unfortunately, member states do not always interpret Directives correctly, so where you are dealing with a field of law covered by an EC Directive and you have any doubt as to what the law is, it is important to compare the domestic law instrument used to give it effect in domestic law with the Directive to see if the Directive has been properly implemented. Domestic law must be interpreted to give effect to Directives wherever possible.[14]

Furthermore, the articles of a Directive may have direct effect and be used by an individual against an emanation of the state ('vertical direct effect') if the measure in question is intended to confer rights upon individuals, and is sufficiently precise and unconditional.[15] An emanation of the state is 'a body whatever its legal form, which has been made responsible pursuant of a measure adopted by the State for providing a public service under the control of the state, and has for that purpose special powers beyond those which result from normal rules applicable in relations between individuals.'[16]

Local authorities, the DSS, the Benefits Agency, social security appeal tribunals, disability appeal tribunals, medical appeal tribunals and child suport appeal tribunals, commissioners and courts are all emanations of the State, and appropriate social security Directives are directly effective as against them or before them.

Decisions are only binding on the parties to whom they are addressed.[17]

Commission **Recommendations** are what is known as 'soft law'. They are not binding on anybody, but courts and tribunals should take them into account in reaching their decisions.[18]

Sometimes people are deprived of EC legal rights to which they are entitled because a European legal instrument does not have direct effect in their member state, and neither has it been incorporated into the domestic law. In some such circumstances, where a Directive gives a clear and ascertainable right to an individual, and the failure by the state to implement the Directive has caused the individual to suffer loss, EC law may give a right to sue the state for damages for its failure to implement an EC Directive properly.[19]

The precise scope of this doctrine has not yet been worked out but it has recently been held that damages can only be awarded where the state's failure was 'manifest and serious'.[20]

CHAPTER TWENTY THREE

EC social security law – an introduction

This chapter covers:

1. The two routes for claiming social security benefits (p280)
2. The objectives of EC social security law (p281)

This part of the book concerns the rights and benefits to which you may be entitled if you are travelling to, from or around the European Economic Area (EEA). It describes the rights you may have as a citizen of a country within the EEA including the European Union (EU), or as a dependant of one of these citizens.

Note: Unless you are already familiar with the structure of European social security law, you will need to read Chapters 22 and 25 before referring to individual benefits. Some people may be able to claim benefits by one route, others by both or neither. So when you consider your claim for a particular benefit you should refer to the checklist on p283.

The EEA consists of the member states of the European Union (EU) (see glossary), and Iceland, Liechtenstein and Norway.[1] The EEA Agreement came into force on 1 January 1994.

The foundation of the European Community (EC) is the Treaty of Rome which was incorporated into English law by the European Communities Act 1972. The Treaty has since been amended so that the EC became the European Union (EU). Different countries have joined the EU at different times. EU law continues to be called community or EC law.

For the different terms used in this part of the book, see p314.

Terminology

Some of the terminology used in Part 4 is different from that used in other parts.

A 'regulation' in domestic social security law is secondary legislation made by a minister using powers given by a statute. In EC social security law, however, a regulation is a provision which is directly applicable in the legal systems of the various member states regardless of what domestic law might say.

> If an English statute or English regulation contains a provision which is inconsistent with an EC regulation, then the European provision will override the English legislation.

I. THE TWO ROUTES FOR CLAIMING SOCIAL SECURITY BENEFITS

There are two routes set down by EC law under which you may be able to claim certain social security benefits in the UK, either from the social security system of the UK, or that of another EU or EEA member state, or a combination of the two. In this book we call the two routes the **co-ordination rule** based on rights given by Regulation 1408/71 (see pp282, 293-95, 297-307 and 311-12), and the **social advantages rule** based on rights given by Regulation 1612/68 (see pp282, 286-93 and 308-12).

These two rules can be used by EU and EEA nationals and their dependants in the UK (see below). If you have worked in the UK and wish to go to another European country, you may also be able to take certain benefits earned in the UK abroad with you (see p304).

Some countries outside the EU and the EEA have signed association agreements with the EU. These agreements give nationals of these countries limited rights including some rights of access to social security or other welfare benefits as they would get under the co-ordination rule or social advantages rule (see p395).

You may have rights under the co-ordination rule or the social advantages rule if you are:

- a national of an EU member state;
- a national of an EEA member state;
- a dependent family member of an EU/EEA national;
- a third country national from a country which has an association agreement with the EU;
- a dependent family member of a third country (see glossary) national from a country which has an association agreement with the EU.

The system which governs the rights and benefits you can claim when you come to the UK from an EU, EEA or association agreement country, is very complex. This is because EC welfare law does not aim to make social security provisions the same in every member state. The national systems and standards of living in the member states are at present too different for that to be feasible. Instead, EC law aims to ensure that there is continuity of social protection for people who move between member states. Although this objective is clear, the measures adopted to achieve it are convoluted; and the case law of the European Court of Justice (ECJ) which interprets the relevant European legislation is not always clear or consistent.

2. THE OBJECTIVES OF EC SOCIAL SECURITY LAW

It is a fundamental principle of European social security law that nationals of member states should be able to move freely from one member state to another in order to seek work. The right to mobility is not absolute but is generally confined to economically active groups. The legislation seeking to provide these rights is found in:

- Article 48 of the EC Treaty which confers on workers a right of free movement between member states; *and*
- Article 52 of the EC Treaty which permits 'freedom of establishment' and confers similar rights on the self-employed.

For an explanation of how free movement operates in the EU and EEA, see pp285-87.

The aim is to achieve social as well as economic integration, and the rules are based on the general rule against discrimination:

Within the scope of application of this Treaty, and without prejudice to any social provision contained therein, any discrimination on grounds of nationality shall be prohibited.[2]

However, EC law recognises that there is more to removing barriers to free movement than the abolition of immigration controls. The objective of free movement would in practice be frustrated if a migrant were to lose out on social security benefits guaranteed under the law of a member state.[3]

Examples
An English woman is unlikely to take up a job in France if she cannot rely upon national insurance contributions made in both countries when it comes to receiving her pension, whether she returns to England or retires in France.

A Greek couple may be deterred from coming to England to set up a business if they cannot bring their dependent children with them, and if they cannot get child benefit for them when they are in England.

An Italian man may decide not to seek work in England if he cannot get child benefit for children who stay living in Italy.

> A Belgian woman who has worked for ten years in Belgium may be discouraged from accepting a job in England if she cannot return to Belgium and still claim sickness benefit, having become ill in England.

For this reason, EC law has developed two methods to help reduce these financial and social barriers to free movement.

Methods used to achieve EC objectives

The two methods developed under EC law designed to overcome social barriers to people's freedom of movement are:

- The 'co-ordination rule'. This was developed under the 'social security' provisions of EC law and is set out in Regulation 1408/71[4] and Regulation 1247/92. It seeks to co-ordinate the social security systems of member states so that neither workers nor their families lose out on social security protection by moving within the EU or EEA. In general, it only applies to social security provisions (ie, contributory benefits) and not to social assistance or means-tested benefits (see p298 for definitions). Special rules apply to non-means-tested non-contributory benefits (see p337) and some means-tested benefits (see p299).
- The 'social advantages' rule. This was developed under the free movement provisions of EC law and is set out in Regulation 1612/68.[5] The aim is to ensure that certain people moving from one member state to another are not financially disadvantaged as a result, and that they acquire the same rights of access to social security and social assistance as citizens of the host state. In other words, after moving they should have access to the same 'social advantages' which they receive in their state of residence (the 'receiving state') as citizens of that state.

Deciding which rule to use

The social advantages rule and the co-ordination rule both have the same objectives: to make it easier for workers to move freely from member state to member state. But the 'personal scope' (ie, the range of people) and the 'material scope' (ie, the range of benefits)[6] covered, and the degree of protection given by each set of arrangements to particular people or particular benefits, are not identical.[7]

In general, it is more beneficial if you can claim a benefit under the co-ordination rule rather than the social advantages rule (see p308 for why this is the case). So, generally, the first question to ask is: does the benefit you are concerned with come within the range of benefits covered by co-ordination rule? If it does, you need not consider the social advantages rule.[8] However, in some cases the European Court of Justice has decided that a person is not within the range of people covered by the co-ordination rule and has gone straight on to consider whether the benefit is covered by the social advantages rule. This was done without considering whether another person who was within the range of people covered by the co-ordination rule could claim the benefit under that provision.[9]

The European Court of Justice has said that some benefits (such as a benefit for the support of young work-seekers) are within the scope of both the social advantages and co-ordination rules.[10] It recognises that the two systems can overlap, and that the same benefit can be covered by both schemes of protection.[11]

Some people may be able to use either rule to claim a particular benefit, while others may be covered by only one rule. Alternatively, the benefit may not be one covered, or wholly covered, by the co-ordination rule, in which case you should always consider whether you can claim the benefit as a social advantage instead.

You should always ask:

- Am I a person who comes within the range of people covered by the co-ordination rule?
- Is this a benefit which I can claim from the UK social security system and/or another European social security system under the co-ordination rule ?
- Am I a person who can claim protection under the social advantages rule?
- If not, is it a benefit which I can claim under the social advantages rule – ie, is this benefit which falls within the material scope of Reg1612/68?

CHAPTER TWENTY FOUR

People who can claim social security benefits under EC law

This chapter covers:

I. WHO CAN CLAIM BENEFITS UNDER THE SOCIAL ADVANTAGES AND/OR CO-ORDINATION RULES

People who can benefit from the social advantages rule may not necessarily be able to benefit from the co-ordination rule, and vice versa.

- If you are an EU/EEA national (see glossary) and a 'worker' (see p287), or you are the dependant of such a person, you may be able to claim benefits in the UK under the social advantages rule.
- If you are a national of an EU/EEA member state, and are covered as a worker under the social security scheme of such a state (see p294), or if you are the family member of such a person, you may be able to claim social security benefits in the UK, or take them abroad with you under the co-ordination rule.
- Certain other people can claim under the co-ordination rule (see pp293-94).

Note: Both rules can be used by EU/EEA nationals who are 'workers', and by relevant dependants. But each rule has its own *different* definitions of 'worker' and 'family member'.

For the extent to which third country nationals are protected other than as family members of EU/EEA nationals, see Part 5.

Definitions of an EU national and an EEA national for co-ordination rule purposes are the same as those used for the social advantages rule under the free movement provisions (see below).

2. AN IMMIGRATION OUTLINE

Freedom of movement within the EU/EEA

If you are a citizen of an EU/EEA member state, you and your dependants will have rights under EC law, and therefore also under UK law, to enter and reside in the UK.[1] As a citizen of an EEA country outside the EU, your free movement rights are the same as those of citizens of the EU. For example, if you are a 'worker'(see p287), you are entitled to enter and reside here. The term 'worker' includes people in current employment and people seeking work. The self-employed, people who have retired after exercising an economic activity in the UK, students, pensioners and self-sufficient but economically inactive people are entitled to reside here. Each of these categories has a particular meaning in EC law which may not be the same as the ordinary meaning. For example, a 'worker' can be someone who is unemployed. You need to check whether you meet the requirements to benefit under one of these categories (see pp287-90).

The rights of people who are EEA nationals but not citizens of the EU are virtually the same as regards freedom of movement. These rights are explained below. It is confusing that UK implementing legislation refers to EEA nationals primarily, grouping together the two categories. In fact, the right of free movement is a fundamental principle of EC law which is conferred directly on citizens of the EU. By virtue of the EEA Agreement, those rights have also been extended to nationals of Iceland, Liechtenstein and Norway. In this book we therefore refer to EU/EEA nationals and EU/EEA member states.

EC law relating to people's freedom of movement applies directly in the UK whether or not it has been implemented into UK law correctly or at all. Therefore, while reference will be made to UK implementing legislation, this does not always reflect the rights which have been recognised in EC law. Nevertheless, you, as an EU/EEA national, can rely directly on EC law to establish your right of residence even if there is no relevant provision of UK law specifying this.

Providing evidence for your right to free movement

Under EC law, work-seekers, as well as people with a job offer, are entitled to move to the UK without any requirement to obtain leave to enter the UK.[2] After you come to the UK, EC law allows the UK authorities to require you to obtain a residence permit if you are likely to remain in an

economic activity for more than three months.[3] This permit is only providing evidence of your right to free movement; it does not confer the
right of residence itself.[4] In practice, the UK authorities do not penalise
you for failing to obtain a residence permit as evidence of your right to
free movement in the UK. However, failure to obtain a residence permit
can have disadvantages, since you may have trouble proving that you
have exercised your right under EC law as a worker or self-employed
person and that you are therefore entitled to benefits. You can get a residence permit by presenting a valid identity card, or passport issued by an
EU/EEA member state, to the Home Office, together with evidence of
work, self-employment or other grounds for qualifying. Permits are normally valid for five years.

British citizens and the EU/EEA

If you are a national of Austria, Belgium, Denmark, Finland, France,
Germany, Greece, Italy, Luxembourg, the Netherlands, Portugal, the
Republic of Ireland, Spain or Sweden, you are a citizen of the EU.[5]
British citizens are citizens of the EU and part of the EEA.[6] However, if
you are British, you can only rely on rights deriving from EC provisions
relating to freedom of movement if you have exercised your free movement right and worked or been self-employed in another EU/EEA member state.[7] In theory, on your return to the UK, you should be entitled to
the same rights in EC law as other citizens of the EU, but see p356.

As a citizen of the EU, you have the right to move and live freely within
the territory of its member states.[8] If you are a dual national possessing,
for instance, British citizenship as well as the citizenship of another member state, you are entitled to rely on the citizenship of that other state if
this will give you better access to benefits or other advantages.[9] This
applies even if you were born and have lived since birth in the UK.[10] You
can exercise your rights under EC law, provided you can produce a passport or identity card properly issued to you by your member state of
nationality. If you can do this, the UK authorities are not entitled to question whether or not you also have the nationality of a third state.[11] You
may not be treated differently because of the time when, or the manner in
which, you acquired nationality of a member state, provided that, at the
time when you rely on that nationality, you do in fact possess it.[12]

3. PEOPLE COVERED BY THE SOCIAL ADVANTAGES RULE

The rights of free movement conferred by Article 48 of the Treaty of
Rome enable some EU/EEA nationals to qualify for benefits using the

social advantages rule.[13] However, it is always worth checking first whether you can use the co-ordination rule (see p293).

If you are a worker, self-employed, or retired or incapacitated (see below), you are entitled to equal treatment with British citizens as regards access to benefits.[14] The only exception is the category of work-seekers who are subject to limitations on access to benefits (see p359).

Three other categories of people are entitled to remain the UK, even though they are not engaging in economic activities: students, pensioners and economically inactive people. However, the terms of their residence rights do not permit them to claim some benefits.

Rights in EC law can overlap. Sometimes a person may be entitled to residence under one or more categories. It is then up to the individual to choose the one which is most beneficial to her/him. For instance, if you are a pensioner or an economically inactive person, you may qualify for residence as a former worker who has now retired in the state where you last worked. This would give you the best residence status. However, if you are a pensioner with sufficient income, you could also possibly qualify for a right of residence as an economically inactive person.

The following groups of people are covered by the social advantages rule except where stated.

Workers

Free movement of workers is a fundamental principle of EC law.[15] Although the term 'worker' is not defined in EC law it has an EC meaning nonetheless. In other words, national definitions of who is and is not a worker cannot be applied for the purpose of determining who is a worker under EC law.[16] The concept of a 'worker' includes many people who are not actually in work at a particular time. For example, it includes people coming to the UK to look for work,[17] people who are working[18] and people who are involuntarily unemployed.[19]

According to the European Court of Justice, **you must be treated as a worker exercising your free movement right under EC law if:**

- **you are looking for work.** You must be allowed a reasonable period of time to find employment and, in principle, a period of six months has been held sufficient. If, however, at the end of that period you can show that you are continuing to seek employment, and that you have a genuine chance of being engaged, you cannot be required to leave the UK. (But note the limitations for work-seekers, see p359);[20]
- **you are working in the UK, either full or part time.** For EC law purposes, the essential feature of an employment relationship is that, for a certain period of time, you perform services for, and under the direction of, another person, in return for which you receive

remuneration.[21] It is not necessary for the employer to make an undertaking. All that is required is the existence of, or the intention to create, an employment relationship.[22]

You are entitled to the status of a 'worker' while you are pursuing effective and genuine activities, excluding those on such a small scale as to be regarded as marginal or ancillary.[23] Provided that you pass this test, you cannot be excluded from the benefits of being a 'worker' in EC law just because your income is so low that, in order to survive, you have to supplement it with income from other sources, or even financial support from public sources – ie, benefits.[24] Your low productivity does not prevent you from being a worker in EC law.[25] Trainees employed over the summer months may be workers,[26] as may be a member of a religious or spiritual community undertaking various jobs, such as plumbing, housekeeping and participating in the external economic activities of the community.[27]

However, you will not be a worker within the meaning of EC law if the work pursued merely constitutes a means of rehabilitation or reintegration for you, and the purpose of the paid employment, which is adapted to your physical and mental possibilities, is to enable you to recover your capacity to take up ordinary employment or to lead as normal a life as possible.[28]

You will still be a worker if your pay, in return for services performed, is less than the basic minimum index-linked wage for a particular sector.[29] It may be 'a share' and calculated on a collective basis – eg, if you are a fisherman.[30] Generally, the origin of the remuneration is irrelevant[31] and the remuneration may be in kind (eg, food, clothing or housing) and be considered as indirect payment for services performed by you (see also 'currently working', p359);[32]

- **you have worked in the UK but have become involuntarily unemployed or temporarily incapable of work.**[33] If you become involuntarily unemployed, you must notify the relevant employment office to be sure of retaining your status as a worker;[34]
- **you have worked in the UK but have become involuntarily unemployed and must take occupational retraining to compete in the job market;**[35]
- **you have been temporarily laid off and are seeking to return to work with the same employer in the UK.**[36]

*****Note:** If you are voluntarily unemployed your position is not entirely clear in law. At the very least, however, you would have to enjoy rights as a work-seeker if you had begun to look for work again (see also p361).

Self-employed people

You are entitled to enter and reside in the UK if you are planning to establish yourself as self-employed here which includes the right to take up and pursue activities as a self-employed person and to set up and manage undertakings in particular companies or firms.[37]

You will be a self-employed person as opposed to a worker if your activity is not carried out in the context of a relationship of subordination.[38] This means that, if you are not under the direct control of a person or undertaking, your right to move to and reside in the UK is based on your self-employment. The principles governing entry into, and residence on, the territory of the UK[39] are the same for self-employed people as they are for workers (see above). Accordingly, so long as your self-employed activities are not on such a small scale as to be regarded as purely marginal or ancillary, you will be self-employed for the purposes of EC law in the UK. It is likely that the guidelines relating to remuneration for workers will also be the same for you as a self-employed person.

People who have retired or who are incapable of working

If you have reached statutory retirement age and worked in the UK for the 12 months before that date and have been resident here continuously for more than three years, you continue to be entitled to the status of worker in EC law.[40] The same applies if, after living in the UK continuously for two years or more, you cease working as a result of permanent incapacity arising from an accident at work or an occupational disease.[41] Special provisions apply to protect frontier workers.[42] Identical rules apply in respect of self-employed people who have reached statutory retirement age in the UK.[43]

Students

If you come to the UK for the purpose of studying here, then your right to remain in the UK is dependent on your having sufficient resources to avoid becoming a burden on the social security system and sickness insurance in respect of all risks.[44] However, you retain your status as a worker if you came to the UK to work and did so, but subsequently began to study as a result of involuntary unemployment and a need to retrain yourself.[45] On the contrary, if, while studying, you are also working or are self-employed, but that work or self-employment is ancillary or marginal, your residence right derives from being a student only.[46] If you are the child of an EU/EEA worker in the UK[47] or of a self-employed person,[48] or the child of a worker who since working in the UK has retired and thereby acquired a residence right,[49] then your right of residence is not exclusively because you are a student but on the basis of being the child of a worker.

'Child' in EC law, for the purposes of a right to education, includes all children of a worker (or self-employed person).[50] Your right, as a child of a worker, to reside in the UK in order to study, continues even if you are over 21 and no longer dependent on your parents, and even if your parents no longer live in the UK. Indeed, even if you have already taken employment, if you lose your job you may rely on your status as a child of a worker.[51] However, while you may be entitled to benefits as a worker yourself who is involuntarily employed and retraining, you may not be entitled to them as a child of a worker if you are not dependent on your parents and the benefit does not constitute an advantage to them (see p311).[52]

Pensioners

If you have come to the UK as a pensioner and are claiming an early retirement pension, old-age benefit or pension in respect of an industrial accident, but you have never worked in the UK, you are still entitled to reside in the UK.[53] However, the terms of your residence require that you have sufficient funds to avoid being a burden on the social security system, and that you have sickness insurance in respect of all risks in the UK during your residence.[54] Provided that the resources you have available are equal to, or greater than, those you would receive in social security benefits in the UK, you are entitled to reside here.

Economically inactive people

If you do not come within any of the other categories as an EU/EEA national, you are entitled to reside in the UK if you have resources available to you which are at least equal to , or greater than, those you would receive in social security benefits in the UK, and you have sickness insurance in respect of all risks in the UK during your residence.[55]

Family members of EU/EEA nationals

The definition of family members for the purposes of EC law is not uniform. There is one definition relating to free movement rights under the social advantages rule, and another for the purpose of determining eligibility for social security benefits under the co-ordination rule (see p295). However, where an EU/EEA national has exercised a free movement right to work or be self-employed in the UK, her/his family members are entitled to equal treatment in access to all benefits which constitute social advantages for the EU/EEA national (see pp311-12). This section is limited to an explanation of which family members have a right to join an EU/EEA national who is exercising a free movement right in the UK. It is therefore a brief outline of your rights to family reunion as regards immigration only.

If you are a **worker** or **self-employed person** under EC law, you are entitled to be joined in the UK by the following family members irrespective of their nationality:

- your spouse;
- your children and grandchildren (and other descendants) as well as those of your spouse who are under the age of 21;
- your children and grandchildren (and other descendants) or those of your spouse of any age who are dependent upon either of you;
- any relatives in the ascending line (eg, parents, grandparents) of you or your spouse who are dependent upon either of you.[56]

If you are a **pensioner** who has not worked here, or you are **economically inactive**, under UK law you are entitled to be reunited with the same family members listed above. This is more generous than required by EC law which limits family reunion with children to those dependent upon you or your spouse.[57] However, if the only ground for your right of residence in the UK is because you are studying, you are only entitled to be joined by your spouse and dependent children.[58]

Family members who are not nationals of an EU/EEA member state, who seek to come to the UK as the family members of an EU/EEA national exercising a free movement right, must obtain a visa abroad. This is known as an EEA family permit and it must be presented to the immigration officer on arrival in the UK.[59] The EEA family permit must be issued free of charge[60] and the family members must be given every facility to obtain an EEA family permit.[61] If your family members are already in the UK, and you are exercising your right to work or be self-employed in the UK, your family members should not be required to return to the country of origin in order to obtain an EEA family permit.

Your family members are entitled to reside in the UK and pursue economic activities here even while their application for a residence permit or residence document is under consideration by the Home Office.[62]

Your right to family reunion begins when you take up employment or become self-employed, but does not cease if you become involuntarily unemployed. In this case, you remain, for EC law purposes, a worker.[63] However, there is no guidance on how long this status will last if you are unable to find new work or become self-employed.

In transposing EC law into national law, the Home Office has specified that 'spouse' does not include a party to a marriage of convenience.[64] No such specification exists in EC law. The interpretation of the concept of a 'marriage of convenience' has not been included in the UK legislation and has not yet been clarified by the courts. It is different, however, from Britain's recently abolished primary purpose test.

Your family members are entitled to reside in the UK as long as you remain here and they remain your family members.[65] If the marriage breaks down while you are resident in the UK and you cease to live together under the same roof, your spouse continues to be entitled to remain in the UK under EC law until your divorce is final,[66] or until you leave the UK permanently. However, if your children are in education in the UK, they are entitled to remain in order to continue studying after you leave.[67] Therefore their right of residence is not dependent on them living under the same roof as you.

If you are entitled to have your family members with you because they are dependent on you or your spouse, their dependence is a matter of fact. It does not matter why the family member is dependent on you or whether they could support themselves by paid employment.[68] The fact that a dependent family member may be eligible for a social security benefit, and claims it, should not result in the loss of that person's status as a dependent member of the family.[69]

Your family members are entitled to residence permits or documents of the same validity as yours.[70] In practice, this takes the form of a stamp in the family members' passports if they are not themselves EU/EEA nationals.[71] Because non-EU/EEA national members of your family have only a derived right of residence in EC law – based on your presence in the UK – it is very important that you seek the benefit of an independent and durable domestic immigration status for them at the earliest opportunity. This status is indefinite leave to remain. It is available to EU/EEA nationals (other than students) and members of their families who have obtained a five-year residence permit (or stamp in their passports for the non-EU/EEA national family members). They must also have been in the UK for four years fulfilling the requirements of one of the categories for residence.[72] It is only when your family members have obtained this immigration status that they will be able to remain in the UK after your departure, or cease to be dependent on you or your spouse without risk of losing their residence right here.

General immigration outline

UK immigration law is governed by a series of primary acts of Parliament[73] which provide a framework under which secondary legislation, in the form of immigration rules, set out the specific detail.[74] However, these acts and rules cannot be applied to people entitled to rely on rights of entry and residence in the UK under EC law, unless the national provisions conform to EC obligations.[75]

If you have a right to enter and live in the UK under EC law, you cannot be prevented from doing so by national law. Three categories of people have rights of entry, residence and to engage in economic activities in the UK as a result of EC law. They are:

- EU/EEA nationals;
- family members of any nationality of EU/EEA nationals;
- nationals of states outside the EU/EEA to whom rights are granted by way of agreements between their state and the EU/EEA (see Part 5).

A fourth category may be emerging from the case law of the European Court of Justice covering nationals of states outside the EU who are employed by enterprises based in the EU, and who are required to travel from one member state to another to carry out economic activities for their employers. This category, which lacks clarity and definition at this time, is not covered here.

If EC law gives you a right to enter and reside in the UK, national law cannot affect that right by requiring, for instance, that you ask for permission to enter the UK or to reside here.[76] However, you can be required to let the UK authorities know that you have taken up residence here. Your right of residence in the UK can only come to an end if you cease to qualify under EC law, or your personal activities constitute a threat to public policy, public security or public health.[77] If the UK authorities wish to expel you from the UK, you are entitled to a right of appeal against that decision.[78]

3. PEOPLE COVERED BY THE CO-ORDINATION RULE

The co-ordination rule seeks to co-ordinate the social security systems of member states so that neither workers nor their families lose out on social security protection by moving within the EU/EEA. The rule covers the following groups of people:

- people who are employed or self-employed and who are, or have been, subject to the legislation of one or more EU/EEA member states (see glossary);
- pensioners who are EU/EEA nationals (even if they became pensioners before their country joined the EU), and their families or survivors, whatever their nationality;
- people who are 'stateless persons' or 'refugees' residing within the territory of one or more EU/EEA member state, and their families and survivors, whatever their nationality.[79]

- civil servants not insured under a special scheme for civil servants.

To date, co-ordination provisions do not cover:

- the non-employed (unless they are family members); *or*
- people insured under a special scheme for civil servants; *or*
- students; *or*
- people who are not EU/EEA nationals or their families; *or*
- survivors (except for stateless persons or refugees and their families and survivors).

In the near future, the scope of the co-ordination provisions is likely to be extended to apply to students, the non-employed and some civil servants.

Workers under the co-ordination rule

For the purposes of the co-ordination rule, a worker is someone who has insurance as a worker under the social security system rather than someone who is pursuing 'effective and genuine activities'.[80] An employed or self-employed person is defined as:

> …any person who is insured compulsorily or on an optional basis, for one or more of the contingencies covered by the branches of a social security scheme for employed or self-employed persons.[81]

You are also included under this definition if:

- you ought to be affiliated to the social security scheme (because you fulfil the statutory criteria) even if your contributions have not in fact been paid;[82]
- you have, in the past, been insured under the relevant scheme of insurance;[83]
- you are no longer economically active.[84]

If you are a part-time worker you will still be covered under the co-ordination rule, no matter how much or how little time you devote to your activities.[85] However, you must still satisfy the insurance definition (see above). If you earn less than the lower earnings limit, then you are probably not covered.[86]

The concept of a worker (and a self-employed person) for social security purposes has an EC law meaning which overrides any definition in the national legislation.[87]

Family members of an EU/EEA national under the co-ordination rule

A member of the family is any person defined or designated as a member of the household by the legislation under which benefits are provided. However:

> where...the said legislations regard as a member of the family or a member of the household only a person living under the same roof as the worker, this condition shall be considered satisfied if the person in question is mainly dependent on that worker.[88]

This means that the decision as to whether or not you count as the family member of an insured person is largely a matter of national law. In the UK, you are a 'member of the family' if you are a dependant.[89] However, the European Court of Justice has, on occasion, extended the definition of the family when it considered it necessary to do so in order to promote freedom of movement for workers.[90]

Survivors

You are defined as a 'survivor' if you are a survivor in national law – eg, in the UK, a widow or widower is a 'survivor'. Note that this is subject to the same proviso that you can be a dependant, and do not have to have been living under the same roof as the worker.[91]

People subject to UK legislation

There is a general rule that a worker for co-ordination rule purposes is subject to the legislation of a single member state only (see p316).[92]

You only come under the co-ordination arrangements if you have been subject to the legislation of a member state,[93] and can only qualify for UK social security benefits under the co-ordination rule if the UK is the Competent State (see p316). In order to avoid duplication of benefits, only one state can be the Competent State. There are specific rules for determining which legislation applies and, therefore, which is the Competent State.

CHAPTER TWENTY FIVE

Benefits covered by the co-ordination and social advantages rules

This chapter covers:

This chapter explains, in general terms, the mechanisms for ensuring continuity of protection of social security benefits under the 'co-ordination rule' and the 'social advantages rule'.

The co-ordination rule, set out in Regulation 1408/71, seeks to co-ordinate the social security systems of member states so that neither workers nor their families lose out on social security protection by moving within the EU/EEA.

The social advantages rule, set out in Regulation 1612/68, aims to ensure that certain people moving between member states are not financially disadvantaged as a result but that they receive the same 'social advantages' as they would if they were in their own state of residence.

The chapter outlines:

- how the two rules work;
- which benefits you may be able to claim in the UK if you come within the range of people who can use one or both of the two rules (see p283); *and*
- how the co-ordination rule may help you take certain UK-based benefits abroad.

References are made to the main EC regulations and articles of the Treaty of Rome that are the foundations of these rules.

A more detailed benefit-by-benefit explanation of what to do if you want to claim a particular benefit in the UK and in the EU/EEA is given in Chapters 26 and 27. Part 5 deals with what you should do if you want to claim benefits and are not an EU/EEA national.

In respect of each of the rules, you have to consider 'the personal scope' (that is, the range of people who can use the rule), and 'the material scope' (that is, the range of benefits covered by the rule).

1. THE CO-ORDINATION OF SOCIAL SECURITY BENEFITS

The legal basis for the co-ordination rule

Regulations which contain the co-ordination rule are made under Article 51 EC. Article 51 is designed to secure the following safeguards for migrant workers and their dependants:

- the aggregation of all qualifying periods taken into account under the laws of the different countries, for the purpose of acquiring, retaining and calculating benefit entitlement; *and*
- payment of benefits to people resident in the territories of member states other than their state of origin.

The mechanism adopted by the EC to achieve this is Council Regulation (EEC) 1408/71.[1]

Benefits covered by co-ordination rule

Benefits fully covered: social security benefits

The co-ordination rule covers social security benefits designed to protect against certain risks. These are:

- sickness and maternity benefits;
- invalidity benefits, including those intended for the maintenance or improvement of earning capacity;
- old-age benefits;
- survivors' benefits;
- benefits in respect of accidents at work and occupational diseases;
- death grants;
- unemployment benefits;
- family benefits.[2]

It does not matter whether these benefits are created under a general or a special social security scheme, nor whether the scheme under which they arise is contributory or non-contributory.[3] However, you cannot use the co-ordination rule unless you have paid national insurance contributions in an EU/EEA member state or are the family member[4] of a person who has, but see p349 on income-based JSA. The co-ordination rule also applies to schemes where employers are liable to pay benefit.[5]

Benefits partially covered: special non-contributory benefits

Since 1992, the co-ordination rule also covers special non-contributory benefits, to a more limited extent (see p299). These benefits are provided under legislation or schemes other than those already covered,[6] or specifically excluded from cover.[7] Attendance allowance, invalid care allowance and disability living allowance are classed as special non-contributory benefits though special rules apply. (See p337 for more information about these benefits.)

Special non-contributory benefits are intended *either*:

- to provide supplementary, substitute or ancillary cover to the risks catered for by the branches of social security (see p297); *or*
- solely as specific protection for the disabled.[8]

Benefits not covered – social and medical assistance

The categories of risks listed as being covered by social security benefits and special non-contributory benefits[9] are exhaustive. Any branch of social security not mentioned in the list is not covered by the co-ordination rule.[10] In addition, the co-ordination rule is specifically said not to apply to:

- social and medical assistance;
- benefit schemes for victims of war or its consequences;
- special schemes of civil servants or persons treated as such.[11]

Those benefits not covered by the co-ordination rule will be referred to as 'social and medical assistance'.

How to distinguish between 'social security' and 'social and medical assistance'

Setting out the theory concerning which categories of benefits fall inside or outside of the co-ordination rule is easier than applying it in practice. The application of the categories is made more difficult because of the inconsistent and unpredictable case law on this subject from the European Court of Justice (ECJ).

To add to the confusion, the ECJ has held that sometimes a benefit can have links with both social security and social assistance.[12] Working out whether a particular type of benefit is 'social security', 'social assistance' or a (hybrid) 'special non-contributory benefit' is, however, an important exercise, because getting the right category enables you to work out whether, and how, the co-ordination rule applies to it.

The category into which a benefit falls depends upon factors relating to each benefit, in particular its purpose and the conditions for its eligibility,[13] and not on whether or not it is described as 'social security' by the national legal system.[14]

Under EC law, a social security benefit is one which confers upon an individual a legally defined position entitling them to benefits in particular circumstances without any individual or discretionary assessment.[15] For example, an allowance to which all employed pregnant women are entitled is a social security benefit.

Under EC law, social assistance is a benefit or measure which makes the claimant's need one of the essential criteria for eligibility. It is a means-tested benefit rather than an entitlement linked primarily to the risk. For example, a means-tested grant for a pregnant woman to buy baby clothes is social assistance.

The situation has become even more complicated since 1992, when special non-contributory benefits were introduced (see p298). The ECJ used to struggle with what it called 'hybrid' benefits which are those with the characteristics both of social security (ie, giving a legally defined right in the event of a defined risk occurring), and social advantage (ie, being generally available to the population as a whole provided they satisfy the 'need' criterion). It tended to come down on the side of defining such hybrid benefits as social security.[16]

It is not clear how the new category of 'intermediate' (special non-contributory) benefits will be interpreted. The ECJ has been asked whether disability living allowance (DLA) is an invalidity benefit fully covered as social security under the co-ordination rule,[17] or a special non-contributory benefit which is solely for the specific protection of the disabled under Regulation1408/71[18] and so only partly covered.[19] At the time of going to press, the court had not reached a decision, but the Advocate General's opinion is that DLA is a special non-contributory benefit.

Member states' declarations and Annex IIa of Regulation 1408/71

Each member state has to list the benefits which are treated as social security benefits and those which are treated as special non-contributory benefits for the purpose of the Regulation.[20]

They do this in special 'declarations' which you can find in the Compendium of European Social Security Law (see Appendix 3). Many are not up-to-date. Benefits which the member states themselves think of as special non-contributory benefits are listed as an annex to Reg1408/71.[21] The relationship between the annex and the declaration has yet to be clarified by the ECJ.

If a member state has listed a benefit as social security, then you are entitled to rely on the declaration to prove that the benefit is social security and, therefore, comes under the co-ordination rule.[22]

However, even if a benefit is not listed in the declaration as social security it does not necessarily mean that the ECJ may treat it as such if, in fact, it has the characteristics of a social security benefit.[23]

How a benefit is characterised is a matter of law, which can only finally be resolved in cases of dispute by the ECJ.[24] In practice, the DSS is not likely to treat a benefit as social security unless it is in the UK declaration, so if you want to use the co-ordination rule to claim a benefit which might be treated as social security, but could also be a hybrid benefit, or social assistance, you should take legal advice.

The UK has not altered its declaration since 1986 because of changes to UK social security law. Benefits which are now included in the UK declaration as social security are:

- the Social Security Act 1975 (excluding Sections 37 and 37A) and amending legislation and equivalent Northern Irish legislation;
- Parts I and II of the Social Security Pensions Act 1975 (excluding section 22) and amending legislation and equivalent Northern Irish legislation;
- Industrial Injuries and Diseases (Old Cases) Act 1975;
- Part I of the Social Security and Housing Benefits Act 1982 and amending legislation and equivalent Northern Irish legislation;
- benefits in kind under the National Health Service Act 1977 and amending legislation and the Northern Irish and Scottish equivalents;
- child benefit.

Because the UK's declaration of what counts as a social security benefit has not been amended since special non-contributory benefits were included under Reg 1408/71, two problems arise. First, there is no UK declaration concerning special non-contributory benefits and, second, the UK declaration of social security benefits includes benefits which, according to Annex IIa of Reg 1408/71 are special non-contributory benefits – eg, attendance allowance.

Annex IIa lists the following as special non-contributory benefits:

- invalid care allowance;
- family credit;
- attendance allowance;
- income support;
- income-based jobseeker's allowance;[25]
- disability living allowance;
- disability working allowance.

The relationship between a benefit being listed in Annex IIa and its actual legal status has not yet been defined, so we do not know what happens if:

- a benefit is listed in a declaration (or in Annex IIa) as a special non-contributory benefit, but, in fact, has the characteristics of a social security benefit; *or*
- there is an apparent contradiction between the statement in the declaration and the content of Annex IIa.

A good example of this confusion surrounds attendance allowance (AA). Attendance allowance is in the UK declaration as a social security benefit, and mobility allowance (MA) was held to be a social security benefit in a decision of the ECJ.[26] Disability living allowance (DLA), however, is not in the UK's declaration as social security, but is listed as a special non-contributory benefit in Annex IIa. Since DLA replaced AA and MA for many people – covering the same risks, and granted on the same terms – it is arguable that DLA should also be treated as a social security benefit. However, for the time being, the DSS will not treat it as such. The DSS says it is a special non-contributory benefit designed solely as specific protection for the disabled. This is important because special non-contributory benefits are not exportable (see below). The decision determining how a benefit such as DLA should be characterised is awaiting resolution by the ECJ (see p299).[27]

How social security provision is co-ordinated

Co-ordination is achieved by applying the following principles:

- equality/non-discrimination on grounds of nationality;
- in most cases, by applying the legislation of one state only;
- by ensuring that a person does not receive overlapping benefits;
- by aggregating and apportioning benefit entitlement between the different member states where a person has been a 'worker' (see p294);
- by allowing the portability of social security benefits between member states.

What follows is a basic outline of how the principles are applied in practice. There are specific arrangements in relation to maternity and sickness benefits, unemployment benefits, old age, invalidity and death benefits, special non-contributory benefits and family benefits. For more details about UK benefits see CPAG's *Rights Guide to Non-Means Tested Benefits* and *Jobseeker's Allowance Handbook*.[28] For more information about how the co-ordination rule applies to different types of benefits, see Chapter 26.

In general, the state which pays you benefits is called the 'Competent State'. Even though your benefits may have been earned in a different member state and be funded by that state, you claim them from the Competent Institution of the Competent State (see p316).

Equality of treatment[29]

If you are covered by the co-ordination rule, you are entitled to enjoy the same benefits under the legislation of the Competent State as a national of that state. This does not just outlaw direct discrimination against you based on your nationality, but also rules out disguised or 'indirect' forms of discrimination. This arises in measures which, although apparently neutral and non-discriminatory, have, in practice, a greater adverse impact on those who are not nationals of the Competent State. For example, if a woman with children cannot claim benefit for them unless the children are nationals of the Competent State, the ECJ has said that such a condition about the nationality of the children causes indirect discrimination against nationals of member states other than the Competent State, and that the rule of national law which creates the condition must not be applied.[30]

The non-discrimination principle also prevents 'reverse' discrimination – ie, discrimination in favour of non-nationals of the Compent State. If you are a national of the UK, you are entitled to UK benefits on terms which are as favourable as those applying to nationals of other EU/EEA member states.[31]

Preventing discrimination

The non-discrimination principle has been used to extend the rights of EU/EEA claimants and their families in relation to widows' rights,[32] disabled people's allowances,[33] allowances for large families[34] and non-contributory old-age allowances.[35] However, on its own, it is not enough to prevent some of the types of problems identified in Chapter 23 from occurring (see examples, p281).

If you have come to the UK, or want to go from the UK to another EU/EEA member state, and you want to know your benefit entitlement, you need to ask:

- Which member state's legislation applies to you?
- If the benefit you are claiming is contributory, will the contributions you have made in another EU/EEA member state count towards your entitlement?
- Can you continue claiming the benefit you have earned in one benefit system if you go to live in another EU/EEA member state?

Deciding which member state's legislation applies to you: the 'Single State Rule'

There are rules deciding which state's legislation applies.[36] The general rule[37] is that it is the state in which you are employed or in which you were last employed – ie, the Competent State (see pp316-19). This is called the *lex laboris* rule. The exceptions to this rule are discussed in more detail on pp317-19. The Competent State's social security institution is the Competent Institution. The DSS (and the Benefits Agency) is the UK's primary Competent Institution. For example, if you last worked in Germany and have just arrived in the UK to look for work, Germany is the Competent State and its social security institution will still be the Competent Insitution responsible for paying you benefit, even though you will make your claim to the local UK JobCentre.

Aggregating and apportioning your insurance contributions made in different member states

Aggregation and apportionment of insurance periods for the purpose of calculating entitlement to benefit are key co-ordinating mechanisms. The principle is that you should be entitled to benefits on the basis of your contributions to all of the social security schemes in all of the EU/EEA member states in which you have been insured.

If the national rules of the Competent State give you a non-contributory entitlement to a particular social security benefit, you can claim it in the Competent State as you could if you had always been insured in that member state.

Otherwise, your benefit will be calculated by taking account of aggregation or apportionment procedures, which are used in different ways for different types of benefit.

Aggregation

Aggregation tends to be applied to short-term benefits like unemployment, maternity, sickness and some invalidity benefits.

There are no general aggregation provisions: each type of social security benefit to which aggregation provisions are applied has its own rules and you will need to take account of these when claiming.[38] (For more information, see Chapter 26).

If the acquisition, retention or recovery of benefits is conditional upon completion of periods of residence, employment or insurance, then, to the extent necessary, the Competent Institution must:

- decide whether you are entitled to benefits; *and*
- calculate the amount of your benefit entitlement.

It must do this by aggregating (adding up) all your periods of residence, employment or insurance in the different EU/EEA member states.

What constitutes a period of residence, employment, or insurance is determined by the legislation of the member state in which it took place.[39]

Apportionment

Apportionment is the technique used in relation to longer-term entitlements such as old age, survivors' and some other types of invalidity benefit.

In the case of certain longer-term benefits, apportionment is coupled with aggregation. For example, if you have contributed to the state pension scheme in a number of EU/EEA member states, each state must pay a proportion of the rate to which you would have been entitled if you had spent your whole working life in that state. The proportion is calculated by dividing your working life by the length of time actually worked in each member state (see p341 for how this is done).

Prevention of overlapping of benefit entitlement

To avoid duplication of benefit entitlement, only the Competent State (see p316) carries out the aggregation exercise, and you will only receive a pro rata amount of any aggregated benefit[40] (see 'calculating your pension', p341).

Exporting benefits

This is the other principal coordinating mechanism in the co-ordination rule, often referred to as 'portability'. Its aim is to abolish residence and presence conditions which restrict entitlements to benefit, and to enable people to export certain social security benefits when they cease to be resident in the member state where the entitlement arose.

The portability mechanism means that, except where the co-ordination rule specifically provides otherwise, the following benefits acquired under the legislation of one or more member states may not be reduced, modified, suspended, withdrawn or confiscated just because you live in a different member state to the one where the Competent Institution responsible for payment is situated:[41]

- invalidity benefits;
- old-age benefits;
- survivors' cash benefits;
- pensions for accidents at work or occupational diseases;
- death grants.

Only certain types of benefits can be exported. Portability does not work for the new special non-contributory benefits,[42] and applies only on a restricted basis to unemployment, sickness and maternity benefits. The policy justifications for this are that:

- there should be a social link between the paying state and the recipient;

- the paying state may wish to monitor a person's condition;
- the wish to prevent people from maximising benefit entitlement by moving between member states, claiming and taking benefits with them as they go – 'benefit tourism' as it is called.

How the co-ordination rule applies to different types of benefit

The ways in which the co-ordination rule is applied to different kinds of benefits (under Reg 1408/71), are extremely complex. This chapter provides a brief overview of how the conditions apply to different types of benefit. They may be relevant to you if:.

- you have no entitlement to benefit under UK law, but may be able to claim some benefits under the benefit system of another member state;
- your right to benefits in the UK may be subject to periods of contribution, residence or employment abroad, *or*
- you can only get a proportion of your overall benefits from the UK system and need to seek the other proportion (under apportionment provisions) from elsewhere.

You will need to make further enquiries of the Competent Institution of the relevant Competent State. The way in which portability operates in relation to UK benefits is described in Chapter 26.

Maternity and sickness benefits

There is enormous variation in the types of benefits (in cash and in kind) provided by the different EU/EEA social security systems to cover maternity and sickness.[43] Aggregation is carried out by the Competent State.[44] There is no apportionment. A limited degree of exportability is allowed[45] if:

- your pregnancy or sickness means you need to claim benefit while you are in a member state other than the Competent State; *or*
- you become entitled to those benefits in the Competent State and then move to, live or stay in another member state.

For practical reasons, benefits in kind are provided by the state of residence, though the cost is borne by the Competent Institution.

Unemployment benefits

(Note that in the UK, unemployment benefit is now called jobseeker's allowance (JSA). This section refers to the contribution-based element of JSA.)

Unemployment benefits can be aggregated under tightly controlled conditions[46] but there is no apportionment. You can export unemployment benefits, but only for a limited period. In general, to claim unemployment benefit from the Competent State, you must have been registered and available for work there for the first four weeks of unemployment and then register as seeking work in each member state to which you go in search of work. Your entitlement to benefit from the Competent State will cease after three months' absence unless you return to it within three months. Thus, a British national who has satisfied the conditions for getting contribution-based JSA for four weeks in Britain, who then moves to France to look for work, will be entitled to three months' benefit from Britain – provided that s/he registers/signs on for work in France. However, s/he will cease to be entitled if s/he does not return to Britain after three months.

Old age, invalidity and death benefits

In most cases, these long-term benefits are subject to a combined aggregation and apportionment procedure,[47] with different procedures applying to different categories of benefits. You need to consult the precise terms of Reg 1408/71 if you think you have some entitlement from another member state and some from the UK and you wish to aggregate them. These categories of benefits are also fully exportable[48] (provided they are social security and not special non-contributory benefits).

Note that death benefits mean survivors' benefits such as widows' pensions and do not mean death grants. Note also that different techniques apply to different kinds of invalidity benefits (see types A and B invalidity benefits – pp335-36).

Family benefits

Some member states pay family benefits conditional upon residence (in other words, anyone who lives in the member state can qualify for them). Other member states pay family benefits conditional upon employment (in other words, you must be working in that member state to claim). This creates serious problems of overlapping. Reg 1408/71 differentiates between 'family benefits' (ie, benefits in cash or in kind under social security legislation) and 'family allowances' (ie, cash benefits payable according to the number of children you have and/or their ages).

The basic mechanism used to co-ordinate family benefits and allowances is aggregation with no apportionment.[49] For more information about family benefits see Chapter 26, p346.

Where the Competent State makes family benefits dependent upon periods of insurance or employment, such benefits are paid by the Competent Institution in the worker's last state of employment or residence, even if the worker's children (in respect of whom the benefits are paid) are resident in other EU/EEA member states. For example, if you are a worker entitled to be paid family benefits by the Competent State because of periods of insurance or employment in that and/or other member states, you will receive family benefit in respect of your children whether or not your children live in another state.[50]

There may be a problem if the worker is subject to the legislation of a Competent State in which entitlement to family benefits relates to periods of work/contribution, but the family members live in a state where entitlement to family benefits relates to residence. In those circumstances, the family benefits from the family's state of residence are suspended, but only up to the level of the contributory benefits in the first member state. However, if the worker in the different member state is not the parent responsible for the children, and the responsible parent is in fact working in the member state where the children reside, then that state, and not the non-caring parent's state of employment, must pay the benefit.[51]

Example

Sarah's husband John goes to work in another EU/EEA member state, leaving Sarah and their two children in England. She is a full-time carer and does not pay National Insurance contributions. In the state where John works, family benefits depend on following an occupation in that member state. That state pays John family benefits, calculated by aggregating his periods of insurance there with his periods of National Insurance in the UK. Family benefits are higher in that state, so the Benefits Agency suspends the child benefit which was payable in the UK. However, if Sarah starts to work in the UK, then the benefit entitlement from the state where John works will cease, and the family will be entitled to UK child benefit instead.

If, however, Sarah does not go to work, and the family benefits are lower in the state where John is working, then the family would get child benefit from both countries: child benefit paid by the member state where John works, topped up by UK child benefit.

---

2. THE PROTECTION OF SOCIAL ADVANTAGES

The importance of the social advantages rule

The social advantages rule, set out in Regulation 1612/68, is another means of preventing discrimination on grounds of nationality, and is important to people who cannot be helped by the co-ordination rule.

Under the co-ordination rule in Reg 1408/71, you cannot be discriminated against on grounds of nationality in relation to entitlement to social security benefits and hybrid benefits (see p302). It also allows you to export benefits. Therefore, if you *can* use the co-ordination rule to claim a benefit, it is generally more beneficial.

Not every person, or every benefit, is covered by the co-ordination rule. But potentially every benefit is covered by the social advantages rule and is a 'social advantage'.

If you cannot use the co-ordination rule, or if a benefit which you would like to claim is not covered by the co-ordination rule, the social advantages rule may help you. Whether a benefit counts as a 'social advantage' for the purpose of the social advantages rule is a different question to whether it is social security, social assistance or a hybrid benefit under the co-ordination rule (see p298). The social advantages rule covers a different and wider range of people and benefits to help ensure that you are not discriminated against when you claim benefits in the UK.

The social advantages rule may help you if:

- You are not covered by the co-ordination rule, but you are a 'worker' (see pp287-89). For example, you are from another member state and are working in the UK, and you fall below the lower earnings limit so do not pay National Insurance. In this case, you will not be insured as a worker and so cannot claim under the co-ordination rule; but you are a 'worker' under the social advantages rule.
- If the benefit you claim is classed as 'social or medical assistance'[52] (see pp298-99) and therefore not covered by the co-ordination rule, it may still count as a social advantage, in which case you may be able to claim under the social advantages rule in the UK (see below).[53]

Example

You are Finnish, and have been insured in the UK as a worker, and so come under the co-ordination rule (as well as being a 'worker' for social advantage/ free movement purposes). But now that you are unemployed and your entitlement to contribution-based JSA has ended, you want a crisis loan from the social fund. Social fund payments are social assistance, and are not covered by the co-ordination rule. However, a social fund payment is classed as a social advantage, so you can make your application under the social advantages rule.

Benefits covered by the social advantages rule

If benefits are covered by the social advantages rule they may be referred to as coming within 'the material scope' of the rule.

Under the social advantages rule, a migrant 'shall enjoy the same social and tax advantages as national workers' while employed in the territory of another member state.[54] In other words, national workers and other EU/EEA nationals (within the range of people covered – see pp286-93) must be treated equally.

Social advantages can include social security benefits (see p297) and other benefits in kind (see pp309-10).

Regulation 1612/68, which sets out the social advantages rule, applies to:

- benefits which are generally granted to national workers primarily because of their objective status as 'workers' (see pp287-89); *or*
- benefits for which national workers qualify because they live in the member state, and which would help workers who are nationals of other member states to be mobile within the EU/EEA.[55]

Although the social advantage rule is aimed at workers, it does not just prevent discrimination in relation to benefits arising under a contract of employment, but also extends to a wide range of other benefits and assistance, some of which fall within the statutory scheme for social security.[56]

What are social advantages?

Benefits granted on a discretionary basis, such as social fund payments, are classed as social advantages, as well as benefits accorded as of right.[57]

The following are examples of rights and benefits which have been held to be social advantages:

- fare reduction cards issued by a railway authority;[58]
- an allowance for handicapped adults;[59]
- an interest-free childbirth loan granted on the basis of state subsidy to low-income families;[60]
- an income guarantee for old people or a special old-age allowance;[61]
- unemployment benefits granted to young work-seekers;[62]
- a social benefit guaranteeing a minimum income in case of need (a Belgian benefit called 'the minimex', similar to income support);[63]
- a grant award for maintenance and training at school or university;[64]
- the right to claim a grant for a worker's child who continues to be dependent while studying;[65]
- a benefit for maternity and childbirth;[66]
- a means-tested funeral payment, whether or not the burial or cremation is to take place in the receiving state.[67]

Specific provisions in the social advanatages rule prohibit discrimination in relation to access to training[68] and in relation to all rights and benefits in matters of housing[69] (including housing benefit).

The prohibition of discrimination applies to indirect as well as to direct discrimination. This means that provisions which appear to be neutral but do, in fact, operate to the detriment of EU/EEA nationals from member states other than the one providing benefit, may be unlawful. The only defence against this is where the discrimination can be objectively justified as being 'proportionate and necessary' to achieve the end in question.

Examples

Mr Sotgui, an Italian working in Germany, applied for a separation allowance payable to those working away from their homes. A higher allowance was paid to people working away from a residence in Germany than to those whose residence was outside Germany. Although the differentiation was based on residence and not nationality, in practice it adversely affected those who were not German nationals. The ECJ decided that the differential residence condition might indirectly discriminate and so, unless the distinction could be objectively justified, it contravened EC law.[70] Whether or not it could be justified was a matter for the national court.[71]

Mr O'Flynn's son was an Irish national and former worker resident in the UK. When his son died in the UK the family buried him in Ireland. Mr O'Flynn's application for a burial grant (a means-tested social benefit) was refused on the ground that the burial had not taken place in the UK. The UK government argued that there was no discrimination because the grant was payable to Irish nationals on the same terms as to UK nationals – ie, only if the burial took place in the UK. The ECJ held that the condition constituted indirect discrimination unless it could be objectively justified.[72]

---

3. RIGHTS OF FAMILY MEMBERS UNDER THE CO-ORDINATION AND SOCIAL ADVANTAGES RULES

Although the definitions of 'family member' are slightly different under the co-ordination rule (see p295) and the social advantages rule (see pp290-91), the principles which may help a family member of a 'worker' (see pp287-89) to claim social security or social advantages are the same.

The European Court of Justice (ECJ) recognises that you will be deterred from exercising a right to mobility if your family lose social advantages by moving with you, and gives a wide interpretation to the rights of family members.

The co-ordination rule therefore applies to family members and survivors of insured people.[73]

Under the social advantages rule, EU law gives relevant family members of a worker the right to accompany her/him to the receiving state,[74] and gives her/his children residing in an EU/EEA member state a right to non-discriminatory access to 'general educational, apprenticeship and vocational training courses'.[75]

In addition, because the rights which your family have are treated as 'social advantages', your family members are entitled to receive social advantages on non-discriminatory terms too.[76] These are called derived rights.[77] These rights exist irrespective of the nationality of the family member, but note that they are dependent on the worker coming within either the co-ordination or social advantage rule.[78]

Examples

Surinder, an Indian national, is the dependent father of Rajdeep, a British national living and working in the UK. He wishes to live with Rajdeep, but Surinder has no free movement rights of his own under European law. He only 'has derived rights' as Rajdeep's dependent family member. Because Rajdeep has never worked in a member state other than his own, he has no EC law status for these purposes and, accordingly, neither does Surinder.[79]

Marie is a Burundian national and the dependent mother of Nicole, a French national. Marie lives with Nicole in France. Nicole gets a job in the UK and wants to take Marie with her. Because Nicole is an EC worker exercising her free movement rights, she comes under the social advantage rule.[80] Marie has a 'derived right'[81] to enter the UK with Nicole. She has a derived right[82] to receive social advantages (including social assistance) on the same terms as a UK national, and she can use the co-ordination rule to take any social security benefits to which she may be entitled with her from France to the UK.

Christina was married to Giuseppe, an Italian who worked in England. They stayed in England when Giuseppe retired, and then he died. Christina is entitled to a pensioner's bus pass on the same terms as a UK national because it is a social advantage and she is Guiseppe's widow.[83]

As a family member you can retain your derived rights even when you are not living permanently with the worker.[84]

Until recently, EC law drew a clear distinction between those rights which you could obtain yourself as a worker under the co-ordination rule and the more limited rights which could be claimed as derived rights by a family member under the social advantages rule. However, a recent decision of the ECJ suggests that the scope of 'derived rights' may be interpreted broadly, and in favour of claimants, as from April 1996, because the social security entitlement of a worker's family under the co-ordination rule is a social advantage for the purposes of the social advantages rule.[85] It seems that earlier decisions, which distinguished between the rights of workers and the rights of members of their families and survivors, are now limited to the aggregation and co-ordination rules relating to unemployment benefits[86] and that, in respect of all other social security benefits, family members and survivors of workers can benefit from the co-ordination rule on the same terms as workers themselves.

CHAPTER TWENTY SIX

Using the co-ordination rule to claim social security benefits

This chapter covers:

1. Common terms and benefits covered (below)
2. Insurance, contributions and general rules (p316)
3. Benefits and the co-ordination rule (p321)

Chapter 25 identified the co-ordination arrangements set out in Regulation (EEC) 1408/71, which sets out provisions relating to benefit rights. The co-ordination arrangements are made under Article 51 EC in order to protect the position of migrant workers and their dependants. Regulation (EEC) 574/72 sets out the procedures for implementing the provisions.

We call the co-ordination arrangements the co-ordination rule (see also p280). You should refer to Chapter 24 to see if you are a person who can claim under the co-ordination rule. This chapter tells you about the practical details of how to determine which EU/EEA states' legislation you are subject to. It is divided into three sections:

- section 1 lists the benefits covered and explains common terms central to the operation of the co-ordination rule and other aspects of EC law;
- section 2 explains how the mechanisms of the principles in Reg 1408/71 for co-ordinating social security (see also Chapter 25) are applied, who benefits from the co-ordination rule and which member state is responsible for paying benefits;
- section 3 describes the arrangements for particular benefits, looking at unemployment, maternity, sickness and invalidity, occupational diseases and industrial accidents, retirement and widowhood, and the benefits paid for child dependants.

1. COMMON TERMS AND BENEFITS COVERED

Common terms

Some terms commonly used in the operation of the co-ordination rule are explained here. For the terms United Kingdom (UK), European Community (EC), European Economic Area (EEA) and European Union (EU), see glossary.

Competent State

The Competent State is the EU/EEA member state responsible for paying your benefits.

Exportable benefits

This is a term commonly used in EC law to describe a benefit which a person wishes to 'export' to another member state where they live either temporarily or permanently (see p304).

'Habitual residence' under EC law

'Habitual residence' is a term used in both EC and UK law but the meaning in each is not same.[1] For a full explanation, see p105 and glossary.

'Past presence' test

It is sometimes a condition of entitlement to a benefit that you must have been present in the UK for a certain length of time.

Subject to the legislation of a member state

Normally you are subject to the legislation of only one member state. That member state is known as the Competent State and is the EU/EEA state responsible for paying your benefits. See pp301-7 and 316-20.

UK benefits covered by the co-ordination rule

Sickness and maternity benefits

Sickness and maternity benefits available in the UK under the co-ordination rule are:

- short-term incapacity benefit;
- maternity allowance;
- statutory sick pay;
- statutory maternity pay.

Invalidity benefits

Invalidity benefits available in the UK under the co-ordination rule are:

- long-term incapacity benefit;
- severe disablement allowance; and

- in certain circumstances, attendance allowance (AA), invalid care allowance and disability living allowance (DLA) The *extent* to which AA and DLA are covered is, at the time of writing, the subject of two cases being taken to the European Court of Justice (ECJ).[2]

Increases of long-term incapacity benefit and severe disablement allowance for child dependants are family benefits, not invalidity benefits.

Old-age benefits

Old-age benefits available in the UK under the co-ordination rule are:

- additional pension (AP)
- graduated retirement benefit;
- increments;
- adult dependency increases of retirement pension;
- retirement pension;
- age addition; and
- Christmas bonuses.

Increases of retirement pension for child dependants are family benefits, not old-age benefits.

Survivors' benefits

Survivors' benefits available in the UK under the co-ordination rule are:

- widowed mother's allowance;
- widow's pension (including AP);
- widow's payment;
- widows' benefits. (There are currently no benefits for widowers. At the time of writing, this is being challenged as contrary to the European Convention on Human Rights.[3])

Benefits for accidents at work and occupational diseases

Benefits for accidents at work and occupational diseases available in the UK under the co-ordination rule are:

- disability benefit;
- reduced earnings allowance;
- constant attendance allowance;
- exceptionally severe disablement allowance;*
- hospital treatment allowance;*
- benefits under the Old Cases Act.*

(*Not available to new claimants)

Death Grants

There are no UK death grants covered under the co-ordination rule. (For Social Fund funeral expenses payments in the UK, see Chapter 27.)

Unemployment benefits

The only unemployment benefit available in the UK under the co-ordination rule is contribution-based jobseeker's allowance, but see p349.

Family benefits

Family benefits available in the UK under the co-ordination rule are:

- child benefit (paid at a higher rate to lone parents);
- family credit;
- guardian's allowance;
- child's special allowance (transitional entitlement);*
- child dependency increases for non-means-tested benefits.

(*Not available to new claimants.)

For a full description of each of the non-means-tested benefits listed above, see CPAG's *Rights Guide to Non-Means-Tested Benefits* and *Jobseeker's Allowance Handbook*. Means-tested benefits are described in CPAG's *National Welfare Benefits Handbook* and income-based JSA in the *Jobseeker's Allowance Handbook* (see Appendix 3).

2. INSURANCE, CONTRIBUTIONS AND GENERAL RULES

The Single State and Competent State rules

The general rules applying to insurance and contributions under the co-ordination rule are that:

- you are normally subject to the legislation of only one member state at a time.[4] This is known as the **Single State rule** (see p302). (See below for exception to this rule.)
- you are normally subject to the legislation of the member state where you work, even if you live in another member state.[5] This is known as the **Competent State rule**. If you work in the UK, then the UK will usually be the Competent State and you will be subject to UK social security regulations. If you go to work in another member state, that will usually be the Competent State and you will be subject to that member state's social security regulations. (See below for exceptions to this rule.)

Exception to the Single State rule

If you are simultaneously employed in one EU/EEA member state and self-employed in another, you may, in certain circumstances, be subject to the legislation of both.[6] You should ask the Benefits Agency if this may be the case.

Exceptions to the Competent State rule

You may not be subject to the legislation of the member state where you work in the following circumstances.

You work temporarily in another EU/EEA member state for a UK employer

If the company that employs you sends you to work in another EU/EEA member state for less than a year, then you will remain subject to the legislation of the original member state. However, if you are replacing another employee whose period of posting is ending, you will be subject to the legislation of that member state.[7]

If you are being sent to another EU/EEA member state from the UK to work for less than a year, you should get form E101 from the DSS before you go abroad. This certifies that you remain covered by UK legislation. If the job is extended for up to a year due to unforeseen circumstances, then you can apply for an extension using form E102. Your employer must apply for this extension before the end of the first 12-month period.[8]

You are temporarily self-employed in another EU/EEA member state

The same rules apply if you are self-employed and go to work in another EU/EEA member state for less than 12 months.[9] If you go from the UK to take up temporary self-employment in another member state you will pay self-employed earner's contributions (Class 2 and 4) as if you were still in the UK. You will not have to contribute to the other member state's insurance scheme.[10]

You will normally be accepted as self-employed if you have been self-employed for at least 12 weeks during the last two tax years or since then, although it may be possible to classify you as self-employed even if you do not fully meet this condition. To clarify the position you should contact the Contributions Agency (see Appendix 2).

People working in the German construction industry have, in the past, experienced difficulties when registering as self-employed in Germany. If you go to work in the construction industry in Germany you must register at the local office of the Chamber of Handicrafts (Handwerkskammer) taking your form E101 with you. In order to register with the

Handwerkskammer, you will need to prove that you are qualified in your trade. You must provide a 'Certificate of Experience' which will cost you £80 from the British Chamber of Commerce. If you do not register with the Handwerkskammer, you are not allowed to be self-employed in Germany.

You are employed in two or more EU/EEA member states[11]

If you are employed in two or more EU/EEA member states, unless you are an international transport worker (see below), you will be insured under the UK scheme if:

- you normally live in the UK, and the UK is one of the EU/EEA member states you work in; *or*
- you work for several companies that are based in different EU/EEA member states; *or*
- you do not normally live in any EU/EEA member state that you work in but your employer is based in the UK.

If when you start work you are sent abroad immediately by an employer or agency, you will usually carry on paying UK national insurance contributions.

If you are taken on while abroad you will normally be insured under that member state's scheme.

However, there are special rules if an agency hires you to work for a client in the Netherlands or Germany. You may have to pay UK national insurance contributions for up to nine months if you are in Germany and six months if you are in the Netherlands. After this period you will be insured in the member state in which you are working. Your employer needs to get form E101 to inform the social security authority in the other member state that you will remain insured in the UK, and then form CZ 3822 to inform the UK Contributions Agency.

International transport workers

If you are an international transport worker and work in two or more member states, you will be insured under the UK scheme if:

- your employer's registered office is in the UK; *or*
- your employer's registered office is in another EU/EEA member state and you work for a branch office in the UK; *or*
- you live in the UK and work mainly in the UK even if your employer does not have an office here.

If none of the above apply, you are insured under the scheme of the EU/EEA member state where your employer has its main office.

Special arrangements

In some circumstances, it may be to your advantage to remain insured in the UK even if you are working in another member state.[12] If so, the UK Contributions Agency and its counterpart in the other member state must agree to this. You should write to the Contributions Agency to find out about your position (for address, see Appendix 2).

Special rules also apply to mariners, civil servants, diplomatic or consular staff and people called up for service in the Armed Forces. You should get advice from the appropriate authority – the Contributions Agency in the UK.

Voluntary contributions

You can choose to pay voluntary contributions to the UK national insurance scheme while you are working in another EU/EEA member state, unless you are already paying voluntary contributions in another EU/EEA member state.

If you want to find out whether it makes sense for you to pay voluntary contributions while working in another EU/EEA member state, you should contact the Contributions Agency (for address, see Appendix 2). Do this as soon as possible as there are time-limits for voluntary contributions counting towards benefit entitlement.

Overlapping benefits

The general principle of the co-ordination rule is that a claimant should not use one period of compulsory insurance to obtain a right to more than one benefit derived from that period of insurance.[13]

In general, you will only be insured in one EU/EEA member state for any one period,[14] so you cannot use insurance from that one period to obtain entitlement to benefits of the same kind from two member states. Usually, benefits will be adjusted to ensure either that only one state (the Competent State) pays the benefit, taking into account periods of insurance in other EU/EEA member states; *or* that the benefit is paid pro-rata according to the lengths of periods of insurance in different member states. Aggregation *or* portability provisions apply, but not both (see pp303-5).

The co-ordination rule allows a member state to introduce provisions to prevent 'double recovery'. In the UK these are contained in the Overlapping Benefits Regulations.[15]

In certain cases, however, you *may* be paid both the full level of a UK benefit *and* a proportion of the benefit from another member state which has been accrued as a result of insurance contributions there. Following a decision of the ECJ,[16] member states are not allowed to apply provisions preventing the overlapping of their own benefits with those of other member states where it would have the effect of reducing what you would have received from your years of contribution in the first member state alone.

This means that no adjustment can be made to your benefits under the Overlapping Benefits Regulations if the 'duplicate' benefits which you are receiving are:

- a UK benefit based only on years of insurance in the UK (without seeking to bring in periods of insurance from work abroad) and a benefit paid by another EU/EEA member state based only on your contribution in that member state; *or*
- a UK benefit based only on years of insurance in the UK (without seeking to bring in periods of insurance from work abroad) and a benefit paid as a result of contributions in another EU/EEA member state, where entitlement to the benefit from the second member state arises on other provisions of the co-ordination rule.

For benefits – like old-age and death benefits – which are paid pro rata by different member states, depending on the length of the period of insurance in each member state, the overlapping provisions do not apply to 'adjust' benefits downwards. Each member state must pay you either the benefit you have earned under its system, pro rata, or the rate payable under its own legislation for the years worked, whichever is higher. In such cases the Single State rule does not apply.

Example

In the UK, if you have been employed for 90 per cent of the qualifying years of your working life, you are entitled to the basic rate state retirement pension at the full rate. If you have spent the remaining 10 per cent of your working life in another member state, you can now receive your *full* UK pension as well as the 10 per cent pro-rata pension which you are entitled to from the other member state.

There are further detailed exceptions to the overlapping provisions in relation to benefits paid for invalidity, old age, occupational disease or death.[17] Broadly speaking, a member state is not allowed to apply its overlapping provisions to reduce benefits you receive from it which are of the same kind just because you are receiving other benefits in respect of those risks from another member state.

3. BENEFITS AND THE CO-ORDINATION RULE

This section explains how the new aggregation and apportionment rules (see Chapter 25) are applied to particular types of benefit. In relation to each benefit, it describes:

- the general contribution conditions;
- those benefits available in the UK (for more about UK benefits, see CPAG's Handbooks listed in Appendix 3);
- how those benefits are affected by the co-ordination rule;
- what happens if you want to go to another EU/EEA state; *and*
- what happens if you want to come to, or return to, the UK.

Unemployment benefits[18]

General rules

If you become unemployed in an EU/EEA member state, and have worked in other member states, you must find out which is the Competent State (see p316). The general rule is that you will be paid unemployment benefit by the member state in which you were last employed[19] and that you can take it with you to other member states while seeking employment abroad.

An exception to this general rule is where you are living in one member state and working or paying contributions in another. In this case you can claim from either the member state you are living in or the one in which you are working or paying contributions.

If you are potentially entitled to unemployment benefit both from the member state where you last worked *and* the member state in which you are 'habitually resident' (see p105), you must choose where to register for work and claim unemployment benefit.[20]

You continue to be entitled to unemployment benefit from the Competent State for a period of up to three months whether you stay there while looking for work or travel to seek work in another EU/EEA member state (though only for one journey – see p325). After three months you must return to the Competent State to continue receiving unemployment benefit.

If you are a person from another EU/EEA member state who is seeking work in the UK, you are entitled to exportable unemployment benefit from another member state. You cannot receive contribution-based job-seeker's allowance from the UK.[21]

Unemployment benefits available in the UK

Jobseeker's allowance

Jobseeker's allowance (JSA) is the only social security benefit for unemployment available in the UK under the co-ordination rule. It replaced unemployment benefit in October 1996. JSA is based on both contributions and a means test but only contribution-based JSA is social security and therefore covered by the co-ordination rule (although the non-contributory element can be claimed by appropriate people under the social advantages rule – see note 23 and p286).

You can get contribution-based JSA if you:

- are unemployed; *and*
- are capable of, available for, and actively seeking work; *and*
- have a current jobseeker's agreement; *and*
- satisfy the contribution conditions (see below).

To satisfy these conditions you must:

- have paid, in one of the last two tax years, Class 1 employed earner's contributions producing an earnings factor of at least 25 times that year's lower earnings limit; *and*
- have paid or been credited with contributions producing an earnings factor equal to 50 times the lower earnings limit in each of the last two complete contribution years, before the relevant benefit year.[22]

For full details of JSA see CPAG's *Jobseeker's Allowance Handbook* and for the contribution conditions, the *Rights Guide to Non-Means-Tested Benefits* – see Appendix 3.

You can use periods of insurance or employment completed as an employed person under the legislation of any other member state to satisfy either or both of these conditions, *provided that you were subject to UK legislation immediately before claiming contribution-based JSA.* Each week of employment completed as an employed person in any other member state is treated as a contribution paid into the UK scheme on earnings of two-thirds of the present upper earnings limit for contribution purposes.

What happens if you go to another EU/EEA member state

Contribution-based JSA is the only element of JSA which can be exported. Contribution-based JSA paid in another EU/EEA member state is referred to as 'exportable' JSA. This is because you remain entitled to UK contribution-based JSA and do not become entitled to the other EU/EEA member state's unemployment benefit. EC law overrides domestic legislation which says that JSA is not payable abroad.[23]

If you are going to look for work in another EU/EEA member state you will be entitled to contribution-based JSA abroad if:

- **you are wholly unemployed immediately before you leave the UK.** This means you are without any employment except for partial and intermittent unemployment.[24] Partial unemployment means you are short-time (not part-time) working. Intermittent unemployment means you are temporarily laid off; *and*
- **you satisfy the conditions for contribution-based JSA before you leave the UK.**[25] You will qualify even if you have claimed contribution-based JSA but no decision has been made yet on your entitlement, but you are getting JSA hardship payments pending the decision; *and*
- **your entitlement to contribution-based JSA arises from aggregating insurance payments you made in different member states.**[26] Your entitlement to contribution-based JSA must not arise as a result of a reciprocal Convention between the UK and a state that is not a member of the EU/EEA (for how to determine this, see p372).[27]
- **you are going to the other EU/EEA member state to seek work.**[28] You are not entitled to exportable contribution-based JSA if you are going on holiday, visiting a sick relative or accompanying your spouse. If you give up work to accompany your spouse or partner on a posting abroad it is very unlikely that you will be able to export your UK contribution-based JSA. In order to establish entitlement you must show that;
  - there was just cause for voluntarily leaving your employment; *and*
  - you were capable of, available for, and actively seeking, work.

  Usually it will be accepted that if you left work to accompany your partner on a foreign posting, you had just cause as long as you left no earlier than was reasonable to organise your affairs before travelling.[29] However, you may still lose entitlement because you will find it difficult to establish that you were available for work during this time. If, on the other hand, you were already unemployed and you take the opportunity of accompanying your spouse or partner abroad to seek work, you may be accepted as satisfying this condition.
- **you have been registered as available for work for at least four weeks in the UK.**[30] In exceptional circumstances you may be allowed to leave the UK before the four weeks is up and still qualify. You must get authority in advance to do so from Overseas Benefits Directorate in Newcastle (see Appendix 2);
- **you are registered for work in another EU/EEA member state.**[31] If you are looking for work in another member state, you must register for work there within seven days of leaving the UK and comply with that member state's regulations unless there are exceptional circumstances.[32]

The employment services of that member state will pay contribution-based JSA in accordance with its own legislation. This includes the method and frequency of payment.[33] The requirement to attend at a JobCentre is satisfied if:

– you attend at an equivalent office in the other member state; or
– you comply with that member state's control procedures, showing that you are available for work as its rules require.

That member state will carry out checks on entitlement to JSA in accordance with its own procedures. If there is doubt about whether you meet the registration and availability conditions of the member state in which you are living this will be reported to the Benefits Agency in the UK. On the advice of the other EU/EEA state, the Benefits Agency will make a decision about whether you continue to be entitled or not. While the question is referred to the Benefits Agency your benefit may be suspended by the other state. It is important that the decision is made in the UK because you have the right to appeal. In some EU/EEA states there is no right of appeal against the decision of an adjudication officer.

If all of the above six conditions are met, you will be entitled to UK contribution-based JSA abroad in an EU/EEA member state for one of the following periods, whichever is the shortest:[34]

• three months from the date when you ceased to be available to the UK employment services;[35] or
• until your entitlement to UK contribution-based JSA is exhausted after six months/26 weeks;[36] or
• if you are a seasonal worker (see below), until the end of the season.[37]*

* A **seasonal worker** is a person who:

• is 'habitually resident' (see p105 and glossary) in one member state and goes to work in another EU/EEA member state; and
• does seasonal work in that second member state for a period of up to eight months; and
• remains in that member state for the whole period of that season's work.[38]

Seasonal work is work which happens every year and is linked to a particular season of the year.

Example

A Spanish man came to Somerset to pick potatoes. He was made redundant during the normal potato-picking season and became entitled to contribution-based JSA. He returned to Spain and kept entitlement to contribution-based JSA until the end of the potato-picking season.

He was 'habitually resident' in Spain throughout the time he did seasonal work in the UK, and was entitled to contribution-based JSA because he had paid contributions in Spain.

If you satisfy all the conditions for exporting contribution-based JSA, it can be awarded in advance for three months.[39]

On request a statement will be issued to you by the Pensions and Overseas Benefits Directorate (see Appendix 2) for you to give to the employment services of the member state where you are going to look for work.[40] The statement will give:

- the rate of contribution-based JSA that is payable;
- the date from which contribution-based JSA can be paid;
- the time-limit for registration in the other EU/EEA member state;
- the maximum period of entitlement;
- any other relevant facts that might affect your entitlement.

You can export contribution-based JSA to more than one EU/EEA member state during the same period of absence from the UK.

Example

A man went to the Netherlands to seek work and retained entitlement to contribution-based JSA. Later he went directly from the Netherlands to Germany to look for work. He remained entitled to UK contribution-based JSA.

But contribution-based JSA can only be exported once from the UK during any one period of unemployment. You cannot return to the UK and then go abroad a second time in the same period until you have worked and paid more contributions in the UK.[41]

Example

A woman went to Denmark to look for work and continued to receive contribution-based JSA. She could not find work so returned to the UK and continued to get contribution-based JSA. Finding no work in the UK, she returned to Denmark again to look for work. During this second absence she could not receive contribution-based JSA.

If you have not found a job within three months and return to the UK before the three-month period is up, you will continue to get contribution-based JSA in the UK, assuming that the six- month period for which JSA can be paid is not exhausted.[42]

If you fall sick or become pregnant while looking for work in another EU/EEA member state, you may be entitled to UK short-term incapacity benefit or maternity benefit but only for the period until your contribution-based JSA entitlement runs out.[43] For example, if you have already used up four months while in the UK, you will only be entitled to two months' contribution-based JSA abroad. To claim these benefits you will need form E119.

If you become unemployed while working abroad and are insured in that member state's unemployment insurance scheme, then that member state is responsible for paying unemployment benefit if you are entitled to it. If you were previously insured in the UK you will normally be able to use periods during which you paid national insurance and aggregate them with periods of insurance in the member state you last worked in, to enable you to get the unemployment benefit of the member state where you have been working.[44]

If you are entitled to receive UK contribution-based JSA while in another EU/EEA member state, you should get a letter from your local JobCentre to help register for work in the other member state.

If you are going to look for work in Austria, Belgium, Finland, France, Germany, Greece, Iceland, Italy, Norway, Portugal, Spain or Sweden, you will be given form E303. If you are going to look for work in another EU/EEA member state, then form E303 will be sent directly to that member state.

If you are going abroad, you should always give the Department for Education and Employment advance warning to enable them to advise you on procedures and make the necessary arrangements on your behalf.

What happens if you come to the UK and are unemployed

If you are a returning resident or an EU/EEA national coming to the UK to work or to seek work, the following applies to you.

If you have worked and paid insurance contributions under the legislation of another EU/EEA member state (see p303), the periods of insurance in that state may count towards your entitlement to contribution-based JSA on your return to the UK. This will apply if, after your return to the UK, you get employment, pay Class 1 contributions but then become unemployed again.[45] You are then subject to UK legislation (ie, the UK is the Competant State) and the UK is resonsible for paying you the appropriate amount of contribution-based JSA.

If you were not subject to another member state's legislation while abroad (because you were an exception to the rule that the Competent State is the state where you work – see p317) the unemployment insurance you paid while abroad may nevertheless still be taken into account when assessing your entitlement to contribution-based JSA if it is decided that, while you were abroad, you remained 'habitually resident' (see p105 and glossary) in the UK.

If you are coming to or returning to the UK to look for work and have been insured in another EU/EEA member state, you may be able to get the other member state's unemployment benefit for up to three months if:[46]

- you were getting that member state's unemployment benefit immediately before coming to the UK;[47] *and*
- you have been registered as available for work for four weeks (or less if the member state's rules allow) in the other member state;[48] *and*
- you register and claim UK JSA within seven days after you were last registered in the other member state;[49] *and*
- you satisfy the UK's availability for work rules.[50] The UK Benefits Agency will carry out checks and pay benefit where unemployment benefit has been exported from another EU/EEA member state to the UK. However, the UK Benefits Agency cannot decide whether or not there is entitlement to the other member state's unemployment benefit. If a doubt arises about your continuing entitlement, the UK Benefits Agency will inform the employment authorities of the other member state and, if appropriate, may suspend payment of your unemployment benefit while awaiting a reply. For how member states co-operate to make decisions about availability, see p324.

Before you leave the other member state you must get form E303.[51]

If members of your family are living in another EU/EEA member state and the amount of your unemployment benefit is determined by the number of people in your family, then they will be taken into account as if they were living in the member state that pays your benefit.[52]

If your dependant lives in another member state you will need form E302. This form may be obtained from the employment institution of the member state in which your dependant lives.

There is no provision in UK legislation defining 'a member of your family' for benefit law. The Benefits Agency counts any child or person for whom an increase of benefit could be payable *or* any child, where benefit could be payable to an adult for that child as a family member, but that is arguably contrary to EC law[53] (see p295).

Note: If you come to Britain to look for work and are paid, for example, German unemployment benefit, you will get an addition for dependants. If you then get work in the UK and then become unemployed after that period of work, you will get British unemployment benefit (contribution-based JSA) instead, which will not include additions for dependants.

Maternity benefits

General rules

If you are pregnant or have just had a baby in another member state, the following rules apply.[54]

- Maternity benefits are always paid according to the rules of the member state where you are subject to the legislation (ie, the Competent State), regardless of where you are living.
- Whenever the completion of a waiting period is required before you become entitled to benefit, the benefits authorities must take account of periods of insurance, residence or employment completed under the legislation of other member states.

Maternity benefits available in the UK

There are two UK benefits payable if a woman is expecting a child or has recently had one. They are statutory maternity pay and maternity allowance.

Statutory maternity pay

Statutory maternity pay (SMP) is payable for up to 18 weeks by your employer if you have given up work and are expecting a child, or if you have recently given birth, and meet certain conditions (see CPAG's *Rights Guide to Non-Means-Tested Benefits*). SMP has been payable worldwide since 18 August 1996.

Maternity allowance

Maternity Allowance (MA) is payable for up to 18 weeks (the MA period) if you have given up work and are expecting a child, or have recently given birth and are employed, or have recently been employed, or are self-employed but not entitled to SMP. You must also satisfy the contribution conditions (see CPAG's *Rights Guide to Non-Means-Tested Benefits*).

What happens if you go to another EU/EEA member state
Claiming UK maternity benefits
If you are entitled to UK SMP you can claim it in another EU/EEA member state. If you are not entitled to SMP, but you last paid insurance in the UK, you may instead be able to claim UK MA in another EU/EEA member state if:[55]

- you move to live or work in another EU/EEA member state; *or*
- you are looking for work in another EU/EEA member state and you are getting UK contribution-based JSA; *or*

- you are already getting MA in the UK and you go back to the member state where you usually live, or you go to live in another EU/EEA member state. However, you need to agree this with the DSS in advance; *or*
- the Department of Health tells you that you can go to another EU/EEA member state to get medical treatment.

If you have your baby in another EU/EEA member state, you are entitled to UK MA on the same basis as if your baby was born in the UK, unless you are getting the same sort of maternity allowance from the other member state (see overlapping benefits, p319).

If your MA period starts while you are in another EU/EEA member state looking for work, you will be entitled to MA instead of 'exported' contribution-based JSA. Exported contribution-based JSA is usually paid for three months but the MA period may be extended by the Secretary of State if you are prevented from returning to the UK.[56]

If you are going abroad you should give the DSS plenty of advance warning to enable them to advise you on procedures and to make the necessary arrangements on your behalf.

Claiming maternity benefits from another EU/EEA member state
If you have been working in another EU/EEA member state before your period of entitlement, that state is the Competent State and you should claim maternity benefits under that member state's rules (see p305). You can use periods of insurance paid in the UK and aggregate them with periods of contributions in that member state to qualify for that member's state's maternity benefits under its rules.[57]

What happens if you are coming to the UK
If the last place you have worked and been insured in is another EU/EEA member state, then that is the Competent State. You should claim exported benefits under its scheme. But if you have worked and been insured under the legislation of another EU/EEA member state (see p316) but have since returned to the UK where you have then worked and paid national insurance contributions, you are entitled to UK MA. The insurance contributions that you paid in the other member state may count towards your entitlement to UK MA.[58] Before you return to the UK you should ask the other member state's authorities for a record of your sickness insurance (form E104).

Claiming benefits from two or more EU/EEA member states
You will usually only be able to claim maternity benefit from the member state where your baby is born, even if you were eligible to claim it in more than one EU/EEA member state. If you cannot get benefit in the

member state where your child was born, you can claim it from the member state to whose legislation you were last subject (see p302).

Sickness benefits

General rules

The general rules governing sickness benefits in EC law are that:[59]

- sickness benefits are always paid according to the rules of the Competent State (see p316), regardless of where you are living; and
- whenever the completion of a waiting period is required before you become entitled to benefits, the benefits authorities must take account of periods of insurance, residence or employment completed under the legislation of other member states. But see p99 – the residence requirements laid down by the DSS may be contrary to EC law.

Sickness benefits available in the UK

Statutory sick pay

Statutory sick pay (SSP) is paid and administered by your employer for up to 28 weeks if you are incapable of work for four or more days in a row. To qualify you must be working under a contract of service. For details, see CPAG's *Rights Guide to Non-Means-Tested Benefits*.

SSP is payable worldwide. If you do not qualify for SSP, you may be entitled to incapacity benefit – see below.

Incapacity benefit

Incapacity benefit (ICB) is paid at three different rates but only the short-term rates are 'sickness benefit' and payable outside of the UK.

- The short-term lower rate is payable for the first 28 weeks of incapacity.
- The short-term higher rate is payable for weeks 29-52.
- The long-term rate is payable after 52 weeks. It counts as an invalidity benefit (see page 332). However if you get the disability living allowance (DLA) care component paid at the highest rate or are terminally ill, the long-term rate can be claimed from week 29 after you become ill.

You can qualify for ICB if:

- you are incapable of work; and
- you satisfy the contribution conditions (unless the incapacity is the result of a prescribed disease or an industrial injury).

To satisfy the contribution conditions you must:

- have actually paid, in *any* one contribution year, the appropriate class of contributions producing an earnings factor of at least 25 times that year's lower earnings limit. (**Note:** different contribution rules applied before 6 April 1975.); *and*
- have either paid or been credited with contributions producing an earnings factor equal to 50 times the lower earnings limit in each of the last two complete contribution years, before the relevant benefit year.[60]

For details about ICB, the test for incapacity (the 'own occupation' test for the first 28 weeks and after that the 'all-work' test) and the contribution conditions, see CPAG's *Rights Guide to Non-Means-Tested Benefits*.

What happens if you go to another EU/EEA member state

You may be able to get UK short-term ICB in another EU/EEA member state if you last paid contributions in the UK, and if you satisfy one of the following conditions:

- you fall sick while you are living or working in another EU/EEA member state;[61] *or*
- you fall sick while you are looking for work in another EU/EEA member state and you are getting UK unemployment benefit[62] (jobseeker's allowance) (during your first three months there); *or*
- you are already getting short-term ICB in the UK and you go back to the member state where you usually live or you go to live in another EU/EEA member state. However, to ensure payment you need to agree this with the DSS in advance; *or*
- the Department of Health tells you that you can go to another EU/EEA member state to get medical treatment.

Even if none of the above apply to you, you may still be able to get short-term ICB in another EU/EEA member state for up to 26 weeks. However, if you go abroad to receive medical treatment, you must also have been unable to work for the past six months to get UK ICB abroad. Claiming UK ICB while receiving medical treatment is not an automatic right as it depends on permission granted by the Department of Health.

If you are going abroad you should give the DSS plenty of advance warning to enable them to advise you on procedures and make the necessary arrangements on your behalf.

Claiming benefit from another member state

If you are working in, and insured for sickness in, another EU/EEA member state and get sick, you need to claim benefit for short-term sickness under that state's social security scheme. Periods of insurance contributions in the UK may be aggregated with periods of insurance in that member state and count towards your entitlement to such a benefit.[63]

What happens if you come to the UK

If you have been working in and are insured in another EU/EEA member state and become ill, you may wish to return to the UK. In these circumstances you may be entitled to the other member state's sickness benefit in the UK. However, in order to benefit, you should make your claim before you leave the other member state.

If you have worked abroad but last worked and paid insurance contributions in the UK before making a claim for short-term ICB here, the insurance contributions you paid in another EU/EEA member state may be aggregated with you UK contributions and so count towards calculating your entitlement to ICB.[64] If you have been working in another member state you should always get a Form E104 which is a record of the social insurance that you have paid in that member state, before returning to the UK.

Invalidity benefits

General rules

EC law treats sickness benefits and invalidity benefits differently. There are no provisions in EC law defining which are sickness and which are invalidity benefits. It is decided by looking at the conditions of entitlement to each benefit and the reason for, and length of, the incapacity. Nor is EC law very clear at present about what is an 'invalidity benefit' (ie, social security and within the co-ordination rule) and what is a benefit specifically for the protection of disabled people (ie, a special, non-contributory benefit) and only partly covered by the co-ordination rule. The ECJ decisions in two cases presently before it should clarify the situation.[65]

Invalidity benefits available in the UK

Long-term incapacity benefit and severe disablement allowance are available as invalidity benefits in the UK. Special rules apply to attendance allowance, invalid care allowance and disability living allowance which, on 1 June 1992, were declared to be special non-contributory benefits for the purposes of EC provisions (see below and p337) although whether in fact they are special non-contributory benefits or social security is at the time of writing the subject of the two references to the ECJ.[66]

Long-term incapacity benefit

Long-term incapacity benefit (ICB) is paid after 52 weeks. The short-term rates of ICB are classified as sickness benefits for the purposes of EC regulations and cover shorter-term incapacities (see p330).

In the UK, long-term ICB is paid when a person is incapable of work. In some other EU/EEA member states, invalidity benefit may be payable where a person is not fully incapable of work. This means that a person may receive an (exportable) invalidity benefit from that member state while remaining disqualified in the UK because s/he is capable of some work.[67]

Severe disablement allowance

Severe disablement allowance (SDA) may be paid after 28 weeks of incapacity if you cannot satisfy the contribution conditions for ICB (see CPAG's *Rights Guide to Non-Means-Tested Benefits*).

To qualify for SDA you must:

- satisfy the 'ordinary residence' test[68] (see p99 for what this is, but note that the DSS may be applying the residence and presence requirements wrongly – see p335); *and*
- satisfy or be exempt from an immigration status test[69] (see p121). If you are an EU/EEA national or the family member of an EU/EEA national, you are treated as satisfying this test for the purposes of receiving this benefit in the UK.

To get SDA, you will also usually need to qualify for disability living allowance, see p334. For special rules applying to this benefit, see pp337-38.

Attendance allowance

Attendance allowance (AA) is paid to help towards the extra costs of disabled people over the age of 65 with care needs and who satisfy the residence and immigration conditions[70] (see pp99 and 121). If you are an EU/EEA national or the family member of an EU/EEA national, you are treated as satisfying the immigration test for receiving this benefit in the UK.

On 1 June 1992 the UK government declared AA to be a special non-contributory benefit outside the jurisdiction of the EU provisions.[71] How much weight this declaration has is to be determined in proceedings before the ECJ at the time of writing. If you want to export AA from the UK, you should check with the present state of the law (see pp300-1 and 337).[72] Different rules apply depending on whether or not you were entitled to AA before 1 June 1992. For details, see p337.

Invalid care allowance

Invalid care allowance (ICA) is paid to a carer between the ages of 16 and 65 who satisfies the residence and immigration conditions (see pp99 and 121).[73] If you are an EU/EEA national or a family member of an EU/EEA national, you are treated as satisfying the immigration test for receiving this benefit in the UK.

On 1 June 1992, the UK government declared ICA to be a special non-contributory benefit outside the jurisdiction of the EU provisions. Again, it is arguable that this declaration does not have effect, so that ICA may be exportable (see above and pp300 and 337). Different rules apply depending on whether or not you were entitled to ICA before 1 June 1992. See p337 for details.

Disability living allowance

Disability living allowance (DLA) is paid to help towards the extra costs of disabled people with care and/or mobility needs who satisfy the residence conditions and immigration test.[74] If you are an EU/EEA national or a family member of an EU/EEA national, you are treated as satisfying the immigration test for receiving this benefit in the UK.

On 1 June 1992, the UK government declared DLA to be a special non-contributory benefit outside the jurisdiction of the EU provisions. The worth of this declaration depends on court challenges (see attendance allowance above). Different rules apply depending on whether or not you were entitled to DLA before 1 June 1992. See p337 for details. (**Note:** DLA replaced AA from 6 April 1992 for people under 65 on that date.)

Disability working allowance

Disability working allowance (DWA) is a means-tested benefit paid to top up the wages of low-paid workers with a disability. It is not covered by the co-ordination rule (see p354).

What happens if you go to another EU/EEA member state

If you are covered by EC provisions and you are entitled to long-term incapacity benefit (ICB) or severe disability allowance (SDA) in the UK, you remain entitled if you go to another member state provided that:[75]

- you are 'habitually resident'[76] in the other member state (see page 105 and glossary); *or*
- you are temporarily resident in the other member state; *or*
- you are staying temporarily in the other member state (eg, you are on holiday).[77]

If you are 'habitually resident' in another EU/EEA member state but are temporarily outside the EU/EEA, you remain entitled to long-term ICB and SDA. This is because, although you are *temporarily* outside the

EU/EEA, you are nevertheless 'habitually resident' in an EU/EEA member state.

Example
A man is who is entitled to long-term ICB (previously invalidity benefit) went to live in France. He continued to live there from 1984 until 1996. In the summer of 1996 he took a holiday in South Africa for six weeks. He remains entitled to long-term ICB because he is still 'habitually resident' in France.

What happens if you come to the UK

To be entitled to SDA (but not ICB) in the UK, you need to satisfy the ordinary residence test (see p99) and presence test (see p98). When deciding these tests, periods of employment or self-employment from 29 July 1991 when you were subject to the legislation of another EU/EEA member state (see p316) count as presence and residence in the UK.[78] DSS policy is that from 1 June 1992, periods of insurance *and* residence in another EU/EEA member state are taken into account when considering whether you satisfy the ordinary residence test but not the presence test. It is arguable that this is not a correct interpretation of EC law.[79]

What happens if you become entitled to long-term ICB or SDA while in another member state

If you have been entitled to short-term ICB, sickness benefit or statutory sick pay for 364 days, you can become entitled to long-term ICB or SDA while you are 'habitually resident' or 'temporarily resident' in another EU/EEA member state.[80]

If you are living in another EU/EEA member state and are subject to that member state's legislation (ie, it is the Competent State), any sickness insurance you have paid in the UK may help you qualify for an invalidity benefit in the other member state.[81]

Claiming from more than one EU/EEA member state

There are two types of invalidity benefit under EC regulations, Type A and Type B.

Type A invalidity benefit

The amount of benefit you receive does not depend on the amount of contributions paid. It is paid at a standard rate.[82] (Incapacity benefit is a Type A invalidity benefit.)

If you have worked and paid insurance contributions only in member states with Type A invalidity benefits you are entitled to invalidity benefit under one member state's legislation only. Which member state is responsible depends on:

- where you became sick; *and*
- whether you worked in that member state or, if not, in which member state you were last employed.

Type B invalidity benefit

The rate of your benefit depends on the amount of your contributions.[83] You may be able to get Type B invalidity benefit from two or more EU/EEA member states if you have paid insurance contributions in any of the following member states: Austria, Denmark, Finland, Germany, Greece (except under the agricultural insurance scheme), Iceland, Italy, Liechtenstein, Luxembourg, Norway, Portugal, Sweden, France (but only under the French miners' insurance scheme, or if you were self-employed in France).

How much you get from each member state is worked out according to a formula. It is calculated by two different methods and you get whichever is higher.[84]

Where you have paid contributions in member states paying Type A benefits and others paying Type B, your benefit may be calculated according to the Type B formula.

If you were paying contributions in any one of the above states and you are getting benefit from only one of those, you should ask the authorities there to send your details to the other member states where you have been subject to the legislation/paying contributions. You may be entitled to a higher level of benefit.

Medical examinations

Medical examinations will usually be carried out by the member state in which you are living, but you may be required to return to the state which is paying your pension for an examination if you are able to travel. So if you are living in France, for example, that member state will check your incapacity, but you could be asked to return to the UK to be examined by a BAMS (Benefits Agency Medical Services) doctor.

Adult dependency increases[85]

If you are only receiving invalidity benefit from one EU/EEA member state (either ICB or SDA from the UK or an invalidity benefit from one other member state), it may be increased if you have an adult who is dependent on you. An adult dependency increase is only payable with ICB if:

- your husband/wife is aged 60 or over; *or*
- you are 'residing with' (see p112 and glossary) and you have entitlement to extra benefit for one or more children.

This increase is payable even if your dependant is in another member state. An increase is also payable for the children provided there is entitlement to UK child benefit, but increases for children count as family benefits, not invalidity benefits. Payment of adult and child dependency increases are subject to the amount of your husband or wife's earnings. If you receive an invalidity pension from the UK and from another member state, special rules apply. You will need to contact the Benefits Agency Overseas Directorate (see Appendix 2) for more information.

Special non-contributory benefits

General rules

Whether a benefit is an invalidity benefit (and therefore covered by the co-ordination rule, including exportability conditions) or whether it is a special non-contributory benefit (which cannot be exported from the Competent State) is hard to determine. In particular, the position of attendance allowance (AA) and disability living allowance (DLA) is unclear. This sub-section deals with the rules which will govern AA, DLA and invalid care allowance (ICA) *if* they are held to be special non-contributory benefits. Otherwise they will continue to be governed by the rules relating to invalidity benefits.

Under Regulation 1408/71 each member state has to specify the legislation and schemes to which the Regulation applies. On 1 June 1992, the UK listed AA, ICA and DLA as being special non-contributory benefits outside the jurisdiction of the EC provisions.[86] There is a legal debate as to whether it is possible for two of these benefits (AA and DLA) to have been demoted from social security benefits to special non-contributory benefits (cases have been referred to the ECJ, see p315). If the applicants in these two cases are successful, then DLA and AA continue to be exportable under the co-ordination rule. If they are not, different rules will apply to these benefits depending on whether or not you were entitled to them before 1 June 1992. The Benefit Agency's present approach is to treat these as special non-contributory benefits.

Entitlement to AA, ICA and DLA before 1 June 1992

If you were entitled to AA, ICA or DLA before 1 June 1992 (and subject to the reference to the ECJ at the time of writing), you can export your benefit if you take up 'habitual residence' (see p105) in another EU/EEA member state, provided that you satisfy all the other conditions of entitlement, except the 'residence' and 'presence' conditions; *and either*

- you are working in the UK (this counts whether or not you are paying national insurance contributions); *or*
- you have worked in the UK as an employed or self-employed person

and, at the time you apply to take your AA/ICA/DLA to another EU/EEA member state, you have an entitlement to an insurance benefit based on your past contributions.[87]

Entitlement to AA, ICA and DLA after 1 June 1992

If AA/ICA and/or DLA *are* treated as special non-contributory benefits, then they cannot be exported. They are payable only in, and at the expense of, the member state of 'habitual residence'. This means that if these are special non-contributory benefits and you became entitled to one of them on or after 1 June 1992, you cannot take your entitlement with you if you take up 'habitual residence' in another EU/EEA member state. You may, however, claim a similar special non-contributory benefit from the EU/EEA member state where you are 'habitually resident' if there is an equivalent benefit there.

You are treated as satisfying the immigration status test (see p121) if you are an EU/EEA national or family member of an EU/EEA national.

Satisfying residence and presence conditions

Assuming the ECJ uphold the legality of the UK's 'residence' and 'presence' tests for AA/ICA/DLA, you may be able to satisfy these if:

- you are an EU/EEA national or a family member of an EU/EEA national; *and*
- you come 'within the personal scope' of the co-ordination rule[88] (see p293); *and*
- you are 'habitually resident' in the UK (see p105). If you are 'habitually resident' in the UK you will normally be able to satisfy the 'ordinary residence' requirement. Any periods of residence, employment, or self-employment in another EU/EEA member state can be taken into account to satisfy the 'past presence' conditions for these benefits.[89] For details of past presence test, see CPAG's *Rights Guide to Non-Means-Tested Benefits*.

Example

An Italian national who lived and worked for 20 years in Italy sold her home there and came to live with her family in the UK on 10 December 1996. She claimed attendance allowance immediately on arrival and satisfied the Benefits Agency that she was 'habitually resident' in the UK. The 'past presence' condition was satisfied by using her periods of residence in Italy before 10 December 1996.

Accidents at work and occupational diseases

General rules

Disablement benefit and related allowances are paid to you if you have had an accident at work or contracted a prescribed industrial disease. These benefits and allowances are covered by EC Regulations.[90] However, they only apply to employed earners and not to self-employed people.[91]

You should claim at your local social security office as soon as the first signs of disablement appear.

If you are receiving one of the above benefits in the UK and are 'habitually resident' in another member state[92] (see p105), or are staying there temporarily[93] (which includes taking a holiday), you are entitled to the benefit at the same rate it would have been paid to you in the UK.[94]

Benefits available in the UK

Disablement benefit is payable if you are still disabled 15 weeks after the accident at work or the onset of the disease. The benefit is payable in addition to any incapacity benefit and the amount depends on the degree of incapacity as assessed by a medical board.[95]

You may also be entitled to related allowances with disablement benefit. These are:

- constant attendance allowance, which you may receive if you are getting 100 per cent disablement benefit and need somebody to look after you;[96]
- exceptionally severe disablement allowance, which you may receive if you are getting constant attendance allowance at one of the two highest rates, and your need for constant attendance is likely to be permanent;[97]
- reduced earnings allowance which you may receive if your accident occurred or your disease started before 1 October 1990, and you cannot do your normal job as a result.[98]

For detailed information about these benefits, see CPAG's *Rights Guide to Non-Means-Tested Benefits*.

What happens if you go to another EU/EEA member state

Disablement benefit and related allowances are payable if you go to another EU/EEA member state. If you are intending to travel, you should consult the office which pays you benefit well in advance so that arrangements can be made for payment in the other member state.

What happens if you have worked in other EU/EEA member states

If you were insured in another EU/EEA member state, you will be paid directly by the appropriate institution of that state according to its rules for determining whether or not you are eligible and how much you should be paid. That institution may arrange for the DSS to make your payments, but this will not alter the amount you receive.

If you have worked in two or more EU/EEA states in a job that gave you a prescribed industrial disease, you will only get benefit from the member state where you last worked in that job. There are special rules for sclerogenic pneumoconiosis (see CPAG's *Rights Guide to Non-Means-Tested Benefits*).

If your condition deteriorates and you are getting, or used to get, benefit from an EU/EEA member state, then that state will be responsible for carrying out any necessary further medical examinations and paying any additional benefit.

Retirement Pensions

General rules

If you have worked in more than one member state, your insurance record is preserved in that member state until you reach pensionable age. You will get a retirement pension from each member state where you have worked for a year or more, based on your insurance record in that member state or, where residence counts for benefit purposes, the length of your residence in that member state.

If the period during which you have been insured in a member state or, where residence counts for benefit purposes, lived in a member state, is not long enough to qualify you for a pension, then any periods of insurance or residence which you have completed in other EU/EEA member states will be taken into account.

Your retirement pension will be paid to you regardless of where you live or stay in the EU/EEA without any reduction or modification.[99]

Pensionable age

Pensionable age in the UK for a man is 65, for a woman 60. However, from 6 April 2010 the pension age for women will increase from 60 to 65 over a ten-year period. The age at which you may be entitled to a retirement pension differs from member state to member state. Because of this you may be entitled to an old-age benefit in one EU/EEA member state before you reach retirement age in another. Correspondingly, if you have been incapable of work before you reached pension age you may be entitled to pro rata invalidity benefits in the member state where you have not yet reached pension age. In the UK this is long-term incapacity benefit – see pp332-37.

In Greece the pension age for men and women is lower than in the UK while, in Belgium, Finland, France and Spain it is lower for men only.

Benefits available in the UK

The co-ordination rule refers to old-age benefits.[100] In the UK, retirement pensions of any category are included. There are four types of retirement pension in the UK: Categories A, B C and D. Categories A and B are contributory while category D carries a residence test and is paid in strictly limited circumstances. (Category C is no longer relevant as it applies only to people who were of pension age in 1948.)

- additional pension (AP);
- graduated retirement benefit;
- retirement pension
- increments;
- adult dependency increases of retirement pension;
- age additions;
- Christmas benefits.

Although incapacity benefit and child dependency increases can be paid to someone over pension age, they are not classed as old-age benefits.[101]

For detailed information about these benefits, see CPAG's *Rights Guide to Non-Means-Tested Benefits*.

Entitlement to a pension

If you have worked and paid contributions in more than one member state you may be entitled to a pension under EC law, even if you do not qualify for a pension solely under the legislation of the country in which you are resident. A person who has paid contributions in the UK but does not qualify for a Category A or B pension under British legislation but who worked in another EU/EEA state may qualify for a retirement pension when those contributions are taken into account. The retirement pension is then worked out according to a formula (see below).

Calculating your pension

The following rules apply wherever you are in the EU/EEA. If you have been subject to the legislation of more than one member state, each of them must calculate your pension entitlement as follows in accordance with EC law. This is one field where migrants may be better off than others because of an exception in the overlapping provisions (see p319).

Each member state should calculate the pension you are entitled to (if any) under its own legislation.[102] For example, if you have been insured in the UK for 20 years you would be entitled to a UK pension of approximately 50 per cent of the standard rate. On the other hand, under UK domestic legislation, if you had only worked for eight years in the UK you would have no entitlement.

Each member state should then calculate a theoretical pension as if your entire career in the EU/EEA had been spent in that member state.[103] This theoretical amount is then reduced in proportion to the actual time you worked in that state compared with the time worked in the EU/EEA as a whole. The resulting amount is known as your pro-rata entitlement.

Each member state then pays you whichever is the greater of the amount you are entitled to under its own domestic legislation, and the pro-rata amount of its benefit which you are entitled to from that member state calculated in accordance with the co-ordination rule.[104]

Example

Mr Coiro from Italy has worked for 43 years in different member states:

8 years in the UK

15 years in Italy

20 years in Ireland

His entitlement in the UK based on UK domestic legislation (based on periods of insurance) amounts to nothing.

However, if his entitlement to a UK pension was calculated as if his entire EU/EEA career of 43 years' work had been carried out in the UK, he would be eligible for 100 per cent of the UK standard rate (this is his 'theoretical entitlement'). He can therefore claim the 'pro-rata' amount of this entitlement in respect of his years of work in the UK.

His pro-rata entitlement is worked out as follows:

His pro-rata entitlement *equals*

$$\frac{\text{his theoretical rate} \times \text{his UK period of insurance}}{\text{his EU/EEA period of insurance}}$$

which is:

$$\frac{100\% \times 8 \text{ years}}{43 \text{ years}}$$

Answer: 19%

So Mr Coiro will be entitled to the pro-rata rate of 19 per cent of the UK standard rate. Since the alternative amount which he could claim from the UK based on his eight years' contributions is nil, the pro-rata amount is the higher of the two possible entitlements to a UK pension and that is what Mr Coiro can claim.

In this example, Italy and Ireland would perform similar calculations and Mr Coiro would receive a pension from each on the same basis. It could be that for either or both of these member states the calculation based on their domestic legislation turned out to be higher, and Mr Coiro would receive that larger pension.

Because of the way the calculation rules work for UK pensions, entitlement under domestic legislation alone[105] will almost invariably be equal to or higher than the pro-rata amount calculated in accordance with the co-ordination rule.[106] (For example, you may qualify for a Category D pension – see p341.) In order to be considered in this way, you will, of course, have had to have paid sufficient contributions to qualify you for a UK pension.

If you worked in a member state that only recently joined the EC and you were entitled to a retirement pension before that country joined, check the rules under reciprocal arrangements (see p372).

The provisions in the co-ordination rule in relation to entitlement to a UK pension are therefore most likely to be of use to people who have worked in the UK but for an insufficient period to qualify for a pension under UK rules alone, and who have also worked for a period in another EU/EEA member state. A similar situation exists in most other member states.

If you have worked for a period of less than one year in an EU/EEA member state, your pension is calculated differently and you receive no pension from that state.[107] But the period is included in the calculation of your total period of employment in the EU/EEA.[108]

Graduated retirement benefit in the UK is not included in the pro-rata rate calculation, but your UK entitlement is added on after the calculation under the co-ordination rule has been carried out.[109]

Adult dependency increases (ADIs) are paid at the same pro-rata rate as the basic pension.[110]

A child dependency increase is a family benefit. It is not paid at a pro-rata rate, but in full.

The pro-rata equation is not recalculated when benefits are uprated. But the rate of retirement pension is increased.[111]

Extra retirement pension for your dependants

If you are entitled to a retirement pension from an EU/EEA member state you are also entitled to an extra amount for a dependent adult. The extra amount will be calculated in the same way as the rest of your pension. You can claim this benefit even if the person who depends on you is in another EU/EEA member state.

If you are living in the EU/EEA member state that pays your pension, it will also pay any benefits to which you are entitled for your children. In the UK this would be child benefit or extra pension or both – see pp346-47.

If you are living in a member state that does not pay you a retirement pension, then the member state that is paying your retirement pension will pay the benefits for your children.

If you are getting a retirement pension from two or more member states, then the member state where you were insured for the longest time will pay any benefits you are entitled to for your children.

What happens if you have made pension contributions in more than one EU/EEA member state

You can claim your pension directly from any EU/EEA member state in which you have been insured in accordance with the calculation set out on p342, or you can claim from the member state in which you are living when you approach pension age (which will be the present Competent State). That state will pass details of your claim to any other EU/EEA member state where you have been insured so that each one can do its calculation. The Competent State will inform you whether you can claim more under domestic law alone or with your entitlement calculated under the co-ordination rule.[112]

Each member state decides how to pay your pension and pays it itself. If you are in the UK and you get a pension from any other EU/EEA member state, this will count as income when calculating any income support to which you may be entitled (for information about the income support rules and EU/EEA nationals, see p349).

Receiving your UK pension in another EU/EEA member state

You can be paid a UK pension in any other EU/EEA member state at the same rate as you would get if you were living in the UK or at the rate calculated in accordance with the formula in the co-ordination rule.[113] The calculation as to what you are entitled to will be carried out as above (see p342). Your pension may be paid directly into a bank in the member state you are living in, or in the UK. Alternatively, the pension can be paid by payable order normally issued every four weeks. Payment is always made in sterling.

Receiving income-based benefit pending payment of your pension in the UK

If you get paid arrears these will usually be sent directly to you. However, you should bear in mind that if you have claimed income support while waiting for your pension to arrive from another member state, you will have to repay that amount when your pension arrives. Similarly, if you have been getting an income support type benefit in another EU/EEA member state while waiting for your UK retirement pension, you may have to pay that amount back when your UK pension arrives.

Category D retirement pension

You may be entitled to this if you are 80 years of age or over, but it is paid only in limited circumstances.

Residence in another EU/EEA member state can count towards satisfying the ten-year residence conditions for a category D pension provided that either:

- residence in the other EU/EEA member state counts towards entitlement to old-age benefits in that member state; *or*
- you were insured in the other member state and you have at some time been subject to UK legislation. For example, you have been liable to pay UK class 1 or class 2 national insurance contributions.

If you satisfy these conditions, the period of residence in the other EU/EEA member state is added to the periods of residence in the UK and pro-rata Category D retirement pension is awarded. The UK pays the percentage of benefit which is equivalent to the number of years of residence in the UK used to satisfy the ten-year residence condition.

Survivors' benefits (widows and orphans)

General rules

In general, the co-ordination arrangements for survivors' benefits are the same as those for retirement pensions (see pp340-45) in that you can elect whether to take the amount you are entitled to (under the co-ordination rule) from all the EU/EEA member states in which the deceased made contributions or to take the pro-rata amount from the state in which you are living.

Survivors' benefits can be exported to any EU/EEA member state without reduction or modification.[114] If the deceased person was insured in more than one EU/EEA member state, the pension for the surviving spouse is calculated on the same basis as would have applied to the insured person. If the person was drawing pensions under the legislation of two or more member states, the spouse will be entitled to widows' or widowers' pensions under the legislation of these member states. The rules are the same as those for retirement pensions – see pp340-45.

If you are a widow and your husband was only insured in one member state, that member state pays any benefits to which you may be entitled for your children. If your partner was insured in more than one member state, it will normally be the member state where the child lives that will pay the benefit.

Benefits available in the UK

The UK benefits for widowhood are:

- widow's payment
- widowed mother's allowance;
- widow's pension

For a full description of these benefits and when they are paid, see CPAG's *Rights Guide to Non-Means-Tested Benefits*.

The fact that there are not widowers' benefits in the UK is the subject of a legal challenge under the European Convention on Human Rights. (See CPAG's *Welfare Rights Bulletin* for updates.)

Family benefits

General rules

For a basic introduction to the rules relating to family benefits, see pp306-7. This covers residence provisions and insurance and employment conditions for getting these benefits.

Family benefits available in the UK

Family benefits available in the UK are:

- child benefit (paid at a higher rate for lone parents);
- family credit (paid to parents in work but on low pay);
- guardian's allowance;
- child dependency increases.

For a full description of these benefits, see CPAG's *Rights Guide to Non-Means-Tested Benefits* and the *National Welfare Benefits Handbook* (see Appendix 3).

Family benefits for children of pensioners

Under EC law, family benefits are payable for the dependent children of pensioners. To qualify you must be claiming:[115]

- an old-age benefit; *and*
- an invalidity benefit; *or*
- a benefit for an accident at work or an occupational disease.

If you are getting your pension from only one EU/EEA member state, family benefits are payable by that member state regardless of where in the EU/EEA you or your children are living.

If you are receiving a pension from more than one member state, family benefits are payable by the member state where you live, provided there is entitlement under that member state's scheme. If there is no entitlement under its scheme, then the member state to which you have been subject to the legislation for the longest period, and under which you have entitlement to family benefits, will be responsible for paying you.[116]

What happens if you go to another EU/EEA member state

Usually the general rules (see pp306-7) will apply in deciding which state pays family benefits. But if you are posted to work in another EU/EEA member state for less than 12 months you remain subject to the legislation of the member state from which you have been posted. (The 12-month period can be extended for a further 12 months in certain circumstances.) The member state from which you are posted will therefore be responsible for paying family benefits.[117] If you are a member of the Armed Forces serving in another EU/EEA member state, you remain subject to UK legislation.

What happens if you work outside the EU/EEA

If you have worked outside the EU/EEA but remain subject to the legislation of an EU/EEA member state (see p316), you may retain the right to family benefits.[118]

When you are unemployed

If you are unemployed[119] and

- you were previously employed or self-employed; *and*
- you are getting unemployment benefit from an EU/EEA member state

you are then entitled to family benefits from that member state for members of your family who are living in an EU/EEA member state.

You are entitled to family benefits from your state of residence for members of your family living with you if:[120]

- you are unemployed; *but*
- you were previously employed; *and*
- during your last period of employment you were resident in a different EU/EEA member state to the one you were working in; *and*
- you are receiving unemployment benefit from the member state where you are living.

CHAPTER TWENTY SEVEN

Using the social advantages rule to claim means-tested benefits

This chapter covers:

1. The benefit rules (below)
2. British citizens with EC rights in the UK (p356)
3. Habitual residence and exemptions (p357)
4. The requirement to leave (p365)
5. Deportation or removal from the UK (p368)

It deals with the rules affecting the rights of EU/EEA nationals and family members to the following benefits: income support (IS), income-based jobseeker's allowance (JSA), housing benefit (HB), council tax benefit (CTB), family credit (FC), disability working allowance (DWA) and the social fund.

Terminology

In this chapter, we refer to EC legislation by name and number. This is because the British regulations often refer to EC law definitions. These definitions often overlap. If we used our own definitions, it would lessen the book's accuracy and usefulness in helping you formulate your arguments. The references you will see throughout are:

- Reg (EEC) 1612/68: which covers workers;
- Reg (EEC) 1251/70: which covers retired and incapacitated workers;
- EC Directive 68/360: which covers workers;
- EC Directive 73/148: which covers self-employed people, and people who are in receipt of services.

I. THE BENEFIT RULES

The rules for means-tested benefits treat people with EC rights differently from other migrants and British citizens who do not have those rights. Some of the rules treat EU/EEA nationals worse than British citizens, but most of the rules are more favourable. Almost all of these rules are in British benefit regulations, unlike most of the EC rules for non-means-tested benefits (see Chapter 26). These rules have been included in British regulations because of the 'social advantages rule' (see p308). There are still some favourable rules for EU/EEA nationals which are not part of British regulations but which come straight from the social advantages rule and the 'co-ordination rule'.

There are two sets of rules for people with EC rights:

- the rules for IS, income-based JSA, HB and CTB (see below); *and*
- the rules for FC and DWA (see p353).

There are no special British regulations for the social fund (see p365), but the social advantages rule may apply to some situations.

IS, income-based JSA, HB and CTB

If you are an EU/EEA national (see glossary) or a family member of an EU/EEA national (see p355), you are entitled to these benefits on the same basis as a British citizen (Chapter 11) unless you are a person from abroad (see p350). If you are a person from abroad you are not entitled to these benefits (see Chapter 10).[1]

British citizens may be able to use the rules for EU/EEA nationals to get exemption from the habitual residence test (see p356).

If you are being paid IS or income-based JSA, you are exempt from the HB and CTB rules about people from abroad.[2] The local authority which deals with your HB/CTB claim should not make enquiries about your immigration status or habitual residence.[3]

EC rules allowing you to take benefit abroad do not apply to IS.[4]

Taking income-based JSA outside the UK

It is not clear whether you can keep entitlement to income-based JSA while you are looking for work in the EU/EEA outside of the UK (apart from the UK rules for temporary absence – see p248). Under the co-ordination rule, you can keep entitlement to contribution-based JSA in these circumstances for three months (see p322). The UK government has included income-based JSA in the list of benefits *excluded* from the EC rules allowing you to take the benefit abroad.[5] However, we consider that this may breach EC law. Under the co-ordination rule, unemployment benefits are exportable for three months. If JSA is an unemployment benefit under the co-ordination rule, then you are entitled to income-based JSA as well as any contribution-based element of JSA.[6] We consider that both types of JSA are an unemployment benefit.[7] This would apply to any EU/EEA national (including a British citizen) going elsewhere in the EU/EEA to look for work.

EU/EEA nationals

If you are an EU/EEA national you are a person from abroad if:[8]

- you are *not* habitually resident in the UK, Ireland, Channel Islands or Isle of Man *and* you are not exempt from the habitual residence test (see p357);
- the Home Office has written to you stating that you are not lawfully in the UK. This is called a 'requirement to leave' (see p365);
- the Home Office has made an order for your deportation from the UK (see p368); *or*
- an immigration officer disputes that you are an EU/EEA national (see p370) and has *either*:
  - given you temporary admission; *or*
  - decided that you are an illegal entrant.

Family members

If you are a British citizen and a family member of an EU/EEA national, you may be able to use these rules to be exempt from the habitual residence test. If you are not an EU/EEA national but are the family member of an EU/EEA national, you may be able to use the rules about entitlement to IS, income-based JSA, HB and CTB for EU/EEA nationals. Remember that the definition of 'family member' includes not only a spouse and children, but possibly relatives who do not live with the EU/EEA national – eg, a separated spouse, parents and adult children (see p355).

Using these rules may depend upon your immigration history. If you have been given permission to enter or remain in the UK because of your relationship with an EU/EEA national, you should have a 'residence document'. This is a stamp in your passport or on a Home Office letter called a 'residence document' (see p292).

You will not have a residence document if:

- you do not have permission to be in the UK, or you have limited leave to be in the UK. For whether you are better off under the rules for EU/EEA nationals or the rules which apply to you because of your 'leave to remain', see below. *A claim for benefit may affect your immigration position* (see p187). *You should seek immigration advice before claiming*; *or*
- you have indefinite leave to remain under the UK Immigration Rules (see Chapter 12), but you do not have a residence document. This is likely if the EU/EEA national whose family member you are is British or Irish, or is from a member state which joined the EU/EEA after you were given leave to remain; *or*

- you have been given leave to remain in the UK as a refugee or have been given exceptional leave to remain. If this applies to you, the rules for refugees (see Chapter 13) or exceptional leave to remain (see Chapter 14) are always more favourable so you should use them.

If you have a residence document

If you are a non-EU/EEA national but are a family member of an EU/EEA national *and* you have a residence document (see p350), you are a person from abroad if:[9]

- you are *not* habitually resident in the UK, Ireland, Channel Islands or Isle of Man *and* you are not exempt (see 357); *or*
- the Home Office has made an order for your deportation from the UK (see p368); *or*
- an immigration officer has *either*:
  – given you temporary admission (see p24); *or*
  – decided that you are an illegal entrant (see p206).

If you do not have a residence document

If you are a non-EU/EEA national but are a family member of an EU/EEA national *and* you do *not* have a residence document (see p350), you are a person from abroad if:[10]

- you are a sponsored immigrant (see p153) – but your EU/EEA status may override these rules (see below); *or*
- you have no leave (see Chapter 16) or only limited leave (see Chapter 15) to remain in the UK, but your EU/EEA status may override these immigration status rules (see p352);
- you are *not* habitually resident in the UK, Ireland, Channel Islands or Isle of Man *and* you are not exempt (or only some exemptions apply to you – see p357); *or*
- the Home Office has made an order for your deportation from the UK (see p368); *or*
- an immigration officer has *either*:
  – given you temporary admission (see p24); *or*
  – decided that you are an illegal entrant (see p206).

Using your EU/EEA status to override sponsored immigrant rules

Under the sponsored immigrant benefit rules, only a person with leave to enter or remain in the UK can be a sponsored immigrant (see p154). This does not seem to apply if you also have a right under EC law to remain in the UK, for two reasons:

- since you have an EC law right to remain in the UK, you do not require leave to remain in the UK.[11] However, even though you still

formally have indefinite leave to remain, it will not count under the benefit rules; *and*
- the Home Office cannot require an undertaking from your sponsor if you have an EC law right to enter the UK (see pp290-92).

So, if you have an EC law right to remain, relying on a sponsorship undertaking to deny you benefit would seem to breach EC law – even if you only got your EC law right after you were given leave to enter. This is most likely to apply if your sponsor is a British citizen who has exercised the right to free movement. It is not necessary for you to have moved within the EC (see example below). If this applies to you, take independent advice. CPAG would be interested to hear from advisers dealing with this situation.

Example

Noor is a British citizen, but his mother, Shafla, is an elderly Indian national living abroad. Noor signs a RON 112 form undertaking to maintain and accommodate Shafla in the UK. Shafla is given indefinite leave to enter the UK as Noor's mother. She lives with Noor who works and maintains her. After a year, Noor moves to Germany. He works there for one year while Shafla remains in the UK, maintained by Noor. Noor returns to the UK and again finds work but is made redundant six months later. He claims JSA (both income- and contribution-based) and Shafla claims IS. Because Noor has exercised his EC law right of free movement to work in Germany, he now has an EC law right to live in the UK. This includes the right to have his mother living with him as an elderly dependent relative. Shafla can argue that the sponsored immigrant rule no longer applies to her because her EC law right to reside with her son is now based on her right as a family member of an EU/EEA national with an EC law right to live in the UK. She no longer has indefinite leave to remain for the purposes of the benefit rules, so refusing her IS is a breach of EC law.

Using your EU/EEA status to override immigration status rules

You may be able to use your status as an EU/EEA family member to override the immigration status rules. This is because, as a family member, you have an EC right to stay in the UK and do not need leave to remain.[12] Therefore, any conditions on your limited leave do not apply and you cannot be here without leave – for example, as an overstayer – because you do not need leave. Any decision that you were an illegal entrant, or to give you temporary admission, no longer has legal effect once you have an EC right to stay in the UK, unless these are actions taken as part of Home Office action to remove you from the UK under the rules for family members of EU/EEA nationals (see p292).

EU/EEA family members and habitual residence

Only the claimant is subject to the habitual residence test.[13] If there is a chance you may fail the habitual residence test and your partner is an EU/EEA national (including certain British citizens – see p356), you should consider making your partner the claimant, though there may be disadvantages in this (see CPAG's *National Welfare Benefits Handbook*).

If you are not habitually resident (see p357), you may be exempt, but you can only use some of the exemptions available for EU/EEA nationals (see p358). You are exempt if:

- you have a residence document showing that you are the family member of an EU/EEA national (see p350). This proves that you have a right to reside in the UK under Directive 68/360 or 73/148;[14] *or*
- you do not have a residence document, but are the family member of an EU/EEA national who has a right to reside in the UK under Directive 68/360 (see p362) or 73/148 (see p363). This is because you have the same right to reside as the EU/EEA national whose family member you are.[15]

However, if the EU/EEA national does not have a right of residence in the UK under Directive 68/360 or 73/148, you cannot use any status s/he has as a worker within the meaning of Regulation 1612/68 or 1251/70 to be exempt from the habitual residence test. That is because the benefit regulations only refer to 'workers' and not to family members of workers,[16] and the definition of 'worker' under Regulations 1612/68 or 1251/70 for these purposes does not include family members.[17] This means that the benefit regulations may breach EC law.[18] You should seek specialist advice.

FC for EU/EEA nationals

If you are an EU/EEA national (see glossary) you are exempt from the FC immigration condition.[19]

There is no habitual residence test for FC, but under British law you (and any partner) must be ordinarily resident in the UK (see p138).[20] The co-ordination rule (see Chapter 25) means that these rules do not apply to EU/EEA nationals. FC is a family benefit under the co-ordination rule so:[21]

- if you are working in the UK, there is no ordinary residence or presence test for you (or any partner);
- if you are working outside the UK but in the EU/EEA, the state where you are working is responsible for paying you family benefits. If you are entitled to FC under UK benefit rules (including meeting the ordinary residence and presence test) the Benefits Agency can offset from your FC the amount of any family benefit from that state to which you

are entitled (or would be entitled if a claim were made). (This also applies to child benefit and guardian's allowance – see p346.) You should end up with the benefit you would have received if you lived and worked in the member state which pays the most family benefit. `

If you have a partner, these rules apply regardless of who is the FC claimant. For example, a woman living in Ireland can claim FC even if her partner works in the UK.

FC for family members of EU/EEA nationals

The rules are the same as for DWA (see below).

DWA for EU/EEA nationals

If you are an EU/EEA national (see glossary) you are entitled to DWA on the same basis as a British citizen (see p138). This is because EU/EEA nationals are exempt from the DWA immigration condition.[22]

If you are not entitled to DWA under UK regulations because you are not ordinarily resident in the UK, you may be able to use the co-ordination rule to get DWA.[23]

If you are not entitled to DWA under UK regulations because your partner is not ordinarily resident in the UK, or because all of her/his earnings come from outside the UK, you may be able to use the co-ordination rule or social advantages rule to get DWA. The condition that your partner must be ordinarily resident in the UK may be unlawfully discriminatory.[24] If this applies to you, take specialist advice. You may be able to argue that your partner is not your partner for DWA purposes (see p111).

FC/DWA for family members of EU/EEA nationals

If you are an EU/EEA family member but are not an EU/EEA national, you are entitled to FC or DWA on the same basis as a British citizen (see p138). This is because EU/EEA family members are exempt from the FC/DWA immigration condition.[25] If you are an EU/EEA national yourself, see p353.

There is no definition in the FC/DWA rules of a 'family member of an EU/EEA national'. If you have a residence document (see p350) showing that you are an EU/EEA family member, you ought to be accepted as one by the Benefits Agency.

If you do not have a residence document, the Benefits Agency will consider whether or not you are an EU/EEA family member. If you do not have permission to be in the UK, or you have limited leave to be in the UK, *a claim for benefit may affect your immigration position* (see p187). *You should seek immigration advice before claiming.*

There is no case law on who is an EU/EEA family member for FC/DWA purposes. The same wording is used for attendance allowance, disability living allowance and severe disability allowance, so any case law on those benefits will be useful for FC/DWA purposes. We consider that the term 'EU/EEA family member' should be given its ordinary meaning, but that it must be broad enough to include anyone who comes within the definition of EU/EEA family member for the EC right of free movement (eg, adult children – see p291). This is because the purpose of the exception for EU/EEA family members is that UK law follows EC law, and therefore the UK definition should be interpreted to give effect to EC law. The commissioners may give guidance on who is an EU/EEA family member. Until this happens, we consider that it includes:

- any person who has a right to join that EU/EEA national as a family member (see p290);[26]
- an EU/EEA national's unmarried partner;
- an EU/EEA national's former unmarried partner;
- any other relative of the EU/EEA national or her/his partner, whether related by blood, adoption or marriage, who:
  - is dependent on the EU/EEA national or spouse (for meaning, see p292);[27] *or*
  - 'lived under the same roof' as the EU/EEA national or spouse in their country of origin;[28] *or*
  - taking into account their ties to the EU/EEA national or partner, is a member of that person's family.

Benefits Agency advice is that a 'family member of an EU/EEA national' for FC/DWA is limited to the FC/DWA definition of family, which is:[29]

- a married or unmarried couple and any child or young person in the household for whom one or both are responsible;
- a single person and any child or young person in the household for whom one or both are responsible.

We disagree with this advice because it does not take account of the EC law on who counts as a family member.

If you are refused FC/DWA on the grounds that you are not an EU/EEA family member, you should seek specialist advice.

Social fund

There are no special UK rules relating to the social fund for EU/EEA nationals or family members. However, some of the social fund rules which affect EU/EEA nationals and their family members may be unlawful under the social advantages rule (see p308) in particular:

- for **funeral payments,** the rule that the burial must take place in the UK. This is unlawful and does not apply to EU/EEA nationals who have an EC law right to be in the UK (see p149);
- for **community care grants** (made to help you re-establish yourself in the community following a stay in institutional or residential care), the rule that they can be made only if you have previously lived in GB (see p150). This may be unlawful in the case of a person intending to join an EU/EEA national in GB as that national's family member. This rule is discriminatory because an EU/EEA national is more likely to have a relative in care in another EU/EEA country than is a British national;[30]
- for **payments or loans from the discretionary social fund,** the rule is that they can only be made for a need which occurs in the UK.[31] This may be unlawful discrimination in the case of an EU/EEA national or a family member, because it is a condition which s/he is less likely to be able to meet than a UK national.[32] For example, if an Italian retired worker living in the UK wishes to visit his sick mother in Italy, he may not be excluded because the need is *his* need to visit, and it arises in the UK. If, however, the need is his mother's, he can apply if she lives in Bolton, but not in Italy. The rule is discriminatory because it is more likely to affect an EU/EEA national than a British citizen.[33]

If any of these apply to you, you should ask for an internal social fund review and quickly seek specialist advice.

2. BRITISH CITIZENS WITH EC RIGHTS IN THE UK

All British citizens are EU/EEA nationals but do not always have EC law rights. You may be exempt from the habitual residence test using the exemptions for EU/EEA nationals, but only if:[34]

- you have travelled to another EU/EEA member state; *and*
- you went to that member state to use an EC right there, *and*
- you later returned to the UK to exercise an EC right here.

The EC rights which carry the right to free movement are:

- the right to work, including the right to seek work (see p287);[35]
- the right to establish yourself as self-employed, including the right to seek to do that (see p289);[36]
- the right to receive and provide services (see p364).[37]

Benefits Agency guidance states that you have not exercised your right to free movement if you claimed IS or income-based JSA on your return to the UK. This is because you have not returned to the UK 'to work'.[38] This advice is *wrong*. If you return to the UK to seek work, then you have exercised your right to free movement, regardless of any claim for benefit.[39]

If you are treated as an EU/EEA national under these rules, then the habitual residence exemptions apply to you as they apply to other EU/EEA nationals (see p358).

3. HABITUAL RESIDENCE AND EXEMPTIONS

The habitual resident test applies to IS, income-based JSA, HB and CTB. It does not apply to FC or DWA.

The habitual residence test applies only to the person claiming IS.[40] It does not apply to any partner or child for whom IS is being claimed. If there is a chance you might fail the test, but you have a partner who is more likely to pass, s/he could claim instead, though there may be disadvantages to this (see CPAG's *National Welfare Benefits Handbook*).

You pass the habitual residence test if you are habitually resident (see p102) in the UK, Ireland, the Channel Islands or the Isle of Man. If you are an EU/EEA national who is not habitually resident, and you are not exempt (see p358), you are a person from abroad[41] and are not entitled to IS, income-based JSA, HB or CTB.[42]

In *Sarwar* the Court of Appeal decided that the habitual residence test was not unlawful under EC law.[43] The claimants argued that the test discriminates in favour of Irish nationals and against nationals of other EU/EEA member states. The test applies to people habitually resident in the Republic of Ireland, even though that is outside of the UK. Irish nationals are more likely to be habitually resident in Ireland than nationals of other EU/EEA member states, therefore the test is discriminatory. Discrimination between nationals of EU/EEA member states on the grounds of nationality is unlawful under EC law, if it affects something covered by the EC Treaty. The Court of Appeal decided that the discrimination in the habitual residence test only affected work-seekers (see p359) and that discrimination against work-seekers in relation to possible entitlement to IS is not covered by the EC Treaty. The Court also decided that the habitual residence test was not unlawful under British law. The claimants may appeal against both parts of the decision.

Lawfulness of habitual residence test for income-based JSA

We consider that the habitual residence test for income-based JSA may be unlawful under a different part of EC law from that used by the claimants in *Sarwar* (see above). The case was brought before JSA was introduced. Under EC law, JobCentres must give EU/EEA national work-seekers the same assistance as British citizens.[44] We consider that income-based JSA may count as assistance under EC law because it is an essential and inseparable part of a co-ordinated programme of assistance to help the unemployed find work – including advice, training and JobClub. If income-based JSA is assistance, then provision which discriminates on nationality grounds is in breach of this part of EC law. This applies to work-seekers as well as workers,[45] while the EC rule considered in *Sarwar* only applied to workers.[46] Non-EU/EEA national family members of an EU/EEA national can only use this argument if the EU/EEA national is a work-seeker or worker.[47]

Exemption from the habitual residence test

As an EU/EEA national you are exempt from the habitual residence test if:[48]

- you are a worker for the purposes of EC Regulations 1612/68 or 1251/70; *or*
- you have a right to reside in the UK under EC Directives 68/360 or 73/148.

You may qualify as a worker under Regulation 1612/68 if:

- you are working in the UK (see p359);
- you have been a worker in the UK (see p360); *or*
- you have never worked in the UK but have worked elsewhere in the EU/EEA (see p361).

You may be a worker under Regulation 1251/70 or have a right to reside if:

- you are working in the UK (see p362);
- you have retired from work because of old-age or incapacity (see p363);
- you are, or intend to be, self-employed in the UK (see p363);
- you are in receipt of certain services in the UK (see p364); *or*
- you live in the UK but work in another EU/EEA member state, called a frontier worker (see p365).

If you are a British citizen and do not have the nationality of any other EU/EEA member state, these rules may exempt you from the test. For British citizens who can do this, see p356.

The Benefits Agency should accept that you are exempt if you hold a current EU/EEA residence permit (see p285) issued by the Home Office. However, Benefits Agency staff are advised that they can decide that the right of residence has been lost, even if you have a current residence permit.[49] For details of when this may happen, see p362.

You do not need to have a residence permit to be exempt. Your rights come from EC law and not from having a permit.[50] If you do not have a permit, the Benefits Agency will have to decide whether or not you are a 'worker' and/or have a 'right to reside'. The law on this is complicated and unclear. You may be covered by more than one exemption so you should check each one. Benefits Agency staff find it difficult to deal with these rules and are reluctant to treat claimants as exempt. If the Benefits Agency decides that you are not habitually resident and not exempt, you should appeal and take independent advice.

Work-seekers

A social security commissioner has decided that looking for work in the UK is not enough to make you a worker for the purposes of the social advantages rule.[51] You must have actually worked in the EU/EEA to qualify. A person who has not worked in the UK but who has worked elsewhere in the EU/EEA may count as a worker (see p361).

Currently working

If you are an EU/EEA national and you are working in the UK, you are a worker for the purposes of Regulation 1612/68.[52] The UK does not include the Channel Islands and Isle of Man for this purpose.[53]

There is no precise definition of a 'worker', only guidelines from case law. Work includes all 'genuine and effective'[54] economic activity carried out for an employer[55] (for self-employment, see p363). This means that you must be doing work now in order to receive an income (in cash or in kind), either now or in the future.

The case law does *not* lay down:

- a minimum period of work,
- a minimum number of hours per week, *or*
- minimum pay,

for an activity to count as work. It does not matter if you are paid in kind rather than cash.[56] It is irrelevant that the income from the work is not enough to support you.[57] Voluntary work from which you can expect no benefit is not 'work'. However, a person who works for nothing for a period of time, under an agreement which is intended to lead to payment, may qualify as a worker. Work for your rehabilitation may not count as work under this rule.

The following activities have been considered as work:

- teaching music for 12 hours a week;[58]
- work for 60 hours over 16 weeks under a contract with no fixed hours but which requires the person to be available to work;[59]

- training over the summer in a hotel school;[60]
- distributing magazines for four hours a week for £18 a week.[61]

For full details, see p287.

People who formerly worked in the UK – under Regulation 1612/68

An EU/EEA national who has worked in the UK may count as a worker for the purposes of Regulation 1612/68, but it is not clear when this will happen. Because of this, you should always check to see if you count as a worker under Regulation 1251/70 (see p363), or have a right to reside as a retired person (see p363) or as a person receiving services (see p361).

Benefits Agency advice (see below) states that Regulation 1612/68 only applies to former workers in certain special situations. We believe this advice may be wrong and that all former workers may be exempt. This is because of the wording of the benefit rules. These state that you are exempt if you are 'a worker for the purposes of Regulation 1612/68'. They do *not* use the words 'a person with equal rights to benefits as a worker for the purposes of Regulation 1612/68'.[62] Therefore, this exemption covers a person who is treated as a worker under Regulation 1612/68 for *any* purpose. Some workers have fewer rights than other workers under Regulation 1612/68, but Regulation 1612/68 protects all workers who become unemployed from discrimination on grounds of nationality for the purposes of reinstatement or re-employment.[63] This protection does not depend on that unemployment being involuntary.[64] The status as worker under this rule does not end while the undertaking which employed you still exists because, as long as it does, you are protected against discrimination by that undertaking. Therefore, even though this may be the only right you have as a worker under Regulation 1612/68, you are still a worker for the purposes of Regulation 1612/68 and so exempt (see example below).

The cases referred to in the Benefits Agency advice only deal with whether a decision is wrong because of a person's *rights* as a worker under *one part* of Regulation 1612/68, and not with whether a person is a 'worker for the purposes of Regulation 1612/68'.[65] Where the European Court of Justice decides that a person does not have a particular right as a worker, this does not mean that the person has lost the status of 'worker' for all purposes of Regulation 1612/68.[66]

Example

Andreas, a Greek national, found work in a department store. This temporary work lasted for four weeks. A few months later he approached the store and asked to be re-employed. He was refused on the grounds that he is Greek. This is a breach of his right as a worker to equal treatment for re-employment. This protection, and therefore the status of 'worker', continues as long as Andreas needs it, which is as long as the store (or any other firm which takes over that undertaking) exists.

Benefits Agency advice states that you only remain a worker for the purposes of Regulation 1612/68 if:[67]

- you voluntarily gave up work in the UK to undergo vocational training linked to that work;
- you became involuntarily unemployed and have taken on occupational retraining in another field because of the state of the job market;
- you have been temporarily laid off and are seeking reinstatement or re-employment with the same employer.

The Benefits Agency does not explain why this advice is limited to people who are *temporarily laid off*. Those words are not in EC law.[68]

Voluntary unemployment
The Benefits Agency may refuse to treat you as a former worker because they consider that you are not involuntarily unemployed. There is no definition of involuntary unemployment under EC law. If you were dismissed or resigned from your job, but the JobCentre has not disqualified you from JSA (see CPAG's *Jobseeker's Allowance Handbook*), then you should be considered involuntarily unemployed for the purpose of the habitual residence test. If the JobCentre has disqualified you or does not allow you to sign on (eg, because you cannot show that you are available for work) you may still qualify as unemployed under EC law (see p368).

People who formerly worked elsewhere in EEA
A social security commissioner has decided that work in the EU/EEA outside the UK cannot exempt a person from the habitual residence test as a worker for the purposes of Regulation 1612/68.[69] This is important for British citizens returning here after working in the EU/EEA (see also p356). The basis for the decision was EC case law that a person only has *rights* as a worker under EC law in the UK *once that person has worked in the UK* (or, in the case of a British citizen, has worked after exercising EC rights – see p356).[70] We consider that the commissioner's decision may be wrong. Under UK benefit regulations a claimant does not have to be a worker for the purposes of Regulation 1612/68 *in the UK* – the emphasised words are not there.[71] This is different from the exemption for people with a right to reside *in the*

UK (see p362).[72] If you work in an EU/EEA member state other than your own, you become a worker for the purposes of Regulation 1612/68 even though that gives you no rights in other EU/EEA member states. This argument was not considered by the commissioner dealing with the case. The EC cases considered by the commissioner do not deal with this because it is not about EC law, but about the wording of the British regulation.

Right to reside as a worker – Directive 68/360

Directive 68/360 deals with entitlement to a residence permit. Benefits Agency guidance states that the right of residence lasts:[73]

- where a permit has been issued, for the period of the permit; *or*
- where no permit has been issued, for the period over which a permit would have lasted, if an application had been made.

In practice, the length of a permit issued by the Home Office is five years. However, Benefits Agency staff are advised that if you applied for a permit, one would be issued for:[74]

- up to three months where your work is expected to last for three months or less;
- up to a year where your work is expected to last for more than three months but less than a year; *or*
- at least five years where the employment is expected to last for more than one year.

If you worked in a job that was not for a fixed period, you should try to get your old employer to confirm that your job was for an indefinite period. The Benefits Agency should then treat your case as if a permit lasting five years had been issued.

If you worked in a job on a fixed length contract of more than three months, you should be treated as if you had been issued with a permit lasting until the expected end of the contract, even if your employment ended earlier – for example, you were made redundant.[75]

Benefits Agency staff are advised that the right of residence *only* ends before the permit (or the permit that would have been issued) if:[76]

- you 'leave the UK for more than six months (except for military service in your own country)'.[77] The six months must be consecutive. The relevant EC rule refers to 'residence' (see Chapter 8) in the UK, not presence, which means that the six-month period only starts running once you are no longer residing in the UK. There is no time limit on absence for military service; *or*
- you become 'voluntarily unemployed' (see p361).[78]

It is not clear if the Benefits Agency can decide that your right of residence has ended. We consider that only the Home Office can do this (whether or not a permit has been issued).[79] This is because EC law does not state that the right of residence ends automatically, only that the residence permit may not be withdrawn except for either of the reasons above.[80] This means that a decision to end the right to reside is a discretionary one which must take into account all the circumstances of your case. Only the Home Office is in a position to make that decision. If the Benefits Agency decides that you are not exempt from the habitual residence test because you have lost the right to reside, seek specialist advice. You should also consider whether you are exempt under any of the other rules.

Retired or incapacitated people – Regulation 1251/70

You may have a permanent right to remain in the UK as a worker if you have stopped working because of old age or incapacity.[81] You must have been a worker (see p358) in the UK, unless you were a frontier worker (see p365 below).[82] Even if you do not qualify under the rules below, you may qualify under Regulation 1612/68 (see p358).

You are a worker for the purposes of Regulation 1251/70 if:

- you retired on or after pensionable age (60 for women, 65 for men),[83] and either:[84]
  - you had worked in the UK for at least the last 12 months before retirement and resided continuously in the UK for more than three years; *or*
  - your spouse is a British citizen (or lost that citizenship because s/he married you);[85] *or*
- you stopped working because of permanent incapacity, and either:[86]
  - at the date you stopped working you had resided continuously in the UK for more than two years; *or*
  - your incapacity was caused by an industrial injury or disease which entitles you to a UK invalidity benefit (see p332); *or*
  - your spouse is a British citizen (or lost that citizenship because s/he married you).[87]

When working out your period of 'continuous residence', ignore:[88]

- absences from the UK of up to three months a year;
- longer absences due to your country's rules about military service.

When working out your period of employment, ignore:[89]

- days of unemployment recorded with the JobCentre (even if you were not paid JSA – eg, because of an inadequate contribution record);
- absence from work due to illness or accident.

Self-employed – Directive 73/148

If you are self-employed in the UK, you have a right to reside in the UK.[90] Self-employment includes professional activity. The guidelines for which activities count as work (see p359) also apply to self-employed work. There is no minimum period of residence or of work.

Your right to reside is permanent, but may be taken away if:

- you stop residing in the UK for longer than six consecutive months (ignoring any absence for military service);[91] or
- you stop being self-employed, unless this is because of temporary incapacity due to illness or accident.[92]

Benefits Agency staff are advised that the right of residence ends if either of these events happens.[93] We consider that the right of residence (whether or not a permit has been issued) can only be taken away by the Home Office (see p362).[94] If the Benefits Agency decides that you are not exempt from the habitual residence test because you have lost the right of residence, seek specialist advice.

Benefits Agency staff are advised that someone who intends to be self-employed in the UK does not have the right of residence.[95] This advice may be wrong since a person intending to be self-employed in the UK is considered by the Home Office to have a right of residence and is entitled to a residence permit.[96] If you intend to be self-employed, and you fail the habitual residence test, keep evidence of your efforts to become self-employed (correspondence, advertisements) and seek specialist advice.

If you have retired from self-employment because of old age or incapacity, you may have a right to reside under Directive 75/34.[97] The rules are the same as those for retired workers[98] (see p363), except that your self-employment in the UK counts as work. Even though you have a right to reside, this does not exempt you from the habitual residence test because the benefit exemptions do not refer to Directive 75/34. This seems to be a DSS oversight and may be in breach of EC rules about equal treatment.[99] If you fail the habitual residence test seek specialist advice.

Receiving services under Directive 73/148

If you are receiving services in the UK, you have a right to reside in the UK.[100] That right continues as long as the services are being received (see example below). Services include:

- tourism,[101] but this must be more than visiting friends;[102]
- education, except for education provided as part of the national education system;[103] and
- medical treatment.[104]

Benefits Agency guidance does not mention the right to reside while receiving services. If you may have this right take specialist advice.

Example

Ettore, an Italian man, came to Manchester to study languages part time at a private college. He paid the annual college fees and intended to support himself by working part time. He is unable to find any part-time work and claims income-based JSA. He is exempt from the habitual residence test because he has a right to reside in Manchester to receive the services provided by the college.

Frontier workers

You are a frontier worker if you live in one EU/EEA member state but work in another. You have a right to reside in the UK by virtue of Directive 68/360 if:[105]

- you work in another EU/EEA member state; *and*
- you return to your home in the UK as a rule at least once a week.

If you have retired because of old age or incapacity, you may have a right to remain and therefore be exempt from the habitual residence test as a worker for the purposes of Regulation 1251/70. The same rules apply to you as apply to retired workers who had worked in the UK (see p363) except that your work, while you were a frontier worker, counts as work in the UK.[106]

4. THE REQUIREMENT TO LEAVE

The requirement to leave applies to IS, income-based JSA, HB and CTB.[107] It does not apply to FC or DWA. The rules for IS and income-based JSA apply to partners and children as well as the claimant,[108] but we are not aware of any cases where the 'required to leave' letter (see p366) has been sent to partners or children.

If you are an EU/EEA national and you are 'required to leave' the UK by the Home Office, you are a person from abroad and are not entitled to IS, income-based JSA, HB or CTB.[109] The requirement to leave does not affect entitlement to FC or DWA.

A British citizen cannot be required to leave.[110] This applies even if you are also a national of another EU/EEA member state. If you are a British Dependent Territories citizen because of your connection with Gibraltar and you do not have leave to remain, you could be required to leave.[111]

An EU/EEA national who has indefinite leave to remain in the UK cannot be required to leave.[112] It may also be unlawful under British law for the Home Office to send you a 'requirement to leave' letter if you are an EU/EEA national who is exempt from deportation (see pp8-10).[113]

If you are the family member of an EU/EEA national but are not an EU/EEA national yourself, you cannot be sent a Home Office letter requiring you to leave. If you were admitted to the UK as the family member of an EU/EEA national and that EU/EEA national receives a Home Office letter requiring her/him to leave, that does not make you a person from abroad and you may claim IS, income-based JSA, HB or CTB in your own right. *If you do not have a residence document and you do not have indefinite leave to remain (see p32), you should not claim these benefits or allow your partner to claim for you unless you have taken immigration advice.* Any IS/income-based JSA will be paid at a reduced rate because your partner is a person from abroad (see p123). If the Benefits Agency or a tribunal later decides that your partner is not a person from abroad, your benefit will be made up to the ordinary amount for a couple, including the arrears due.

How the requirement to leave works

The requirement to leave letter is from the Immigration and Nationality Directorate of the Home Office. It states that

> in view of the fact that you are in the UK in a non-economic capacity and that you have become a burden on public funds, the Secretary of State is not satisfied that you are lawfully resident here under EC law and you should now make arrangements to leave the UK...If you do not leave the UK on a voluntary basis then, in the present circumstances of your case, we will not take steps to enforce your departure from the UK.[114]

This letter has no effect on your immigration status in the UK.[115] You are not really being required to leave! You cannot appeal in the immigration appeal system (see p293) against the letter itself, because it is not an immigration decision.[116] The only reason the letter is issued is to end your entitlement to IS/income-based JSA/HB/CTB.

In *Remilien and Wolke*, the Court of Appeal decided that the Home Office letter is a requirement to leave the UK.[117] For details of this decision, see below. The House of Lords has heard the claimants' appeal and, at the time of publication, a decision is awaited.[118]

There are no rules about when the letter will be issued. CPAG is not aware of any Irish nationals who have received the letter. The letter seems to have been issued only to claimants receiving IS[119] for more than six months who are not working part time. This may happen even if you are signing on.

The Benefits Agency or Employment Service tells the Home Office that you are claiming IS/income-based JSA. The Employment Service may then consider whether you have a realistic prospect of finding work, but that does not seem to happen normally, especially if you are signing on. The Home Office then issues the letter and tell the Benefits Agency or Employment Service that this has been done.

If you receive a requirement to leave letter, the Benefits Agency will stop your IS/income-based JSA. The local authority may then stop any HB/CTB.

If you have a partner who has not also been required to leave, s/he should consider claiming instead (see 366).

Challenging the requirement to leave

The law on your rights to challenge this decision is not clear. You should seek expert advice. You may be able to challenge the decision by:

- asking for a judicial review of the Home Office letter. You should do this through a solicitor or law centre; *or*
- appealing to a social security appeal tribunal against the Benefits Agency decision (see below). If your HB/CTB has been stopped, you should ask the local authority to review this decision, using the argument below. If the authority refuses, ask for a review board hearing. For details of appeals, see CPAG's *National Welfare Benefits Handbook*.

You can appeal to a tribunal on the basis that the Home Office letter is wrong to state that you are 'not lawfully in the UK'. If the letter is wrong, then the requirement that you leave the UK is not effective and the decision(s) to stop your benefit is wrong. The tribunal has the power to consider whether the Home Office letter is correct because a person whose EC rights are disputed has a right under EC law to the same kind of appeal hearing as a British citizen.[120] A British citizen whose IS/income-based JSA is taken away because, for example, s/he is not actively seeking and available for work, has a right to have all the facts of her/his case considered by the tribunal. An EU/EEA national has the same rights. The barrister representing the Chief Adjudication Officer in *Remelien and Wolke* told the Court of Appeal that a claimant who is required to leave can challenge the Home Office letter on an appeal to a social security appeal tribunal, on the grounds that it was wrongly issued.[121] Despite that statement, the Benefits Agency may argue at your appeal that the tribunal can only consider if you have been required to leave the UK, not whether you are lawfully here. There are at least two cases on appeal to a commissioner where the tribunal's powers to allow requirement to leave appeals, will be considered.[122]

The tribunal hearing your appeal should consider whether you can properly be required to leave the UK. It should consider whether:

- you have a right to reside in the UK as a worker (see p358), a retired or incapacitated worker (see p363), a self-employed person (see p363) or a person providing or receiving services (see p364); *or*
- you have a right to reside in the UK as the family member of a national of an EU/EEA member state, including the UK (see p350);
- you have a right to be present in the UK as a work-seeker[123] or because you want to establish yourself in self-employment (see below).[124]

You are a work-seeker if:[125]

- you are actively seeking employment; *and*
- you have a genuine chance of finding employment.

You can be a work-seeker under EC law, even if you do not qualify as unemployed under normal rules. This is because the definitions of 'work' and 'unemployment' under EC law differ from those under British law. For example, you may be available only for part-time work because you are a single parent and could not afford after-school childcare. In this case, you would not be 'unemployed' under British law because you are not 'available for work' (see CPAG's *Jobseeker's Allowance Handbook*). But because part-time work counts as work under EC law (see p359), you would count as a work-seeker under EC law.

You do not have to sign on as unemployed to qualify as a work-seeker. If you are a person who does not have to sign on (see CPAG's *National Welfare Benefits Handbook*), and you are concerned that you may be required to leave or are appealing to a tribunal about a requirement to leave, you should sign on if you can (see CPAG's *Jobseeker's Allowance Handbook*).

However, even if the JobCentre allows you to sign on as unemployed, that does not *always* mean that you qualify as a work-seeker. This is because under EC law you must have a genuine chance of finding work, even though under British law you can be unemployed where there is no chance of finding work.

If you want to establish yourself in self-employment, there are no clear rules for when you have a right to be present. We believe that the above rules for work-seekers apply.

5. DEPORTATION OR REMOVAL FROM THE UK

It is very rare for the Home Office to remove an EU/EEA national from the UK whether s/he has a right to reside or not. In practice, the Home

Office usually only removes those who are convicted of a serious criminal offence, or who are believed to be a threat to national security. This is because of EC rules about deportation. The Home Office has two methods of removing EU/EEA nationals. These are different from a requirement to leave letter where the so-called requirement is never carried out (see p365). :

- by making a deportation order;[126] *or*
- by making a 'decision to remove'.[127]

During this process, you may be given temporary admission which affects your entitlement to benefits (see below).

Your benefit entitlement may depend upon the method used by the Home Office:

- if a deportation order is made, you become a person from abroad[128] and are not entitled to IS, income-based JSA, HB or CTB.[129] This only applies once the deportation order is signed. However, if your removal from the UK is deferred in writing by the Home Office, you stop being a person from abroad for HB/CTB purposes.[130] If this applies, you are also exempt from the HB/CTB habitual residence test.[131] You do not become a person from abroad just because of a 'decision to deport' (see p206).
- if a decision to remove is made, it is not clear whether you become a person from abroad. This is because a decision to remove would seem to be neither a deportation order[132] nor a requirement to leave,[133] in which case it does not make you a person from abroad so your entitlement to IS, income-based JSA, HB and CTB would not be affected.

You can still use the FC/DWA rules for EU/EEA nationals (see pp353-54) because there are no special rules for a person subject to deportation.

As part of this process an immigration officer may:

- give you temporary admission (see p24 – if you are detained, see p370); *and/or*
- decide that you are an illegal entrant (see p73).

If this happens, then until the Home Office reverses the decision or gives you a residence permit, you cannot use the rules for EU/EEA nationals for IS, income-based JSA, HB and CTB.[134] The rules for other migrants will apply to you, so you may still be entitled to benefit (see Chapter 16). However, if your removal from the UK as an illegal entrant is deferred in writing by the Home Office, you stop being a person from abroad for HB/CTB (see p215).[135] If this applies you are also exempt from the HB/CTB habitual residence test.[136]

If the Home Office later accepts that you are an EU/EEA national and you have lost benefit, you should seek expert advice about compensation.

If you are detained, you do not become a person from abroad, because none of the parts of that definition apply to you. You are not a prisoner under IS/income-based JSA rules unless you are also detained having been charged with an offence.[137] However, you may lose entitlement to some benefits, particularly income-based JSA, because of the normal conditions of entitlement (see CPAG's *National Welfare Benefits Handbook*).

All these rules also apply to family members of EU/EEA nationals who have been recognised as such by the Home Office. If the Home Office applies the ordinary immigration rules to you and not the immigration rules for EU/EEA family members, you may still be able to argue that this does not affect your benefit entitlement (see p352).

Disputed nationality

If you have a valid passport or identity card issued by an EU/EEA member state, then the Home Office and the Benefits Agency must accept that you are an EU/EEA national. If you do not have a valid passport or identity card, the Home Office may refuse to accept that you are an EU/EEA national. In this very unlikely event the following steps can be taken:

- if it happens at a port, an immigration officer may detain you (see p70) or give you temporary admission to the UK (see p24); *or*
- if you are already in the UK, an immigration officer may decide that you are an illegal entrant (see p73) and either detain you (see p70) or give you temporary admission to the UK (see p24).

These actions have the same effect on entitlement to IS, income-based JSA, HB and CTB as they do in the cases of deportation or removal (see above). For FC/DWA the Benefits Agency must make its own decision about your nationality and if it decides you are an EU/EEA national, the special rules for EU/EEA nationals apply (see p353). These rules are not overridden by an immigration officer's decision.

All these rules also apply to any family members of a person whose EU/EEA nationality is disputed.

PART FIVE

International agreements

CHAPTER TWENTY EIGHT

International agreements

This chapter covers:

1. UK reciprocal agreements (below)
2. Multilateral agreements (p378)

1. UK RECIPROCAL AGREEMENTS

The UK has reciprocal agreements covering social security with both EU/EEA member states and with countries outside the EU/EEA (see Appendix 7). The provisions of reciprocal agreements apply directly and are part of UK law.[1] You may claim either in the UK or in the country with which the UK has made the agreement. If you are an EU/EEA national, see Part 4.

Benefits not covered by reciprocal agreements

The following benefits are not covered by any of the agreements:

- disability working allowance (DWA);
- severe disability allowance (SDA);
- family credit (FC);
- social fund payments;
- income-based jobseeker's allowance (JSA); *and*
- income support (IS).

The provisions concerning contribution-based JSA only apply insofar as they relate to the contribution conditions.

Applicable legislation

All UK reciprocal agreements with member states which have insurance-based schemes contain provisions to ensure that you do not find yourself in either of the following situations:

- that you are not insured in either country's scheme; *or*

- that you are insured in both countries' schemes.

Specific provision is made if you have been sent by your employer as a 'detached worker' (see p37) to work in the other country. If this applies to you, you will remain insured only in your home country, provided that the secondment is not expected to last for longer than an agreed period – one year in older conventions and up to five years in later ones.

Scope for new agreements between the UK and other countries is limited because of the 'frozen' pension policy. Under new agreements, the UK would normally be expected to pay annual cost of living increases to pensioners and widows living in the other country. This would lead to pressure to 'unfreeze' pensions in Canada, Australia and New Zealand. The UK government regards this as too costly. However, the UK is currently negotiating limited agreements providing for the potential problem of double, or no, contribution liability with a small number of countries.

Benefits covered by reciprocal agreements

The agreements differ in which benefits are covered and the provisions made. Some provide for aggregation of periods of presence or residence, or contributions that you have paid in one country to count towards fulfilling the conditions in the other country. Others provide for the benefits of one country to be paid to you in the other.

Unemployment benefits

None of the agreements allow you to receive unemployment benefits (contribution-based JSA in the UK) outside the country where you paid your insurance contributions. However, a number provide for insurance that you have paid in one country to count toward satisfying the conditions of entitlement in the other. This is the case with the UK agreements with Austria, Cyprus, Malta, Iceland, Finland, New Zealand and Norway.

Sickness benefits

Other short-term benefits are also covered by some of the agreements. If you are entitled to sickness and/or maternity benefits, some of the agreements allow you to receive your benefit in the other country. This is subject to certain other conditions being satisfied. In other cases, contributions that you have paid under one country's scheme may be taken into account to help you satisfy the conditions of entitlement in the other.

In the UK, the relevant sickness benefit is short-term incapacity benefit, and the relevant maternity benefit is maternity allowance (MA).

You may be entitled to MA, or continue to be paid MA, if absent from the UK, under the reciprocal agreements with the following non-EU/EEA countries: Barbados, Cyprus, the Isle of Man, Jersey and Guernsey, Switzerland, Turkey and the former Republic of Yugoslavia.

The circumstances under which you may be able to claim or retain MA differ from agreement to agreement.

Invalidity benefits

A number of the agreements allow you to receive invalidity benefits in the other country. The relevant benefit in the UK is long-term incapacity benefit (ICB). In some of these agreements, the provisions relating to persons abroad (see Part 2) are not modified, and payment abroad is still restricted – eg, in Australia and New Zealand.[2] The agreements with Norway, Sweden, Austria, Iceland and Cyprus allow you to continue to receive your long-term ICB in the other country – subject to medical controls being undertaken in the agreement country. Correspondingly, you are able to receive the other country's invalidity benefit in the UK.[3] The agreement with Barbados allows a certificate of permanent incapacity to be issued, permitting you to receive long-term ICB without medical controls.

Benefits for industrial injuries

Most of the agreements include benefits for industrial injuries. The arrangements determine which country's legislation will apply to new accidents or diseases depending on where you are insured at the time. Most agreements include arrangements to allow you to receive all three of the British benefits for industrial injury indefinitely in the other country.

Retirement pensions and widows' benefits

All the agreements include retirement pensions and widows' benefits. In the UK, the relevant benefits are retirement pensions, widows' pensions and widowed mothers' pensions. In most cases, you can receive a retirement pension or widows' benefit in the agreement country at the same rate you would be paid in the country where you are insured. This is the case under all of the agreements except those with Australia, Canada and New Zealand, which do not permit the uprating of these benefits. If you go to live in one of these countries, your retirement pension (and any other long-term benefit) will be 'frozen' at the rate payable either when you left the UK, or when you became entitled to your pension abroad.

If you do not qualify for a retirement pension or widows' benefit from either country, or you qualify for a pension or widows' benefit from one country but not the other, the agreements with the following countries allow you to be paid basic old-age and widows' benefits on a pro rata basis, with your insurance under both schemes taken into account:

Austria, Barbados, Bermuda, Cyprus, Finland, Iceland, Israel, Jamaica, Malta, Mauritius, Norway, the Philippines, Mauritius, Sweden, Switzerland, Turkey, the USA and the former Republic of Yugoslavia.

Family benefits

In the UK, the relevant family benefits are child benefit and guardian's allowance. The provisions concerning these two benefits enable periods of residence and/or presence that you may have spent in the other country to be treated as residence and/or presence spent in GB. The extent to which reciprocity exists varies, however, according to the particular agreement. For example, residence or contributions paid in the following countries count towards your satisfying UK residence conditions for guardian's allowance: Cyprus, Israel, Jamaica, Jersey/Guernsey, Mauritius and Turkey.

Reciprocal agreements with EU/EEA member states

The UK has reciprocal agreements with all EU/EEA member states except Greece. EC provisions replace agreements between EU/EEA member states.[4]

You cannot qualify for benefits using reciprocal agreements if you:

- fall within the 'personal scope' of the co-ordination rule (see Chapter 24);[5] *and*
- acquired your right to benefit on, or after, EC provisions applied.[6]

If you are not covered by the the co-ordination rule, you may be able to get benefits using the reciprocal agreements. Table 1 in Appendix 7 shows the countries with which GB has social security agreements, and the benefits covered by each. Agreements between EU/EEA member states continue to apply if you do not fall within the personal scope of the co-ordination rule[7] but you do fall within the scope of the reciprocal agreement.

Agreements between EU/EEA member states can also continue to apply if:

- the provisions of an agreement are more beneficial to you than the EC provisions; *and*
- your right to use the reciprocal agreement was acquired before:
  - EC provisions applied to the UK on 1 April 1973; *or*
  - the other member state joined the EU/EEA.[8]

This is likely to help nationals of member states that joined the EU/EEA only recently.

Example

Ms Collier, a teacher from the UK, was teaching in France under the cultural convention when she was injured in the course of her work. She was able to claim:

- long-term incapacity benefit; *or*
- UK industrial injuries benefits .[9]

The UK's agreement with Denmark continues to apply in both the Faroes and Greenland as they are not part of the EU/EEA. Greenland left the EC on 1 February 1985.

People covered by the agreements

Some of the agreements cover nationals of the contracting parties, while others apply to 'people going from one member state to another'. This may be particularly significant if you are a non-EU/EEA national who has worked in two or more EU/EEA member states but cannot benefit under the co-ordination rule (see p316).[10] Of the member states which now form the EU/EEA, the agreements with Belgium, Denmark, France, Italy, Luxembourg are confined to nationals only.[11] The convention with the Netherlands has recently been re-negotiated and now extends to all people moving from one member state to the other who fall within its scope.

The reciprocal agreements define who is counted as a national for the purpose of the reciprocal agreement where nationality is an issue. In all of these, a UK national is defined as a 'Citizen of the United Kingdom and Colonies'.[12]

The category of people termed 'Citizens of the United Kingdom and Colonies' disappeared on 1 January 1983 when the new British Nationality Act 1981 came into force. From that date on, a person who had previously held Citizenship of the United Kingdom and Colonies became:

- a British citizen; *or*
- a British dependent territories citizen; *or*
- a British overseas citizen; *or*
- a British subject.

For the purposes of the UK social security 'nationals only' conventions with Belgium, Denmark, France, Italy and Luxembourg a national in relation to the UK now includes anyone in one of the above four categories.

For a detailed explanation of British citizenship, see Chapter 2.

The definition of nationality contained in the agreements[13] with Denmark, Italy, Luxembourg is simply that of a 'Danish' or 'Italian' or 'Luxembourger' national. These agreements confer no rights if you are not a national of one of these member states. The agreement with Belgium, however, covers a 'person having Belgian nationality or a native of the Belgian Congo or Ruanda-Urundi'. The agreement with France refers to 'a person having French nationality' and 'any French-protected person belonging to French Togoland or the French Cameroons'.

When these agreements came into force in 1958, the Belgian Congo and Ruanda-Urundi and French Togoland and the French Cameroons were Belgian and French territories respectively. The question concerning who is presently covered by these agreements, insofar as Belgian and French nationals are concerned, is a matter for the Belgian and French authorities. If you come from one of these countries you should enquire of the Belgian or French authorities whether you are covered by these agreements.

The agreements[14] confer equal treatment on the nationals of the contracting countries, stating that a 'national of one Contracting Party shall be entitled to receive the benefits of the legislation of the other Contracting Party under the same conditions as if he were a national of the latter Contracting Party'.

The agreements with Finland, Iceland, Ireland, Portugal, Spain and Sweden are not confined to nationals but confer rights on:

- 'people who go from one country to another' (Ireland);
- 'a person subject to the legislation of one Contracting Party who becomes resident in the territory of the other Party' (Portugal);
- 'a national of one Contracting Party, or a person subject to the legislation of that Party, who becomes resident in the territory of the other Contracting Party' (Spain); *and*
- 'a national of the state and person deriving their rights from such nationals and other people who are, or have been, covered by the legislation of either of the states and people deriving their rights from such a person' (Sweden).

The agreements with Austria and Norway have nationality restrictions which apply to the protocol on benefits in kind (eg, medical treatment) but not to social security contributions and benefits. A national of the UK is defined as anyone who is recognised by the UK government as a UK national, provided that s/he is 'ordinarily resident' in the UK. A person can be treated as ordinarily resident from the first day of her/his stay in the UK.

The agreement with Germany is not restricted to nationals of either agreement member state insofar as social security benefits are concerned.

However a nationality provision applies to the articles relating to contribution liability.

Even if you are not a national of one of the contracting parties to these agreements you may still be able to benefit from their provisions.

Of the agreements with countries which are not EU/EEA member states, those with Bermuda, Cyprus, Jamaica, Mauritius, New Zealand and the USA make provision for a person 'subject to the legislation of one member state', who becomes resident or takes up employment in the other.

The agreements with Israel, Switzerland, Turkey and the former Yugoslavia refer to nationals, in each case the respective member state's nationals and Citizens of the United Kingdom and Colonies.

2. MULTILATERAL AGREEMENTS

The UK is a signatory to a number of multilateral social security agreements.

The European Convention on Social and Medical Assistance (ECSEMA)

This convention has been in force since 1954. It requires that ratifying states provide assistance in cash and kind to nationals of other ratifying states who are lawfully present in their territory and without sufficient resources, on the same conditions as their own nationals. It also prevents ratifying states repatriating lawfully present nationals of other ratifying states simply because the person is in need of assistance.

The countries that have signed this agreement are all now, with the exception of Turkey, within the EU/EEA. Therefore if you are Turkish you may only benefit from this agreement if you are Turkish and legally present in this country. If this is the case then your immigration status does not make you a person from abroad for IS, income-based JSA, Council Tax or HB. (For a fuller description of the person from abroad regulations, see p121.)

The 1961 Council of Europe Social Chapter

Again all the signatories to this agreement are now members of the EU/EEA and covered by the EC social security arrangements (see Chapters 26 and 27) with the exception of Turkey and the Republic of Cyprus. It should be noted that North Cyprus is now the Turkish Republic of North Cyprus which is only recognised as a country by

Turkey. The Republic of Cyprus recognises people as its nationals who were born in North Cyprus before the Turkish invasion of 1974. The nationality of people born after 1974 in North Cyprus is unclear though some may have another nationality – eg, Turkish.

The effect of this Agreement is that if you are Turkish or a Greek Cypriot the persons from abroad regulations do not apply to you. (For a description of the persons from abroad regulations, see p120.)

The co-operation and association agreements between the EC and third countries

There are an increasing number of these agreements in force, or under negotiation, with third countries, including: Maghreb (Algeria, Morocco and Tunisia), the Maghrag (Egypt, Israel, Jordan and Lebanon), Central and Eastern European, Baltic and former Soviet Union states. At present, the only agreements which directly affect benefits in the UK are the four co-operation agreements with Algeria, Morocco, Tunisia and Slovenia.

The co-operation agreements

The practical effect of these agreements is that if you are an Algerian, Moroccan, Tunisian or Slovenian national or a member of their family and are lawfully working in the UK you are treated as satisfying the new immigration/residence test for AA, CB, DLA, DWA, FC, ICA and SDA introduced in February 1996.[15]

The agreements do not cover IS. However, with the extension of the definition of public funds to cover non-contributory benefits, the UK government has, in order to comply with its obligations under these four agreements, exempted people from these four countries who are workers or members of their families from the requirement of meeting the public funds criteria in respect of DWA, income-based JSA and FC.[16]

The association agreements

The association agreements generally have the potential to assist migrant workers, legally employed in the UK and members of their families who are legally resident, to qualify for UK benefits.

Although the European Court of Justice (ECJ)[17] has said that the provisions of association agreements can be directly applicable if they are sufficiently clear and precise and do not require further implementing procedures, a recent judgment[18] has confirmed that specific benefit provisions are not directly applicable without the adoption of detailed implementing decisions and regulations by the member states. No such measure has yet been taken under any association agreement.

The protocol of the Turkish association agreement has been the subject of a number of cases before the ECJ. The question of the direct effect of the social security provisions contained in Decision 3/80 of the Association Council continues to be a matter of controversy[19] and a further case is due to go before the Court in 1997 which may decide that the provisions concerning social security[20] can be relied on by Turkish workers and members of their families in the UK.

The Lome Convention

The EC has now concluded the Lome IV Convention with 69 states in Africa, the Caribbean and Pacific (ACP). The convention includes provisions about workers. It provides that the contracting states shall 'ensure through the legal or administrative measures which they have or will have adopted, that migrant workers, students and other foreign nationals legally within their territory are not subjected to discrimination on the basis of racial, religious, cultural or social difference, notably in respect of housing, education, health care, other social services and employment'.[21]

The Convention states[22] that 'workers who are nationals of an ACP state legally employed in the territory of a member state, and members of their families living with them, shall, as regards social security benefits linked to employment in that member state, enjoy treatment free from any discrimination based on nationality in relation to nationals of that member state.'

The real scope of this convention has not yet been interpreted by the European Court of Justice.[23] At present it is very unlikely that, if you are national of one of the African, Caribbean and Pacific signatory countries, you can benefit from the provisions of this treaty.

Getting further advice on immigration and social security

The procedure in immigration appeals is outlined in Part 1 of this *Handbook* but appellants should seek advice from their local law centre or one of the agencies listed below. If there is no local law centre and you cannot contact any of the agencies listed below you should contact your local Citizens Advice Bureau.

Independent advice and representation on immigration issues

Local law centres can often help with applications and appeals. In addition contact one of the following:

Joint Council for the Welfare of Immigrants
115 Old Street
London ECV 9JR
tel: 0171 251 8706

Immigration Advisory Service
County House, 190 Dover Street
London SE1 4YB
tel: 0171 357 6917
(there are other offices in the regions and at the ports)

Afro Asian Advisory Service
53 Addington Square
London SE5 7LB
tel: 0171 701 0141

AIRE Centre (Advice on Individual Rights in Europe)
74 Eurolink Business Centre
49 Effra Road
London SW2 1BZ
tel: 0171 924 0927

African Churches Council for Immigration and Social Justice (ACCIS)
Unit 6-7, 321 Essex Road
London N1 3PS
tel: 0171 704 2331

Refugee Arrivals Project
Room 2005, 2nd floor, Queens Building
Heathrow Airport TW6 1DL
tel: 0181 759 5740

Refugee Council
Bondway House, 3-9 Bondway
London SW8 1SJ
tel: 0171 582 6922/1162

Refugee Legal Centre
Sussex House, 39-45 Bermondsey Street
London SE1 3XF
tel: 0171 378 6242

(For a fuller list of agencies concerned with immigration issues including policy, race relations and civil liberties see JCWI's *Immigration, Nationality and Refugee Law Handbook*.)

Independent advice and representation on social security

It is often difficult for unsupported individuals to get a positive response from the Benefits Agency. You may be taken more seriously if it is clear you have taken advice about your entitlement or have an adviser assisting you.

If you want advice or help with a benefit problem the following agencies may be able to assist.

- Citizens Advice Bureaux (CABx) and other local advice centres provide information and advice about benefits and may be able to represent you.

- Law Centres can often help in a similar way to CABx/advice centres.
- Local authority welfare rights workers provide a service in many areas and some arrange advice sessions and take-up campaigns locally.
- Local organisations for particular groups of claimants may offer help. For instance, there are Unemployed Centres, pensioners groups, centres for disabled people etc.
- Claimants Unions give advice in some areas. For details of your nearest group contact the Plymouth Claimants Union, PO Box 21, Plymouth PL1 1QS or the Swindon Unemployed Movement, Room 20, Pinehurst People's Centre, Beech Avenue, Pinehurst, Swindon, Wiltshire.
- Some social workers and probation officers (but not all) help with benefit problems, especially if they are already working with you on another problem.
- Solicitors can give free legal advice under the green form scheme (pink form in Scotland). This does not cover the cost of representation at an appeal hearing but can cover the cost of preparing written submissions and obtaining evidence such as medical reports. However, solicitors do not always have a good working knowledge of the benefit rules and you may need to shop around until you find one who does.

If you cannot find any of these agencies in the telephone book your local library should have details.

Unfortunately, CPAG is unable to deal with enquiries directly from members of the public but if you are an adviser you can phone the advice line, which is usually open from 2 to 4pm on Monday to Thursday – 0171 253 6569. This is a special phone line; do not ring the main CPAG number. Alternatively, you can write to us at Citizens' Rights Office, CPAG, 4th Floor, 1-5 Bath Street, London EC1V 9PY. We can also take up a limited number of complex cases including appeals to the Social Security Commissioners or courts if referred by an adviser.

Useful addresses

Immigration issues

**Home Office Immigration and
Nationality Directorate**
Lunar House
40 Wellesley Road
Croydon CR9 2BY
Main telephone number: 0181
686 0688
(There are direct lines to groups
dealing with individual cases – for
details see JCWI's *Immigration,
Nationality and Refugee Law
Handbook*)

Asylum Directorate
Quest House
11 Cross Road
Croydon CR9 2BY
(There are different lines according
to the case that is being dealt with)
Appeals Support Section
tel: 0181 760 4722/2334/1701
Application Forms Unit
tel: 0181 760 2233

Asylum Screening Unit
tel: 0181 760 1303/1728

Nationality Directorate
Home Office
3rd floor, India Buildings,
Water Street

Liverpool L2 0QN
tel: 0151 237 5200

Immigration Service Office
Beckett House
66-68 St Thomas' Street
London SE1 3QU
tel: 0171 238 1300

Passport Agency Offices
Clive House
Petty France
London SW1H 9HD
tel: 0171 799 2290

Aliens Registration Office
10 Lamb's Conduit Street
London WC1X 3MX

**Department for Education
and Employment**
Overseas Labour Service
Porter Brook House, W5 Moorfoot
Sheffield S1 4PQ
tel: 0114 259 4074

Foreign and Commonwealth Office
Migration and Visa Division
1 Palace Street,
London SW1H 5HE
tel: 0171 270 3000

(Addresses of some of the main High Commissions and Embassies abroad are listed in the JCWI's *Immigration, Nationality and Refugee Law Handbook*.)

Treasury Solicitor
Queen Anne's Chambers
28 Broadway
London SW1H 9JS
tel: 0171 210 3000

Home Office (Minister's Private Office)
Queen Anne's Gate
London SW1H 9AT
tel: 0171 273 4604

European Commission
London Office
8 Storey's Gate
London SW1P 3AT
tel: 0171 973 1992

Social Security issues

Benefits Agency addresses

Benefits Agency Chief Executive
Mr P Mathison
Quarry House
Quarry Hill
Leeds LS2 7UA
tel: 0113 232 4000

Central Adjudication Services
Quarry House
Quarry Hill
Leeds LS2 7UA
tel: 0113 232 4000

Overseas Benefits Directorate
Tyneview Park
Whitley Road, Benton
Newcastle-upon-Tyne NE98 1YX
tel: 0191 218 7878

Contributions Agency
Longbention
Newcastle-upon-Tyne NE98 1YX

Attendance Allowance Unit
Norcross
Blackpool FY5 3TA

Child Benefit Centre
Washington
Newcastle-upon-Tyne NE88 1BR
tel: 0541 555501

Disability Benefits Unit
Warbreck House
Warbreck Hill Road
Blackpool FY2 0YE
tel: 0345 123456

Invalid Care Allowance Unit
Palatine House
Lancaster Road
Preston PR1 1NS
tel: 01253 856 123

Medical Services (BAMS)
Room 124
Alberty Edward House
3 The Pavilion
Ashton-on-Ribble
Preston PR2 2PA
tel: 01772 898052

Disability Working Allowance Unit
Diadem House
2 The Pavilion
Ashton-on-Ribble
Preston PR2 2GN
tel: 01772 883300

Family Credit Unit
Government Buildings

Cop Lane
Penwortham
Preston PR1 0BR
tel: 01253 500050

Severe Hardship Claims Unit
  (16/17-year-olds)
174 Pitt Street
Glasgow G2 4DZ
tel: 0141 225 4259

Benefits Agency helplines for claimants

The following freephone numbers are available for clients to seek general advice. Specific advice on claims should be sought from the local office dealing with the claim. If English is not your first language, ask the Benefits Agency to arrange for advice to be given in your own language.

Benefits enquiry line
(for disability benefits)
0800 882200

Forms completion service
(for completing disability benefit
forms)
0800 441144

Incapacity Benefit line
0800 868868

Senior line
0800 650065

Appeal bodies

The President
HH Judge K Bassingthwaighte
The President's Office
4th Floor, Whittington House
19-30 Alfred Place
London WC1E 7LW
tel: 0171 814 6500

The President (Northern Ireland)
Mr CG Maclynn
6th Floor, Cleaver House
3 Donegal Square North
Belfast BT1 5GA
tel: 01232 539900

Social Security Appeal Tribunals

National Chairperson
Mr R Huggins
The President's Office
4th Floor, Whittington House
19-30 Alfred Pkace
London WC1E 7LW
tel: 0171 814 6500

Ombudsman addresses

Local Government

England
21 Queen Anne's Gate
London SW1H 9BU
tel: 0171 915 3210

Scotland
23 Walker Street
Edinburgh EH3 7HX
tel: 0131 225 5300

Wales
Derwen House
Court Road
Bridgend CF31 1BN
tel: 01656 661325

Northern Ireland
Progressive House
33 Wellington Place
Belfast BT1 6HN
tel: 01232 233821

The Parliamentary Ombudsman
Office of the Parliamentary
Commissioner
Church House
Great Smith Street
London SW1P 3BW
tel: 0171 276 2130

Useful publications

Immigration reference material

Macdonald's Immigration Law and Practice by Ian Macdonald and Nicholas Blake, 4th edn, Butterworths 1995. Supplement 1997
British Nationality Law by Laurie Fransman, Fourmat Publishing, 1989
Immigration Law and Practice by David Jackson, Sweet & Maxwell, 1997
Immigration, nationality and refugee law handbook: a user's guide, 1997 edn, Joint Council for the Welfare of Immigrants, £12.99
European Directory of Migrant and Ethnic Minority Organisations, JCWI, 1996, £27.50
JCWI Bulletin – this is quarterly and contains changes to the law, explains how law is interpreted and includes a digest of important immigration appeal tribunal decisions.
Legal Action, Legal Action Group, recent developments in immigration law appears three times a year
Tolley's Immigration and Nationality Law and Practice, Tolley Publishing, quarterly journal
Butterworth's Immigration Law Service Vols I-III, looseleaf with regular updates

Social Security reference material

Many of the books listed here will be in your main public library. Stationery Office books are available from Stationery Office bookshops and also from many others. They may be ordered from The Publications Centre, PO Box 276, London SW8 5DT tel: 0171 873 9090; fax: 0171 873 8200. General enquiries tel: 0171 873 0011; fax 0171 873 8247.

1. CPAG Handbooks

National Welfare Benefits Handbook, £8.95 (£3 for claimants)
Rights Guide to Non-Means-Tested Benefits, £8.95 (£3 for claimants)

Jobseeker's Allowance Handbook, £6.95 (£2.50 for claimants)
Child Support Handbook, £9.95 (£3.30 for claimants)
Council Tax Handbook, £9.95
Debt Advice Handbook, £9.95
Fuel Rights Handbook, £8.95
Rights Guide for Home Owners, £8.95
Available from CPAG Ltd, 4th Floor, 1-5 Bath Street, London EC1V 9PY. Prices include p&p.

2. Textbooks

The Law of Social Security by AI Ogus, EM Barendt and N Wikely, 4th edn 1995, Butterworths. This is the standard textbook on social security law.
Compensation for Industrial Injury by R Lewis, Professional Books, 1987
Tolley's National Insurance Contributions, Tolley Publishing Company, 1994-95

3. Case law and legislation

Social Security Case Law – Digest of Commissioners Decisions by D Neligan, Stationery Office (looseleaf in two volumes). Summaries of commissioners' decisions grouped together by subject.
The Law Relating to Social Security, Stationery Office (looseleaf in 11 volumes)
The Law Relating to Child Support, Stationery Office (looseleaf in one volume)
Child Support: the legislation by E Jacobs and G Douglas, 3rd edn, Sweet & Maxwell, £36 including p&p from CPAG if you are a CPAG member.
CPAG's Income Related Benefits: the legislation (Mesher) 1997/98 edn, updated by P Wood, Sweet & Maxwell, £45.95 with Dec supplement, incl p&p from CPAG
CPAG's Housing Benefit and Council Tax Benefit Legislation by L Findlay, R Poynter and M Ward, CPAG Ltd 1997/98 available late 1997, £43.95 (incl Supplement) incl p&p)
Medical and Disability Appeal Tribunals: the legislation by M Rowland, 3rd edn 1997, Sweet & Maxwell, available from late 1997, £36 incl p&p from CPAG if you are a CPAG member
Compendium of Community Provisions on Social Security, 4th edn, Office for Official Publications of the European Communities, 1995 (Available from Stationery Office)
Cases and materials on EC Law, S Weatherill, Blackstones, 1996

4. Official Guidance

Adjudication Officers' Guide, Stationery Office (looseleaf in 13 volumes). Volume 3 deals with international issues.
Child Support Adjudication Guide, Stationery Office (looseleaf in one volume)
Child Support Guides, Child Support Agency, series on specific issues, eg The Child Support Requirement to Co-operate Guide
Field Officers' Guide, Child Support Agency (looseleaf in one volume)
Housing Benefit and Council Tax Benefit Guidance Manual, Stationery Office (looseleaf in one volume)
The Social Fund Guide, Stationery Office (looseleaf in two volumes).

5. Tribunal handbooks

Social Security Appeal Tribunals: A Guide to Procedure, Stationery Office

6. Leaflets

The Benefits Agency publishes many leaflets which cover particular benefits or particular groups of claimants or contributors. They have been greatly improved in recent years and the bigger ones extend to 48-page booklets. They are free from your local Benefits Agency office or on Freephone 0800 666 555. If you want to order larger numbers of leaflets, or receive information about new leaflets, you can join the Benefits Agency Publicity Register by writing to the Benefits Agency, 3rd Floor South, 1 Trevelyan Square, Leeds LS1 6EB or by phoning 0645 540 000 (local rate). Free leaflets on HB/CTB are available from the relevant department of your local council.

7. Periodicals

The *Welfare Rights Bulletin* is published every two months by CPAG. It covers developments in social security law and updates this Handbook between editions. The annual subscription is £21 but it is sent automatically to CPAG Rights and Comprehensive Members.

8. Other Handbooks

Guide to Housing Benefit and Council Tax Benefit, £12.95
Disability Rights Handbook, £9.95.
Unemployment and Training Rights Handbook (Unemployment Unit, £9.95).
These are available from CPAG Ltd, 4th Floor, 1-5 Bath Street, London EC1V 9PY. Prices incl p&p.

Standard forms and letters

The forms and standard letters reproduced on the following pages are those most commonly used by the Home Office. They are:

- Undertaking of support – RON 112 (also attached to Home Office application form SET(F))
- Grant of temporary admission – IS96
- Letter granting indefinite leave to remain – RON 60
- Letter granting exceptional leave to remain – GEN 19
- Standard letter after appeal has been dismissed – RON 67

Other forms and standard letters (not reproduced in this appendix) are:

- Entry clearance application – form IM2A
- Letter granting one year's leave to remain as a spouse – RON 124
- Application form to apply for settlement after a year's leave on marriage grounds has been granted – SET(M)
- Refusal of leave to remain, with right of appeal – APP 101A
- Decision to make a deportation order – APP 104

Undertaking of support (RON 112) also attached to Home Office application form SET(F)

SPONSORSHIP DECLARATION

Completion of this declaration by the applicant's sponsor is not compulsory but an application will normally be refused if the sponsor refuses to do so. This form should only be completed if the sponsor is resident in the UK.

1. I,.. (name), of
(full postal address - see **Note 4** below) ....
.... (house number and street)
.... (post town)
.... (county)
.... (postcode)
hereby declare that my date of birth is ....
and that I am employed as .... (occupation)
at (full work address) ....
.... (company name and street)
.... (post town)
.... (county)
.... (post code).

My National Insurance number is ....

2. I hereby undertake that if .... (name of
sponsored person) who was born in .... on
.... (place and date of birth of sponsored
person) is granted leave to enter or remain in the UK I shall be responsible for his/her maintenance and accommodation in the UK throughout the period of leave and any variation of it.

3. During his/her stay in the UK, the sponsored person will reside at: (full postal address) ....
.... (house number and street)
.... (post town)
.... (county)
.... (postcode)

4. I understand that this undertaking shall be made available to the Department of Social Security in the UK who will take appropriate steps to recover from me the cost of any public funds paid to or in respect of the person who is the subject of this undertaking.
Signed:
Date:

FOR OFFICIAL USE ONLY

Certificate

I certify that this document, apart from this certificate, is an undertaking given in pursuance of the Immigration Rules within the meaning of the Immigration Act 1971.

Signed by .... , being a person authorised to make this certificate on behalf of the Secretary of State.
Signature:

Personalised date stamp:

Note 4: The sponsor/principal wage earner should provide evidence that he/she lives at the address claimed. This should be in the form of a certified copy of the deeds or a letter from the Building Society/Bank which holds the mortgage (if the house is privately owned) or a housing association/council rent book or letter from the council certifying that the sponsor lives at the address (if the house is rented from a housing association or the local authority). If the house is privately rented, correspondence addressed to the sponsor at the address should be provided from at least 3 of the following sources:

(i)   **Local authority: notification of council tax**
(ii) **Utility Company (Gas, water, etc)**
(iii) **Local Health Authority**
(iv) **Department of Social Service**
(v)   **Inland Revenue**
(vi) **Any other government department.**

Grant of temporary admission IS96

HOME OFFICE
ind
IMMIGRATION SERVICE

Port Reference:

Home Office Reference:

IS 96

HM IMMIGRATION OFFICE

Telephone:

IMMIGRATION ACT 1971 – NOTIFICATION OF TEMPORARY ADMISSION TO A PERSON WHO IS LIABLE TO BE DETAINED

To ....

LIABILITY TO DETENTION
 A. You are a person who is liable to be detained*

TEMPORARY ADMISSION/ RESTRICTIONS
 B. I hereby authorise your (further) temporary admission to the United Kingdom subject to the following restrictions**:

- You must reside at:-. ....
....
.... Telephone: ....

- You may not enter employment, paid or unpaid, or engage in any business or profession.

- You must report to:

Tick ☑ as appropriate

an Immigration Officer ⎫ at ....
the Police   ⎬ ....
on .... 19......., at .... hrs.
each .... day at .... hrs. until further notice.
on a date and at a time to be notified to you in writing
....

ANY CHANGE OF RESTRICTION
  If these restrictions are to be changed, an Immigration Officer will write to you.

- **Although you have been temporarily admitted, you remain liable to be detained**
- **You have NOT been given leave to enter the United Kingdom within the meaning of the Immigration Act 1971**

Date

Immigration Officer

* Paragraph 16 of Schedule 2 to the Act
** Paragraph 21 of Schedule 2 to the Act

(IS 96 Temporary Admission)

Letter granting indefinite leave to remain RON 60

Immigration and Nationality Directorate

HOME OFFICE

ind

Lunar House 40 Wellesley Road
Croydon CR9 2BY
Tel 0181-760-
Fax 0181-760-

Your Reference

Our Reference

Date

Dear   RON 60

I am writing to say that there are no longer any restrictions on the period for which you may remain in the UK. Your passport, which is enclosed, has been endorsed with vignette number
....

You can now remain indefinitely in the UK. You do not need permission from a Government Department to take or to change employment and you may engage in business or a profession as long as you comply with any general regulations for the business or professional activity.

If you are thinking of going to live or work in the Isle of Man or one of the Channel Islands, you should first consult the Immigration authorities of the Island concerned.

If you leave the UK, you will normally be readmitted for settlement as a returning resident provided that you did not receive assistance from public funds towards the cost of leaving this country; that you had indefinite leave to enter or remain here when you last left; that you have not been away for longer than 2 years; and that you are returning for the purpose of settlement. In order to be considered as settled here, you will have to be able to show that you are habitually and normally resident in this country, and that any absences have been of a temporary or occasional nature. You will not be readmitted as a returning resident if you are resident overseas and only return here for short periods.

If your absence from the UK is for longer than 2 years, but you can still demonstrate that you had indefinite leave to enter or remain here when you last left, and you are returning for the purpose of settlement, you may still qualify for admission as a returning resident if, for example, you have maintained strong connections with this country.

You do not require a visa to return to the UK provided you are returning for settlement after an absence of 2 years or less. However, if you are returning for settlement to the UK after an absence of over 2 years you are advised to apply for an entry clearance at the nearest British Diplomatic Post in the country in which you are living as this will facilitate your re-admission to the UK.

If you obtain a new passport, you may ask us to stamp it to show your immigration status before you travel. You should send or bring it to this Directorate at the address at the top of this letter, or take it to one of our local Public Enquiry Offices. You should also bring or send the enclosed passport and this letter. If you send your passport by post, you should do so at least 2 months before you intend to travel.

If you do not have your passport stamped before you travel, when you return to the UK you will have to satisfy the immigration officer that you had indefinite leave to remain when you left. To do this, you will need to produce either the enclosed passport or other documentary evidence such as bank statements, notices of income tax coding, school or employment records etc relating to the earlier years of your residence in the UK. It may also be helpful to carry this letter with you.

A child born to you in the UK since 1 January 1983 who is not a British citizen may now be entitled to be registered as such a citizen and any child born to you while you remain settled here may be a British citizen automatically at birth. However, you should note that where the parents of a child have never been married to each other British Citizenship can only be derived from the mother. More information about all aspects of British Citizenship including by birth in the UK, and an application form for registration, are available from the Nationality Directorate of the Home Office, 3rd floor, India Buildings, Water Street, Liverpool L2 0QN, telephone 0151 237 5200.

Yours sincerely

Letter granting exceptional leave to remain GEN 19

Immigration and Nationality Directorate

Lunar House 40 Wellesley Road
Croydon CR9 2BY
Tel 0181-760-
Fax 0181-760-

Your Reference

Our Reference

Date

Dear

Your application for refugee status in the United Kingdom has been carefully considered but I have to tell you that it has been refused. It has been decided, however, that although you do not qualify for refugee status it would be right because of the particular circumstances of your case to give you exceptional leave to remain in the United Kingdom until
. . . .

You should, however, fully understand that if during your stay in the United Kingdom you take part in activities involving, for example, the support or encouragement of violence, or conspiracy to cause violence, whether in the United Kingdom or abroad, the Secretary of State may curtail your stay or deport you.

POLICE REGISTRATION

* You must now register with the police: please take this letter to your local police station as soon as possible.

* I enclose your police registration certificate which has been suitably endorsed.

* Please send (or take) your police registration certificate, your passport and this letter to your local police registration officer so that the certificate can be endorsed.

If you change your address or any other details of your registration you should tell your local police registration officer (either in person or by letter) within 7 days. Ask at your local police station if you do not know how to contact your police registration officer.

EMPLOYMENT

You do not need the permission of the Department of Employment or the Home Office before taking a job. The Employment Service can help you find a job or train for work - any job centre or unemployment benefit office will be able to help you and you can apply for a place on a government-sponsored training scheme if you meet the normal conditions for these schemes. You are free to set up in business or any

Letter granting exceptional leave to remain GEN19, page 2

professional activity within the general regulations that apply to that business or profession.

If you want to live or work in the Isle of Man or one of the Channel Islands you must ask the Island's immigration authorities.

HEALTH AND SOCIAL SERVICES

You are free to use the National Health Service and the social services and other help provided by local authorities as you need them. You will be able to get social security benefit (including income support) if you meet the ordinary conditions. If you need any of these services, take this letter with you and show it if there is any question about your entitlement to the service. Your local Social Security Office will give you advice on social security benefits, the British Refugees Council (Bondway House, 3-9 Bondway, London SW8 1SJ; telephone 071-582 6922) can advise you on other welfare services, and your local Citizens Advice Bureau will help you with general questions.

FAMILY REUNION

This grant of exceptional leave to remain does not entitle your spouse or children under 18 to join you. An application for them to do so cannot normally be considered until 4 years from the date of this letter. This is subject to your having received further grants of exceptional leave. The normal requirements of the Immigration Rules regarding support and accommodation of relatives would have to be satisfied. An application for family reunion may be granted at an earlier point if there are compelling compassionate circumstances.

TRAVEL ABROAD

You should be aware that, if you travel abroad, the leave you are now being granted will lapse. Any application to return will be considered as an application for fresh leave.

You should keep your present passport valid. If, however, your national authorities will not renew or replace your passport, or you can show it would be unreasonable to expect you to approach your Embassy or Consulate here, you can apply for a Home Office travel document from the Travel Document Section (telephone 081-760 2345) at the Home Office, Lunar House, Croydon, CR9 2BY.

FURTHER LEAVE TO REMAIN

Your passport is enclosed, endorsed with leave to remain until .... Any application you make for further leave to remain will be carefully considered.

Yours sincerely

* Delete as appropriate
ENC(S)

Standard letter after appeal has been dismissed RON 67

Immigration and Nationality Directorate

Lunar House 40 Wellesley Road
Croydon CR9 2BY
Tel 0181-760-
Fax 0181-760-

Your Reference

Our Reference

Date

Dear

Your appeal against the Secretary of State's decision of ....
was withdrawn/dismissed by the adjudicator on ....

* and we have no evidence that you have an appeal against the dismissal
pending before the Immigration Appeal Tribunal.

* and your application to the Immigration Appeal Tribunal has been
refused.

* and the Immigration Appeal Tribunal has dismissed your appeal.

You therefore have no basis of stay in this country and must now leave
the United Kingdom immediately.

If you fail to embark, you will be liable to prosecution for an offence
under the Immigration Act 1971 (as amended by the Immigration Act
1988). You will also be liable to deportation under administrative
powers contained in section 3(5)(a) of the 1971 Act. If you fail to
embark, the Secretary of State will consider whether on the basis of
facts known to him it would be right to make a deportation order
against you.

Yours sincerely

* Delete as appropriate

People admitted for temporary purposes

People admitted for temporary purposes

A = Applicant

Category	Rule (HC395)	Employment conditions	Additional employment requirements	Requirement that applicants and dependants are adequately maintained and accommodated without recourse to public funds	Entry clearance required for non-visa nationals
Visitor	40-46	Employment prohibited	Must not intend to take employment in the UK or produce goods/provide services within the UK	Yes, out of resources available to A without taking employment or will be maintained and accommodated by relatives	No
Visitors in transit	47-50	Employment prohibited	None	None	No
Visitors seeking medical treatment	51-56	Employment prohibited	Must not intend to take employment in the UK or produce goods/provide services within the UK	Yes, out of resources available to A without taking employment or will be maintained and accommodated by relatives	
Student	57-62	Freedom to take employment restricted	Must not intend to engage in any business or take employment except part time or vacation work without the consent of the Secretary of State for Employment	Yes, and without taking employment or engaging in business	No
Student nurse	63-69	Freedom to take employment restricted	Must not intend to take employment or engage in business other than in connection with the training course	Yes, must have 'sufficient funds available' to satisfy the requirements without engaging in business or taking employment (except in connection with the training course). A Department of Health bursary may be taken into account in determining whether the requirements are met.	No

For explanation in text, see pp 37-38

Post graduate doctors and dentists	70-75	None	Must *either* intend to undertake pre-Registration House Officer employment for up to 12 months as required for full registration with the General Medical Council; *or*, if a doctor or dentist eligible for full or limited registration with the General Medical Council or with the General Dental Council must intend to undertake post graduate training in a hospital	Yes, A must be able to so maintain and accommodate	No
Spouses of students/ prospective students	76-78	Employment prohibited except where the period of leave being granted is 12 months or more	Must not intend to take work other than that permitted according to the conditions of leave	Yes, the parties must be 'able' to so maintain and accommodate	No
Children of students/ prospective students	79-81	Employment prohibited except where the period of leave being granted is 12 months or more	None	Yes, the child must show that s/he 'can and will' be so maintained and accommodated	No
Prospective students	82-87	Employment prohibited	None	Yes, must be able to meet the costs of these requirements without working	No

Au pairs	88-94	Prohibited from working except as an au pair	Must intend to take up an au pair placement	Yes, A must be able to so maintain and accommodate her/himself	No (although rules advise entry clearance is obtained)
Working holidaymakers	95-100	Freedom to take employment is restricted	Must intend to take employment incidental to a holiday but not to engage in business, provide services as a professional sportsman or entertainer or pursue a career in UK	Yes, A must be 'able' and must 'intend' to so maintain and accommodate her/himself	Yes
Children of working holidaymakers	101-103	None	None	Yes and without parent(s) engaging in business or taking employment except as permitted as incidental to the holiday. Must show that child can and will be so maintained and accommodated	Yes
Seasonal workers at agricultural camps	104-109	Condition imposed restricting freedom to take employment to a period of no more than 3 months or until 30th November of the year in question (whichever is the shorter period)	Must not intend to take employment other than as a seasonal worker at an agricultural camp	Yes, A must be able to so maintain and accommodate	Yes, in form of a valid Home Office work card issued by the operator of a scheme approved by the Secretary of State

Teachers and language assistants under approved exchange schemes	110-115	None	Must not intend to take employment other than in an established educational establishment in the UK under an exchange scheme approved by the Department for Education and Employment or administered by the Central Bureau for educational visits and exchanges or the League for the Exchange of Commonwealth Teachers	Yes, A must be able to so maintain and accommodate	Yes
Department for Education and Employment approved training or work experience	116-121	Freedom to take or change employment restricted	Must intend to only take employment as specified in the work permit, ie, training or work experience under the scheme administered by the Department for Education and Employment (TWES)	Yes, A must be able to so maintain and accommodate	No, but must have a work permit issued under TWES or if applying for leave to remain was admitted or allowed to remain as a student
Spouses and children of those with limited leave as teachers/ language assistants	122-127	None	None	Yes, the parties must be able to so maintain and accommodate in accommodation which they own or occupy exclusively. The child must show that s/he can and will be so maintained and accommodated which her/his parents own or occupy exclusively	Yes
Person exercising rights of access to a child resident in the UK	246-248	Employment prohibited	Must not intend to take employment in the UK or to produce goods/ provide services within the UK	Yes, A must show that s/he will be so maintained and accommodated out of resources available to him or will be so maintained by relatives or friends	Yes

Alternative sources of help

Many migrants are excluded from means-tested benefits (see Part 2). Most people affected are asylum-seekers, but British citizens are also excluded if they fail the habitual residence test. Also, many people who are subject to immigration control are now excluded from local authority housing, even when homeless.

A person in need of 'care and attention' with no other means of obtaining it may apply to the social services department of their local authority for accommodation and other assistance.[1] This provision remained in place when the government removed rights to local authority housing and benefits in 1996. As a result, many migrants (especially asylum-seekers) apply for assistance under this Act.

The Court of Appeal has decided[2] that the Act is broad enough to cover people whose need for care and attention arises only from exclusion from means-tested benefits. This does not mean that every asylum-seeker is entitled to assistance. Local authorities must assess each application to see if the individual needs assistance and how it is to be provided.

Providing assistance

The High Court has ruled that the local authority may only provide assistance if it is providing accommodation.[3] The local authority does not have to wait, however, until the applicant is roofless before helping. The High Court has also ruled that destitute asylum-seekers need at least 'shelter, warmth and food'[4] so we consider that a person lacking one or more of these should normally qualify for assistance.

Although the most important form of assistance is accommodation, a person who is accommodated under the Act must also be given 'board and other services, amenities and requisites provided in connection with the accommodation'.[5]

Local authority practice varies: accommodation has been provided from authority housing stock or bed and breakfast or, in some cases, payment to the applicant's landlord. Food has been provided by way of food parcels, vouchers, or hot meals at a particular site within the borough such as at a hospital canteen. Vouchers have been provided for toiletries and some have provided vouchers to obtain winter clothing. In one case,[6] a local authority was to be challenged where it had provided bed and breakfast only and directed the individual to the nearest soup kitchen but the authority agreed at the last minute to provide meals.

In all cases, the local authority must deliver the services directly. The authority cannot pay cash to applicants for them to make their own arrangements.[7]

Children Act 1989

Local authorities must promote the welfare of 'children in need' in their area.[8] The local authority may also accommodate a child in need with her/his family.[9] Many local authorities have used the Act to meet the family's housing costs and pay cash to the parent(s) or carer(s). This is often paid at the urgent cases rate of income support.

Disabled and mentally ill people

Local authorities must assess the needs and provide appropriate services to migrants who appear to be disabled[10] and to those who have been suffering from mental illness and who are discharged from hospital.[11]

Reciprocal arrangements

TABLE 1: BENEFITS COVERED IN CONVENTIONS WITH EU/EEA MEMBER STATES

	Jobseeker's allowance	Short-term incapacity benefit	Long-term incapacity benefit	Maternity benefit	Disablement benefit	Retirement pension	Widow's benefit	Guardian's allowance	Child benefit	Attendance allowance
Austria	x	x	x	x	x	x	x	x	x	
Belgium	x	x	x	x	x	x	x	x	x	
Denmark	x	x	x	x	x	x	x	x	x	
Finland	x	x	x	x	x	x	x		x	
France		x	x	x	x	x	x			
Germany	x	x	x	x	x	x	x	x	x	
Iceland	x	x	x		x	x	x	x		
Ireland	x	x	x	x	x	x	x	x		
Italy	x	x	x	x	x	x	x	x		
Luxembourg		x	x	x	x	x	x	x		
Netherlands	x	x	x	x	x	x	x	x		
Norway	x	x	x	x	x	x	x	x	x	x
Portugal	x	x	x	x	x	x	x	x	x	
Spain	x	x	x	x	x	x		x	x	
Sweden	x	x	x	x	x	x	x	x	x	

Note: There is no agreement with Liechtenstein; an agreement with Greece is currently being negotiated.

TABLE 2: BENEFITS COVERED IN CONVENTIONS WITH NON-EU/EEA MEMBER STATES										
	Jobseeker's allowance	Short-term incapacity benefit	Long-term incapacity benefit	Disablement benefit	Industrial injuries benefit	Retirement pension	Widow's benefit	Guardian's allowance	Child benefit	Attendance and disability living allowances
Australia	x	x	x			x	x	x	x	
Barbados		x	x	x	x	x	x	x	x	
Bermuda					x	x	x			
Canada	x					x			x	
Cyprus	x	x	x	x	x	x	x	x		
Israel		x		x	x	x	x	x	x	
Jamaica[1]			x		x	x	x	x		
Jersey & Guernsey		x	x	x	x	x	x	x	x	x
Malta	x	x	x		x	x	x	x		
Mauritius					x	x	x	x	x	
New Zealand	x	x				x	x	x	x	
Philippines					x	x	x			
Switzerland		x	x		x	x	x	x	x	
Turkey		x	x	x	x	x	x	x		
USA[2]		x	x			x	x	x		
(Former) Yugoslavia[3]	x	x	x	x	x	x	x		x	

See notes on page 452.

Abbreviations used in the notes

AC	Appeal Cases
All ER	All England Reports
Art(s)	Article(s)
CA	Court of Appeal
CMLR	Common Market Law Reports
Crim App R	Criminal Appeal Reports
DC	Divisional Court
ECHR	European Court of Human Rights
ECJ	European Court of Justice
ECR	European Court Reports
EEA	European Economic Area
EHRR	European Human Rights Reports
FLR	Family Law Reports
HBRB	Housing Benefit Review Board
HC	House of Commons
HL	House of Lords
HLR	Housing Law Reports
HO	Home Office
IAT	Immigration Appeal Tribunal
ICR	Industrial Cases Reports
Imm AR	Immigration Appeal Reports
IRLR	Industrial Relations Law Reports
LGR	Local Government Reports
New LJ	*New Law Journal*
OJ	Official Journal of the European Communities
PC	Privy Council
QBD	Queen's Bench Division
r.	rule
reg	regulation
s(s)	section(s)
SFI	Social Fund Inspector

SJ	*Solicitors' Journal*
SSAT	Social Security Appeal Tribunal
SSHD	Secretary of State for the Home Department
SSSS	Secretary of State for Social Security
WLR	Weekly Law Reports

Acts of Parliament

AIA 1996	Asylum and Immigration Act 1996
AIAA 1993	Asylum and Immigration Appeals Act 1993
BNA 1948	British Nationality Act 1948
BNA 1981	British Nationality Act 1981
FLRA 1969	Family Law Reform Act 1969
IA 1971	Immigration Act 1971
IA 1988	Immigration Act 1988
IntA 1978	Interpretation Act 1978
JSA 1995	Jobseekers Act 1995
SSAA 1992	Social Security Administration Act 1992
SSCBA 1992	Social Security Contributions and Benefits Act 1992

European law

Secondary legislation is made under the Treaty of Rome 1957, the Single European Act and the Maastricht Treaty in the form of Regulations (EEC Reg) and Directives (EEC Dir).

Regulations

Each set of regulations has a statutory instrument (SI) number and date. You ask for them by giving their date and number

AA(P) Rules	The Asylum Appeals (Procedure) Rules 1996 No.2070
AIA(Comm 2)O	The Asylum & Immigration Act 1996 (Commencement No.2) Order 1996 No.2127
CB Regs	The Child Benefit (General) Regulations 1976 No.965
CB(Amdt) Regs	The Child Benefit (General) Amendment Regulations 1996 No.2327
CB(Amdt 2) Regs	The Child Benefit (General) Amendment (No. 2) Regulations 1996 No. 2530
CB(RPA) Regs	The Child Benefit (Residence and Persons Abroad) Regulations 1976 No.963
CB&SS(FAR) Regs	The Child Benefit and Social Security (Fixing and Adjustment of Rates) Regulations 1976 No.1267
CF(A)O	The Consular Fees (Amendment) Order 1986 No.1881

CTB Regs	The Council Tax Benefits (General) Regulations 1992 No.1814
DWA Regs	The Disability Working Allowance (General) Regulations 1991 No.2887
FC Regs	The Family Credit (General) Regulations 1987 No.1973
HB Regs	The Housing Benefit (General) Regulations 1987 No.1971
HBCTBIS(Amdts) Regs	The Housing Benefit, Council Tax Benefit and Income Support (Amendments) Regulations 1995 No.625
I(CERI)O	The Immigration (Control of Entry through the Republic of Ireland) Order 1972 No.1610
I(EEA)O	The Immigration (European Economic Area) Order 1994 No.1895
I(EC)O	The Immigration (Exemption from Control) Order 1972 No.1613
I(VL)O	The Immigration (Variation of Leave) Order 1976 No.1572
IA(N) Regs	The Immigration Appeals (Notices) Regulations 1984 No.2040
IA(P) Rules	The Immigration Appeals (Procedure) Rules 1984 No.2041
IRB(Montserrat) Regs	The Income-related Benefits (Montserrat) Regulations 1996 No.2006
IRBS(MA) Regs	The Income-related Benefits Schemes (Miscellaneous Amendments) (No.3) Regulations 1994 No.1807
IS Regs	The Income Support (General) Regulations 1987 No.1967
IS(JSACA) Regs	The Income Support (General) (Jobseeker's Allowance Consequential Amendments) Regulations 1996 No.206
JSA Regs	The Jobseeker's Allowance Regulations 1996 No.207
JSA(Amdt) Regs	The Jobseeker's Allowance (Amendment) Regulations 1996 No.1516
SFCWP Regs	The Social Fund Cold Weather Payments (General) Regulations 1988 No.1724
SFCWP(Amdt) Regs	The Social Fund Cold Weather Payments (General) Amendment Regulations 1996 No.2544
SFM&FE Regs	The Social Fund Maternity and Funeral Expenses (General) Regulations 1987 No.481

SFM&FE(Amdt) Regs	The Social Fund Maternity and Funeral Expenses (General) Amendment Regulations 1996 No.1443
SMP Regs	The Statutory Maternity Pay (General) Regulations 1986 No.1960
SMP(PAM) Regs	The Statutory Maternity Pay (Persons Abroad and Mariners) Regulations 1987 No.418
SS(AA) Regs	The Social Security (Attendance Allowance) Regulations 1991 No.2740
SS(Adj) Regs	The Social Security (Adjudication) Regulations 1995 No.1801
SS(C&P) Regs	The Social Security (Claims and Payments) Regulations 1987 No.1968
SS(Con) Regs	The Social Security (Contributions) Regulations 1979 No.591
SS(Cr) Regs	The Social Security (Credits) Regulations 1975 No.556
SS(DLA) Regs	The Social Security (Disability Living Allowance) Regulations 1991 No.2890
SS(EEEIIP) Regs	The Social Security (Employed Earners' Employment for Industrial Injuries Purposes) Regulations 1975 No.467
SS(GA) Regs	The Social Security (Guardian's Allowance) Regulations 1975 No.515
SS(IB-ID) Regs	The Social Security (Incapacity Benefit – Increases for Dependants) Regulations 1994 No.2945
SS(ICA) Regs	The Social Security (Invalid Care Allowance) Regulations 1976 No.409
SS(IIAB) Regs	The Social Security (Industrial Injuries) (Airmen's Benefits) Regulations 1975 No.469
SS(IIMB) Regs	The Social Security (Industrial Injuries) (Mariners' Benefits) Regulations 1975 No.470
SS(IIPD) Regs	The Social Security (Industrial Injuries) (Prescribed Diseases) Regulations 1985 No.967
SS(MB) Regs	The Social Security (Mariners' Benefits) Regulations 1975 No.529
SS(NIRA) Regs	The Social Security (Northern Ireland Reciprocal Arrangements) Regulations 1976 No.1003
SS(OB) Regs	The Social Security (Overlapping Benefits) Regulations 1979 No.597
SS(PFA)MA Regs	The Social Security (Persons from Abroad) Miscellaneous Amendments Regulations 1996 No.30
SS(SDA) Regs	The Social Security (Severe Disablement Allowance) Regulations 1984 No.1303

SS(WB&RP) Regs	The Social Security (Widow's Benefit and Retirement Pensions) Regulations 1979 No.642
SSB(Dep) Regs	The Social Security Benefit (Dependency) Regulations 1977 No.343
SSB(PA) Regs	The Social Security Benefit (Persons Abroad) Regulations 1975 No.563
SSB(PRT) Regs	The Social Security Benefit (Persons Residing Together) Regulations 1977 No.956
SSFA(PM) Regs	The Social Security and Family Allowances (Polygamous Marriages) Regulations 1975 No.561
SSP Regs	The Statutory Sick Pay (General) Regulations 1982 No.894
SSP(MAPA) Regs	The Statutory Sick Pay (Mariners, Airmen and Persons Abroad) Regulations 1982 No.1349
TF(IA)O	The Transfer of Functions (Immigration Appeals) Order 1987 No.465

Other information

AOG	The *Adjudication Officers' Guide.*
GM	The *Housing Benefit and Council Tax Benefit Guidance Manual*
SF Dir	Direction(s) on the discretionary social fund. They are printed in the *Social Fund Guide* and Mesher and Wood.

Notes

PART ONE: IMMIGRATION LAW

You will find references in the notes to this Part to HC 395, HC 31 and HC 329. These are House of Commons Papers 'Statement of Changes in Immigration Rules' and are available from the Stationery Office. HC 31 and HC 329 are session 1996/97; HC 395 is session 1994/95. Command Papers are also available from the Stationery Office.

Chapter 1: Immigration control
(pp2-10)

1 s1(3) IA 1971
2 For details of these categories, see s9(4) and (6) IA 1971 and Immigration (Control of Entry through the Republic of Ireland) Order 1972 (as amended) and para 15 HC 395
3 s3(1)(b) IA 1971
4 s3(1)(c) IA 1971
5 For all addresses and telephone numbers of relevant Home Office Departments see *JCWI Handbook*
6 s4(1) IA 1971
7 Sch 2 IA 1971
8 See *R v SSHD ex parte Oladehinde* [1991] AC 254
9 See s4(1) IA 1971
10 s3(2) IA 1971
11 Sch 5 IA 1971 as amended by Transfer of Functions (Immigration Appeals) Order 1987 SI No.465
12 s22 IA 1971, Sch 2 paras 4 and 5 AIAA 1993
13 s4(3) IA 1971
14 See s24(2) IA 1971
15 Sch 2 para 17 and Sch 3 para 2(4) IA 1971
16 ss1(4) and 3(2) IA 1971
17 para 4 HC 395
18 See most recently *ECO Bombay v Stanley Walter De Noronha* [1995] Imm AR 341
19 s19 and Sch 2 para 1(3) IA 1971, *R v SSHD ex parte Hosenball* [1977] 1 WLR 766, *Pearson v IAT* [1978] Imm AR 212
20 s1 IA 1971
21 s2 IA 1971 as substituted by s39(2) BNA 1981
22 s1(2) and Sch 2 paras 2-4 IA 1971
23 s3(8)(a) IA 1971
24 paras 88-90 HC 395 and para 4 HC 329, 2 April 1996 with effect from 4 April 1996
25 paras 95-100 HC 395
26 paras 186-193 HC 395
27 paras 211-223 HC 395 and paras 5 and 6 HC 329
28 s3(5)(a) IA 1971
29 See Sch 2 paras 8 and 9 IA 1971
30 s3(5)(b) and (c) IA 1971
31 s8(3) IA 1971, International Organisations (Immunities and Privileges) Act 1950, International Organisations Act 1968, Commonwealth Secretariat Act 1966 and associated Orders in Council
32 *Kandiah* (2699)
33 See *Florentine* [1987] Imm AR 1
34 See for some guidance *Gupta* [1979-80] Imm AR 52 and footnote reference to QBD decision at 52 and 78
35 See s8(2) IA 1971 (Exemption from Control) Order 1972 SI No.1613 as amended
36 s8(3) IA 1971
37 s8(5) IA 1971
38 See s8(4)(6) IA 1971
39 s8(1) IA 1971
40 See s33(1) IA 1971 and *Diestel* [1976] Imm AR 51
41 s8(1) IA 1971

Chapter 2: Nationality
(pp11-19)

1 For further detail see *Macdonald* and *Fransman* (see Appendix 3)
2 s12 BNA 1948
3 *East African Asians v*

UK [1981] EHRR 76

4   s2 IA 1971, now repealed

5   Parts I, II, III BNA 1981

6   s2(1)(a) IA 1971

7   s2(1)(c) IA 1971 repealed

8   s4(1) BNA 1981

9   s2(1)(b) IA 1971 as substituted

10 s2(1) BNA 1981

11 Falklands Act 1983

12 Hong Kong Act 1985

13 s4(1) BNA 1981

14 British Nationality (Hong Kong) Act 1990

15 Hong Kong Selection Scheme Order

16 s40 BNA 1981

17 s12 BNA 1981

18 para 17 HC 395

19 paras 18-19 HC 395

20 paras 249-251 HC 395

21 paras 252-254 HC 395

22 para 16 HC 395

23 s2(1)(2) BNA 1981

24 See now s50(3) BNA 1981

25 s50(2)(3)(4) BNA 1981

26 s1 BNA 1981

27 s1(5) and (6) BNA 1981

28 s48 BNA 1981

29 See s47 and s50(9) BNA 1981

30 s2(1)(a) BNA 1981

31 See s14 BNA 1981 for definition of 'by descent'

32 s4(1) BNA 1981

33 s1(3) BNA 1981

34 Sch 2 BNA 1981

35 s3 BNA 1981

36 Sch 1 and s6 BNA 1981

Chapter 3: The process of controls and determining immigration status
(pp20-50)

1   para 25 HC 395

2   para 24 HC 395

3   para 24 HC 395

4   para 12 HC 31

5   para 24 HC 395

6   para 90 HC 395

7   The Foreign and Commonwealth office publishes a list of such designated posts abroad

8   para 28 HC 395

9   para 30 HC 395 and see Consular Fees (Amendment) Order 1986 SI No.1881

10 This practice was condoned in *R v Hoque and Singh* [1988] Imm AR 216

11 s18(1)(2) IA 1971; paras 3-4 IA(N) Regs

12 para 26 HC 395

13 para 27 HC 395

14 See para 2 HC 31 from 1 November 1996

15 Sch 2 para 2(1) IA 1971

16 Sch 2 para 16 IA 1971

17 Sch 2 para 6 IA 1971 as amended

18 para 328 HC 395 under the criteria of the 1951 UN Convention

19 See *Bagga* [1991] 1 QB 485 and *Badaike* [1977] *Times* 4 May 1997 DC

20 Sch 2 para 6(1) IA 1971 as amended

21 Sch 2 para 6(1) IA 1971 prior to amendment

22 *Rehal v SSHD* [1989] Imm AR 576

23 para 10 HC 395

24 rule 3 1A(N)Regs

25 Sch 2 para 8 IA 1971

26 para 321 HC 395

27 s3(3)(b) IA 1971 as amended by s10 and para 1 of Schedule to IA 1988; para 20 HC 395

28 s13(3) IA 1971; *Oloniluyi* [1989] Imm AR 135 CA

29 See s33(1) IA 1971 for definition of 'illegal entry' and s11 IA 1971 for construction of 'entry' to the UK

30 s4(1) IA 1971

31 See *Davoren* 1996 Imm AR 307

32 para 32 HC 395

33 para 33 HC 395

34 s3(3)(a) IA 1971

35 See for example para 284(i), 322(3) HC 395

36 s14(1) IA 1971, s8(2) AIAA 1993

37 s3(5)(a) IA 1971

38 s24 IA 1971

39 See *ex parte Oyele* [1994] Imm AR 265, *Adepoju* (12573) and commentary in *Immigration Nationality Law and Practice* Vol 10 No. 2 1996 p68

40 para 2 HC 329 and para 32 HC 395

41 para 34 HC 395

42 regs 3-4 para 31 HC 395

43 *ex parte Subramaniam* [1977] QB 190, *Suthendran v IAT* [1977] AC 359

44 s14(1) IA 1971, s8(2) AIAA 1993

45 para 3(1) I(VL)O

46 IA(P) Rules; AA(P) Rules

47 See para 3(2) I(VL)O

48 s14(1) IA 1971; *Subramaniam* [1977] QB 190

49 s14(1) IA 1971, Sch 2
    para 7 AAIA 1993
50 For computation of
    time see para 3(1)(3)
    I(VL)O
51 rule 4(5) IA(P) Rules
52 rules 5(1) and 11(4)
    IA(P) Rules
53 para 323 HC 395, s7
    AIAA 1993 as
    amended by Sch 3
    para 1 AIA 1996
54 s3(3)(a) IA 1971, s7
    AIAA 1993
55 s33(1) IA 1971 as
    amended
56 ss3(5)(a)(aa) and 5 IA
    1971 as amended by
    Sch 2 para 1(3) AIA
    1996
57 ss3(5)(b)(c), (6) and 6
    IA 1971
58 paras 325-326 HC
    395
59 Immigration
    (Registration with
    Police) Regs 1972 SI
    No.1758
60 ss1 and 3 IA 1971
61 s3(1)(b) IA 1971
62 *R v SSHD ex parte
    Smith* [1996] Imm
    AR 337
63 s3(1)(c) as substituted
    and Sch 2 para 7 IA
    1971, para 8 HC 395
    as amended
64 Although this has
    been a requirement in
    the rule for a long
    time, it is only since 1
    November 1996 that
    it has been elevated
    into a *condition* upon
    which leave may be
    granted – see para 8
    HC 395 as amended
    by para 3 Command
    Paper 3365 (August
    1996)
65 s3(3)(a) IA 1971
66 paras 42, 45 HC 395
67 paras 58, 61 HC 395
68 s3(5)(a) IA 1971
69 s24(1)(b)(c) IA 1971

        as amended by s6
        AIA 1996
70 para 323 HC 395
71 paras 320(11)(17)
    and 322(3) HC 395
72 See s3(3)(a) IA 1971
73 s3(5)(b), (6) IA 1971
74 paras 18-19 HC 395
75 para 6 HC 395 as
    amended and see
    Chapter 5
76 s33(2A) IA 1971 as
    amended; see also
    para 6 HC 395
77 ss4, 6 and Sch 1 to
    BNA 1981
78 s1 BNA 1981
79 para 8 HC 395
80 para 32 HC 395 as
    amended
81 paras 57-58 HC 395
82 para 320 HC 395
83 para 59 HC 395
84 para 58 HC 395
85 s3(1)(c) IA 1971 as
    substituted by Sch 2
    para 1 AIA 1996
86 paras 334 and 345
    HC 395 as amended
    by Command Paper
    3365 August 1996
87 Art 1A(2) UN
    Convention on
    Refugees 1951
88 paras 101(ii), 102,
    103 HC 395
89 paras 277-280 HC
    395
90 paras 277-280 HC
    395
91 HC 395 23 May
    1994, as amended
92 paras 186-193 HC
    395
93 paras 211-223 HC
    395
94 paras 281-289 HC
    395
95 paras 317-319 HC
    395 and see also for
    certain children paras
    297-303, 310-316
    and 304-309
96 paras 327-352 HC
    395

97 paras 95-103 HC 395
98 paras 103-109 HC
    395
99 paras 110-115 HC
    395
100 paras 116-121 HC
    395
101 paras 57-62 HC 395
102 See para 7 HC 329
103 para 8 HC 329
104 paras 63-69 HC 395
105 paras 82-87 HC 395
106 para 92 HC 395
107 paras 246-247 HC
    395
108 paras 249-254 HC
    395
109 para 26 HC 395
110 See paras 320-323
    HC 395
111 paras 320-323 HC
    395
112 para 320(3) HC 395
113 para 320(11)(12) HC
    395
114 para 322(6) HC 395
    and see further now
    para 10 HC 31 from
    1 November 1996
115 See *Bagga* [1991] 1
    QB 485 and *Badaike*
    [1977] *Times* 4 May
    1977 DC
116 Sch 2 para 6(1) IA
    1971 as amended
117 Sch 2 para 6(1) IA
    1971 prior to
    amendment
118 *Rehal v SSHD* [1989]
    Imm AR 576
119 s3(3)(b) IA 1971
120 Articles 27-28 and
    Schedule to the UN
    Convention on
    Refugees 1951

**Chapter 4: What is
exceptional leave**
(pp51-56)

1   s19(2) IA 1971, Sch 2
    para 1(3) IA 1971; *R
    v SSHD ex parte
    Hosenball* [1977];
    WLR 766, *Pearson v*

IAT [1978] Imm AR 212

2 HO evidence given in case of *R v SSHD ex parte Alakesan* unreported 22 April 1996 QBD

3 Within the meaning of the 1951 Geneva Convention on Refugees to which the immigration rules refer

4 Secretary of State, HC *Hansard* 17 July 1984 col 85

5 HC Standing Committee A 12/11/92 ministerial comment during the passage of the AIAA 1993

6 *Luzarevic and Others v SSHD* [1997] Imm AR 251 CA

7 HO minister, HC *Hansard* 28 July 1988 col 425

8 See *ex parte Miranda* CO/960/1995 unreported, *AS Abdi* (13172) at pp19-20

9 See HC *Hansard* 22 February 1996 col 450; reproduced in *Immigration Law Digest* (IAS) Vol. 2 No. 4 p6

10 s3(2) IA 1971

11 *DS Abdi v SSHD* [1996] Imm AR; *Hersi and Others v SSHD* [1996] Imm AR 569; *Reem Louis Shekouri* (13711)

12 paras 330 and 335 HC 395

13 HO evidence to HC sub-committee on race and immigration (SCORRI) 1984-85 17 December 1984 HC 72-iv

14 SCORRI evidence HC 72-iv para 8; HO

minister, HC *Hansard* 18 January 1995

15 This is just one aspect of the policy provisions set out in the letter of 17 May 1990 to Tower Hamlets Law Centre reported in the note to *R v SSHD ex parte Diria* [1993] Imm AR 35 pp40-46 but now withdrawn see HO minister HC *Hansard* 25 January 1994 col 166. The current policy on family reunion for Somali nationals is set out in an HO letter to Immigration Law Practitioners Association 29 February 1996

16 See SCORRI evidence above para 24 and para 8.3 of letter of 17 May 1990 above at [1993] Imm AR 35

17 See policy set out as a note to *Conteh v SSHD* [1992] Imm AR 594 CA; and on transfer of refugee status, see eg *Jinnah Rahman* [1989] Imm AR 325

18 See Ministerial letter of Tim Renton 8 October 1987. For a full discussion on the, sometimes conflicting, policy statements on long residence see Jackson, *Immigration Law and Practice* paras 7-50 to 7-64

19 DP/2/93, reproduced in *Immigration and Nationality Law and Practice* Vol 7, 100-102

20 Now contained in

policy statements DP/3/96, DP/4/96, DP/5/96 reproduced in *Immigration and Nationality Law and Practice* Vol 10 No.4 1996 and Vol 11 No.1 1997 (Practice Note)

21 The instructions are much informed by the jurisprudence of the ECJ and Commission in cases such as *Berrehab* [1988] 11 EHRR 322 and *Abdulaziz, Cabales, Balkandali v UK* [1985] 7 EHRR 471

22 Note of B1 Management Unit to HO caseworkers, January 1994

23 The latest is BDI 3/95

24 See *George Davoren v SSHD* [1996] Imm AR 307

25 HO minister HC *Hansard* 16 May 1991 col 73 as amplified in HO letter to Rev I Paisley 22 September 1992

26 See statement of Nicholas Baker MP HC *Hansard* 9 December 1994 col 379

27 para 364 HC 395

28 Letter to JCWI 18 July 1989, *R -v- SSHD ex parte Amoa* [1992] Imm AR 218 QBD

29 BDI 2/95 issued April 1995

30 For further details, see Macdonald's *Immigration Law and Practice*, 4th edn, paras 2.65-2.61; ILPA Training Document on ELR, 1989

31 paras 76-78 HC 395

32 Letter of HO Minister Nicholas Baker to Tony Banks MP, 26 July 1995

Chapter 5: Recourse to public funds
(pp57-69)

1 paras 47-50 HC 395
2 paras 249-254 HC 395
3 paras 304-309 HC 395
4 paras 327-352 HC 395
5 paras 18-20 HC 395
6 paras 3, 6, 7, 8 and 9 HC 31
7 s3(1) IA 1971 as amended by Sch 2 para 1(1) AIA 1996 and para 8(ii) HC 395 as substituted by para 3 Command Paper 3365 August 1996
8 s3(5)(a) IA 1971
9 s24(1)(b) IA 1971
10 paras 320(11), 322(3)(4) HC 395
11 para 323 HC 395
12 'Policy and Practice' *Immigration and Nationality Law and Practice*, January 1988 p102
13 para 322(4), 323 HC 395
14 s3(3)(a) IA 1971
15 s14 IA 1971 as amended by Sch 2 para 3 AIA 1996
16 See s9(1)(2)(3) AIA 1996; Housing Accommodation and Homelessness (Persons Subject to Immigration Control) Order 1996 SI No.1982; Housing Act 1996; Homelessness Regulations (1996) SI No.2754; Allocation of Housing Regulations 1996; and in terms of benefits, ss10, 11 and Sch 1 AIA 1996 and Social Security (Persons from Abroad) Miscellaneous Amendments Regs 1996
17 See *Dumerville* (9395); *Stein* (7978)
18 para 6 HC 395 as amended by para 1 HC 329 and para 1 HC 31
19 Under Housing Act 1985, parts III Housing (Scotland) Act 1987 or part II Housing (Northern Ireland) Order 1988
20 Under part III SSCBA 1992 or part III SSCBA (Northern Ireland) 1992
21 *Ibid*
22 *Ibid*
23 *Ibid*
24 Under part VII SSCBA 1992 or part VII SSCBA (Northern Ireland) 1992
25 *Ibid*
26 *Ibid*
27 *Ibid*
28 *Ibid*
29 Under JSA 1995
30 Under part IX SSCBA 1992 and part IX SSCBA (Northern Ireland) 1992 and s10 AIA 1996
31 para 1 HC 329
32 para 1 HC 31
33 See comments in *R v IAT ex parte Shaim Begum* [1995] *Times* 15 February 1995 QBD per Schiemann J; also noted in *Legal Action* (1995) July p21; and see *Zia v SSHD* [1993] Imm AR 404; *ex parte Aslam* 12 May 1997 (unreported)
34 *Azem* (7863)
35 *Tedeku* (6024)
36 *Dumerville* (9395)
37 *Egal* (ISD35)
38 See *Begum* (3811) and see *Mushtaq* (9343)
39 ss324-325 Housing Act 1985
40 see HO instructions set out in *Immigration and Nationality Law and Practice*, July 1987 vol 2 p26
41 See s326 Housing Act 1985
42 See *Kasuji* [1988] Imm AR 587; *Musrat Jabeen* (14925)
43 *Ahmed* (8260); *Zia v SSHD* [1993] Imm AR 404 (obiter) cf *Kausar* (8025)
44 See *R v IAT ex parte Chhinderpal Singh and Gurdip Singh* [1989] Imm AR 69 and *R v SSHD ex parte Islam Bibi and Dilshad Begum* [1995] Imm AR 157
45 *Chhinderpal Singh* (above)
46 *Azem* (7863), *Buchaya* (9025), *Quiambo* (12416), *Uddin* (12429), *Shah* (12444)
47 See *Bashir Ahmed* [1991] Imm AR 30, *Ahmed* (9028), *Pervez Hussain* (7509), *Ishaque* (6752)
48 *Buchanan* (11280); *Uddin* (9170); *Singh* (7387)
49 *Agub* (9547); *Begum* (8582); *Mohd Ramzan* (11185); *Patel* (11278)

50 *Mukhtar Ahmed*
(9028)

51 *Legal Action* (1995)
July p21 and *IAS
Law Digest,* 26
October 1995 for text
of letters of Nicholas
Baker MP (Minister)
to Max Madden MP
and 26 April 1995
and 2 October 1995
respectively. See also
letter of 12 March
1997 to BM Birnberg
and Co in relation to
CB

52 The letter is set out in
more detail in *Legal
Action* (1995) March
p20

53 See for further detail
of HO stated
interpretation
'Recourse to public
funds and indirect
reliance',
*Immigration and
Nationality Law and
Practice* Vol 10, No.
2 1996, pp 50-53;
*Immigration Law
Digest* Vol 1 26
September 1996
pp22-24; and in
earlier articles in
*Immigration and
Nationality Law and
Practice* Vol 9:1 1995
p29, and Vol 6:3
1992 p99

54 See *Reem Louis
Shekouri* (13711),
Clevon Marcus Scott
(13389); *Neharun
Begum* (13489)
although see the
contrary view in
Javaid Iqbal (12528)
but this latter case
was decided prior to a
key decision in
relation to appellate
authority jurisdiction
of *SSHD v DS Abdi*
[1996] Imm AR 148

55 See *Mohammed
Yousaf* (9190)

56 *Azem* (7863),
Buchiya (9025),
Ahmed (9028),
Yousaf (9190),
Ishaque (6752) and
Muhmood (12833)

57 *Azem* (7863)

58 See *Munir Jan* (1517);
Sultan Begum (3155)

59 *Bakiserver* (1151)

60 *Bashir Ahmed* [1991]
Imm AR 130, *Sabir
Hussain* (5990)

61 *Kazmi* (5866)

62 *Afzal* (11853)

63 *Akhtar* (7837)

64 See also *Keyani*
(5662) for anticipated
earnings

65 *Sabir Hussain* (5990)

66 See paras 232-239
HC 395

67 *Ibid*

68 paras 128-135 HC
395

69 paras 95-100 HC 395

70 paras 110-115 HC
395

71 paras 116-121 HC
395

72 paras 57-62 HC 395

73 paras 57(v) and 58
HC 395

74 paras 40-46 HC 395

75 paras 40-46 HC 395

76 paras 51-56 HC 395

77 See Jackson,
*Immigration Law
and Practice,* Sweet
and Maxwell, 1996;
paras 6036, 6-37, 11-
109

78 *Hussain* (5990), *Azad*
(5993), *Sadiq* (6017),
Saleem (6017),
Akhtar (7837), *Kaur*
(12838), *Akhtar*
(9903), *Khan* (6283),
Yousaf (9190)

79 eg see *Azra Tubeen*
[1991] Imm AR 178;
Ansar Mahmood
(8402), *Ishaque*

Ahmed (12992),
Nanjo (9730)

80 *Kauser* (8025),
Mahmood (8402),
Wray (9022),
Rafaqat (9445),
Mistry (12160),
Akhtar (11658)

81 See *Jabeen* [1991]
Imm AR 178 where
the sponsor was
detained and there
was no actual
evidence of third
party support,
Ildaphonse (8464),
Begum (8582), *Wray*
(9022), *Mohammed
Hussain* [1991] Imm
AR 476; *Hussain*
(11372), *Azad* (5993)

82 See paras 263-270
HC 395

83 para 200-210 HC
395

84 para 211-223 HC
395

85 para 232-239 HC
395

86 Introduced in 1994
(statement of
immigration rules HC
395)

87 Letter from Nicholas
Baker MP (minister)
to Sir Giles Shaw MP,
October 1994 (the
time when the rules
came into force)
Legal Action (1995)
March p20

88 para 35 HC 395

89 para 35 HC 395;
ss78, 105 and 106
SSAA 1992; SSAA
(Northern Ireland)
Act 1992

90 Parliamentary answer
29 January 1986 of
Secretary of State for
Social Services and
letter 4 January 1991
from DSS to JCWI

91 paras 320(14) and
322(6) HC 395

Chapter 6:
Enforcement and
appeals
(pp70-81)

1 The Bail Act does not apply to immigration detainees, so there is no presumption that you will be released on bail by immigration appellate authorities. Where the Home Office or the immigration service have a power to detain they always have a discretion to temporarily admit or release you into the community on conditions as to residence, employment and/or reporting.
2 s8(3) IA 1971; Immigration (Exemption from Control) Order 1972 SI No.1613
3 See s7 IA 1971 for details
4 ss2(2) and 5(2) IA 1971
5 s3(5)(6) IA 1971 amended by para 1(2) AIA 1996; paras 8 and 363 HC 395
6 s3(5)(a) IA 1971
7 s3(6) IA 1971
8 s3(5)(b) IA 1971
9 s3(5)(aa) IA 1971 as added by Sch 2 para 1(2) AIA 1996
10 s3(5)(c) IA 1971
11 *Offeh* (9662)
12 para 364 HC 395
13 para 367 HC 395 as substituted
14 para 365 HC 395 as substituted
15 s5(i)(2) IA 1971
16 paras 390-392 HC 395
17 s8 AIA 1996
18 s33(1) IA 1971 as

amended by Sch 2 para 4(1) AIA 1996
19 Arts 15, 17 I(EEA)O
20 Visiting Forces Act 1952
21 s86 Mental Health Act 1983
22 If you need to know more about extradition, you should consult *Jones on Extradition*, Alun Jones QC, Sweet & Maxwell 1995
23 See para 2 HC 329 amending para 32 HC 395
24 s14(1) IA 1971, s8(2) AIAA 1993
25 s13(3A) IA 1971 as amended
26 s13(3B)(3C) IA 1971; s14(2A)(2B) IA 1971 as amended by Sch 12 para 3(2) AIA 1996
27 s13(5), 14(3), 15(3)(4) IA 1971; Sch 2 para 6 AIAA 1993
28 *R v SSHD ex parte Radiom and Shingara* 3 February 1995; joined cases C-65/95 and C-111/95 17 June 1997
29 s14(2ZA) IA 1971 as added by Sch 2 para 3(1) AIA 1996
30 s18 IA 1971; rules 3-4 IA(N) Regs
31 IA(P) Rules; AA(P) Rules
32 s13 IA 1971
33 s15(5) IA 1971
34 s13 IA 1971
35 s14 IA 1971
36 para 32 HC 395 as amended
37 s15 IA 1971
38 s5 IA 1988
39 s16 IA 1971
40 s8 AIAA 1993; ss1-3 AIA 1996
41 IA(P) Rules; AA(P) Rules
42 s3(2) AIA 1996

43 rule 8 IA(P) Rules
44 s1 AIA 1996
45 s15(7) IA 1971
46 Sch 2 para 5(7) AIAA 1993 as substituted by s1 AIA 1996
47 IA(P) Rules; AA(P) Rules
48 s9 AIAA 1993
49 Sch 2 para 28(1) IA 1971
50 s14(1) IA 1971
51 s15(2) IA 1971
52 Sch 2 para 28(2) IA 1971
53 Sch 2 para 28(5) IA 1971
54 s33(4) IA 1971 as amended by Sch 2 para 4(2) AIA 1996
55 s6 AIAA 1993
56 Sch 2 paras 7, 8, 9 AIAA 1993; para 333 HC 395
57 s2 AIA 1996
58 s2(1)(2)(3) and s3(1)(2) AIA 1996
59 s13(3) IA 1971
60 Sch 2 para 28(1) IA 1971
61 *Lokko* [1990] Imm AR 111

PART TWO:
IMMIGRATION
AND BENEFITS
Chapter 7:
Immigration and
benefits
(pp84-96)

1 *R v Inhabitants of Eastbourne* [1803] 4 East 103 (cited in *R v SSSS ex parte JCWI* [1996] & All ER 385) which considered the rights to poor relief of a German baker, his English-born wife and their four children
2 Requirement to leave: see p365

3 Habitual residence test: see p102

4 HB/CTB Circular A1/96 para 4

5 This replaced the joint HO/DSS unit in late 1996/early 1997

6 See Dummett and Nicol, *Subjects, Citizens, Aliens and Others*, Weidenfeld & Nicholson, 1990 p233 nl

7 Version 4.0

8 The current forms (version 4.0) wrongly include 'JSA' in the list of public funds benefits, rather than limiting it to income-based JSA

9 s2(1)(a) SSCBA 1992

10 Reg 119(1)(a) SS(Con) Regs

11 Reg 119(2) SS(Con) Regs

12 Reg 119(3) SS(Con) Regs

13 Reg 120(2)(b) SS(Con) Regs

14 Reg 120 SS(Con) Regs

15 s2(1)(b) SSCBA 1992; reg 119(1)(d) SS(Con) Regs

16 Reg 119(1)(c) SS(Con) Regs

17 Reg 123A SS(Con) Regs

18 Reg 58(b) SS(Con) Regs

19 s2(1)(b) SSCBA 1992; reg 119(1)(d) SS(Con) Regs

20 This has been the case since the late 1970s

21 According to the CA, this may not happen in sensitive cases (unspecified)

22 Also, the *Guardian*, 15 February 1997 reported the case of a man aged about 50 born in GB whose

birth had not been registered and about whom there were no official records. The DSS reportedly refused to pay him IS because of lack of evidence of identity

23 IS was refused but later awarded on review

24 IS was refused but awarded following an appeal

25 *Re Taylor* [1961] WLR 9, CA. For more cases see Keane, *The Modern Law of Evidence*, Butterworths

26 Sch 10 SSCBA 1992

27 s37(2) SSCBA 1992

28 see *Keane*

29 *The Poulet Peerage Case* [1903] AC 395. In Scotland s5(1)(a) Law Reform (Parent and Child)(Scotland) Act 1986

30 For possible sources of evidence see Keane

31 s26 FLRA 1969; *S v S* [1972] AC 24 at 41. In Scotland s5(4) Law Reform (Parent and Child)(Scotland) Act 1986

Chapter 8: Presence and residence
(pp97-105)

1 see *Failing the Test*, NACAB, February 1996, for a detailed account of the habitual residence test in practice

2 CIS/1067/95

3 *R v Barnet London Borough Council ex parte Shah* aka *Akbarali v Brent London Borough Council* [1983] 2 AC

309; [1983] 2 WLR 16, [1983] 1 All ER 226 [1983] 127 SJ 36; [1983] 81 LGR 305; [1983] 133 New LJ; HL, Lord Scarman at p343H

4 s172 SSCBA 1992; s35(1) JSA 1995 'GB'

5 Territorial Sea Act 1987. Before 15 May 1987 territorial waters were only those three miles from the shore

6 R(S) 1/66; vol 3 para 20630 AOG

7 Reg 1(3) CB(RPA) Regs

8 s147(1) SSCBA 1992 'week'

9 Reg 1(3) CB(RPA) Regs

10 R(M) 1/85

11 *R v Barnet London Borough Council ex parte Shah*

12 p343H *Shah*

13 p344G *Shah*

14 *Levene* v *Inland Revenue Commissioners* [1928] AC 217, HL

15 *Levene; Inland Revenue Commissioners* v *Lysaght* [1928] AC 234, HL

16 eg Lysaght was found to be ordinarily resident in England even though he was clearly also ordinarily resident in the Irish Free State

17 p345E-H *Shah*

18 R(F) 1/62; vol 3 para 20806 AOG

19 *Macrae* v *Macrae* [1949] p397; [1949] 2 All ER 34; 93 SJ 449; 47 LGR 437, CA. In CIS/1067/ 1995 para 27 the commissioner doubts

Macrae because he considers it used a test very close to the 'real home' test rejected in *Shah*. He does not seem to have heard any argument about this: *Macrae* was cited in *Shah* and was not one of the cases mentioned there as wrong: pp342-3

20 [1949] 2 All ER 34 p37A

21 *Lewis* v *Lewis* [1956] 1 WLR 200; [1956] 1 All ER 375; 100 SJ 134, High Court

22 The facts are in the Court of Appeal's judgment: *R* v *Barnet London Borough Council ex parte Shah* [1982] QB 688 at p717E; [1982] 2 WLR 474, [1982] 1 All ER 698; (1982) 80 LGR 571

23 p344C-D *Shah*

24 p344C-D *Shah* Education was the purpose in R(F) 1/62

25 *Levene*

26 eg Macrae's decision to move to Scotland was not made long before he went

27 eg *Shah*

28 p344G *Shah*

29 R(F) 1/82; R(F) 1/62; R(P) 1/62; R(P) 4/54; vol 3 paras 20815-6 AOG

30 R(F) 1/62; R(M)1/85; vol 3 paras 20818-20 AOG

31 *Hopkins* v *Hopkins* [1951] p116; *R* v *Hussain* (1971) 56 Crim App R 165, CA; *R* v *IAT ex parte Ng* [1986] Imm AR 23, QBD

32 *Shah*; CG/204/49; vol 3 para 20808

AOG *R* v *IAT ex parte Siggins* [1985] Imm AR 14, QBD

33 *Levene*; *Lysaght*

34 Relying on vol 3 Para 20826 AOG example 1 suggests the opposite but this conflicts with *Levene* R(P) 1/78

35 p342D *Shah*

36 *Stransky* v *Stransky* [1954] p428; [1954] 3 WLR 123; [1954] 2 All ER 536

37 *Haria* [1986] Imm AR 165, IAT

38 *Shah*

39 *Lysaght*

40 In *Re Mackenzie* [1941] 1 Chancery Reports 69

41 *Gout* v *Cimitian* [1922] 1 AC 105, PC: deportation of an Ottoman subject from Egypt did not stop him becoming ordinarily resident in Cyprus

42 *Re A (A Minor: Abduction: Child's Objections)* [1994] 2 FLR 126: on habitual residence, but applies to ordinary residence also

43 In Scotland, parental rights and responsibilities

44 *Re M (Minors: Residence Order: Jurisdiction)* [1993] 1 FLR 495: on habitual residence, but applies to ordinary residence also

45 *Re A (A Minor) (Abduction: Acquiescence)* [1992] 2 FLR 14: on habitual residence, but applies to ordinary residence also

46 There is transitional

protection for people entitled to benefit on 31 July 1994: regs 2-4 IRBS(MA) Regs

47 In particular, Peter Lilley's speech to Conservative Party conference 1993

48 see *Failing the Test* from which the statistics are taken

49 Reg 21(3) IS Regs 'person from abroad': habitual residence; reg 85(4) JSA Regs 'person from abroad': habitual residence; reg 7A(4)(e) HB Regs reg 4A(4)(e) CTB Regs

50 Command Paper 9512

51 Command Paper 2643

52 Art 13 European Social Charter; Art 1 European Convention on Social and Medical Assistance

53 This argument was not resolved in *Sarwar* v *Secretary of State for Social Security*, CA 24 October 1996 because the CA decided any discrimination would be outside the scope of the EC Treaty

54 *R* v *SSHD ex parte Brind*, HL [1991] 1 AC 696; [1991] 1 All ER 720; [1991] 2 WLR 588

55 CIS/1067/95 para 17; CIS/2326/95 para 17

56 CIS/1067/95 para 27; CIS/2326/95 para 20; both applying comments in *Re J*

57 CIS/2326/95. The claimant's appeal to the CA is due to be

heard in November
1997

58 *Kapur* v *Kapur*
[1984] FLR 920; CIS/
1067/95 para 27;
CIS/2326/95 para 31
in which the
commissioner set
aside the tribunal's
decision because only
ordinary residence
was considered and
not also whether
there was an
appreciable period
of residence

59 In particular *Nessa* v
CAO, the claimant's
appeal from CIS/
2326/95

60 CIS/2326/95 lists
most of the important
cases on habitual
residence. See also
Jacob & Douglas,
*Child Support: the
Legislation*, notes to
habitual residence
test in s44(1) Child
Support Act 1991

61 CIS/1067/95 para 15

62 CIS/1067/95 para 19

63 CIS/1067/95 para 27;
CIS/2326/95 para 24;
both applying
comments in *Re J*

64 *Cameron* v *Cameron*
[1996] *Scots Law
Times* 306;
CIS/1067/95 para 28

65 CIS/2326/95 para 24

66 *Cameron* v *Cameron*
followed in
CIS/2326/95 para 24;
vol 3 para 20748.6
AOG

67 CIS/2326/95 para 26;
vol 3 para 20748.7
AOG

68 CIS/1067/95 para 28-
30; CIS 2326/95 para
28; vol 3 para
20748.8-9 AOG

69 CIS/2326/95 para
30; para 20748.13

vol 3 AOG

70 Art 1(h) EEC Reg
1408/71

71 Art 71(1)(b)(ii) EEC
Reg 1408/71

72 Case 76/76 *Di Paolo*
[1977] ECR 315

73 R(U) 7/85; R(U) 8/88
and the cases listed in
that case

74 CIS/2326/95 para 22

75 CIS/564/94

Chapter 9: Special rules for family members
(pp106-119)

1 Reg 2 and Sch 1
SS(NIRA) Regs

2 s137(1) SSAA 1992
'married couple'

3 s137 SSAA 1992
'unmarried couple';
R(SB) 17/81

4 *Santos* v *Santos*
[1972] 2 WLR 889;
[1972] 2 All ER 246,
CA

5 R(SB) 8/85

6 R(SB) 4/83

7 CIS/671/92

8 s124(1)(c) SSCBA
1992; s3(1)(e) JSA
1995

9 Reg 23(1) IS Regs; reg
88(1) JSA Regs

10 The rules say 'resume
living with': reg 16(2)
IS Regs; reg 78(1) JSA
Regs

11 Reg 16(1)-(3) IS Regs;
reg 78(1)-(3) JSA
Regs. Only the rules
relevant to partners
abroad are dealt with
here

12 Reg 16(2)(a) IS Regs;
reg 78(2)(a) JSA
Regs: either person's
lack of intention
counts because the
rules refer to the
'person who is living
away from the other

members of his
family' and both
partners are living
away from each other

13 See CIS/508/92 and
CIS/484/93 on a
similarly worded IS
housing costs rule:
now Sch 3 para 3(10)
IS Regs

14 Until 4 October 1993
the rules referred to
absence from the
home

15 Reg 21(1) and Sch 7
paras 11 and 11A IS
Regs; reg 85(1) and
Sch 5 paras 10 and 11
JSA Regs

16 Reg 16(1) IS Regs; reg
78(1) JSA Regs

17 Reg 21(1) and Sch 7
paras 11 and 11A IS
Regs; reg 85(1) and
Sch 5 paras 10 and 11
JSA Regs

18 Sch 4 para 4 and Sch
5 para 5 HB Regs;
Sch 4 para 4 and Sch
5 para 5 CTB Regs

19 Reg 23(1) IS Regs; reg
88(1) JSA Regs

20 HB Guidance manual
para A3.16

21 These comments do
not apply to arrears

22 Reg 51(3) CTB Regs:
reg 51(4) no longer
applies. Every
resident of a dwelling
is jointly and severally
(ie collectively and
individually) liable to
pay all the council
tax. If there are more
than two people liable
for council tax on
your accommodation,
your CTB will be
worked out on the
basis that the total
liability is divided
equally between them

23 Reg 15 HB Regs; reg
7 CTB Regs

24 Reg 3(1)(d) FC Regs; reg 5(1)(d) DWA Regs

25 Reg 3(1)(b) FC Regs; reg 5(1)(b) DWA Regs

26 Reg 10(1) FC Regs; reg 12(1) DWA Regs

27 Reg 47(1) FC Regs

28 Reg 52(1) DWA Regs

29 This is because you may be entitled under Community law to social security benefits linked to employment on the same basis as UK nationals: para 2 Annex VI Council & Commission Decision 91/400/ECSC, EEC: OJ No L 229, 17/8/91, p249. These rules about your partner may be indirectly discriminatory because they are more likely to apply to people from African, Caribbean and Pacific countries than UK nationals

30 Reg 9(1) FC Regs; reg 11(1) DWA Regs

31 Because the rules refer to 'resume living together': reg 9(1) FC Regs; reg 11(1) DWA Regs

32 see CIS/508/92 and CIS/484/93 on a similarly worded IS housing costs rule: now Sch 3 para 3(10) IS Regs

33 Reg 9(2) FC Regs; reg 11(2) DWA Regs. There are also rules for mental patients but these only apply in the UK

34 Sch 2 para 8 IS Regs; Sch 1 para 9 JSA Regs

35 Reg 2(2)(b)

CB&SS(FAR) Regs

36 Reg 11(1) CB Regs made under s147(4) SSCBA 1992

37 CF/1/81. The commissioner decided that the political situation in Vietnam meant the claimant's wife would probably never join him in the UK. See also *Welfare Rights Bulletins 75* and 79

38 Reg 11(2) CB Regs

39 Reg 2(2)(c) CB&SS(FAR) Regs

40 Reg 11(3) CB Regs treats unmarried parents as residing together during any temporary absence, but the higher rate rules refer to living, not residing, together, so reg 11(3) does not seem to make a difference to higher rate

41 Reg 13 SSB(PA) Regs disapplying s113 SSCBA 1992

42 Reg 2(4) SSB(PRT) Regs made under s122(3) SSCBA 1992

43 CSS/18/88

44 Reg 2(2) SSB(PRT) Regs

45 Regs 10(2)(c) and (3) and 12 and Sch 2 para 7(b)(iv) SSB(Dep) Regs; reg 14 SS(IB-ID) Regs The general disqualification in s113 SSCBA 1992 does not apply to adult dependant increases

46 Reg 2(4) SSB(PRT) Regs made under s122(3) SSCBA 1992

47 CSS 18/88

48 Reg 17(b) IS Regs; reg 83(b) JSA Regs

49 s137(1) SSCBA 1992 'family' (b) and (c); s35(1) JSA 1995 'family' (b) and (c)

50 Reg 16(5)(aa)(ii) IS Regs; reg 78(5)(b)(ii) JSA Regs

51 Reg 16(5)(a)(ii) IS Regs; reg 78(5)(a)(ii) JSA Regs

52 Reg 16(5)(a)(i) and (aa)(i) and (5A) IS Regs; reg 78(5)(a)(i) and (b)(i) and (6) JSA Regs

53 Reg 16(b) HB Regs; reg 8(b) CTB Regs

54 s137(1) SSCBA 1992 'family' (b) and (c)

55 Reg 15(1)-(3) HB Regs. Only the rules relevant to partners abroad are dealt with here

56 Reg 15(2)(a) HB Regs: either person's lack of intention counts because the rules refer to the 'person who is living away from the other members of his family'

57 s128(1)(d) SSCBA 1992. If you are responsible for a child, s/he is treated as a member of your household: reg 8(1) FC Regs

58 Reg 7(1) FC Regs; reg 9(1) DWA Regs

59 CFC 1537/95

60 Reg 7(2) FC Regs; reg 9(2) DWA Regs; CFC 1537/95

61 Reg 7(3) FC Regs; reg 9(3) DWA Regs

62 ss80(1) and (5) and 90 SSCBA 1992; reg 12 and Sch 2 para 2 SSB(Dep) Regs. The general disqualification in s113(1) SSCBA 1992

63 Reg 13A(3) SSB(PA) Regs

64 Reg 13A(6) SSB(PA) Regs cancels the effect of reg 8 SS(OB) Regs

65 ss 121(1)(b) and 133(1) SSCBA 1992; reg 2(1) IS Regs 'polygamous marriage'; reg 1(3) JSA Regs 'polygamous marriage'; reg 2(1) HB Regs 'polygamous marriage'; reg 2(1) CTB Regs 'polygamous marriage'; for child benefit: reg 12(2)(a) CB Regs; for other non-means-tested benefits: reg 1(2) SSFA(PM) Regs

66 s6 IntA 1978; reg 1(4) SSFA(PM) Regs

67 *Re Bethell, Bethell and Hildyard* [1888] 38 Chancery Division 220

68 Reg 2(1) IS Regs 'partner' para (b); reg 1(3) JSA Regs 'partner' para (b); reg 2(1) HB Regs 'partner' para (b); reg 2(1) CTB Regs 'partner' para (b)

69 Reg 18 IS Regs; reg 84 JSA Regs; reg 17 HB Regs; reg 9 CTB Regs

70 Reg 18(2) IS Regs; reg 84(2) JSA Regs

71 Reg 46(2) FC Regs; reg 51(2) DWA Regs

72 Reg 23(3) IS Regs; reg 88(4) JSA Regs; reg 19(3) HB Regs; reg 11(3) CTB Regs; reg 10(2) FC Regs; reg 12(2) DWA Regs

73 Reg 2 SSFA(PM) Regs

74 R(G) 1/93

75 See CPAG's *Rights Guide to Non-Means-Tested Benefits* or *Bonner*, notes to s38 SSCBA 1992 for an outline

76 Reg 21(3) IS Regs 'person from abroad'; reg 85(4) JSA Regs 'person from abroad'. The habitual residence test only applies to the claimant, not any family member

77 Reg 21(3) IS Regs 'person from abroad' para (g); reg 85(4) JSA Regs 'person from abroad' para (g)

78 Reg 21(3) IS Regs 'person from abroad' para (c); reg 85(4) JSA Regs 'person from abroad' para (c)

Chapter 10: Means tested benefits
(pp120–129)

1 Reg 21(3) 'person from abroad' IS Regs and Sch 7 para 17; reg 85(4) 'person from abroad' Sch 5 para 4 JSA Regs; reg 7A HB Regs ; reg 4A CTB Regs

2 These types of people cannot be on that list. Only people on the list of persons from abroad count as such.

3 Reg 21(3F) IS Regs This only applies from 28 August 1996: reg 1 IRB(Montserrat) Regs. Before that date, extra-statutory IS payments were made to persons from abroad from Montserrat: Income Support Bulletins 63/96 and 82/96

4 Reg 21(3) 'person from abroad' IS Regs

5 Reg 21(3F) IS Regs; See note 3

6 s124(1)(e) SSCBA 1992; reg 4ZA and Sch 1B para 21 IS Regs

7 Sch 7 para 17(a) IS Regs

8 Sch 7 para 17(c)(ii) and (iii) IS Regs

9 Sch 7 para 17(c)(i) IS Regs

10 Sch 7 para 17(e) IS Regs

11 plus any 'protected sum' paid because you were boarded before 10 April 1989: Sch 3A IS Regs

12 Sch 7 para 17 IS Regs

13 Sch 7 para 17(d)(ii) IS Regs

14 Sch 7 para 17(d)(i) IS Regs

15 This apparent anomaly is because Sch 7 para 17(d) IS Regs does not apply to this situation, so even though the claimant is a person from abroad, the only person from abroad rule to apply is para 17(e) Sch 7 IS Regs

16 Reg 9(1) SS(Cr) Regs

17 Reg 9(1) SS(Cr) Regs

18 Para 12(1)(b) Sch 2 IS Regs

19 Reg 71(1)(a) IS Regs

20 Reg 71(1)(a) IS Regs. The rules for people who lost out in the change from supplementary benefit to IS also apply in the usual way (see: Income Support (Transitional) Regulations 1987)

except that the special
rules for people who
are not entitled to a
transitional addition
do not apply because
reg 71(1)(a) IS Regs
does not include an
amount under reg
17(1)(b) IS Regs
21 Reg 22A IS Regs. The
20% reduction only
applies to people to
whom none of the
paragraphs of Sch 1B
IS Regs apply (apart
from para 25 re
appealing the all
work test) and para
21 applies to a person
entitled to urgent
cases rate
22 Reg 72(1) IS Regs
23 Reg 72(1)(a) and
Sch 9 paras 5, 40 and
42 IS Regs.
Also, for IS, any
compensation paid
for loss of housing
benefit supplement.
This supplement was
paid under the
supplementary
benefit scheme and
abolished in April
1988
24 Reg 72(1)(a) IS Regs
25 Reg 72(1)(a) and sub-
paras 39(2) and (3)
Sch 9 IS Regs
26 Sch 9 Sub-para 39(5)
IS Regs does not
apply to urgent cases:
reg 72(1)(a) IS Regs.
27 Reg 72(1)(a) and
Sch 9 sub-para 39(4)
IS Regs
28 Reg 72(1)(a) and sub-
paras 39(2) and Sch 9
(3) IS Regs
29 Reg 72(1)(a) IS Regs
30 Reg 72(1)(a) and
Sch 9 paras 5, 52 and
57 IS Regs
31 Reg 48(1), (2), (3)
and (9) IS Regs

32 Reg 72(1)(c) IS Regs
33 Reg 72(1)(b) IS Regs
34 Reg 72(2) IS Regs
35 Also taken into
account are family
income supplement
and supplementary
benefit (which were
abolished in April
1988) and mobility
allowance (which was
replaced by DLA in
April 1992)
36 Reg 72(2) and Sch 10
paras 47 and 57 IS
Regs
37 Sutton SSAT,
represented by J Parr,
Refugee Council
38 Sch 10 Para 7(b) IS
Regs
39 Reg 4ZA(1) and Sch
1B para 21 IS Regs
40 Reg 85(4) JSA Regs
41 Reg 147(3) JSA Regs
42 Reg 147 JSA Regs
43 Regs 148 and 149
and Sch 5 para 14
JSA Regs
44 Reg 7A(5)(g) HB
Regs; reg 4A(5)(g)
CTB Regs
45 HB/CTB Circular
A1/96 para 4
46 You are treated as
having no liability to
pay rent: reg 7A HB
Regs. This is within
the Secretary of
State's powers:
Sarwar v *Secretary of
State for Social
Security* CA, 24
October 1996
47 Reg 7A(4)(c) HB
Regs; reg 4A(4)(c)
CTB Regs
48 Reg 7A(4)(b) HB
Regs; reg 4A(4)(b)
CTB Regs
49 Reg 7A(4)(e)(v) and
(vi) HB Regs; reg
4A(4)(e)(v) and (vi)
CTB Regs

**Chapter 11: British
citizens and others
with the right of abode**
(pp130-151)

1 s124(1) SSCBA 1992
2 s137(2)(b) SSCBA
1992; reg 4 IS Regs
3 Reg 21(3) IS Regs
'person from abroad':
habitual residence
4 Reg 21(3) IS Regs
'person from abroad':
habitual residence
5 None of the urgent
cases provisions
apply to people with
an undisputed right
of abode: reg 70(3) IS
Regs
6 *Sarwar* v *Secretary of
State for Social
Security*, CA, 24
October 1996
7 Reg 21(3F) IS Regs as
amended by reg 4
IRB(Montserrat)
Regs. This only
applies from 28
August 1996. Before
that date, extra-
statutory payments
were made to persons
from abroad from
Montserrat: *Income
Support Bulletins*
63/96 and 82/96
8 Reg 21(3)(e) and (f)
IS Regs 'person from
abroad'
9 Reg 21(3)(g) IS Regs
'person from abroad'
10 Reg 21(3F) IS Regs
See also note 7 above
11 Reg 85(4) JSA Regs
12 Reg 7A(5)(d) and (e)
HB Regs and reg 2
IRB(Montserrat)
Regs; reg 4A(5)(d)
and (e) CTB Regs
13 HB/CTB Circular
A1/96 para 4
14 Reg 7A HB Regs; reg
4A CTB Regs
15 s130(1)(a) SSCBA

1992; reg 5 HB Regs
16 s131(3)(a) SSCBA
    1992
17 Reg 7A(5)(f) HB
    Regs; reg 4A(5)(f)
    CTB Regs. This only
    applies from 28
    August 1996. Before
    that date, extra-
    statutory payments
    may have been made
    – see note 7 above
18 Reg 7A HB Regs; reg
    4A CTB Regs
19 s146A SSCBA 1992
    as inserted by
    s10(1)(a) AIA 1996;
    s13(2) AIA 1996
    'person subject to
    immigration control'.
    In force from 7
    October 1996: AIA
    (Comm 2)O
20 s146(2) and (3)
    SSCBA 1992
21 Reg 2 and Sch 1
    SS(NIRA) Regs
22 Reg 4(2) CB(RPA)
    Regs
23 Regs 4(3) and 1(3)
    CB(RPA) Regs;
    s147(1) SSCBA 1992
    'week'
24 Reg 4(2A) CB(RPA)
    Regs
25 Reg 2(2) CB(RPA)
    Regs
26 Reg 2(2)(c)(ii)
    CB(RPA) Regs
27 Reg 2(2)(c)(iii)
    CB(RPA) Regs
28 Reg 2(3) CB(RPA)
    Regs
29 Reg 5(4) CB(RPA)
    Regs
30 Reg 3(4) CB(RPA)
    Regs
31 Reg 5(2)(b) CB(RPA)
    Regs
32 Reg 5(2)(d)(i)
    CB(RPA) Regs
33 Reg 5(2)(d)(ii)
    CB(RPA) Regs
34 Reg 5(2)(c) CB(RPA)
    Regs

35 Reg 5(2)(a) CB(RPA)
    Regs
36 Reg 3(2)(a) CB(RPA)
    Regs
37 Reg 3(2)(c) and (3)
    CB(RPA) Regs
38 Reg 3(2)(b) CB(RPA)
    Regs
39 Regs 6(1) and 7(1)
    CB(RPA) Regs
40 Reg 6(2) CB(RPA)
    Regs
41 Reg 7(2) CB(RPA)
    Regs
42 Reg 7(3) CB(RPA)
    Regs
43 s144(2) and Sch 9
    para 4 SSCBA 1992;
    reg 9(1) CB Regs
44 s77 SSCBA 1992
45 Reg 2 and Sch1
    SS(NIRA)Regs
46 Reg 3(2)(b) CB(RPA)
    Regs
47 Reg 6(1) SS(GA)
    Regs. The normal
    rule that benefits are
    not payable to a
    person absent from
    the UK (s113(1)
    SSCBA 1992) does
    not apply: reg 4(1)
    SSB(PA) Regs
48 Reg 6(2) SS(GA) Regs
49 s120 SSCBA 1992;
    reg 76 SS(Con) Regs
50 Regs 81 and 86
    SS(Con) Regs
51 Reg 5(3)(f) SSB(PA)
    Regs. See also s113(1)
    SSCBA 1992; reg 4(1)
    SSB(PA) Regs
52 s77(2)(c) and (8)(b)
    SSCBA 1992; reg 5
    SS(GA) Regs
53 Reg 5 SS(GA) Regs
54 *s77(8)(a) SSCBA
    1992; reg 2 SS(GA)
    Regs. The reference in
    reg 2 to s4(3)
    Adoption Act 1968 is
    (because of s17(2)(a)
    IntA 1978), a
    reference to
    ss38(1)(d) and (e) and*

*72(1) and (2)
Adoption Act 1976.*
The Adoption
(Scotland) Act 1978
uses the same
definition as under
English law:
ss38(1)(d) and 65(1)
and (2)
55 Except where the
    adoptive parents were
    entitled to guardian's
    allowance
    immediately before
    adoption: s77(11)
    SSCBA 1992
56 **FC** ss128(1) and
    137(2)(a) SSCBA
    1992;
    DWA ss129(1) and
    137(2)(a) SSCBA
    1992
57 Reg 3(1) FC Regs; reg
    5(1) DWA Regs.
    CFC/16/1991 decided
    that proving actual
    presence in the UK is
    not enough to qualify
    as 'present' for FC
    purposes but that
    these conditions must
    also be satisfied
58 Reg 3(2) FC Regs; reg
    5(2) DWA Regs
59 **FC** s128(1) SSCBA
    1992; reg 3(1)(aa) FC
    Regs;
    DWA s129(1) SSCBA
    1992; reg 5(1)(aa)
    DWA Regs
60 Para 6(b)
    Immigration Rules
    'public funds'
61 Reg 4(2) SS(C&P)
    Regs
62 s129(1) SSCBA 1992
63 Reg 4(3A) SS(C&P)
    Regs
64 Reg 4 FC Regs; reg 6
    DWA Regs
65 s128(1)(d) SSCBA
    1992
66 Reg 46(1)(b) and Sch
    4 paras 2 and 3 FC
    Regs

67 **FC** s128(3) SSCBA
1992;
DWA s129(6) SSCBA
1992
68 **FC** s128(1) SSCBA
1992;
DWA s129(1) SSCBA
1992
69 Regs 49-51A FC
Regs; regs 54-56A
DWA Regs
70 **FC** Regs 16(1A) and
19(1) and Sch 4 para
7(a) and (aa)
SS(C&P) Regs;
DWA Regs 16(4A)
and 19(1) and Sch 4
para 11(a) and (b)
SS(C&P) Regs
71 CFC/25/93; para
43009 AOG
72 s113(1) SSCBA 1992;
s1(2)(i) JSA 1995
73 Regs 2 and 11
SSB(PA) Regs
74 SS(MB) Regs
75 Reg 2 and Sch 1
SS(NIRA) Regs
76 para 6 Immigration
Rules 'public funds'
77 The disqualification
under s113(1) SSCBA
1992 only applies on
a day of absence from
GB
78 Reg 6 SSB(PA) Regs
79 Reg 2 and Sch 1
SS(NIRA) Regs
80 Regs 4(3) and (4) and
5(3)(c) and (d) and
(6) SSB(PA) Regs
81 Regs 4(4) and 5(3)(c)
SSB(PA) Regs
82 Reg 5(8) and Sch
SSB(PA) Regs
83 Reg 5(3)(a) and (aa),
(5)(i) and (6)(i)
SSB(PA) Regs. These
only disqualify where
the husband/former
partner is not
ordinarily resident in
GB
84 Reg 5(7) SSB(PA)
Regs

85 s78 SSCBA 1992;
regs 9, 11 and 12
SS(WB&RP) Regs;
regs 4 and 5(3)(c)
SSB(PA) Regs
86 Reg 10 SS(WB&RP)
Regs
87 Reg 8(1) SSB(PA)
Regs
88 Reg 4(2A) SSB(PA)
Regs
89 s172(a) SSCBA 1992
90 s94(5) SSCBA 1992
91 s109(1) SSCBA 1992;
reg 14 SS(IIPD) Regs
92 ss109(2)(a), 117, 119
and 120 SSCBA 1992
93 Reg 2(1) SS(IIMB)
Regs; reg 2(1)
SS(IIAB) Regs. For
'mariner' and
'airman' see regs 4-7
and Sch 2 SS(EEEIIP)
Regs
94 Reg 2(2) SS(IIMB)
Regs
95 Reg 2(2) SS(IIAB)
Regs
96 Regs 3, 4, 6 and 8
SS(IIMB) Regs; regs 3
and 6 SS(IIAB) Regs
97 Reg 10C(5) and (6)
SSB(PA) Regs
98 Regs 10C(1) and
11(1) SSB(PA) Regs
'prescribed area',
'prescribed
employment' and
'designated area'
99 Reg 10C(2) SSB(PA)
Regs
100 Reg 10C(2) SSB(PA)
Regs
101 Reg 10C(2A)
SSB(PA) Regs
102 Reg 10C(3) and (4)
SSB(PA) Regs;
SS(Adj) Regs
103 Reg 10C(2) SSB(PA)
Regs
104 Reg 3 and Sch 1 Pt II
paras 3 and 4
SS(EEEIIP) Regs
105 Reg 9(3) and (7)
SSB(PA) Regs

106 s113(1) SSCBA 1992;
reg 9(4) and (5)
SSB(PA) Regs
107 Reg 5(b) SS(IIMB)
Regs; reg 4(b)
SS(IIAB) Regs. For
'mariner' and
'airman' see regs 4-7
and Sch 2 SS(EEEIIP)
Regs
108 Reg 17 SS(Adj) Regs
1995
109 Reg 2 and Sch 1
SS(NIRA) Regs
110 Reg 2 and Sch 1
SS(NIRA) Regs
111 Reg 2(1)(b) SS(AA)
Regs; reg 2(1)(b)
SS(DLA) Regs
112 Reg 2(2) SS(AA)
Regs; reg 2(2)
SS(DLA) Regs
113 Regs 81 and 86
SS(Con) Regs
114 s120 SSCBA 1992;
reg 76 SS(Con) Regs
115 Reg 2(3) SS(AA)
Regs; reg 2(4)
SS(DLA) Regs
116 Reg 2(5) SS(DLA)
Regs
117 R(A) 1/94
118 Reg 2(6) SS(DLA)
Regs
119 Reg 2(1)(b) SS(AA)
Regs; reg 2(1)(b)
SS(DLA) Regs
120 Reg 9 SS(ICA) Regs
121 Para 6 'public funds'
para (b) Immigration
Rules
122 Reg 3 SS(SDA) Regs
123 Reg 3(3) SS(SDA)
Regs provides for
exemption from reg
3(1), which includes
the presence rules, as
long as the period of
incapacity continues,
but s113(1) SSCBA
1992 prevents
payment of SDA
abroad unless the
temporary absence
conditions in reg 2

SSB(PA) Regs are met
124 Para 6 'public funds'
para (b) Immigration
Rules
125 Reg 20(1A) SS(SDA)
Regs
126 *Clarke* [1987] ECR
2865
127 Because reg 20(1A)
SS(SDA) Regs ('if she
satisfies the other
requirements for
entitlement') does not
apparently cover a
woman who does not
now meet the
residence
requirements for
SDA, this would
mean arguing that
'has been entitled' in
reg 3(3) SS(SDA)
Regs includes a
woman who would
have been entitled to
non-contributory
invalidity pension
(NCIP) but for the
discriminatory
'normal household
duties' rule found
unlawful by the ECJ
in *Clarke* and does
not require the actual
entitlement to NCIP
given by reg 20(1A).
This may involve
arguing that the
discriminatory effect
of the current rules is
unlawful because a
single woman would
have been entitled to
NCIP in 1984 and
would therefore now
be treated more
favourably.
128 **SSP** ss151(1) and
163(1) SSCBA 1992
'employee' see reg
16(1) SSP Regs; reg
5A SSP(MAPA) Regs;
SMP ss164(1) and
171(1) SSCBA 1992
'employee' see reg

17(1) SMP Regs; reg
2A SSP(PAM) Regs
129 Reg 5 SSP(MAPA)
Regs; reg 2
SMP(PAM) Regs
130 Regs 4 and 8
SSP(MAPA) Regs; reg
8 SMP(PAM) Regs;
s120 SSCBA 1992;
reg 76 SS(Con) Regs
131 Reg 6 SSP(MAPA)
Regs; reg 7
SMP(PAM) Regs; reg
81 SS(Con) Regs
132 Reg 7 SSP(MAPA)
Regs; reg 86 SS(Con)
Regs
133 Regs 6 and 7
SSP(MAPA) Regs; reg
7 SMP(PAM) Regs
134 Reg 5 SMP(PAM)
Regs
135 Reg 5A SSP(MAPA)
Regs; reg 2A
SMP(PAM) Regs.
These rules changed
on 6 April 1996 (SSP)
and 18 August 1996
(SMP). Before that,
entitlement normally
ended when you were
absent from the EU:
reg 10(1) SSP(MAPA)
Regs; reg 9(1)
SSP(PAM) Regs
before amendment
136 Reg 16(2) SSP Regs;
reg 17(3) SMP Regs
137 Reg 119(1)(b)
SS(Con) Regs
138 Reg 14 SSP(MAPA)
Regs; reg 6
SMP(PAM) Regs
139 s138(1)(a) and (2)
SSCBA 1992
140 Reg 5(1)(a) SFM&FE
Regs
141 Reg 7(1)(a) SFM&FE
Regs. See CPAG's
*National Welfare
Benefits Handbook*
for possible limits on
CTB route
142 Reg 7(1)(c) SFM&FE
Regs

143 *R v Secretary of State
for Social Security ex
parte Nessa, Times,*
15 November 1994
144 Case C-237/94
O'Flynn, 23 May
1996 [1996] All ER
(EC) S41
145 *Yahya,* Hounslow
SSAT, 21 March
1997, 7/11/96/17708
146 Reg 7(8) SFM&FE
Regs as amended by
reg 5 Social Fund and
Claims and Payments
(Miscellaneous
Amendments) Regs
1997 S1 No. 792
147 Reg 1A SFCWP Regs
148 SS(C&P) Regs still
apply to cold weather
payments (regs 4 and
2(2)(b)), but the
particular rules and
time limit have been
revoked (reg 15A and
para 9A Sch 4)
149 SF Dirs 12(a),
23(1)(a) and 29
150 SF Dir 25(a)
151 SF Dir 4(a)(i) and
25(b)
152 *R v SFI, ex parte
Amina Mohammed,
Times,* 25 November
1992
153 SF Dir 8(1)(a)
154 SF Dirs 3(a) and
16(b)
155 SF Dir 22
156 SF Dir 18
157 SF Dir 16(b)

**Chapter 12: Indefinite
leave to remain**
(pp152-162)

1 s33(2A) IA 1971
2 s124(1) SSCBA 1992
3 s137(2)(b) SSCBA
1992; reg 4 IS Regs
4 Reg 21(3F) IS Regs as
amended by reg 4
IRB(Montserrat)
Regs. This only

applies from 28 August 1996. Before that date, extra-statutory payments were made to persons from abroad from Montserrat: Income Support Bulletins 63/96 and 82/96

5 Reg 21(3) IS Regs 'person from abroad' para (i). This only applies from 5 February 1996: reg 8(2) SS(PFA)MA Regs. Before that date there were no special rules for sponsored immigrants

6 Reg 21(3) IS Regs 'person from abroad' para (i)

7 para 35 Immigration Rules

8 Reg 21(3) IS Regs 'person from abroad' para (i)

9 s4(1) IA 1971

10 s7(1) IA 1988

11 para 18 Immigration Rules

12 Reg 21(3) IS Regs 'person from abroad' para (i)

13 Vol 13 para 22662 AOG; para 22.3 Memo AOG Vol 3/85

14 Reg 12(2) SS(PFA)MA Regs

15 Vol 3 para 22663 AOG; para 23 Memo AOG Vol 3/85

16 For examples see pp365, 368, 371 and 373 CPAG's *Income-Related Benefits: The Legislation, Mesher and Wood*, 1995/96 edn

17 See examples in note above

18 Reg 70(3)(c) IS Regs

19 Supplementary benefit before 1988

20 s106 SSAA 1992

21 s105 SSAA 1992

22 p165 JCWI *Handbook*, 1995 edn

23 ss78(6)(c) and 105(3) SSAA 1992

24 Reg 21(3) IS Regs 'person from abroad': habitual residence

25 Reg 21(3) IS Regs 'person from abroad': habitual residence

26 None of the other urgent cases provisions apply to people with indefinite leave to remain: reg 70(3) IS Regs

27 *Sarwar* v *Secretary of State for Social Security*, CA, 24 October 1996

28 Reg 21(3F) IS Regs as amended by reg 4 IRB(Montserrat) Regs, see note 4

29 Reg 21(3) IS Regs 'person from abroad': habitual residence para (b)

30 Reg 21(3) IS Regs 'person from abroad': habitual residence para (c)

31 Reg 85(4) JSA Regs

32 Reg 147(3) JSA Regs

33 None of the provisions of JSA (Transitional Provisions) Regs 1996 apply

34 The income-based JSA urgent cases provision does not apply: reg 147(3) JSA Regs

35 ss78(6)(c) and 105 SSAA 1992 as amended by s41(4) and Sch 2 paras 51 and 53 JSA 1995. s106 SSAA 1992 which gives the power to recover income support from a sponsor, was not

amended to cover income-based JSA. NB This does *not* mean the benefit can be recovered from the claimant instead

36 Reg 7A(5)(d) and (e) HB Regs; reg 4A(5)(d) and (e) CTB Regs

37 HB/CTB Circular A1/96 para 4

38 s130(1)(a) SSCBA 1992; reg 5 HB Regs

39 s131(3)(a) SSCBA 1992

40 Reg 7A HB Regs; reg 4A CTB Regs

41 Reg 7A(5)(f) HB Regs; reg 4A(5)(f) CTB Regs; both as amended by IRB (Montserrat) Regs. This only applies from 28 August 1996. Before that date, extra-statutory payments may have been made – see note 4

42 Reg 7A(5)(c) HB Regs; reg 4A(5)(c) CTB Regs

43 Reg 14B(1) CB Regs as amended by reg 2 CB(Amdt) Regs and CB(Amdt 2) Regs

44 Reg 3(1)(aa) FC Regs; reg 5(1)(aa) DWA Regs. Limitations and conditions can only be attached to limited leave to remain: s3(3) IA 1971

45 para 6 'public funds' para (c) Immigration Rules

46 Reg 2(1)(a)(ia) ss(DLA) Regs; reg 2(1)(a)(ia) ss(AA) Regs; reg 9(1)(aa) ss(ICA) Regs; reg 3(1)(a)(ia) (SDA) Regs. Limitations and conditions can only

be attached to limited leave to remain: s3(3) IA 1971

47 para 6 'public funds' para (b) Immigration Rules

48 s78(3)(c) and (6)(c) SSAA 1992

49 para 4054 *Social Fund Decision and Review Guide* – publicly available

Chapter 13: Refugees
(pp163-173)

1 Art 1A(2) Geneva Convention. Similar rules apply to refugees who are stateless: art 1A(2)

2 CIS/564/94 paras 19-24 and 39; *Khaboka v SSHD* [1993] Imm AR 484

3 s124(1) SSCBA 1992

4 s137(2)(b) SSCBA 1992; reg 4 IS Regs

5 Regs 21(3) IS Regs 'person from abroad': habitual residence para (b) and 21ZA(1)

6 Reg 21(3) IS Regs 'person from abroad': habitual residence para (b)

7 Reg 21ZA(2) IS Regs; reg 21ZA(3) IS Regs

8 Reg 6(4D) SS(C&P) Regs

9 s124(1)(f) SSCBA 1992

10 Arts 2(1) and 3(1) EEC Reg 1408/71

11 CIS/564/94

12 The claimants in this case had been recognised as refugees. The Benefits Agency had never challenged their argument that their factual situation had been the same from the date of asylum

claim until recognition. The commissioner decided (paras 20-24 and 39) that a person can be a refugee before being recognised as such. However, if you have not been recognised as a refugee, in the context of this difficult EC argument, it would be very difficult to persuade a tribunal or commissioner to make a decision that you are a refugee. If you do want to argue this, before you do so you should take advice from an adviser who specialises in immigration and social security law

13 The commissioner decided at para 42 that art 3(1) EEC Reg 1408/71 limits equal treatment rights to refugees who are 'employed or self-employed persons' under EC law

14 These comments assume that Art 3 EEC Reg 1408/71 applies to refugees who have not moved between member states. The commissioner did not hear full legal argument about this and leaves this issue open: paras 36-37

15 The commissioner followed CIS/863/94 and decided (paras 32-24) that IS is not a social security benefit under Art 4(1) EEC Reg 1408/71. He

rejected the claimants' argument (which he does not record) that Case 249/83 *Hoeckx* [1985] ECR 973 was no longer good law in light of Case C-78/91 *Hughes* [1992] 4839 in which the ECJ decided that family credit was a social security benefit even though that benefit is entirely means-tested. Arts 4(2a) and 10a(1) and Annex IIa.O(e) added to EEC Reg 1408/71 on 1 June 1992 by EEC Reg 1247/92 mean that IS is covered by the equal treatment rule *from that date*. The commissioner mistakenly thinks (at para 34) that this is because of the UK's declaration under Art 5 EEC Reg 1408/71, but IS is not included in the declaration

16 The equal treatment rule only applies to a refugee habitually residing in the EU/EEA: Arts 1(h) and 3 EEC Reg 1408/71

17 It may be more if your urgent cases IS was reduced because of income or capital

18 Reg 88 SS(Adj) Regs

19 November 1996

20 Reg 85(4) JSA Regs

21 JSA is only payable from 7 October 1996. For any period before that you should seek IS

22 Reg 7A(5)(d) and (e) HB Regs; reg 4A(5)(d) and (e) CTB Regs

23 HB/CTB Circular A1/96 para 4
24 Reg 7A(5)(e)(ii) HB Regs; reg 4A(5)(e)(ii) CTB Regs
25 Reg 7B, Sch A1 and reg 7A(7) HB Regs 'refugee'; reg 4D, Sch A1 and reg 4A(7) CTB Regs
26 Reg 14B(a) CB Regs as amended by reg 2(a) CB(Amdt) Regs
27 Reg 5(1A)(a) DWA Regs; reg 3(1A)(a) FC Regs
28 Arts 2(1) and 3(1) EEC Reg 1408/71 prohibit discrimination against refugees residing in a member state. A commissioner has decided in relation to IS that this can apply for the period before recognition: CIS/564/94
29 The equal treatment rule only applies to a refugee habitually residing in the EU/EEA: Arts 1(h) and 3 EEC Reg 1408/71
30 s1 SSAA 1992; reg 19(2) and (4) SS(C&P) Regs
31 Case C-208/90 *Emmott* [1991] ECR I 4269; [1993] ICR 8; [1991] CMLR 894; [1991] IRLR 387, where the ECJ decided that a time limit which prevented payment of any benefit was contrary to EC law. In C-410/92 *Johnson* 6 December 1994, [1995] ICR 375 the ECJ decided that the old 12-month rule was not unlawful

because, in that case, it did not prevent payment for the whole period. It is not clear if the new rules which replaced 'good cause' comply with EC law in cases where the domestic benefit rules breach EC law
32 November 1996
33 Reg 2(1A)(a) ss(DLA) Regs; reg 2(1A)(a) ss(AA) Regs; reg 9(1A)(a) ss(ICA) Regs; reg 3(1B)(a) ss(SDA) Regs
34 Arts 2(1) and 3(1) EEC Reg 1408/71 prohibit discrimination against refugees residing in a member state. A commissioner has decided in relation to IS that this can apply for the period before recognition: CIS/564/94
35 AA, DLA, SDA and ICA are all covered by Art 4 EEC Reg 1408/71: see pp314-315
36 Reg 17 SS(C&P) Regs
37 para 30 Memo AOG Vol 2/40
38 s30(2)(b) SSAA 1992
39 Reg 3(3) ss(SDA) Regs
40 Reg 2(1A)(a) ss(DLA) Regs; reg 2(1A)(a) ss(AA) Regs; reg 9(1A)(a) ss(ICA) Regs; reg 3(1B)(a) ss(SDA) Regs. These all refer only to a person 'recorded by the Secretary of State as a refugee' *not* 'who has leave as a refugee'

Chapter 14: Exceptional leave to remain
(pp174-179)

1 This is because EC law does not recognise people with UK ELR as a special group
2 Any other approach would lead to absurd results. This has been accepted by a London SSAT
3 AOG Vol 13 para 20714
4 s124(1) SSCBA 1992
5 s137(2)(b) SSCBA 1992; reg 4 IS Regs
6 Reg 21(3) IS Regs 'person from abroad': habitual residence para (c). None of the parts of the 'person from abroad' definition apply to a person with limited leave without 'no recourse to public funds'
7 Reg 21(3) IS Regs 'person from abroad' (a)
8 Reg 85(4) JSA Regs
9 s130(1)(a) SSCBA 1992; reg 5 HB Regs
10 s131(3)(a) SSCBA 1992
11 Reg 7A(5)(d) and (e) HB Regs; reg 4A(5)(d) and (e) CTB Regs
12 HB/CTB Circular A1/96 para 4
13 Reg 7A(4)(e)(iii) HB Regs; reg 4A(4)(e)(iii) CTB Regs
14 Reg 4A(2) HB Regs; reg 5A(2) CTB Regs
15 Reg 14B(b) CB Regs (as amended by reg 2 CB(Amdt) Regs) is not clear, but does not draw any

distinction between
leave to enter and
leave to remain: AOG
Vol 3 para 20714

16 Reg 5(1A)(b) DWA
Regs; reg 3(1A)(b) FC
Regs

17 JSA Regs: the amount
of contribution-based
JSA is set by reg 79
and not reg 83 which
refers to the persons
from abroad rules in
reg 85(4)

18 Reg 2(1A)(b) ss(DLA)
Regs; reg 2(1A)(b)
ss(AA) Regs; reg
9(1A)(b) ss(ICA)
Regs; reg 3(1B)(b)
ss(SDA) Regs

19 Reg 17 SS(C&P) Regs

20 Memo AOG Vol 2/40
para 3

21 Reg 3(3) ss(SDA)
Regs

Chapter 15: Limited leave to remain
(pp180-201)

1 *Shaukat Ali* v *Chief
Adjudication Officer*,
Times, 24 December
1985; *Rajendran* v
SSHD [1989] Imm
AR 512

2 s7 IA 1988

3 Therefore, the part of
reg 21(3) IS Regs
'person from abroad'
para (a) dealing with
EEA nationals with
limited leave to
remain is a dead
letter. The EEA is not
mentioned, but para
(a) covers the EC and
signatories to the
European Social
Charter which
includes two of the
remaining EEA
countries, Iceland and
Norway.
Liechtenstein is the

only EEA country left
out

4 s3(4) IA 1971

5 ss1(3), 3(4) and 11(4)
IA 1971

6 Reg 4ZA and Sch 1B
para 21 to IS Regs

7 Reg 21(3F) IS Regs as
amended by reg 4
IRB(Montserrat)
Regs. This only
applies from 28
August 1996. Before
that date, extra-
statutory payments
were made to persons
from abroad from
Montserrat: Income
Support Bulletins
63/96 and 82/96

8 Reg 21(3) IS Regs
'person from abroad'
para (a) 'has a limited
leave... during that
limited leave'

9 s24(1)(b)(ii) IA 1971

10 Reg 21(3) IS Regs
'person from abroad'
para (a) 'but this sub-
para...1961'. This
refers to signatory
states to the
European
Convention on Social
and Medical
Assistance and
European Social
Charter. The
Convention countries
are the EU/EEA
states, Malta and
Turkey. Cyprus is a
signatory to the
Charter

11 North Cyprus is now
the 'Turkish Republic
of Northern Cyprus',
which is only
recognised as a
country by Turkey.
The Republic of
Cyprus recognises
those born in North
Cyprus before the
1974 Turkish army

invasion as nationals
of Cyprus. The
nationality of people
born after 1974 in
North Cyprus is
unclear, though some
may have another
nationality – eg,
Turkish

12 Reg 21(3) IS Regs
'person from abroad'
para (a) "unless...
1971 Act". Malta
and Turkey are
signatories to the
European
Convention on Social
and Medical
Assistance and not
the European Social
Charter

13 Reg 21(3) IS Regs
'person from abroad'
para (a). This refers
to an application 'for
the conditions of his
leave to remain in the
UK to be varied'

14 s3(3) IA 1971

15 Reg 21(3) IS Regs
'person from abroad':
habitual residence

16 Reg 21(3) IS Regs
'person from abroad':
habitual residence

17 Reg 21(3) IS Regs
'person from abroad':
habitual residence

18 *Sarwar* v *Secretary of
State for Social
Security*, CA, 24
October 1996

19 Reg 21(3F) IS Regs as
amended by reg 4
IRB(Montserrat)
Regs. See note 7

20 Reg 70(3) IS Regs

21 Reg 70(3)(a) IS Regs

22 Reg 71(2)(a) IS Regs

23 We consider the rules
work like this because
reg 71(2) refers to
'any one period of
limited leave...
(including any period

as extended)'. We consider that 'extended' refers to VOLO leave and not to further leave, because VOLO uses the word 'extension' while s3(3)(a) IA 1971 (which deals with further leave) uses the word 'enlargement'

24 Letter from Home Office Minister David Waddington to Max Madden MP in December 1985

25 para 6 'public funds' para (c) Immigration Rules

26 s24(1)(b)(ii) IA 1971

27 para 6 'public funds' para (c) Immigration Rules

28 Reg 85(4) 'person from abroad' JSA Regs

29 ss1(2)(a) and 6(1) JSA 1995

30 s4(1) IA 1971

31 Sch 2 para 6 to IA 1971. This only applies to people whose examination began on or after 10 July 1988. A person whose examination began before that has indefinite leave. For details see Macdonald pp66-69

32 s9(4)-(6) IA 1971; I(CERI)O. For details see Macdonald pp158-9

33 Regs 14(1), 19(1) and 34 JSA Regs

34 s1(2) JSA 1995

35 Reg 141(4) JSA Regs

36 Reg 140(1) JSA Regs

37 Reg 140(1) JSA Regs

38 Reg 145(1) JSA Regs

39 para 6 meaning of 'public funds' para (c) Immigration Rules

40 Reg 7A(5)(d) and (e) HB Regs; reg 4A(5)(d) and (e) CTB Regs

41 HB/CTB Circular A1/96 para 4

42 s130(1)(a) SSCBA 1992; reg 5 HB Regs

43 s131(3)(a) SSCBA 1992

44 Reg 7A HB Regs

45 Reg 7A(2) HB Regs; reg 4A(2) CTB Regs

46 Reg 7A(3) HB Regs; reg 4A(3) CTB Regs. Sub-paras (a) of these paras refer to signatory states to the European Convention on Social and Medical Assistance and European Social Charter. The Convention countries are the EU/EEA states, Malta and Turkey. Cyprus is a signatory to the Charter

47 See note 11

48 Reg 7A(3)(a) HB Regs; reg 4A(3)(a) CTB Regs. These are differently worded from the equivalent in reg 21(3) 'person from abroad' para (a) IS Regs. The IS rule about nationals of Malta or Turkey with VOLO leave does not apply to HB/CTB

49 Reg 7A(4)(f) HB Regs; reg 4A(4)(f) CTB Regs

50 Reg 7A(5)(c) HB Regs; reg 4A(5)(c) CTB Regs

51 Reg 7A(4)(e) HB Regs; reg 4A(4)(e) CTB Regs

52 Reg 7A(5)(f) HB Regs; reg 4A(5)(f) CTB Regs; both

amended by IRB(Montserrat) Regs. This only applies from 28 August 1996. Before that date, extra-statutory payments may have been made – see note 7

53 para 6 'public funds' para (b) immigration rules

54 s146A SSCBA 1992 as inserted by s10(1)(a) AIA 1996; s13(2) AIA 1996 'person subject to immigration control'. This applies only from 7 October 1996: Art 2 and Sch Pt II AIA (Comm 2)O

55 Reg 14B CB Regs as amended by reg 2 CB (Amdt) Regs

56 Reg 14B(d)(i) CB Regs as amended by reg 2 CB (Amdt) Regs. This exemption is included because of the UK's obligations under EC agreements with these countries: see p379

57 Reg 3 CB (Amdt) Regs 1996

58 s25 SSAA 1992

59 s25 SSAA 1992

60 Reg 3 CB(Amdt) Regs 1996

61 Reg 32 SS(C&P) Regs

62 s112 SSAA 1992

63 Reg 3 CB (Amdt) Regs 1996

64 s77(1)(a) SSCBA 1992

65 Reg 5(1)(aa) DWA Regs; reg 3(1)(aa) FC Regs. This applies only from 5 February 1996: regs 5 and 6 ss(PFA)MA Regs

66 para 6 'public funds' para (c) Immigration Rules

67 Reg 3(1A) FC Regs; reg 5(1A) DWA Regs

68 Reg 3(1A)(d)(i) FC Regs; reg 5(1A)(a)(i) DWA Regs. This exemption is included because of the UK's obligations under EC agreements with these countries: see p379

69 This is because you may be entitled under EC law to social security benefits linked to employment on the same basis as UK nationals: para 2 Annex VI Council & Commission Decision 91/400/ECSC, EEC: OJ No L 229, 17.8.91, p249

70 Reg 12(3) SS(PFA)MA Regs 1996. This refers to ss25 and 30 SSAA 1992, but only s25 applies to FC

71 Reg 12(3) SS(PFA)MA Regs 1996. This refers to ss25 and 30 SSAA 1992, but only s25 applies to DWA

72 Reg 12(3) SS(PFA)MA Regs 1996 only gives protection for each benefit you are paid before 5 February 1996, not all the benefits it refers to

73 paras 29 and 32 Memo AOG Vol 12/40

74 For examples see pp365, 368, 371 and 373 *Mesher & Wood*, 1995 edn

75 See examples in note 74

76 Regs 49-51A FC Regs; regs 54-56A DWA Regs

77 eg *E*, Euston SSAT,

2/20/97/01730, 3 April 1997; *Martinez Sutton* SSAT, 7/07/91/15053/5 April 1997.

78 para 6 'public funds' para (c) Immigration Rules

79 Version 3.0 of forms FLR(M), FLR(S), FLR(O), SET(M), SET(F)

80 s24(i)(b)(ii) IA 1971. Any prosecution must be brought within six months of the last breach of conditions: s127 Magistrates Court Act 1980

81 Regs 79 and 82 JSA Regs

82 para 6 'public funds' para (c) Immigration Rules

83 para 6 'public funds' para (c) Immigration Rules

84 Reg 2(1)(a)(ia) SS(DLA Regs; reg 2(1)(a)(ia) SS(AA) Regs; reg 9(1)(aa) SS(ICA) Regs; reg 3(1)(a)(ia) SS(SDA) Regs. This applies only from 5 February 1996: regs 2, 4, 9 and 11 SS(PFA)(MA) Regs

85 para 6 'public funds' para (b) Immigration Rules

86 Reg 2(1A) SS(DLA) Regs; reg 2(1A) SS(AA) Regs; reg 9(1A) SS(ICA) Regs; reg 3(1B) SS(SDA) Regs

87 Reg 2(1A)(d)(i) SS(DLA) Regs; reg 2(1A)(d)(i) SS(AA) Regs; reg 9(1A)(d)(i) SS(ICA) Regs; reg 3(1B)(d)(i) SS(SDA) Regs. This exemption is included because of

the UK's obligations under EC agreements with these countries: see p379

88 Reg 12(3) SS(PFA)MA Regs 1992. This refers to ss25 and 30 SSAA. s25 applies only to ICA and SDA. s30 applies only to DLA/AA

89 paras 29 and 32 Memo AOG Vol 12/40

90 2/32/96/20964, 27 November 1996, by Shepherds Bush Advice Centre, cited in *Legal Action*, January 1997, p12 note 1

91 *R v Adjudication Officer ex parte O and K*, due to be heard 13 August 1997

92 para 6 'public funds' para (c) Immigration Rules

Chapter 16: No leave to remain
(pp202-218)

1 The benefit rules state that you must be 'adjudged by the immigration authorities to be an illegal entrant': reg 21(3) IS Regs 'person from abroad' para (d); reg 85(4) JSA Regs 'person from abroad' para (d); reg 7A(4)(c) HB Regs; reg 4A(4)(c) CTB Regs. The benefit rules define 'immigration authorities' as 'adjudicator, immigration officer, immigration appeal tribunal and

Secretary of State':
reg 2 IS Regs; reg 2(1)
HB Regs; reg 2(1)
CTB Regs; reg 85(4)
JSA Regs as amended
by reg 10(1)(b)
JSA(Amdt) Regs. In
fact only immigration
officers make illegal
entry decisions.
Adjudicators and the
immigration appeal
tribunal have no
power to decide that
a person is an illegal
entrant: *Khawaja v
SSHD* [1984] AC 74;
[1983] 1 All ER 765

2 By quashing it

3 *Khawaja*. Any VOLO
leave also ends

4 Reg 21(3) IS Regs
'person from abroad'
para (e)

5 Reg 21(3) IS Regs
'person from abroad'
para (b)

6 Reg 21(3) IS Regs
'person from abroad'
para (c)

7 Reg 21(3) IS Regs
'person from abroad'
para (d)

8 Reg 21(3F) IS Regs as
amended by reg 4
IRB(Montserrat)
Regs. This only
applies from 28
August 1996. Before
that date, extra-
statutory payments
were made to persons
from abroad from
Montserrat: Income
Support Bulletins
63/96 and 82/96

9 Reg 70(3) IS Regs

10 Reg 12(2)
SS(PFA)MA Regs

11 See comments on
similarly-worded FC
provision, p196

12 Reg 12(2)
SS(PFA)MA Regs
prevents reg 8(3)

SS(PFA)MA Regs
from having effect in
protected cases, and
so keeps the pre- 5
February 1996
version of reg 70(3) IS
Regs

13 Reg 70(3)(i) IS Regs
before amendment by
reg 8(3) SS(PFA)MA
Regs. This only
applies if your
applicable amount
would otherwise be
nil, but it *will* be nil
unless one of the
exceptions which
follows applies

14 Reg 70(3)(e) IS Regs
before amendment by
reg 8(3) SS(PFA)MA
Regs

15 Reg 70(3)(f) IS Regs
before amendment by
reg 8(3) SS(PFA)MA
Regs

16 Reg 70(3)(i) IS Regs
before amendment by
reg 8(3) SS(PFA)MA
Regs

17 Reg 70(3)(b) IS Regs
before amendment by
reg 8(3) SS(PFA)MA
Regs

18 Reg 70(3)(c) IS Regs
before amendment by
reg 8(3) SS(PFA)MA
Regs

19 Reg 70(3)(f) IS Regs
before amendment by
reg 8(3) SS(PFA)MA
Regs

20 Reg 70(3)(g) IS Regs
before amendment by
reg 8(3) SS(PFA)MA
Regs

21 Reg 4ZA and para 21
Sch 1B to IS Regs

22 Reg 21(3) IS Regs
'person from abroad'
para (e)

23 Reg 21(3) IS Regs
'person from abroad'
paras (e) and (j)

24 Unless you are also

on remand or serving
a sentence for a
criminal offence: reg
21(3) IS Regs
'prisoner' paras (e)
and (j)

25 Reg 21(3) IS Regs
'person from abroad'
para (d)

26 Reg 21(3) IS Regs
'person from abroad'
para (g). The Benefits
Agency is confused
about the meaning of
this rule. Vol 3 para
23166 AOG suggests
that the equivalent
JSA rule (reg 85(4)(g)
JSA Regs) applies to a
person seeking an
extension of leave for
the first time

27 Reg 21(3) IS Regs
'person from abroad'
para (a). Nor does it
fit with the Benefits
Agency guidance on
JSA: see previous note

28 R(SB) 11/88

29 CIS/564/94 and
CIS/7250/94 paras 23
and 39

30 Reg 85(4) JSA Regs
'person from abroad'

31 s8 AIA 1996

32 Reg 147(3) JSA Regs

33 Reg 7A(5)(d) and (e)
HB Regs; reg
4A(5)(d) and (e) CTB
Regs

34 HB/CTB Circular
A1/96 para 4

35 Reg 7A HB Regs; reg
4A CTB Regs

36 Reg 7A HB Reg; reg
4A CTB Regs

37 Reg 7A(4)(c) HB
Regs; reg 4A(4)(b)
CTB Regs

38 Reg 7A(4)(b) HB
Regs; reg 4A(4)(b)
CTB Regs

39 Reg 12(2) SS
(PFA)MA Regs

40 Reg 7A(4)(e) and (5)

HB Regs; reg 4A(4)(e) and (5) CTB Regs

41 Sch 2 para 21(1) IA 1971 (temporary admission); Sch 2 paras 24 and 33 IA 1971 (bail)

42 s24(1)(e) IA 1971. Any prosecution must be brought within six months of the last breach of conditions: s127 Magistrates Court Act 1980. It is not clear if breach of bail conditions is an offence

43 Sch 2 paras 23 and 33 IA 1971

44 Regs 79 and 82 JSA Regs

45 para 6 'public funds' para (c) Immigration Rules

Chapter 17: Asylum seekers
(pp219-238)

1 The main definitions are: s1 AIAA 1993 'claim for asylum'; para 327 HC 395; s25(1A) IA 1971 as amended by s5(2) AIA 1996

2 Reg 70(3A)(a) IS Regs before amendment by reg 8(3)(c) SS(PFA)MA Regs; reg 7A(5)(a) HB Regs before amendment by reg 7(b) SS(PFA)MA Regs; reg 4A(5)(a) CTB Regs before amendment by reg 3(b) SS(PFA)MA Regs

3 Reg 70(3A)(a) IS Regs; reg 7A(5)(a) HB Regs; reg 4A(5)(a) CTB Regs

4 *R* v *Secretary of State for Social Security ex*

parte JCWI, [1996] 4 All ER 385.

5 s11(1) and Sch 1 paras 1-6 AIA 1996

6 HEO(AO) 8/96 paras 10-25. Benefits Agency staff were also instructed (para 22) that the Court of Appeal's judgment was not a 'relevant judgment' so the anti-test case rule in s69 SSAA 1992 did not apply

7 Reg 70(3A)(a) IS Regs; reg 7A(5)(a) HB Regs; reg 4A(5)(a) CTB Regs

8 HB/CTB Circular A1/96 pp22-3

9 HEO(AO) 16/96. Several SSATs have allowed appeals in this situation: 2/20/96/21810, 8 November 1996, Chelsea CAB; both cited in *Legal Action*, January 1997, p12 note 2

10 A real case: Euston SSAT; 2/29/96/19748, 16 May 1997

11 s33(1) IA 197 'entrant'

12 Immigration officers are appointed by the Secretary of State: s4(2) and Sch 2 para 1(2) IA 1971, but they are not officers of the Secretary of State acting on his behalf in the same way as civil servants employed at, say, Lunar House

13 Reg 2(1) 'appropriate office' SS(C&P) Regs; reg 57(2)(b) SS(Adj) Regs

14 Constitutionally all Secretaries of State

can carry out each others' powers and duties, so a reference in a regulation to the Secretary of State is a reference to any Secretary of State: Sch1 IntA 1978

15 Para 328 HC 395

16 Though for practical reasons removal to France may not occur before the Dublin Convention is in force

17 Para 15 AOG Vol 3/85 example 4

18 s33(1) IA 1971 'entrant'

19 Because the rules use 'other than on re-entry' and not 'only on his first arrival' so distinguishing between (re)entry and arrival

20 Any leave whether limited or indefinite lapses on a person going outside the common travel area, even if the person does not land in that country: s3(4) IA 1971

21 s3(3)(b) IA 1971

22 Reg 70(3A)(aa)(i) IS Regs; reg 7A(5)(aa)(i) HB Regs; reg 4A(5)(aa)(i) CTB Regs

23 paras 346 HC 395; *Onibiyo* v *SSHD* [1996] Imm AR 370; *R* v *SSHD ex parte* Ravichandran (No.2) [1996] Imm AR 418

24 IS *Bulletin* 47/97

25 At the time of writing these policies only apply to Somalia and Liberia. In Somali cases the Home Office routinely claims that the person is a Kenyan national,

especially if s/he travelled on false Kenyan documents. In Liberian cases there is a questionnaire to test nationality through the asylum-seeker's knowledge of Liberia

26 Reg 12(1) SS(PFA)MA Regs

27 R v *Secretary of State for Social Security ex parte T*, 18 March 1997, *Current Law Digest* 619

28 Reg 70(3A)(a) IS Regs before amendment by reg 8(3)(c) SS(PFA)MA Regs; reg 7A(5)(a) HB Regs before amendment by reg 7(b) SS(PFA)MA Regs; reg 4A(5)(a) CTB Regs before amendment by reg 3(b) SS(PFA)MA Regs

29 Reg 70(3A)(a) IS Regs before amendment by reg 8(3)(c) SS(PFA)MA Regs; Reg 7A(5)(a) HB Regs before amendment by reg 7(b) SS(PFA)MA Regs; Reg 4A(5)(a) CTB Regs before amendment by reg 3(b) SS(PFA)MA Regs

30 Vol 6 para 36049 AOG; HB/CTB A1/96 para 18

31 This is only possible if the claim was made before the new time limits were introduced on 7 May 1997

32 For examples see pp386-93 and 395 *Mesher & Wood*, 1996 edn

33 See examples in note above

34 Reg 12(1) SS(PFA)MA Regs as amended by Sch 1 para 5 AIA 1996

35 HEO(AO) 16/96

36 See HEO(AO) 16/96

37 DSS guidance states that only family members who have not claimed asylum in their own right qualify: HEO(AO) 16/96. This seems to be wrong because, eg, it would treat separated partners differently depending upon whether each had claimed asylum in their own name

38 Despite what DSS guidance states: in HEO(AO) 16/96

39 People who claim asylum *after* certain negative immigration decisions may not be able to appeal against a negative decision of a special adjudicator: Sch 2 para 5 AIAA 1993 as amended by s1 AIA 1996

40 Reg 70(3A)(b) IS Regs before amendment by reg 8(3)(c) SS(PFA)MA Regs; reg 7A(5)(a) HB Regs before amendment by reg 7(b) SS(PFA)MA Regs; reg 4A(5)(a) CTB Regs before amendment by reg 3(b) SS(PFA)MA Regs

41 Reg 70(3A)(b) IS Regs; reg 7A(5A) HB Regs; reg 4A(5A) CTB Regs

42 Memo AOG Vol 3/85 para 10 which was revised by HEO(AO)

16/96 and then incorporated in Vol 6 paras 36069 and 36083 AOG; HEO(AO) Letter 8/96 para 13

43 R v *SSHD ex parte Karaoui and Abbad*. The commentary in the report of this case (*Times*, 27 March 1997) is misleading

44 Reg 70(3A)(b)(ii) IS Regs; reg 7A(5A)(b) HB Regs; reg 4A(5A)(b) CTB Regs

45 The appropriate office is the Home Office official who made the immigration decision being appealed: r.5(3) AA(P) Rules

46 Including an application by the Home Office

47 Under immigration law 'pending appeal' includes where a further appeal can be brought: s33(4) IA 1971

48 Including an application by the Home Office

49 Under immigration law 'pending appeal' includes where a further appeal can be brought: s33(4) IA 1971

50 Including an application by the Home Office

51 Including an appeal by the Home Office. The benefit rules do not expressly cover this situation, but we believe it is covered, either because the whole appeal process is covered or because 'pending appeal' has

the same meaning as in immigration law: s33(4) IA 1971

52 paras 2.1 and 2.3-5, Practice Directions and Standing Orders applicable to Civil Appeals, at p1649, Vol 2, The Supreme Court Practice 1997

53 DSS guidance overlooks this and assumes that all asylum appeals are under the 1993 Act. It seems likely that there will still be outstanding 1971 Act appeals at the end of 1997

54 rr.15 and 16 IA(P) Rules

55 vol 6 para 36069 AOG

56 The Home Office tries to appeal most asylum appeals allowed by adjudicators

57 R v *Secretary of State for Social Security ex parte JCWI*

58 s11(1) and Sch 1 paras 1-6 AIA 1996

59 Sch 1 para 6(1)(b) AIA 1996

60 Reg 6 SS(C&P) Regs; reg 72 HB Regs; reg 62 CTB Regs

61 Reg 70(3A) IS Regs

62 Reg 147(3) JSA Regs

63 Reg 7A(5)(d) and (e) HB Regs; reg 4A(5)(d) and (e) CTB Regs

64 HB/CTB Circular A1/96 para 4

PART THREE: GOING ABROAD
Chapter 19: Temporary absence
(pp242-245)

1 *Chief Adjudication*

Officer v *Ahmed and others* CA 16 March 1994, *Guardian*, 15 April 1994 per Neill LJ

2 R v *Social Security Commissioners ex parte Javed Akbar* 28 October 1991, *Times* 6 November 1992

3 See R(S) 1/85

4 *Ahmed and others* above

5 See also R(S) 10/83

6 paras 20949-20969 AOG

7 *Ahmed and others*

8 R(U) 16/62

9 *Ahmed and others*

10 R(I) 73/54

11 See R(S) 1/85

12 R(S) 1/66

Chapter 20: Entitlement to benefit and going abroad
(pp246-266)

1 See Sch 2 para of 2 JSA 1995 inserting new s124(e) SSCBA 1992; reg 4ZA IS regs as added by reg 4 IS (JSACA) Regs, the 'prescribed categories' of person who remain entitled to IS are set out in Sch 1B IS Regs as added by reg 22 and Sch 1 IS (JSACA) Regs

2 s124(1) SSCBA 1992

3 Reg 4(1), (2)(a) and (b) and 3(a) and (b) IS Regs

4 Reg 4(3)c)d) IS Regs

5 Reg 4(1)a) and (2)(a)-(c) IS Regs as amended by reg 5 IS (JSACA) Regs and reg 6(3) Income-related Benefits Schemes and Social Fund

(Miscellaneous Amendments) Regs 1996 (SI No. 1944)

6 s1(2)(i) JSA 1995

7 reg 50 JSA Regs

8 Regs 50(2)(a), 50(3)(c) and 50(5)(c) JSA Regs

9 Reg 50(2)-(6) JSA Regs

10 s1(2)(a) and (c) JSA 1995

11 Regs 14, 19 and 50 JSA Regs

12 Regs 14(1)m), 19(1)m) and 50(b)(c) JSA Regs

13 Reg 19 JSA Regs

14 Reg 50(1)(2)(i), (3)(b) and, (5)(b) JSA Regs

15 Reg 50(6)(b) and (d) JSA Regs

16 Reg 50(5)(d) and (e) JSA Regs

17 Regs 14(1)(e) and (g) and19(1)(e) and (g) JSA Regs

18 Reg 19(1)(e) and (g) JSA Regs

19 Reg 170 JSA Regs

20 Reg 50(1) and (4) JSA Regs

21 Reg 19(1)(p)(2) JSA Regs

22 Sch 2 para 3(10) JSA regs

23 Sche 2 para 3(10) and (11) JSA Regs

24 s26 JSA 1995; Social Security (Back to Work Bonus) Regs 1996 (SI No.193)

25 Reg 5(8) HB Regs

26 Reg 5(8B), (8C) HB Regs

27 Reg 5(8B) and (d) HB Regs

28 HB/CTB A8/95 para 11

29 Reg 5(8B) and (8C) HB Regs

30 See also paras 3.39-3.41GM and Reg 5(9) HB Regs

31 For further details of

who is treated as occupying a dwelling, see CPAG's *National Welfare Benefits Handbook*

32 *R v HBRB ex parte Robertson, Independent,* 5 March 1988

33 Reg 5(8), 5(8C) HB Regs

34 *R v Penwith DC ex parte Burt* 22 HLR 292

35 s130(1) SSCBA 1992, reg 5(1) and (2) HB Regs

36 See reg 5(2) HB Regs

37 para A3.15 GM

38 s131(3)a) SSCBA 1992

39 s6(5) Local Government Finance Act 1992; ss99(1) Local Government Finance Act (Scotland) 1992

40 Reg 4C CTB Regs as added by reg 4 HBCTBIS (Amdts) Regs

41 reg 6 HBCTBIS (Amdts) Regs

42 Art 3 Council Tax (Exempt Dwellings) Order 1992 (SI No.558)

43 Reg 5(1)(a) SFM&FE Regs as amended by reg 3 SFM&FE (Amdt) Regs

44 Reg 7 SFM&FE Regs 1987 as amended by reg 5(2) SFM&FE (Amdt) Regs

45 Reg 1A SFCWP Regs as amended by reg 3 SFCWP (Amdt) Regs

46 Dirs 12(a), 23(1)(a), 29 SF Dirs

47 Dir 8 SF Dirs

48 Dir 25 SF Dirs

49 Dir 4(a)(i) SF Dirs

50 *R v SFI ex parte Amina Mohammed,*

Times, 25 November 1992

51 Dirs 14-17 SF Dirs

52 Dir 16(b) SF Dirs

53 Dir 22 SF Dirs

54 FC s128(3) and (4) SSCBA 1992; regs 49-51A FC Regs; DWA s129(6) and (7) SSCBA 1992; regs 54-56A DWA Regs

55 Reg 50 FC Regs; reg 55 DWA Regs

56 s128 SSCBA 1992; reg 3 FC Regs; R(FC) 2/93

57 s129 SSCBA 1992; reg 5 DWA Regs

58 See *R v Barnet London Borough Council ex parte Shah* [1983] 2 AC 309

59 s129(1), (2) and (4) SSCBA 1992; reg 7 DWA Regs

60 Reg 3(1) (c) and (d) FC regs; reg 5(1)(c) and (d) DWA regs

61 Reg 4(1)(c) FC Regs; Reg 6(1)(c) DWA Regs

62 Reg 4(6)(a) FC Regs; Reg 6(6)(a) DWA Regs

63 Reg 4(5) FC Regs; Reg 6(5) DWA Regs

64 s21 and Sch 1 para 11(1)(2) JSA 1995; regs 14, 19 50 JSA Regs

65 s1(2)(d)(i) and s2 JSA 1995

66 Reg 11(1A) SSB(PA) Regs as added by reg 165(2) JSA Regs

67 Reg 4A SS(MB) Regs as added by reg 166(3) JSA Regs

68 In order to qualify as a member of the family, you must be the spouse, son, daughter, step-son, step-daughter, father, father-in-law, step-

father, mother, mother-in-law or step-mother of the person in the forces – see reg 2(5)(b) SSB(PA) Regs

69 Reg 2(1)(1A) and (1B) SSB(PA) Regs

70 Reg 2(1)(a) SSB(PA) Regs

71 Reg 2(1) SSB(PA) Regs

72 R(S) 2/86 and R(S) 1/90

73 R(S) 10/51

74 R(S) 1/69; R(S)2/69; R(S) 4/80 and R(S) 6/81

75 s94(1) SSCBA 1992

76 Reg 3 Social Security Benefit (Persons Abroad) Amendment Regs 1994 (SI No. 268)

77 Reg 11(2) SSB(PA) Regs

78 Reg 4A SS(MB) Regs as added by reg 166(3) JSA Regs

79 s35(1)(b) SSCBA 1992

80 s35(2) and s165 SSCBA 1992

81 s2(1)(a)(b) SSCBA 1992

82 Reg 2 Social Security (Maternity Allowance) (Work Abroad) Regulations 1987 (SI No. 417)

83 R(S) 1/75

84 For residence rules, see s78 SSCBA 1992, regs 9, 11 and 12 SS(WB&RP) Regs; Regs 4 and 5(3)c) SSB(PA) Regs

85 Reg 10 SS (WB & RP) Regs

86 Reg 4(1) SSB(PA) Regs

87 Regs 4(3)(4) and 5(3)c) and (6) SSB(PA) Regs

88 Reg 5(3)(a) and (aa)

and (6) SSB(PA) Regs

89 Reg 5(7)SSB (PA) Regs

90 Reg 8(1) SSB(PA) Regs

91 s36(1)b), 37(1) and 38(1) SSCBA

92 Reg 4(2A) SSB(PA) Regs

93 s1(2)a) SSAA 1992 and reg 19(6)b) Social Security (Claims and Payments) Regulations 1987

94 See ss3 and 4 SSAA 1992

95 s94(1), 108, 109 SSCBA

96 s2(1)a) SSCBA 1992

97 s94(5) SSCBA 1992

98 Reg 9(3)(7) SSB(PA) regs

99 Reg 9(3) SSB(PA) Regs

100 s113 SSCBA 1992

101 Reg 9(4) SSB(PA) Regs

102 Reg 9(4) SSB(PA) Regs

103 Reg 9(5) SSB(PA) Regs

104 Reg 9(5) SSB(PA) Regs

105 Reg 9(5)(a)-(c) SSB (PA) Regs

106 Reg 5(b) SS(IIMB) Regs; for the meaning of 'mariner' and 'airman' see regs 4-7 and Sch II of Social SS(EEEIIP) Regs

107 Reg 2(4) SS(DLA) Regs; Reg 2(3) SS(AA) Regs

108 Reg 2(1) SS(DLA) Regs; Reg 2(1) SS(AA) Regs

109 Reg 2(1)(b) SS(DLA) Regs; Reg 2(1)(b) SS(AA) Regs

110 Reg 2(2)(d) SS(DLA) Regs; Reg 2(2)(d) SS(AA) Regs; Reg 10 SSB(PA) Regs

111 Reg 2(2)(e) SS(DLA)

Regs; Reg 2(2)(e) SS(AA) Regs; Reg 10 SSB(PA) Regs

112 Reg 2(2)(a)-(c) SS(DLA) Regs; Reg 2(2)(a)-(c) SS(AA) Regs

113 Regs (1)(a) and 2 SS(DLA) Regs and Reg (1)(a) and 2 SS(AA) Regs

114 See Reg 3 SS(DLA) Regs

115 Reg 9 SS(ICA) Regs

116 Reg 9(2) SS(ICA) Regs; Reg 10B SSB(PA) Regs

117 CG/15/1993

118 Regs 4(2) and 9(2) SS(ICA) Regs

119 Reg 2 SSB(PA) Regs

120 Regs (1)(bb) and 2(1B)a) SSB(PA) Regs

121 Reg 3 SS(SDA) Reg

122 Reg 3(3) SS(SDA) Regs

123 Reg 10 SSP(MAPA) Regs as substituted by reg 3(4) Social Security Contributions, Statutory Maternity Pay and Statutory Sick Pay (Miscellaneous Amendments) Regs 1996 from 6 April 1996; reg 2A SMP(PAM) Regs as added by reg 4 SS(Con) Regs from 6 April 1996 and omitting regs 4 and 9 SMP(PAM) Regs

124 Reg 6 SS(Con) Regs

Chapter 21: Getting paid while abroad
(pp267-272)

1 Reg 38(1) SS(C&P) Regs

2 Reg 38(ZA) SS(C&P) Regs

3 Reg 21 SS(C&P) Regs 1987

4 Reg 72(12) and (13) HB Regs and reg 62(13) and (14) CTB Regs

5 Reg 72(15) HB Regs; 62(16) CTB Regs

6 Sch 2 para14(ZA) IS Regs; Sch 2 para 14(ZA) HB Regs; Sch 1 para 16 CTB Regs; Sch 1 para 17 JSA Regs

PART FOUR: EUROPE

EEC Regulation 1408/71, which deals with the co-ordination of benefits within the EU/EEA, contains a series of annexes. Annex VI covers the legislations of certain member states. The UK is referred to in section 0 of the annex; note that this section was designated J before 1/1/86 and L from 1/1/86 to 31/12/94. All references in the footnotes to Annex VI refer to section 0. (There is a second section 0 which relates to Iceland, but only for the EEA Agreement and we do not refer to it in this book.)

Chapter 22: The European Community's legal system
(pp273-278)

1 The EC Treaty as amended by the Maastricht Treaty is set out at [1992] 1 CMLR 573 and in Blackstone's *EC Legislation* (4th edition)

2 Art B Maastricht, Arts 2 and 3 EC

Treaty. Art 6 prohibits discrimination generally on grounds of nationality and Art 8 establishes the idea of 'citizenship of the union'

3 Arts 155-163 EC Treaty

4 Arts 145-154 EC Treaty

5 Arts 137-144 EC Treaty

6 Arts 164-188 EC Treaty

7 Art 169 EC Treaty

8 Art 170 EC Treaty

9 Arts 5 and 170 EC Treaty

10 *Costa v ENEL* [1964] ECR 585; *Administrazione della Finanze delle State* v *Simmenthal* [1978] ECR 629

11 *Van Duyn v Home Office* [1974] ECR 1337

12 Art 189 EC Treaty

13 Art 189 EC Treaty

14 *Marleasing SA v La Commercial* [1992] 1 CMLR 305; [1986] ECR 1-4135

15 *Marshall v Southampton Area Health Authority* [1986] 1 CMLR 688; [1986] ECR 723; [1986] QBD 401; [1986] 2 All ER 586

16 *Foster v British Gas* [1990] ECR 1-3313

17 Art 189 EC Treaty

18 *Grimaldi v Fonds de maladies Professionelles* [1989] ECR 4407; see *Wadman v Carpenter Farrer Partnership* [1993] IRLR 374

19 *Francovich v Italian State* [1993] 2 CMLR 66; [1991] ECR I

5357; [1992] IRLR 84

20 *R v HM Treasury ex parte British Telecommunications plc* [1996] 3 WLR 203; *Brasserie du Pecheurs SA v Federal Republic of Germany* [1996] QBD 404; [1996] 2 WLR 506

Chapter 23: EC social security law – an introduction
(pp279-283)

1 Technically, the EEA is itself a product of an association agreement, so EEA countries are association agreement countries. But because EEA nationals – unlike nationals of other association agreement countries – are given precisely the same rights as EU nationals, EEA and EU nationals have been dealt with together in the text

2 Article 6 EC Treaty

3 *Kalsbeek v Bestuur der Sociale Verzeteringsbank* [1964] ECR 565; *Petroni v ONPTS* [1975] ECR 1149; *Durighello v INPS* C-196/90, judgment 28.11.91

4 Council Reg of 14.6.71 on the application of social security schemes to employed persons and their families moving within the Community (OJ 1971 416, *Encyclopaedia of European*

Community Law C13-31). Adopted pursuant to Art 51 EC Treaty to replace former EEC reg 3 (OJ 1958, 561). Amended and consolidated on a number of occasions. Last published in a consolidated form by EEC reg 2001/83 (OJ 1983 L230(6)), but since amended by EEC reg 1247/92 (OJ 1992 L136(1)). In its current form published in *Encyclopaedia of European Community Law* (above). It is implemented by EEC reg 574/72 (OJ 1972 159, *Encyclopaedia of European Community Law* C13-465)

5 Council reg of 15.10.68 on Freedom of Movement for Workers within one Community, OJ 1968 475; *Encyclopaedia of European Community Law* Vol. C III C13-177

6 *Hoeckx* [1985] ECR 973

7 *Kits van Heijningen* [1990] ECR 1753

8 *Hughes* [1992] ECR 1-4839

9 *Schmid* [1993] ECR I-3011

10 *Deak* [1985] ECR 1873 (social advantage) and *Kziber* [1991] ECR I-199 (social security)

11 *Commission* v *Luxembourg* [1993] ECR I-187 (childbirth and maternity allowance), *Schmid* (see above)

Chapter 24: People who can claim social security benefits under EC law
(pp284-295)

1 Art 7 Reg 1612/68
2 Art 2(1) Reg 1408/71; Regs 1390/81 added the self-employed to the scope of Reg 1408/71 in 1981 and the scope of Reg 1408/71 with respect to benefits
3 Art 4 Dir 68/360
4 C-48/75 *Royer* [1976] ECR 497, [1976] 2 CMLR 220
5 Art 8A Treaty of Rome (as amended by the Treaty on European Union)
6 The UK implementing legislation (Art 2(1) I(EEA)O specifically excludes British citizens. For EC law purposes British nationals are (a) British citizens, (b) British subjects with the right of abode in the UK, (c) British Dependent Territories citizens who acquired that citizenship from a connection with Gibraltar; 28 January 1983 [1983] OJ C-23 pl; (1983) Command Paper 9062
7 C-370/90 *Singh* [1992] 1 ECR 4265, [1992] 3 CMLR 358
8 Arts 8A, 48-60 Treaty of Rome (as amended by the Treaty on European Union)
9 C-369/90 *Micheletti* [1992] 1 ECR 4239
10 C-235/87 *Matteucci*

[1988] ECR 5589; [1989] 1 CMLR 357
11 C-292/86 *Gullung* [1988] 2 CMLR 57
12 Art 48 Treaty of Rome
13 Art 48 Treaty of Rome; Art 7(2) Reg 1612/68
14 Art 7(2) Reg 1612/68; C-107/94 *Asscher* EC, *Times*, 15 July 1996
15 Art 48 Treaty of Rome
16 C-75/63 *Unger* [1964] ECR 177, [1964] CMLR 319; C-53/81 *Levin* [1982] ECR 1035, [1982] 2 CMLR 454
17 C-292/89 *Antonissen* [1991] 1 ECR 745, [1991] 2 CMLR 373
18 Art 48 Treaty of Rome
19 Art 48 Treaty of Rome; Art 7(2) Reg 1612/68
20 C-292/89 *Antonissen* [1991] 1 ECR 745, [1991] 2 CMLR 373
21 C-66/85 *Laurie - Blum* [1986] ECR 2121, [1987] 3 CMLR 389
22 C-415/93 C-*Bosman* [1996] All ER (EC) 97
23 C-53/81 *Levin* [1982] ECR 1035, [1982] 2 CMLR 454
24 53/81 C-*Levin* [1982] ECR 1035, [1982] 2 CMLR 454; C-139/85 *Kempf* [1986] ECR 1741, [1987] 1 CMLR 764
25 C-344/87 *Bettray* [1989] ECR 1621, [1991] 1 CMLR 459
26 C-27/91 *Le Manoir* [1991] 1 ECR 5531
27 C-196/87 *Steymann* [1988] ECR 6159,

[1989] 1 CMLR 449
28 C-344/87 *Bettray* [1989] ECR 1621, [1991] 1 CMLR 459
29 C-2791 *Le Manoir* [1991] 1 ECR 5531
30 C-3/87 *Agegate* [1989] ECR 4459, [1990] 1 CMLR 366
31 C-344/87 *Bettray* [1989] ECR 1621, [1991] 1 CMLR 459
32 196/87 *Steymann* [1988] ECR 6159; [1989] 1 CMLR 449
33 Art 7(1)(a) and (b) I(EEA)O; C-122/84 *Scrivener* [1985] ECR 1027, [1987] 3 CMLR 638
34 Art 7(1)(b) I(EEA)O
35 C-39/86 *Lair* [1988] ECR 3161, [1989] 3 CMLR 545
36 C-39/86 *Lair* [1988] ECR 3161, [1989] 3 CMLR 545
37 Art 52 Treaty of Rome: Art 6(2)(b) I(EEA)O
38 C-107/94 *Asscher*, ECJ, *Times*, 15 July 1996
39 C-107/94 *Asscher*, ECJ, *Times*, 15 July 1996
40 Art 2(1)(a) Reg 1251/70
41 Art 2(1)(b) Reg 1251/70
42 Art 2(1)(c) Reg 1251/70; Art 6(2)(e) I(EEA)O
43 Dir 74/34
44 Art 1 Dir 93/96; Art 6(2)(h) I (EEA)O
45 C-39/86 *Lair* [1988] ECR 3161, [1989] 3 CMLR 545
46 C-39/86 *Lair* [1988] ECR 3161, [1989] 3 CMLR 545
47 Art 10 Reg 1612/68
48 Art 1 Dir 73/148
49 Art 2 Reg 1251/70;

Dir 75/34

50 Art 12 Reg 1612/68

51 C-7/94 *Gaal* [1995] ECR I-1031, [1995] 3 CMLR 17

52 C-316/85 *Lebon* [1987] ECR 2811, [1989] 1 CMLR 337

53 Art 1 Dir 90/365; Art 6(2)(g) I(EEA)O

54 Art 1 Dir 90/365; Art 6(2)(g) I(EEA)O

55 Art 1 Dir 90/354; Art 6(2)(f) I(EEA)O

56 Art 10(1) Reg 1612/68; Art 1 Dir 73/148; Arts 3(2) and (3) and 4(2) and (3) I(EEA)O

57 Art 2 I(EEA)O; Art 1 Dir 90/364; Art 1 Dir 90/365

58 Art 1 Dir 93/96; Art 9 I(EEA)O

59 Art 3(2) Dir 68/360; Art 3(3) I(EEA)O

60 Art 2(1) I(EEA)O

61 Art 3(2) Dir 68/360

62 Art 11 Reg 1612/68; Art 4(3) I(EEA)O

63 Art 10 Reg 1612/68; Art 1 Dir 73/148; Art 7(1) and (2) I(EEA)O

64 Art 2(2) I(EEA)O

65 Art 4(2) I(EEA)O

66 C-267/83 *Diatta* [1985] ECR 567, [1986] 2 CMLR 164

67 Art 12 Reg 1612/68; C-389, 390/87 *Echternach* [1989] ECR 723, [1990] 2 CMLR 305

68 C-316/85 *Lebon* [1987] ECR 2811; [1989] CMLR 337

69 C-316/85 *Lebon* [1987] ECR 2811; [1989] CMLR 337; C-256/86 *Frascogna* (No 2) [1987] ECR 3431

70 Art 4(4) Dir 68/360; Art 14 I(EEA)O

71 Art 11(2) I(EEA)O

72 para 255 HC 395

73 IA 1971; Immigration (Carriers' Liability) Act 1987; IA 1988; AIAA 1993; AIA 1996

74 The principle rules are found in HC 395

75 s2 European Communities Act 1972

76 C-157/79 *Pieck* [1981] ECR 21711, [1980] 3 CMLR 378

77 Arts 48(3) and 56 Treaty of Rome

78 Art 15 I(EEA)O; Art 8 Dir 64/221

79 Art 2 Reg 1408/71

80 Contrast *Levin* v *Staatssecretaris van Justitie* [1982] ECR 1035, [1982] 2 CMLR 454 with *Heissische Knappschaft* v *Maison Singer et fils* [1965] ECR 965

81 Art 2(a) Reg1408/71

82 *Mouthaan* [1976] ECR 1901

83 *Hoekstra (ne Unger)* [1964] ECR 177; *De Cicco* [1968] ECR 473 (under Reg 3, the predecessor to Reg 1408/71)

84 *Pierik* [1979] ECR 1917

85 *Kits van Heijuningen* [1990] ECR 1753

86 C-317/93 *Nolte* (ECJ judgment 14.12.95) suggests that a lower earnings limit cannot be displaced as constituting indirect sex discrimination, contrary to Dir 79/7, because it can be justified by objectives of social policy

87 *Hoekstra*, see above

88 Article 1(f) Reg 1408/71

89 s137 SSCBA 1992

90 *Mr and Mrs F v Belgian State* [1975] ECR 679; *Piscitello* [1984] CMLR 108

91 Art 1(q) Reg 1408/71

92 Art 13 Reg 1408/71

93 Art 2(a) Reg 1408/71

Chapter 25: Benefits covered by the co-ordination and social advantages rules
(pp296-312)

1 *Official Journal* (English special edn) 1971 Vol I, p416 as amended, updated, and consolidated in Reg 2001/83, *Official Journal* 1983 L230/6. It has now also been amended by Reg 1247/92 (see below). Reg 1408/71 replaced an earlier EEC Reg dealing with co-ordination of social security benefits, Reg 3, so the earlier case law refers to Reg 3 and not Reg 1408/71. The principles in EEC Reg 3 were the same as those in Reg 1408/71

2 Listed in Art 4(1) Reg 1408/71

3 Art 4(2) Reg 1408/71

4 See definition in Ch 24

5 Art 4(2) Reg 1408/71

6 Referred to in Art 4(1) Reg 1408/71

7 Art 4(4), Reg1408/71

8 Article 4(2a) Reg1408/71

9 Arts 4(1)-(2a) Reg1408/71

10 *Scrivner* and *Cole* [1986] I ECR 1027

11 Art 4(4) Reg 1408/71

12 *Giletti* [1987] ECR 955 para 9; *Frilli* [1972] ECR 457 para

13; *Callemeyn* [1974] ECR 553 para 6; *Biason* [1974] ECR 999 para 9; *Newton* C-356/89

13 *Gillard* [1978] ECR 1661 para 12; *Piscitello* [1983] ECR 1427 para 10; *Newton* C-356/89

14 *Scrivner* and *Cole* (above)

15 *Newton* C-356/89

16 Eg *Scrivner* and *Cole* (the Belgian 'minimex' (like income support) and *Newton* (mobility allowance))

17 Art 4(1) Reg 1408/71

18 Art 10(a) Reg 1408/71

19 *Snares* CDLA/913/1994

20 Article 5 Reg 1408/71. The declarations are published in the *Compendium of European Social Security Law*

21 Annex IIa Reg 1408/71

22 *Beerens* [1977] ECR 2249 and *Newton* C-356/89

23 *Beerens* (above)

24 In *Newton* (above) the UK Government said that mobility allowance was not social security because it was not in its declaration and was more akin to social assistance. The ECJ said that it had more the characteristics of social security

25 Annex IIa Reg 1408/71 as amended by Art (8)(b) Reg 3096/95 as from 1/1/96

26 *Newton* (above)

27 *Snares* (above)

28 More detailed explanations can be found in some of the books in the Bibliography

29 Art 3 Reg 1408/71

30 *Caisse Regionale d'Assurance Maladie v Palermo (nee Toia)* [1979] ECR 2645; [1980] 2 CMLR 31

31 C-1/78 *Kenny v Insurance Officer* [1978] ECR 1489

32 *Vandeweghe* [1973] ECR 1329

33 *Costa* [1974] ECR 1251

34 *Palermo* [1979] ECR 2645 (above)

35 *Frascogna* [1987] ECR 3431

36 Arts 13-17 Reg 1408/71

37 Contained in Art 13 Reg 1408/71

38 Sickness and maternity (Art 18 Reg 1408/71), invalidity (Art 38), old age, death (survivors) and certain other invalidity benefits (Art 45(1) to (4)), occupational disease (Art 57) death grants (Art 64), unemployment (Art 67(1) and (2)), family benefit (Art 72)

39 *Mura* [1977] ECR 1699, [1978] 2 CMLR 416; but see also *Frangiamore* [1978] ECR 725 and *Warmerdam-Steggerda* [1989] ECR 1203

40 The general overlapping provisions are contained in Arts 12 and 46 of Reg

1408/71

41 Art 10(1) Reg 1408/71

42 Art 10a Reg 1408/71

43 Arts 18-31 Reg 1408/71

44 Art 18(1) Reg 1408/71

45 Arts 19-22 Reg 1408/71

46 Art 67, 69 and 71 Reg 1408/71

47 Arts 38-51 Reg 1408/71

48 Art 10 Reg 1408/71

49 Art 72 Reg 1408/71

50 Art 72 Reg 1408/71, giving effect to the ruling of the ECJ in *Pinna* [1986] ECR 1. This is a particular application of the non-discrimination principle in Art 3 Reg 1408/71

51 Art 76 Reg 1408/71 and Art 10 Reg 574/72. See *McMenamin v Adjudication Officer* [1993] 1 CMLR 509

52 Art 4(4) Reg 1408/71

53 See eg *Inzirillo* [1976] ECR 2057. Reg 1612/68 contains the provisions necessary to give practical effect to free movement rights under Art 48.

54 Art 7(2) 1612/68. Note that 1612/68 does not just apply to those presently in employment

55 *Even* [1979] ECR 2019; *Reina* [1982] ECR 33; *Castelli* [1984] ECR 3199; *Mutsch* [1985] ECR 2681

56 *Cristini v SNCF* [1975] ECR 1085; [1975] 1 CMLR 573; *Inzirillo* [1970] ECR 2057; [1978] 3

CMLR 596;
Ministere Public v
Even [1979] ECR
2019, [1980] 2
CMLR 71

57 *Frilli -v- Belgium*
[1972] ECR 457,
[1973] CMLR 6

58 *Cristini* [1975] ECR
1085 (see above)

59 *Inzirillo* [1976] ECR
2057

60 *Reina* [1982] ECR 33

61 *Castelli* [1984] ECR
3199; *Commission* v
Belgium [1992] I
ECR 5517; *Frascogna*
[1985] ECR 1739

62 *Deak* [1985] ECR
1873

63 *Hoeckx* [1985] ECR
973; *Scrivner* [1985]
ECR 1027;
Commission v
Belgium [1992] I
ECR 5517

64 *Lair* [1988] ECR
3161; *Brown* [1988]
ECR 3205;
Echternacht [1989]
ECR 723

65 *Bernini* [1992] ECR I
1071

66 *Commission* v
Luxembourg [1993] I
ECR 817

67 *O'Flynn* v *Chief
Adjudication Officer*
(C-237/94), *Times*
7.6.96

68 Art 7(3) Reg 1612/68

69 Art 9(1) Reg 1612/68

70 Art 7(2) Reg 1612/68

71 *Sotgui* v *Deutsche
Bundespost* [1974]
ECR 152

72 ECJ C-237/94, *Times*
7.6.96

73 Art 2 Reg 1408/71

74 Art 10 Reg 1612/68

75 Art 12 Reg 1612/68

76 under Art 7(2) Reg
1612/68

77 See *Cristini* (above)

78 *Kermaschek* [1976]

ECR 1669

79 *Morson and Jhanjan*
v *Netherlands* [1982]
ECR 3205, [1983] 3
CMLR 403

80 Reg 1612/68

81 Art 10(1) Reg
1612/68

82 Art 7(2) Reg 1612/68

83 *Cristini* (above)

84 *Gul* v *Dusseldorf*
[1980] ECR 1573;
[1987] 1 CMLR 501;
Echternach [1989]
ECR 723; *Diatta* v
Land Berlin [1985]
ECR 567; [1986] 2
CMLR 164. The
inconsistent decision
of the House of Lords
in *Re Sandler, Times*
10/5/85 is probably
wrong and should
have been referred to
the ECJ

85 *Cabanis-Issarte* Case
C-308/93 ECJ

86 *Kermaschek* [1976]
ECR 1669, and see
paras 23-24 and 34 of
Cabanis-Issarte
(above)

Chapter 26: Using the co-ordination rule to claim social security benefits
(pp313-347)

1 *Di Paolo* v *Office
National d'Emploi*
[1977] ECR 315;
R(U) 7/85; R(U) 8/88

2 *Partridge; Snares*
CDLA 913/94

3 *Willis* v *UK* ECHR

4 Art 13(1) Reg
1408/71

5 Art 13(2)(a) and (b)
Reg 1408/71

6 Art 14c Reg 1408/71

7 Art 14(1)(a) Reg
1408/71

8 Art 14(1)(b) Reg
1408/71

9 Art 14a(1)(a) Reg
1408/71

10 Art 14a(1)(a) Reg
1408/71

11 Art 14(2) Reg
1408/71

12 Art 17 Reg 1408/71

13 Arts 12 and 48 Reg
1408/71; see also
specific provisions in
relation to particular
benefits; Arts 19(2),
25(1)(b), 34(2), 39(2)
and (5), 68(2), 71(2),
76 and 76(3) Reg
1408/71

14 Art 13 Reg 1408/71

15 SS(OB) Regs

16 *Petroni* [1995] ECR
1149 C-24/75

17 Arts 46a, 46b and
46c Reg 1408/71

18 Arts 67-71 Reg
1408/71

19 Art 13 Reg 1408/71;
C-128/83 *Caisse
Primaire d'Assurance
Maladie de Rouen* v
Guyot; C-20/75
Gaetano d'Amico v
*Landesversicherungs-
anstalt Rheinland-
Pfalz* [1975] ECHR
891; R(U) 4/84

20 C-227/81 *Francis
Aubin* v *ASSEDIC
and UNEDIC* [1982]
ECR 1991

21 Art 69(1)(c) Reg
1408/71; R(U) 7/85

22 s21 and Sch 3 paras 1
and 2 SSCBA 1992

23 s1(2)(i) JSA 1995. In
a letter to the TUC,
November 1996, Mr
Allan Larsson of the
EC said that both
contribution-based
and income-based
JSA would be treated
as falling withing the
scope of Regs
1408/71 and 574/72.
Income-based JSA is a
special non-

contributory benefit
under Arts 4(2a)
and10(a) and Annex
IIa Reg 1408/71
although, given
current domestic case
law, this probably has
little significance

24 Art 69(1) Reg
1408/71

25 Art 69(1) Reg
1408/71

26 Arts 67(1)-(3) and
71(1)(a)(ii) and (b)(ii)
Reg 1408/71

27 Reg 1408/71, Annex
VI section O point 7

28 Art 69(1) Reg
1408/71

29 R(U) 2/90

30 Art 69(1)(a) Reg
1408/71

31 Art 69(1)(b) Reg
1408/71

32 Art 69(1)(b) Reg
1408/71; C-20/75
d'Amico, see above.
Some EU/EEA
member states have
more stringent
conditions than the
UK and may require
people with children
to have formal
childminding
arrangements in
place, including a
contract, before the
unemployed person is
treated as available
for work

33 Art 83(3) Reg 574/72

34 Art 69(1)(c) Reg
1408/71

35 Art 69(1)(c) Reg
1408/71

36 s5(1) JSA 1995; Art
69(1)(c) Reg 1408/71

37 Art 69(1)(c) Reg
1408/71

38 Art 1(c)

39 Art 83(1) Reg 574/72

40 Art 83(1) Reg
574/72; R(U) 5/78

41 Art 69(3) Reg

1408/71

42 Art 69(2) Reg
1408/71; s5 JSA 1995

43 Art 25 Reg 1408/71

44 Art 67 Reg 1408/71

45 Art 67 Reg 1408/71

46 Art 69(1)(a) Reg
1408/71

47 Art 69(1) Reg
1408/71

48 Art 69(1)(a) Reg
1408/71

49 Art 69(1)(b) Reg
1408/71; C-20/75
d'Amico, see above

50 Art 69(1) Reg
1408/71

51 Art 69(1)(c) Reg
1408/71

52 Art 68(2) Reg
1408/71

53 ss80 and 81 SSCBA
1992 (child
dependants); ss82-88
SSCBA (adult
dependants)

54 Arts 18 and 19 Reg
1408/71

55 Arts 19-22 Reg
1408/71

56 Art 25(4) Reg
1408/71; vol 3 para
23446 AOG

57 Art 18 Reg 1408/71

58 Art 18 Reg 1408/71

59 Art 18 Reg 1408/71

60 s31 and Sch 3 part 2
SSCBA 1992

61 Art 13(2)(f) and
Annex VI O(20) Reg
1408/71; R(S) 3/92;
C-215/90, *Twomey* v
CAO [1992] ELR 1-
1823

62 Art 25 Reg 1408/71

63 Art 18 Reg 1408/71

64 Art 18 Reg 1408/71

65 *Partridge; Snares*
CDLA 913/94

66 *Partridge; Snares*
CDLA 913/94

67 R(S) 13/86

68 Reg 3(1) SS(SDA)
Regs

69 Reg 3(1)(a) and (IB)

SS(SDA) Regs

70 Reg 2(1)(SS)(AA)
Regs

71 Art 10a and Annex
IIa O inserted in Reg
1408/71 by Art 1(6)
Reg 1247/92 from
1/6/92. Strictly
speaking no formal
declaration has been
made by the UK
under Art 5a
presumably because
AA is included in
Annex IIa itself (see
pp299-301 for full
explanation)

72 *Partridge; Snares*
CDLA 913/94

73 Reg 9(1) and (1A)
SS(ICA) Regs

74 Reg 2(1)(a) and (1A)
SS(DLA) Regs

75 Art 10(1) and Annex
VI O(12) Reg
1408/71

76 Art 1(h) Reg 1408/71

77 Art 1(i) Reg 1408/71

78 Annex VI O(17)
inserted in Reg
1408/71 by Reg
21955/91 on 29/7/91.
The requirement to
take account of
periods of
employment in the
EEA/EU became part
of EC Regs from July
1991 but point 17
also indicates it is
subject to UK
legislation. This
assumes you have at
some point worked in
the UK

79 Art 39(1) and AOG
Vol 3 para 24026

80 R(S) 9/81

81 Art 18 Reg 1408/71

82 Vol 3 paras 22416
and 22419 AOG; Art
37 Reg 1408/71

83 Vol 3 paras 22467
and 22471 AOG; Art
454(1) Reg 1408/71

84 Art 46(3) Reg 1408/71

85 Art 47.3 Reg 1408/71; Vol 3 para 22476 AOG

86 Art 10a and Annex IIa section 0 inserted in Reg 1408/71 by Art 1(6) of Reg 1247/92 from 1/6/92

87 Art 95b(8) Reg 1408/71; R(A) 5/92

88 Art 2 Reg 1408/71

89 Annex VI O(5) Reg 1408/71

90 Regs 1408/71 and 574/72

91 s95(1)-(4) SSCBA 1992

92 Art 1(h) Reg 1408/71

93 Art 1(i) Annex VI O(12) Reg 1408/71

94 Art 10(1) Reg 1408/71

95 s103 and Sch 7 para 9 SSCBA 1992

96 s104(1) and (2) SSCBA 1992

97 s105 SSCBA 1992

98 Sch 7 para 11(1) SSCBA 1992

99 Arts 1(h) and (i), 10(1) and Annex VI O(12) Reg 1408/71

100 Art 4(1) Reg 1408/71

101 Art 77 Reg 1408/71

102 Art 46(1) Reg 1408/71

103 Art 46(2) Reg 1408/71

104 Art 46(2) Reg 1408/71; Vol 3 para 23863 AOG

105 Art 46(1) Reg 1408/71

106 Art 46(2) Reg 1408/71

107 Art 48 Reg 1408/71

108 Art 46(2)

109 Annex VI O(8) Reg 1408/71

110 Art 47(3) Reg 1408/71

111 Art 51(1) Reg 1408/71

112 Arts 36 and 41 and Annex 3 (O) Reg 574/72; C-108/75 *Balsamo Institut National d'Assurance Maladie Invalidite* [1976] ECR 375; R(S) 3/82

113 Art 10(1) and Annex VI O(12) Reg 1408/71

114 Art 1(h) and (i) and Art 10(1) and Annex VI O(12) Reg 1408/71

115 Arts 77 and 1(t) Reg 1408/71

116 Art 77(2)(b)(i) and (ii) and Art 79(2) Reg 1408/71

117 Art 14(a) and (b) Reg 1408/71

118 C-300/84 *Van Roosmalen* [1986] ECR 3095

119 Art 74 Reg 1408/71

120 Art 72a Reg 1408/71

Chapter 27: Using the social advantages rule to claim means-tested benefits
(pp348-370)

1 Reg 21(3) 'person from abroad' and Sch 7 para 17 IS Regs; reg 85(4) 'person from abroad'; and Sch 5 para 14 JSA Regs; reg 7A(1) HB Regs; reg 4A(1) CTB Regs

2 Reg 7A(5)(d) HB Regs; reg 4A(5)(d) CTB Regs

3 HB/CTB Circular A1/96 para 4

4 Art 10a(1) and Annex IIa O(e) Reg 1408/71 where IS is stated to be non-exportable. IS is not a social security benefit under art 4(1) Reg 1408/71: CIS/863/94 and

CIS/564/94 paras 32-34

5 Art 10a(1) and Annex IIa O(h) EEC Reg 1408/71

6 The DSS has accepted in the case of FC that the inclusion of a benefit in Annex IIa O does not prevent the normal rules under Reg 1408/71 from applying, even if the benefit is then exportable. A commissioner has asked the ECJ to make a ruling on whether the inclusion of DLA in Annex IIa O means it is not exportable: *Snares* CDLA/913/94, *Welfare Rights Bulletin* 129, p14

7 They are both subject to the condition that the claimant is unemployed so clearly relate to one of the risks covered by Art 4(1) Reg 1408/71. The reasoning for FC being covered (*Hughes* – see note 21) applies equally to both parts of JSA

8 Reg 21(3) IS Regs 'person from abroad'; reg 85(4) JSA Regs 'person from abroad'; reg 7A HB Regs; reg 4A CTB Regs

9 Reg 21(3) IS Regs 'person from abroad'; reg 85(4) JSA Regs 'person from abroad'; reg 7A HB Regs; reg 4A CTB Regs

10 Reg 21(3) IS Regs 'person from abroad'; reg 85(4) JSA Regs 'person from abroad'; reg 7A HB Regs; reg

4A CTB Regs

11 s7(1) IA 1988

12 s7(1) IA 1988

13 Reg 21(3) IS Regs 'person from abroad': habitual residence; reg 85(4) JSA Regs 'person from abroad': habitual residence. Under HB/CTB rules the status of partner and children does not affect entitlement: see p128

14 Reg 21(3) IS Regs 'person from abroad': habitual residence para (b); reg 85(4) JSA Regs 'person from abroad': habitual residence para (b); reg 7A(4)(e)(i) HB Regs; reg 4A(4)(e)(i) CTB Regs

15 Art 4(4) Dir 68/306; Art 4(3) Dir 73/148; HEO(AO) 13/96 App 1 paras 6.33 and 6.41

16 Reg 21(3) IS Regs 'person from abroad': habitual residence para (a); reg 85(4) JSA Regs 'person from abroad': habitual residence para (a); reg 7A(4)(e)(i) HB Regs; reg 4A(4)(e)(i) CTB Regs

17 Art 10 Reg 1612/68; Art 1 Reg 1251/70

18 Art 7(2) Reg 1612/68; Art 6(2) Reg 1251/70

19 Reg 3(1A)(c) FC Regs

20 Reg 3(1)(a) and (b) FC Regs

21 Arts 73, 75(1) and 76 Reg 1408/71; C-78/91 *Hughes* [1992] ECR I-4839. Despite the discrimination amendment of Reg 1408/71 by the insertion of Art

10a(1) and Annex IIa O(c) Reg 1408/71 the DSS accepts that these rules still apply to FC: Vol 3 para 21856 AOG

22 Reg 5(1A)(c) DWA Regs

23 DWA is a disability benefit and so within Art 4 Reg 1408/71, so this would involve arguing that Art 18(1) Reg 1408/71 allows for ordinary residence in another EU/EEA member state to count as a period of residence under DWA rules

24 DWA is clearly a social advantage under Art 7(2) Reg 1612/68, so discrimination is unlawful. A residence test for partners may be discriminatory: *Schmid* [1993] I-2011. If you are habitually resident in the UK under EC law you may be able to use Art 3(1) Reg 1408/71 as well, since DWA is a disability benefit

25 Reg 3(1A)(c) FC Regs; reg 5(1A)(c) DWA Regs

26 Art 10(1) Reg 1612/68; Art 1(1)(c) and (d) Dir 73/148

27 Art 1(2) Dir 73/148

28 Art 1(2) Dir 73/148

29 s137(1) SSCBA 1992; Memo Vol 2/40 paras 21-23 AOG

30 Such a grant is clearly a social advantage under Art 7(2) Reg 1612/68, and the discrimination seems incapable of objective justification (see C-

237/94 *O'Flynn* [1996] All ER (EC) 541) so such discrimination is unlawful

31 SF Dirs 12(a), 23(1)(a) and 29

32 Such grants and loans are clearly social advantages under Art 7(2) Reg 1612/68

33 It would seem difficult objectively to justify this absolute rule in the given example in the light of the comments in *O'Flynn* and bearing in mind the discretion available to the social fund officer to limit the amount payable

34 Case C-370/90 *Surinder Singh* [1992] ECR I-4265

35 Art 48 Treaty of Rome

36 Art 51 Treaty of Rome; Art 1(1)(a) Dir 73/148

37 Art 59 Treaty of Rome; Art 1(1)(a) and (b) Dir 73/148. It has not yet been established the circumstances in which a return to the UK after exercising (or to exercise) this right will count under this rule

38 HEO(AO) 13/96 App 3 para 6.13

39 Art 48(3) Treaty of Rome

40 Reg 21(3) IS Regs 'person from abroad': habitual residence; reg 85(4) JSA Regs 'person from abroad': habitual residence. Under HB/CTB rules the status of partner and children does not affect entitlement: see

p128

41 Reg 21(3) IS Regs 'person from abroad': habitual residence; reg 85(4) JSA Regs 'person from abroad': habitual residence; reg 7A(4)(e) HB Regs; reg 4A(4)(e) CTB Regs

42 The only exception is for HB/CTB if a deportation order has been made or if you are declared an illegal entrant: see p368

43 *Sarwar v Secretary of State for Social Security*, CA, 24 October 1996

44 Art 5 Reg 1612/68

45 Art 5 Reg 1408/71 refers to nationals not workers

46 Art 7(2) Reg 1408/71

47 Because Art 5 Reg 1612/68 refers to nationals, non-EU/EEA family members can only use this as a derived right

48 Reg 21(3) IS Regs 'person from abroad': habitual residence para (a); reg 85(4) JSA Regs 'person from abroad': habitual residence para (a); reg 7A(4)(e)(i) HB Regs; reg 4A(4)(e)(i) CTB Regs

49 HEO(AO) 13/96 App 2 paras 6.31 and 6.33

50 C-48/95 *Royer* [1976] ECR 497

51 CIS/4521/95 para 11

52 Arts 7-10 Reg 1612/68

53 Art 227(5)(c) Treaty of Rome; Protocol 3 to Treaty of Accession

54 C-53/81 *Levin* [1982] ECR 1035

55 C-66/85 *Lawrie-Blum* [1986] ECR 2121

56 C-196/87 *Steymann* [1988] ECR 6159

57 C-139/85 *Kempf* [1986] ECR 1741. Earning more than £2 on any one day ought to count as work, because under the rules for unemployment benefit those earnings were too high for you to count as unemployed: reg 7(1)(g)(i) Social Security (Unemployment, Sickness and Invalidity Benefit) Regs 1983 No.1598. On 7 October 1996 UB was replaced by JSA which has no equivalent rule

58 *Kempf*

59 C-357/89 *Raulin* [1992] ECRI-1027

60 C-27/91 *Le Manoir* [1991] ECR I-5531

61 *Rodriguez*, Whittington House West SSAT, 14 February 1995

62 Reg 21(3) IS Regs 'person from abroad': habitual residence para (a); reg 85(4) JSA Regs 'person from abroad': habitual residence para (a); reg 7A(4)(e)(i) HB Regs; reg 4A(4)(e)(i) CTB Regs

63 Art 7(1) Reg 1612/68. See also CIS/4521/95 para 13 and Case 122/84 *Scrivner* [1985] ECR 1027

64 As the right of residence does: Art

7(1) EEC Dir 68/360; Art 7(1)(b) I(EEA)O

65 C-39/86 *Lair* [1988] ECR 3161 and Case C-357/89 *Raulin* [1992] ECR I-1027 dealt with Art 7(2) and 7(3) only of EEC Reg 1612/68

66 This argument has been accepted by at least one SSAT: *Silva*, Walthamstow SSAT, 19 June 1995

67 HEO(AO) 13/96 App 2 para 6.16

68 Art 7(1) EEC Reg 1612/68

69 CIS/4521/95 para 15

70 CIS/4521/95 para 14; *Lair; Raulin*

71 Reg 21(3) IS Regs 'person from abroad': habitual residence para (a); reg 85(4) JSA Regs 'person from abroad': habitual residence para (a); reg 7A(4)(e)(i) HB Regs; reg 4A(4)(e)(i) CTB Regs

72 Reg 21(3) IS Regs 'person from abroad': habitual residence para (a); reg 85(4) JSA Regs 'person from abroad': habitual residence para (a); reg 7A(4)(e)(i) HB Regs; reg 4A(4)(e)(i) CTB Regs

73 HEO(AO) 13/96 App 2 para 6.30 last line

74 HEO(AO) 13/96 App 2 para 6.30

75 Art 6(3) Dir 68/360

76 HEO(AO) 13/96 App 2 para 6.31

77 This refers to Art 6(2) Dir 68/360

78 This refers to Art 7 Dir 68/360

79 Art 16(2) I(EEA)O. If

a residence permit is withdrawn by the Home Office there is a right of appeal to an immigration adjudicator: Art 18 I(EEA)O

80 Art 6(2) Dir 68/360; Art 7 Dir 68/360
81 Reg 1251/70
82 CIS/4521/95 para 15
83 s122(1) SSCBA 1992 'pensionable age'
84 Art 2(1)(a) Reg 1251/70
85 Art 2(2) Reg 1251/70
86 Art 2(1)(b) Reg 1251/70
87 Art 2(2) Reg 1251/70
88 Art 4(2) Reg 1251/70
89 Art 4(2) Reg 1251/70
90 Art 4(1) para 1 Dir 73/148
91 Art 4(1) para 3 Dir 73/148
92 Art 4(1) para 4 Dir 73/148
93 HEO(AO) 13/96 App 2 para 6.40.
94 Art 16(2) I(EEA)O. If a residence permit is withdrawn by the Home Office there is a right of appeal to an immigration adjudicator: Art 18 I(EEA)O
95 HEO(AO) 13/96 App 2 para 6.41
96 Arts 4(1), 5(1) and 6(2)(b) I(EEA)O
97 Art 1 Dir 75/34
98 Art 2(1) last para Reg 1251/70
99 Art 7 Dir 75/34
100 Art 4(2) Dir 73/148
101 Case 186/87 *Cowan* [1989] ECR 195
102 *Tisseyre*, IAT (6052)
103 C-263/86 *Humbel* [1988] ECR 5365
104 C-286/82 and C-26/83 *Luisi and Carbone* [1988] ECR 5365

105 Art 8(1)(b) EEC Dir 68/360
106 Art 2(1) last para EEC Reg 1251/70
107 Reg 21(3) IS Regs 'person from abroad' para (h); reg 85(4) JSA Regs 'person from abroad' para (h); reg 7A(4)(d) HB Regs; reg 4A(4)(d) CTB Regs
108 Under HB/CTB rules the status of partner and children does not affect entitlement: see p128
109 Reg 21(3) IS Regs 'person from abroad' para (h); reg 85(4) JSA Regs 'person from abroad' para (h); reg 7A(4)(d) HB Regs; reg 4A(4)(d) CTB Regs; reg 21(3) IS Regs 'person from abroad' para (h) and reg 85(4) JSA Regs 'person from abroad' para (h) refer to 'national of a member state' but reg 7A(4)(d) HB Regs and reg 4A(4)(d) CTB Regs refer to 'national of an EEA State'. Under s2 European Economic Area Act 1993, the reference in the IS and JSA Regs to 'Member State' has effect as if it refers to EEA State
110 s1(1) IA 1971
111 Because your right to be in the UK is only under EC law. We are not aware of any BDTC being 'required to leave'
112 Because, even if you have no EC right to be here, you are here lawfully because of your leave under

British law
113 If you cannot lawfully be deported, it seems you cannot lawfully be 'required to leave'
114 Quoted in *Chief Adjudication Officer v Remilien and Wolke*, CA, *Times*, 12 July 1996
115 *Castelli and Tristan-Garcia v Westminster City Council*, *Times*, 27 February 1996
116 *Remilien and Wolke*
117 *Remilien and Wolke*
118 The hearing began on 7 July 1997
119 At the time of writing JSA had only recently been introduced
120 C-222/84 Johnston [1986] ECR 1651; C-22/86 *Heylens* [1987] ECR 4097
121 As recorded in the Court's judgment at p38 of transcript
122 Decisions are unlikely before 1998 and will depend upon the House of Lords decision in *Remilien and Wolke*
123 Art 48(3) Treaty of Rome
124 Arts 1(1)(a) and 3(1) Dir 73/148
125 Case C-292/89 *Antonissen* [1991] ECR I-745
126 ss3(5) and 5(1) IA 1971
127 Art 15 I(EEA)O
128 Reg 21(3) IS Regs 'person from abroad' para (c); reg 85(4) JSA Regs 'person from abroad' para (c); reg 7A(4)(b) HB Regs; reg 4A(4)(b) CTB Regs
129 Sch 7 para 17 IS Regs; Sch 5 para 14 JSA Regs; reg 7A(1) HB

Regs; reg 4A(1) CTB Regs

130 Reg 7A(4)(b) HB Regs; reg 4A(4)(b) CTB Regs

131 Reg 7A(4)(e)(v) HB Regs; reg 4A(4)(e)(v) CTB Regs

132 Only a deportation order made under s5(1) IA 1971 counts under the benefit rules. It is not clear whether Art 20(2)(a) I(EEA)O means a deportation order can be made as part of a decision to remove

133 *Remilien and Wolke*

134 Because, as a person with temporary admission or as an illegal entrant, you are a person from abroad under these benefit rules, even if you are also an EU/EEA national: reg 21(3) IS Regs 'person from abroad' paras (d)-(g); reg 85(4) JSA Regs 'person from abroad' paras (d)-(g); reg 7A(4)(c) HB Regs; reg 4A(4)(c) CTB Regs

135 Reg 7A(4)(c) HB Regs; reg 4A(4)(c) CTB Regs

136 Reg 7A(4)(e)(vi) HB Regs; reg 4A(4)(e)(vi) CTB Regs

137 Reg 21(3) IS Regs 'prisoner'; reg 85(4) JSA Regs 'prisoner'

PART FIVE:
INTERNATIONAL
AGGREEMENTS
Chapter 28:
International
agreements
(pp372-380)

1 s179(2) SSAA 1992

2 SS Benefit (Persons Abroad) Regs 1975; SS (Reciprocal Agreement) Order 1995

3 H Bolderson and F Gains, *Crossing National Frontiers: An examination of the arrangements for exporting social security benefits in twelve OECD countries*, HMSO, 1993

4 Art 6 Reg 1408/71

5 Art 2 Reg 1408/71

6 C-82/72 *Walder* [1973] ECR 599; C-4758/93 *Thevenon*

7 Art 2 Reg 1408/71; C-99/80 *Galinsky* [1981] ECR 941; R(P) 1/81

8 C-227/89 *Ronfeldt* [1991] ECR 1-323; C-4758/93 *Thevenon*

9 Annex III A para 60 Reg 1408/71 (reproduced in Vol 9 Part II Blue Books, Convention on Social Security between the UK and France, 10/7/56)

10 Reg 1408/71

11 Art 3 Reg of the relevant reciprocal agreement

12 Art 1 of each agreement

13 Art 1 of the Denmark, Italy and Luxembourg agreements with the UK

14 Art 1 of each agreement

15 SS (PFA) Miscellaneous Amendment Regs 1996

16 Extension of definition of public funds. Statement of changes in Immigration Rules HC (these are constantly revised)

17 *Sevince* and *Kziber* ECJ

18 C-277/94 *Taflan Met and others* v *Bestaur van de Sociale Verzekkeringsbank* [1996] ECR 1-4085

19 Association agreement and Decision 3/80 Association Council

20 1997 case re Decision 3/80

21 para 1 Annex VI Council Commission Decision 91/400/ECSC, EEC: Order No. L229, 17/8/91, p249. Lome Convention countries are Angola, Barbuda, Bahamas, Barbados, Belize, Benin, Botswana, Burkina Faso, Burundi, Cameroon, Cape Verde, Central African Republic, Chad, Comoros Islands, Congo, Cote D'Ivoire, Djibouti, Dominica, Dominican Republic, Equatorial Guinea, Ethiopia, Fiji, Gabon, Gambia, Ghana, Grenada, Guinea, Guinea-Bissau, Guyana, Haiti, Jamaica, Kenya, Kiribati, Lesotho, Liberia, Madagascar, Malawi, Mali, Mauritania, Mauritius, Mozambique, Niger, Nigeria, Uganda, Papua New Guinea, Rwanda, St Christopher (St Kitts) & Nevis, St Lucia, St

Vincent & the Grenadines, Sao Tome & Principe, Senegal, Seychelles, Sierra Leone, Solomon Islands, Somalia, Sudan, Suriname, Swaziland, Tanzania, Togo, Tonga, Trinidad & Tobago, Tuvalu, Western Samoa, Zaire, Zambia, Zimbabwe: OJ No L 229, 17/8/91, pp221-3.

22 para 2 Annex VI (see note 21)

23 *Gisti* 1996

APPENDIX 6

1 s21(1)(a) National Assistance Act 1948 read with Secretary of State's Directions and Approvals, Appendix 1, DoH Circular No. LAC (93)10

2 *R -v- London Borough of Westminster and others ex parte 'M'* [1996] QBD *Times* 10 October 1996, CA 17 February 1997. The Court of Appeal refused leave to appeal to the House of Lords but there is a petition to the House of Lords for leave to appeal

3 *Ex parte Gorenkin and others*, QBD, 13 May 1997, *Times* 9 June 1997

4 *R -v- London Borough of Westminster and others ex parte M* (see note 2)

5 s21(5) National Assistance Act 1948, para 4 Secretary of State's Directions and Approvals; *ex parte Gorenkin* above

6 *R -v- Camden LBC ex parte Al-Shakarchi* [1996] 20 November

7 *R -v- SSH ex parte London Borough of Hammersmith* (*Independent*) 15 July 1997

8 s17 Children Act 1989

9 s20 Children Act 1989

10 National Health Service and Community Care Act 1990; Chronically Sick and Disabled Persons Act 1970

11 s117 Mental Health Act 1993

APPENDIX 7

1 The agreement with Jamaica is being renegotiated.

2 The agreement with the USA has been revised with effect from 1 September 1997.

3 The agreement between the UK and Yugoslavia is now treated as an agreement between the UK and Serbia and Montenegro. Separate agreements are being negotiated with Bosnia, Croatia, the Republic of Macedonia and Slovenia.

Index

H

I

Notes

Notes

Notes

Notes

Notes

Notes

Notes

Notes

Notes

Notes